Dear Mike,

I hope you enjoy this book.

Fondly,
Isabelle
Feb. 9, 2013

SARAH'S TEN FINGERS

Sarah's Ten Fingers

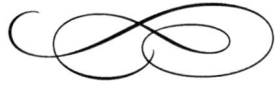

Isabelle Stamler

iUniverse, Inc.
Bloomington

Sarah's Ten Fingers

iUniverse books may be ordered through booksellers or by contacting:

iUniverse
1663 Liberty Drive
Bloomington, IN 47403
www.iuniverse.com
1-800-Authors (1-800-288-4677)

Because of the dynamic nature of the Internet, any web addresses or links contained in this book may have changed since publication and may no longer be valid. The views expressed in this work are solely those of the author and do not necessarily reflect the views of the publisher, and the publisher hereby disclaims any responsibility for them.

Any people depicted in stock imagery provided by Thinkstock are models, and such images are being used for illustrative purposes only.

Certain stock imagery © Thinkstock.

ISBN: 978-1-4759-3682-7 (sc)
ISBN: 978-1-4759-3681-0 (hc)
ISBN: 978-1-4759-3680-3 (e)

Library of Congress Control Number: 2012912186

Printed in the United States of America

iUniverse rev. date: 12/28/2012

Dedicated to Sarah, Bella, and Al; without whose great love *Sarah's Ten Fingers* could not have been written.

Many thanks to my two devoted and hard-working friends Penelope Dion and Francine Rosenthal, and to my grandson Benjamin Stamler and my nephew Long Sam. Without their diligent work I would never have gotten *Sarah's Ten Fingers* from my handwritten manuscript into book form for your reading pleasure.

Table of Contents

Name Changes

Russian/Yiddish	American/English
Fayge	Fanny
Beyla	Bella
Herschel	Harry
Zushe	Sol
Srolik	Irving

Prologue

A veritable "no man's land" exists where the Dneiper River kisses Belarus to the north and Ukraine to the south. Silhouettes of mammoth buildings, from the giant reactor to the worker's tall apartment houses, stand proud in the morning mists; but at closer examination, one sees that they are silent and almost deserted. Skeleton crews remain, wearing what seems to be otherworldly protective gear that shields them from the radioactivity that still escapes and poisons the air. Several tiny, empty hamlets still dot the lovely river landscape.

This enchanting sylvan area, watered by the mighty Dneiper, is virtually uninhabited. Man's careless use of his mighty intellect has rendered the area extremely dangerous. This area is the home of Chernobyl, the huge Soviet atomic complex whose malfunction still poisons the air of large parts of Eastern Europe, and will continue to do so for many years to come. Yet, in spite of the contamination, a small handful of inhabitants remain, even though their futures are deadly and grim.

This blighted area was not always so. In the early twentieth century, in spring and summer, insect and bird song filled the air of this lovely, fertile river valley. Small farms and tiny hamlets surrounded by verdant forests completed the landscape. Nature had blessed the area with great fertility, but the area's inhabitants garnered little from their well-endowed surroundings. Lack of technology and the rule of an iron autocracy bound the people of this region to a grinding poverty. They did not starve, because their rich natural environment fed them; but the many comforts and labor-saving technology that had come to the industrialized world of the nineteenth century were completely absent from this land of agricultural abundance.

IN VASHISHT
SARAH AND HER FATHER

Chapter 1: Vashisht

In 1908, in the tiny Belarussian hamlet of Vashisht, a baby was being born. There was the usual excitement that permeated any household when the midwife arrived. Deprivation due to poverty and the ever-present fear of religious persecution that was rampant in their world were, for now, unspoken and almost disappeared in the excitement of the moment.

The family's four children, who had been exiled to the outdoors, awaited a new baby's cry and information regarding the baby's sex. Through the open door, they heard their mother's low moans and saw their father's anxiety-ridden face. They did not play. There was too much excitement in the air. Instead, the older children quietly spoke of the rumors that were traveling through the town. Marauding Polish bands seeking to harm Jews were galloping through the countryside. They robbed Jewish homes and murdered the inhabitants. Recently, in a nearby town, all of the town's Jews had been herded into the town's small synagogue. The building was then set aflame. Gentile townspeople spoke with horror bout the screams of the victims and the laughter of their murderers.

The four children, anxiously awaiting the arrival of their new sibling, wondered if the Polish anti-Semites would come to Vashisht.

Suddenly a loud cry issued forth from inside their tiny house. It was their mother's voice! Was she dying? There was a short silence followed by the weak cry of a newborn infant. Papa, looking dazed, came to the door. "You have a new sister!"

Now there would be five of them- three girls and two boys. The eldest was a girl of thirteen, who comported herself like "the executive in charge." She ordered Herschel, the oldest boy, to bring some potatoes up from the potato cellar. She then went into the house to meet her new sister and to prepare the family's dinner. Until her mother became stronger, thirteen-year old Anna would be in charge of meals and of her younger siblings. Her father, who would resume his prayers and his studies of the Holy Book, was not to be disturbed. With Anna in charge, she and the children would do any necessary work around the house.

Little Zushe was very mischievous. Most four-year-old boys can get into scrapes, but Zushe was "the king of the mischief-makers." While Anna was in charge, she ordered Fayge to keep Zushe close to her and watch his every move, because Zushe's mischief was particularly unwelcome while Mama was recovering and tending to Beyla, the new baby.

Papa and his four other children sat down at the wooden table opposite the huge Russian stove and thanked *Adenoi* (God) for their food. Fayge brought a bowl of hot potatoes, fresh sour cream, and a glass of milk to Mama, who was lying in bed nursing Beyla. Now they could all eat.

Papa silently thanked God for the four children at the table and for the baby at Sarah's breast. He and Sarah had lost three children, and Papa prayed fervently that these five living children would grow to adulthood. He prayed that by the time they grew up, life would be better in Russia and everyone would feel safe. Little did he know that his lovely wife, Sarah, only shared part of his prayers As Sarah nursed Beyla, she prayed that all five of her children would grow into adulthood somewhere *other* than Russia. To this end, even though the family owned few possessions, Sarah had secreted a small bag of gold coins in a hole under the large Russian stove. In the winter the chickens lived under the stove, so when Sarah needed to add to her hoard, she routed the chickens, retrieved the bag, added a few more gold pieces, and buried the bag once more. Only then would she allow the chickens to return to their warm winter roost, and only then would she feel she was building an escape for herself and her family.

Their grinding poverty caused Sarah's bag of gold to fill very slowly, while evil events in Russia spun around them very quickly. News of pogroms in other towns reached horrified Jewish ears. Nearby villages had been pillaged by marauding Polish or Ukrainian bands. Both Jews and Christians were robbed, but the worst mayhem was unleashed on the Jewish population. Stories describing rape, beatings, and the murder of Jews filled Sarah's frightened ears. She needed to do something.

———————

Michel, Sarah's husband, was usually immersed in the study of Scripture. Mundane day-to-day tasks and worries about survival were left to Sarah. Michel rarely had an opinion about the family's well being, except for a great diligence concerning everybody's observance of their very Orthodox Jewish faith. There could be no deviation from the law, and Michel's sons were expected to study the Holy Word with careful effort and passion.

Michel only interrupted his study and his close scrutiny of his family's piety to visit his parents every Thursday afternoon. On these visits, he would be accompanied by his four children. The five of them would eat their supper with Michel's parents. Sarah and Baby Beyla remained at the market stall that Sarah owned and manned. She sold needles, buttons, thread, and cloth to the Gentile farmers and villagers, and to her fellow Jews. Approximately every three months she went to Kiev to purchase the merchandise she sold. She wished that she could remain in the big city longer, because she wanted to increase her trade and she loved the dynamic life of Kiev's large and vibrant Jewish quarter. Sarah's heart was urban, but her real life was in Vashisht. She could not stay in the big city longer than a few days, because she feared that she was leaving her children on their own. Michel was too preoccupied with his Holy Books to pay much attention to the children, and her surrogate, Anna, often behaved like a flighty teenager and not a serious overseer of the family's well being.

———————

One Sunday, Sarah decided to visit her father in Narovle, the town nearest to Vashisht, which was much larger than the tiny hamlet in which she lived. Its larger Jewish community had a synagogue, a _cheder_ (Jewish school), and a Jewish cemetery. In contrast, Vashisht's Jews were able to gather a *minion* (a quorum of ten or more adult Jewish males necessary for public prayer), but the hamlet's small Jewish population had no synagogue or cheder. Jewish boys were taught by tutors or their fathers. The girls were mostly illiterate, because they did not have the obligation to study the Holy Books, so they rarely were taught to read.

Every Jewish community saw to it that all Jewish boys learned to read the Holy Book, but in Sarah's home, Sarah demanded that Michel teach Anna and Fayge to read too. He did so, and both girls could read Yiddish (the language spoken in Jewish homes) and could read Hebrew (the language of the Holy Books, used by Jews in public prayer).

When a Jew in Vashisht died, the body was taken to Narovle. In this larger town there was a Jewish cemetery, a synagogue, and a burial society to oversee the funeral and make sure that the body was buried with all appropriate Jewish rites.

When Sarah had recovered sufficiently from having given birth to Beyla she went to Narovle to show the baby to her father. He lived there with Sarah's oldest brother and his family. Four-year old Zushe accompanied his mother and baby sister on the trip. It was late autumn and very cold. Sarah and Zushe were bundled up from their noses to their boots and the baby was wrapped in several warm blankets. Boris, Sarah's faithful, hard-working horse, pranced and snorted in the frigid air. Smoke seemed to be coming out of his nose and mouth.

The trip through the forest was more than invigorating. Sarah looked forward to a glass of hot tea at her brother's house. She had not seen her father since her mother's funeral and the mourning period (*Shiva*). Sarah's mother had died three months before Beyla's birth. After her death, Sarah's father decided to live with Yossel, his eldest child. Yossel and his wife were prosperous. They had three sons who would benefit from their grandfather's presence, because he was well versed in Hebrew and the Scriptures, and would be a patient and loving teacher for his grandsons.

As their wagon approached the two-story house on one of Narovle's more prosperous streets in the Jewish quarter, Sarah heard a loud, angry female voice coming through the closed windows. It was Gittel, her brother's wife, berating Sarah's papa.

"Your books, clothes, and tools are left wherever they've been used. You've turned my house into a disorderly barn!"

Gittel's strident, angry voice shocked Sarah, but even worse was the fact that the yelling and scolding was being aimed at her father.

Sarah did not even knock! She strode into Yossel's house and said, "Papa, pack your things. You're coming home to live with us." Gittel and Yossel didn't protest. They agreed that Papa would be happier in Vashisht with Sarah and her family.

Sarah's visit was short. She helped Papa collect his books, shoemaker's tools, and clothing. After bidding her brother and his family a frosty good-bye, Sarah, her small son, Baby Beyla, and Papa settled themselves in the wagon. The trusty Boris pulled them back through the frigid forest, to the warmth and love of Sarah's family in the tiny cottage in Vashisht.

Michel and his father-in-law enjoyed studying the Holy Book together. The children were happy to have their _Zada_ (grandfather) living with them. But everyone's happiness did not last long.

––––––––––

One Thursday, Michel and the four older children went to visit Michel's parents who lived at the other end of the village. _Bubba_ (grandmother) cooked them a dinner that they all loved - potato _latkes_ (pancakes). No one showed any restraint. They ate and ate and ate. Suddenly Michel clutched his abdomen. "I think I have over-eaten," he said, "My stomach is very upset. Let's go right home."

The children and Michel staggered home. When they arrived, Michel took to his bed and moaned. No one slept that night, and when dawn came creeping over the horizon, Sarah told Anna and Herschel to get out of bed and go to Narovle to fetch the doctor. They were directed to bring him back to Vashisht as quickly as possible.

Michel writhed in his bed in a pool of sweat. He moaned, and Sarah wept. The children huddled together in fright as Zada prayed.

It was evening when an exhausted Anna and an extremely tired Herschel came home. They said the doctor was still seeing patients, but that he would come as soon as he could. At 10:00 P.M. they heard the hoof beats of the doctor's horse. Sarah opened the door before he could knock, and Anna and Herschel tended to his horse. The doctor removed his frozen outer clothing, took a few gulps of hot tea, and immediately went to his patient.

Michel's face was dead white. His eyes were closed and sweat poured from every part of his body. The doctor probed and poked around his abdomen and with every poke, the patient cried out. " I think his appendix is infected. I must operate immediately, to remove it," said the doctor.

Sarah quickly cleared space and dragged their heavy wooden table to the center of the one-room cottage. After it had been disinfected and covered with the *Shabbat* (Sabbath) tablecloth, Zada, Sarah, the doctor, and Anna carried Papa to it. Their three kerosene lamps were placed around the table, and everyone stepped back to allow the doctor to do his work.

The doctor soaked a clean rag in chloroform, and rendered Papa unconscious by pressing it over his nose. He then began to cut into Papa's abdomen in order to remove the infected appendix. Just as he was reaching the appendix, the doctor watched in horror as the appendix burst! He valiantly tried to clean the detritus it spewed throughout Papa's abdominal cavity, but his efforts were to no avail. Papa never woke up. At thirty-seven years of age, Michel Sheliznak died on his kitchen table of a burst appendix. Thirty-one year old Sarah was now head of a household consisting of her father who was an old man of sixty-one, Anna thirteen years old, Herschel ten years old, Fayge five years old, Zushe four years old, and the baby Beyla.

———

After Michel's death, Sarah increased the number and lengthened the duration of her trips to Kiev. She was usually away for two weeks and home for one. She now carried her Gentile neighbor's farm produce to Kiev. She sold the produce and bought such manufactured items as buttons, scissors, cloth, and ribbon for the use of the people in Vashisht. She was honest and efficient and her neighbors trusted and respected her. They bought the products she purchased in Kiev, and received money from her in return for their crops, which she had sold in the big city.

When Sarah went on her business trips to Kiev, fourteen and a half year old Anna and Zada were in charge of the family in Vashisht. Zada repaired and made some boots and shoes for the people of the town, but mostly he spent his time reading and studying the Holy Books. Anna cared for Baby Beyla, cooked the family's meals, and ordered the younger children around. Herschel was a big help to her, but Zushe was like a wild child. Although he was five, he ran and played with the wildest boys in the village. Anna paid very little attention to him, because her domestic chores and her consuming adoration of her baby sister took most of her time

Except for the continuing stories of anti-Semitic atrocities in nearby villages and distant cities, life in Vashisht was peaceful and friendly. One day, however, the family's peace was shattered. Almost six-year old Zushe pitched a large stone that went awry, striking the forehead of the town's only mentally challenged child, eleven-year-old Natasha. Natasha, who suffered from a severe form of autism, could not speak. She ran home screaming, crying, and bleeding from her forehead. The boys who had played with Zushe, told her mother that "the Jew, Zushe, threw the stone that opened Natasha's head."

In the meantime, Zushe had run home. He bolted the door and tearfully told his family what had happened. His grandfather and three older siblings trembled behind the bolted door and awaited their neighbors' wrath. Only Baby Beyla remained unafraid.

Soon they heard the tramping feet and angry shouts of the villagers.

"Burn the *Jid's* (Jew's) house down!"

"Send out the Jewish bully who attacks an unfortunate girl. We'll beat him to death!"

"Open the door or we'll smash it in!"

The door remained bolted, while within, the little cottage's inhabitants trembled in terror. Suddenly they heard the sound of a wagon. Sarah was returning from Kiev. She saw the small angry mob at her door and asked what was the matter. Natasha's mother, pointing angrily at her daughter's still bleeding forehead, screamed that Zushe had done this deed.

"Katya," said Sarah soothingly, "he meant no harm. He's a naughty, small boy. I'll give him a good beating."

"In the meantime, please take this bolt of lovely cloth, because I'm filled with sorrow over Natasha's suffering. Let's go into my house and I'll treat the wound. The rest of you – go home! Everything is attended to and you have no business here!"

The small crowd dispersed in all directions, and Katya, carrying the bolt of cloth, led Natasha through the now opened door.

Sarah stopped the bleeding, cleaned the wound, and gave Natasha a kiss on her cheek. She then gave the unfortunate child several yards of red satin ribbon. Natasha, filled with delight, left the cottage with her mother.

Sarah now turned her attention on Zushe. She slapped him soundly on the rump for throwing stones. When he stopped crying, she gathered her four older children around her and said, "Our neighbors have been nice to us, because what I do is necessary for them and because we have always lived together in Vashisht. But, Russians, Poles, and Ukrainians cannot be trusted. From the time they were born they have been taught to hate Jews. Their priests tell lies about us that fan this hatred. When things go wrong for them, they look for someone to blame. The Tsar and the government blame us. We are even accused of killing their God, Jesus!"

"These are bad times in Russia. Jewish people have been attacked by outsiders in towns near and far from us. I am fearful for our safety. If I had enough gold in the bag under the stove, we'd all go to America right now. In America I hear that Jews are not attacked or blamed for everything bad."

Zada interrupted, "I will never go to America. I have heard that in America Jews no longer practice their faith or obey God's commandments. I'd rather die here at the hands of anti-Semites than live a long life without my faith."

Sarah sighed. She knew that she could never change her father's stubborn mind, but she also knew that he was an old man who could not live too many more years. She would never leave him or wrench him away from the pious life he loved, but she would continue to save more gold pieces under the stove, for she was determined to take her family to a free land. She knew little about America, but she felt sure that in America,

Jews still remained Jews. The trip, however, would have to wait until Zada was gone.

————

Anna was now a lush fifteen-year old girl. Male heads turned when she swayed through Vashisht's market place. Her twelve-year old brother Herschel usually accompanied her. She felt very grown up and responsible, because when her mother left Vashisht for Kiev, she and Zada were in charge of the household; and Sarah's trips to Kiev were very frequent.

For Sarah, Kiev wasn't all business. The city had a large bustling Jewish community, which Sarah invaded and became part of. Not only did she do business with Kiev's Jewish merchants, she soon became involved in the numerous social activities of the more modern, young adult community. Unlike the protected, pious, young girls for whom their families would arrange suitable marriages, Sarah was a free, lusty, attractive young widow protected only by her own wits. She met men through her business connections and protected herself from their advances by clever flirtatious maneuvers that kept them at bay, and although she enjoyed their pursuit, she never lost awareness of her responsibilities to her five children and her pious father in Vashisht. She enjoyed musical and dramatic entertainments, lovely kosher restaurants, and the attentions of young widowers and single men. If a widower had children, she turned her attention elsewhere. She did not want to add someone else's children to her household. If a man courted her politely and did not force his attentions upon her, she often became his friend….until she met Avroham.

Avroham swept her off her feet. He was blond, blue eyed, handsome, and younger than she was. At thirty-three Sarah looked twenty-five, but Avroham was truly only twenty-five. He had never been married, because he had left his pious family when they tried to arrange a distasteful marriage for him. He was a city man from Kiev, who successfully ran a large bookstall selling non-religious, and often revolutionary Yiddish books. His deep attraction to the lovely, illiterate, buxom young woman from a hamlet in White Russia (today Belarus) was inexplicable and totally unexpected. Very quickly Avroham sensed and appreciated Sarah's interest in his political pronouncements and in his descriptions of the novels he had read or was reading. Not only did it flatter him when she paid rapt attention to his pronouncements, but she was very insightful in her responses to what he said. What was even more important, he found her as lovely as she found him handsome. Soon the two were not merely intellectually attuned - they had fallen in love.

Sarah told him about her life - her widowhood, her father, and her five children. She protested that she was too old for him, but he swept away all of these facts and fell even more deeply in love with her. She, too, was passionately in love with him, and their idyllic affair went on through several of Sarah's trips to Kiev.

Then the roof fell in! Sarah discovered that she was pregnant. When she told Avroham, he promptly took her to a rabbi, and they were married. Life looked sunny to them as they set out for Vashisht, determined to raise Sarah's family together.

Upon their arrival at Sarah's cottage, they met the first storm clouds; Anna greeted her new stepfather with rage and recriminations. She was only ten years younger than he and she considered her mother's marriage to him a travesty that was shameful for the world to see. She refused to accept him and raged constantly, making scenes during Sarah's difficult pregnancy. Sarah's pregnancy, Anna's histrionics, and the lack of peace in their lives caused Sarah to doubt the wisdom of her marriage to Avroham. When, during one of Anna's numerous outbursts, Anna threatened suicide, Sarah began to fear for the life and sanity of her headstrong daughter. After carefully assessing her situation - the family's lack of peace, Anna's frightening emotional state, Zada'a quiet disapproval, and her young husband's inability to cope with the chaos of her household; Sarah decided to do the unthinkable. She would send Avroham away. They would be divorced. And somehow, she would continue to accumulate gold for the trip to America.

Sarah waited for the baby to be born. She named her newborn son Israel, but called him the diminutive, "Srolik". The baby had his father's blond hair and blue eyes, and Sarah immediately fell in love with him.

Avroham also doted on the baby, but not for long. Anna's histrionics had not abated, and when her daughter's threats of suicide became more frequent, Sarah asked Avroham to return to Kiev and to give her a divorce. The hapless young man refused, but was soon forced to acquiesce, because of Sarah's complete coldness to him, and the untenable emotional conditions in the little cottage in Vashisht. Avroham begged Sarah to let him take their baby. He argued that she had five other children. He said that he wanted to keep and raise Srolik as a memory of their love.

Sarah's retort was unforgettable and unassailable. She said, "I have ten fingers. I cannot spare one of them for you. I have six children and I cannot spare one of them either!" More gently she added, "You are young. You will marry again and have other children. Together with your new young wife, you will raise these children. As for me, I must keep and raise all of my six children. Srolik needs his own mother. I will keep him, because he needs me, and because he will always be *my* memory of our beautiful love."

A forlorn Avroham left Vashisht the next day. On Sarah's next trip to Kiev, a rabbi who had been designated by Avroham, handed Sarah a _get_ (divorce). She never saw Avroham again.

Although Anna's outbursts quieted after Avroham's banishment, it was quite apparent that she still resented her mother and the new baby. Sarah understood this and realized that she too bore resentment toward Anna. It was difficult for her to like the headstrong almost sixteen year old. It would be better if she used some of the buried gold to send Anna and her eldest son Herschel to America. They could establish themselves and perhaps send some more money to add to Sarah's money for the rest of the family's trip to America.

––––––––

The decision was made, and tickets were purchased. Sarah commanded Anna to look after her thirteen-year-old brother. Herschel was to go to an American school and Anna was to procure employment that would support both of them. Sarah's older sister, Chinna, lived in New York City. She would give them a home until they could take care of themselves. Sarah hoped that they would not be a burden on Chinna and would be self-sufficient very quickly.

The year Anna and Herschel left for America was 1910. By 1915, Russia had been at war for a year. Lawlessness and battle raged around Vashisht. Mail from America rarely came. Zada was the adult in the house when Sarah braved her way through the countryside to get to Kiev. Though Beyla was only seven and a half years old, she took care of young Srolik. Necessity had matured Beyla beyond her years. Her two older sisters were gone - Anna to America and Fayge to Kiev, to study dressmaking. Little Beyla, the only girl left, lavished love on her baby brother. Little Srolik adored his young surrogate mother and gave her no trouble at all.

Sarah's trips to Kiev were filled with peril. A plague of marauding bands of anti-Semitic Poles had been ravishing villages on both banks of the Dneiper River. On Sarah's last trip to Kiev, they had shot at the boat that was ferrying her down the river. As the bullets whizzed above her head, Sarah worried about her family's well being in Vashisht.

In Kiev, Sarah conducted her business quickly. Talk in the city was gloomy. The war was going badly and the Tsar had been arrested. Kiev was filled with sickness. Typhus, a disease about which Sarah had never heard, was proliferating throughout the city. She felt great pressure to get home to her young children. She hoped that the marauding Polish bands had stayed away from Vashisht. She prayed that her family was still healthy. Perhaps typhus was only in Kiev and had not come to Vashisht.

After a particularly grueling trip, the lights in the windows of Vashisht's small cottages welcomed Sarah home. Her little village had been spared an invasion by the outlaw Poles. Everything looked peaceful. The one window in her cottage twinkled with lights from the kerosene lamps inside. She quickly dismounted from the wagon and entered her home.

Zushe lay on his bed, flushed with fever. In a corner, Zada quietly wept. Little Beyla was bustling to and fro.

"What's the matter with Zushe?" asked Sarah.

"A week ago, he went to see his friend Serge, who is down with typhus. Now Zushe has typhus too," answered the exhausted little girl. "I keep trying to keep him cool with wet cloths. Zada and I take turns going to the well for buckets of water. Will Zushe die?" asked Beyla.

"Not if I can help it," the worried Sarah replied. "Take a rest, Beyla. I don't want you to get sick too."

Sarah tended Zushe day and night for more than a week. The boy babbled incoherently and continued to burn with fever. Then, just as they were all losing hope for his recovery, rivers of perspiration covered the sick boy's face and body and he began to speak coherently. Two days later, a very weak, but non-feverish Zushe asked for _kasha_ (groat cereal). Beyla promptly gave him a bowl of kasha, as her mother, who collapsed in a chair, covered her face and wept.

Zushe gained strength daily. As he regained his strength, Sarah seemed to be losing hers. Finally, Sarah felt so bad that she took to her bed. Her flushed face and incoherent babbling, told her family that Sarah, too, had caught typhus.

Seven and a half year old Beyla had grown up when her brother Zushe, was ill with typhus. Now, as her mother suffered and tossed with fever, Beyla became her mother's nurse and the family's "general." She issued orders to everyone. Zada fetched water and five year old Srolik stirred soup and disposed of garbage. Even the weakened Zushe helped, by stoking the fire and applying wet cloths to his mother's feverish brow. Beyla was everywhere at once. Even when she caught a few winks of sleep, she remained vigilant, listening for a moan from her mother. Completely exhausted and in tears, every night she begged God to save Sarah.

God must have taken pity on the frightened little girl, because one night, two hours after Beyla had made her impassioned prayer, large beads of perspiration broke out all over Sarah's face and body. She then turned her face to her stricken family and whispered, "Have faith. I will get better."

———————

Just as Sarah was whispering to her family, there was a knock on the door. Zushe opened the door to see Masha, one of their Christian neighbors, and a good friend. Masha was wild-eyed. She spoke rapidly, saying that the day before, a marauding, anti-Semitic Polish band had wreaked havoc in Zletna, a nearby small town, and it was probable that they would soon be coming to Vashisht. Masha offered to take the children to her house, where they could pose as hers. Sarah, however, could not come. Everyone knew that typhus was an infectious disease and some said people who were infected, spread it. Others said it was spread by lice. Whatever was true, Masha would not take the chance of infecting her family. What was more, Zada couldn't come to Masha's house either, because his long beard and *peyes* (ear locks) told everyone that he was a Jew.

Thirteen-year old Zushe took charge. He thanked Masha for her information, but declined her offer of safety for the children. "Zada, the kids, and I will carry Mama into the wheat fields. The wheat has grown very tall, so we can all hide there. If they come, they will take what's in the house, but they won't find us," reasoned the clever thirteen-year old boy.

"To be on the safe side," said Masha, "pack up food and take it out into the field with you. Then come back for your mother. When you're all there, stay in the wheat until I come to tell you that the bandits are gone."

"I'll start packing up the food now. Thank you, Masha," said Zushe.

Within an hour, the three children had carried the food deep into the wheat. Getting Sarah there was another matter. A frail old man and three frightened children, the oldest who was thirteen, struggled and strained as they sometimes supported and other times carried the desperately ill Sarah out into the wheat. When they arrived at the place where they had left the food, they stopped and lay the almost unconscious Sarah on the ground, while they huddled around her, with all eyes looking toward Vashisht.

———

The evil Poles had come! There were approximately fifty of them- all mounted and armed. They galloped to the center of the town where a large wooden cross stood. The town center, with its fourteen market stalls, mostly manned by Jewish women, was deserted. The merchandise remained in the stalls, but no salesperson or customer could be seen. The leader of the horsemen, a burly fellow with piercing blue eyes and a straggly light brown beard, shot his rifle into the air and bellowed, "Who's in charge here?"

The town center remained quiet and deserted. With a sign from his hand, the leader directed his men to the stalls, where they pillaged them and then set all of the stalls ablaze. As the fires burned and smoke filled the air, the leader bellowed, "Come out and show us where the Jews are or we'll burn down every house in this maggoty town."

A small delegation of Vashisht's Christian population slowly emerged. It consisted entirely of middle-aged and elderly women. Masha was among them.

"Where are your men?" shouted the Polish chieftain. "Are they and your young women afraid to show themselves?"

"No Sir," replied a trembling Masha. "We just thought that *we* would be less troublesome. You must know that we share many of your views… You hate the _Jids_ (Jews) and we hate them too."

"Do you now?" laughed the head Pole. "Then you won't mind pointing out the Jews' houses and their synagogues."

"Of course not, Sir," replied the woman. "We'll take you to the house of every dirty Jew in Vashisht. But there is no synagogue here, because our town is small, and thank God our Jewish population is small too."

The Polish leader and his men dismounted. Leading their horses, they noisily followed the female delegation. With their rifles slung over their shoulders, they laughed and called to each other as they strode to the first site in which they planned to commit mayhem. It was the Bernstein house. The Bernstein's were an elderly, deeply impoverished, Jewish couple whose children had all married and moved to Kiev and Narovle. Only a few of the marauders could fit into their tiny, shabby hut. They shot the two elderly Jews and then torched their hovel.

The next house was bigger and better. In the Cohen cottage, they found a silver samovar that the Cohen family had forgotten to take with them when they fled to Narovle. The Poles took the samovar and burned the Cohen cottage to the ground.

Two more Jewish cottages were pillaged. One was deserted, but the other yielded a father, two teen-aged sons, and an elderly grandmother. The sons and their father were beaten to unconsciousness. The old woman was roughly pushed out of the cottage and forced to watch it burn to the ground, with her son and grandsons inside.

When the Poles were led to Sarah's house, Masha entered with them. She stepped forward and angrily said, "This is the house of the dishonest

Jewish woman who buys our produce and sells it in Kiev. She cheats us when she sells, and she cheats us when she procures the goods that we need. Worst of all, because she is so rich, we are sometimes forced to take loans from her. The dirty Jew charges exorbitant interest, and when we are unable to pay, we must give her our most precious belongings. What is more, she even lives in this cottage rent-free. It belongs to Belnikov, the blacksmith, who allows her to live here because she holds a large note that he cannot pay. Masha spit on the floor in disgust.

"Typical Jewish thievery," grunted the leader. "We won't burn this one. But where are the rich Jews who live in Belnikov's house?"

"Sarah and her family left very quickly when they heard that you were coming. They fled to Kiev. When they left, Sarah said that they would remain in Kiev until they could book passage to America. Good riddance!"

The Poles looked around the house. The chickens were still under the stove. Basha, the cow, mooed softly in the lean-to at the side of the house. Fresh wheel tracks could be seen going in the direction of the Dneiper. The Poles assumed that when the Jews left they had no time to take the chickens, the cow, or Boris, who must have been their second horse.

Masha continued, "That thieving, dirty Jewess took my sewing machine when I was a little late in paying my loan. I used to have the only sewing machine in Vashisht, but now Sarah, the Jew, has it!"

"It's still here!" shouted one of the Poles.

"She didn't take it in her wagon!" exclaimed Masha. "She probably couldn't fit it in with all of her possessions and her maggoty family," Masha added.

"You can have it back," said the chieftain. "We are not here to hurt the good Christians who live in this village. We're here only to teach the Jews a lesson. We'll leave this house alone. Tell your blacksmith that we saved his house from the dirty Jews."

The Polish marauders stomped on to the next Jewish cottage. They continued wreaking havoc for over two hours. When they left Vashisht, five Jews were dead, twice that many were badly beaten, and most of the Jewish homes were wrecked or burned. Only Sarah's house and two other

Jewish houses were spared the wrath of the evil Poles. They missed the other two houses, because they were located at the edge of the forest and the female delegation never led the anti-Semitic Poles to them.

———

From their hiding place in the tall wheat, Zada and the children saw the smoke of Vashisht's burning Jewish cottages. They guessed that their Jewish neighbors were suffering greatly, and wondered if Masha or some other Christian friend would come for them when the mayhem stopped. In the meantime, as the smoke poured out of Vashisht, the hidden Jewish family trembled in terror. The only one who showed no fear was Sarah, because the short trek into the wheat had caused her to lose consciousness. As the houses of the Jews of Vashisht burned, Sarah burned with fever.

Masha did not come for the family until late the next day. She feared that the evil Poles might decide to return. Sarah had regained consciousness two hours before Masha's arrival. She smiled weakly at her friend and she whispered her deep gratitude to Masha, for saving their home from destruction. When Masha told them about the atrocities committed against the other Jews in Vashisht, Sarah felt as if her heart was breaking. She begged to be brought home, so with great difficulty, Zada, Masha, and the children helped the stricken Sarah as she stumbled and fell all the way to her cottage.

Vashisht smelled of smoke. Some houses were still smoldering. But Sarah paid them no heed. She was so weak and worn out, that when she entered her home, she was immediately put to bed. She did not emerge from her bed for two weeks. It did not penetrate her weak consciousness, that her most diligent and persistent nurse was her nine-year old daughter, Beyla. She was too weak to see the toll her illness was taking on her very young nurse. It was not until Sarah was a good deal stronger that she was able to assess the situation and delegate some tasks to Zushe, her father, and even little Srolik.

———

In two weeks, a weakened Sarah could walk weakly around the cottage. Beyla, however, had become listless. Sarah ordered her young daughter to bed. She feared that Beyla, her faithful nurse, was coming down with typhus.

Sarah's fears were well founded. Beyla soon became very flushed. She babbled words that made no sense and moaned a great deal. Sarah knew that she was too weakened from the ravages of typhus to properly nurse her sick little girl, so with great anxiety, she asked her father and twelve-year old son, Zushe, to hitch Boris to the wagon and transport Beyla to Mozyr, a much larger town, not too far away from Vashisht. Mozyr had a hospital with a wing for patients with contagious diseases. Beyla would get better care there than she could get from her greatly weakened mother.

Zushe and Zada carried the flushed Beyla to the wagon. She was wrapped tightly in blankets, but was still shivering violently. Sarah stood in the doorway of her cottage watching them and weeping until they were out of sight. Would she ever see her beautiful little girl again?

———————

Because Sarah could not read or write, she asked a friendly Jewish neighbor to write a letter to fourteen-year old Fayge, who was in Kiev, apprenticed to a dressmaker. She wanted Fayge to come home until conditions in Russia became better. The threats of typhus and anti-Semitic gangs caused Sarah to want Fayge to get out of the huge city's crowded Jewish quarter. As bad as conditions were in Vashisht, they seemed better than conditions in Kiev. Besides, Sarah keenly missed her two eldest children now living in America, and she wanted what was left of her family in Russia to be together- with her. Only God knew if she would ever see her precious Beyla alive again. She yearned for news about Beyla and for the return of her father and Zushe from Mozyr.

As Sarah mused about her missing family members, she heard the creak of a wagon and the familiar beat of Boris's hooves. She ran out to welcome her returning son and her father, but it was only Zushe who sat in the wagon.

"Where is Zada?" she demanded.

"Mama," replied Zushe, "the contagious ward of the hospital was very crowded. We were lucky to get a bed for Beyla. She was unconscious and babbling out of her head. Zada feared that the over-worked nurses might neglect a young girl who had no one with her, so he decided to stay at her bedside until she was conscious and strong enough to ask for the attention of the nurses. He said he would find a place to stay, and he asked me to come to Mozyr for them in two weeks. He also asked me to bring more gold when I return."

The worried Sarah sighed as she gave her son a welcoming hug. The two-week wait would be interminable.

———

Sarah fretted for twelve days. On the twelfth day, a drayman delivered fourteen-year old Fayge to her mother's door. Sarah's joy knew no bounds. Lovely fourteen-year old Fayge looked so grown up and citified, with her thick blond braids wound like a crown upon her head. Fayge's face glowed with happiness at being home.

Mother and daughter embraced, and walking arm-in-arm, entered the cottage. Thirteen-year old Zushe carried in the two battered suitcases that housed all of Fayge's belongings.

"Where are Zada and Beyla?" Fayge asked

A tearful Sarah explained Beyla's plight. Though not sure herself, Sarah assured Fayge that they both would come home in a few weeks.

After two weeks had dragged by, a despairing Sarah told Zushe to hitch Boris and see how things were going in Mozyr. Fayge wanted to go too, but Sarah forbade it. "The journey is not safe for a good looking fourteen-year old girl," said Sarah. Zushe would go alone. Sarah sewed a pocket inside Zushe's shirt, in which she placed several gold pieces. She sent up a prayer for an uneventful trip to Mozyr, and a quick and safe return for Zushe, Beyla and Zada.

Zushe's trip to Mozyr was, indeed, uneventful. He passed small farms and farmers at their work. No one would believe that this peaceful region was the target of murderous anti-Semitic bands, or that Russia's soldiers were deserting in huge numbers, leaving the battlefield, and straggling home. Boris flicked at flies with his tail, and Zushe's greatest annoyance on the trip was a persistent fly that kept buzzing about his head. Everything seemed extremely peaceful.

Mozyr was still awake when Zushe arrived. While people were going about their business, Zushe guided Boris toward the outskirts of the town, where the hospital with the wing for contagious diseases was located. When Zushe came to where Beyla lay, he saw Zada frantically trying to dry Beyla's face, as prodigious quantities of perspiration flowed from the sick girl's body.

"I thought she was dying, when two days ago she began to babble and thrash around. She continued this behavior until this morning, when she started to sweat and to speak sensibly. She has been sweating like this all day."

"Thank God," said Zushe. The sweating means that the fever has broken. If the doctors say it is all right, we'll take her home."

"No," said Zada. "She has to be healthier than this to make the trip. Have patience."

Beyla recovered more and more each day. When Zushe had been in Mozyr for five days, the doctors told Zada that Beyla could be moved, but must rest for at least one more week at home.

The old man and his thirteen-year old grandson carefully laid Beyla in the wagon. Pillows and blankets enveloped her, as the faithful Boris bore her, her loving grandfather, and her big brother home on an uneventful return trip, past quiet farms, and through verdant forests, to Vashisht.

For Sarah, Beyla's last week at the hospital in Mozyr was the longest week of her life. She imagined Beyla dead, then tortured herself by imagining Zushe being attacked by bandits and never arriving at the hospital. She even imagined the town of Mozyr being the victim of a pogrom. If her father, with his long beard and peyes were seen, the rampaging anti-Semites would surely kill him and anyone with him.

Sarah sometimes shared these horrible fears with Fayge. Fayge, who was invariably optimistic, rarely succeeded in allaying her mother's fears; and the cottage was shrouded in gloom, until the day its inhabitants heard the beat of Boris' hooves and the creaking of the wagon. They ran to the door and saw their trusty horse pulling the wagon in which an exhausted Zushe and even more exhausted Zada sat. The invalid, Beyla, slept peacefully in the back of the wagon. In years to come, Beyla insisted that she slept peacefully during the whole trip home, but Zada and Zushe said that she moaned and tossed so much, that they feared she would die before they got to Vashisht.

For two weeks, young Beyla was bedridden. She was barely able to feed herself the meager amount of food her wasted body could tolerate, however, the loving care of her family and her strong, young constitution prevailed. Beyla began to recover. In two more weeks a healthy, though pale young Beyla resumed her normal life.

———————

One lovely autumn day, Masha came to the cottage and invited Beyla to join her and five village children on an excursion into the Ukraine to get some pears that grew wild there. These pears were particularly sweet and juicy, and much prized by the people of the region.

Beyla grabbed a basket and tied a scarf around her head. Going with Masha and the other children would be great fun. Bringing home the delicious little pears that grew for such a short season would be a treat for all of them.

The autumn foliage and warm sunshine made the hikers merry and boisterous. By the time they had crossed the river and arrived at the place where the little pears grew, they were tired, but very happy.

After a short rest, Sasha, Masha's thirteen-year old son, quickly scrambled up a pear tree. He shook the branches vigorously, and a storm of pears came cascading to the ground. The children on the ground scrambled for the pears and put them into their baskets. They were all set for a repeat performance from Sasha, when they heard the hoof beats. Three young Ukrainian men cantered their horses to where Masha and the children stood. In the nastiest tone, one of them demanded to know where the group had come from.

Masha told them that they lived in Vashisht, a small village across the river. They had walked and they had taken the ferry to this area to get pears.

The horseman examined the group through squinting eyes. He passed over all of them, but paused at Beyla. "You bring a Jid girl with these children?" he asked in a menacing manner.

Masha laughed. "She's not a Jid. Don't insult my niece!"

The Ukrainian did not share her mirth. "Anyone can see she's a Jid. Her hair is black and her scarf is tied under her chin. Christian girls tie scarves at the back of their necks."

"Why are you protecting the Jid?" he demanded angrily.

Masha answered just as angrily, "Why is a grown man insulting an innocent girl and her aunt? You should be ashamed of yourself!"

A second horseman retorted, "It is easy enough to tell if she's a Jid. They all speak Russian with a Jid accent, or else they can't speak Russian at all." He turned to the trembling Beyla and shouted, "Where do you live and what is your name?"

Beyla answered in a low voice, but she looked squarely into the man's face. "My name is Galina, and I live in Vashisht. Masha is my aunt, and you are a wicked man to shout at us and call me a Jid."

The horseman looked ashamed. The man who had spoken first, apologized to Masha. He justified himself by repeating that her niece looked Jewish, "But," he said, "anyone can hear that she is a Christian child by the way she speaks." He turned to Beyla and said, "Your scarf fooled me, but I should have known better. You're too pretty to be a Jid."

The three horsemen galloped away. Masha and the children left the pear trees and returned to Vashisht with whatever pears they had gotten before the menacing Ukrainians had come.

When Beyla returned home, she told Sarah and the family about her dangerous adventure. Sarah was now more determined than ever to accumulate the money necessary for the family's trip to America. "This is a dangerous place. While there are many wonderful Christians like Masha and some of our other neighbors, there are many more who hate us and want to do us harm. I don't believe it is wise to ever trust a Russian that you don't know very well," Sarah told her family.

The Bolsheviks had come through Vashisht. They were ragged young men who politely asked for permission to enter a home. Sarah, Zada, and the children huddled in a corner when the three of them entered their cottage. The three Bolsheviks politely asked for food, and thanked the trembling Sarah for the bread, cheese and eggs she had given them. They laughed and teased young Srolik. Their leader promised that in the "New Russia," everyone would be equal and life would be good. Beyla and Fayge were starry eyed when they left. They babbled with happiness over the great future the Bolsheviks would bring to everyone.

Sarah quietly shook her head. She knew that it didn't matter. Neither a Russian government run by a Tsar, nor a Russian government run by commissars would be fair to Jews. She would continue to plan her family's escape to America.

When the Bolsheviks left Vashisht, they tore down the large cross that had always stood in the center of town. When the deed was done, their leader bellowed, "Religion is the opiate of the people. Intellect and hard work will deliver Russia. The old beliefs are dangerous. Give them up!"

Most of the Jews felt hopeful. Perhaps these Bolsheviks would bring equality to all. Sarah disagreed. She felt sorrow for her Christian neighbors. The Bolsheviks' disregard and disdain for their Christian beliefs proved to Sarah that the Bolsheviks would show no tolerance for anyone who disagreed with them. She yearned for the end of all roving gangs and battles around Vashisht. She yearned for peace and for more gold under the stove. Sarah wanted her family to get away from Russia. Anna and Herschel were waiting for them in America, and some day, after peace came, the family would leave Russia.

———

A great battle raged in the forest outside of Vashisht. Large explosions rocked the ground and rattled windows in the hamlet. Vashisht's terrified inhabitants huddled in their homes and prayed. Two and a half hours of gunfire and explosions shook the town…then silence. When the silence continued for a few hours, the bravest of Vashisht's residents, Sarah among them, left their homes and picked their way into the smoky forest.

Downed trees and heaps of earth made entry onto the battlefield very difficult. When the first of the locals came to the area of carnage, their horrified eyes could not believe what they saw. Dead and dying horses, and parts of horses, were lying around everywhere. There was an occasional human corpse and many mounds of dirt. The great holes and mounds of earth, the dead and dying animals, and the dead soldiers were the results of the bombardment the villagers had heard. The dying horses sometimes howled eerily in their pain. Weapons, some broken wagons, and downed trees littered the ground. The people from Vashisht stared at the horrific scene and then turned away. They sadly returned to their homes.

———————

When Sarah came home, she took Zushe into a corner and whispered that they would both return to the battlefield. She planned to skin as many of the dead horses as she could. She also planned to collect as many of the abandoned weapons as she could. The horses' skins and the weapons could be sold in Kiev. The bag of gold under the stove would really grow.

Zushe and Sarah hitched Boris to the wagon. Until darkness halted them, they skinned the dead horses and put their skins, along with the weapons they had found, into the wagon. The skinning was hard, disgusting, bloody work. Each skin was so heavy that Sarah and her son strained greatly when they flung it into the wagon.

That night, the boy and his mother slept soundly. At dawn, they awakened, downed a quick breakfast, and hauled their aching bodies onto the wagon. They spent the whole day, until darkness fell, at the same ghoulish labors they had pursued the day before.

Fayge and Beyla brought lunch and dinner to the battlefield laborers. The food remained untouched. The sight of the skinned animals and their blood covered mother and brother turned the young girls' stomachs. Fayge vomited. Both girls hurried home as fast as they could.

When night fell, after the second gory day, Zushe and his mother left their punishing labors. They were both covered with blood. The stench of the battlefield was overpowering. Feeling sick to their stomachs, and numb from tiredness, they slowly made their way home.

At home, Beyla had made borscht for supper. Sarah and Zushe couldn't eat. They washed their bodies and scoured their hands, using water from several buckets that had been hauled home from the well. The blood and stench, brought home from the battlefield by Sarah and Zushe, had caused all of their spirits to drop. Laughter and chatter had ceased.

Suddenly Sarah broke the unhappy silence by exclaiming loudly, "What a good day for us! The skins and weapons we brought home will fetch a lot of money in Kiev. Perhaps we will even have enough money to go to America!"

———

Rumors flew! The Tsar had been executed! The Bolsheviks ruled!

Yet life in Vashisht remained largely the same. One change, however, was that Beyla and Srolik now went to the school that was located on the other side of the forest. Children from Vashisht and from another nearby village attended this one room school. Approximately forty children, ranging in age from six to fourteen went to the school. Since the Bolsheviks had taken over the government, both Jewish and Christian children were required to go to school. Both boys and girls would now be taught to read. In the new Russia, run by the Bolsheviks, there would be no illiteracy.

Beyla was in charge of little Srolik. She saw to it that he was very warmly dressed for their long trek through the snow-covered forest, to their school.

On one winter morning, when it was still dark outside, Beyla woke Srolik for their punishingly cold walk to school. They each ate a bowl of hot kasha, and drank hot milk provided by the family's cow, Basha, who was also Beyla's beloved pet. Each child was bundled up in two handmade knitted woolen sweaters, topped with a warm woolen coat. Their feet were encased in hand-knitted woolen sox and then wrapped in warm rags. Over this they wore stout boots. Hand-knitted woolen mittens and a heavy cap with earflaps completed Srolik's winter attire. Beyla wore the same kind of mittens, but her head and neck were wrapped tightly in a warm _babushka_ (Russian head scarf).

Both children stomped out of the cottage and plodded their way to the forest. A weak sun was rising in the sky. The trees cast strange shadows on the snow and ice crackled in the tree branches, making the familiar forest a very eerie place. Beyla admonished Srolik to stay very close to her. She told him that they were in danger of attack from a wild animal. The terrified young Srolik did not budge from his big sister's side. An hour and a half later, the two nearly frozen children, arrived at the small schoolhouse. The school was heated by a very large Russian stove, around which children of all ages were huddled, trying to get warm.

When the teacher decided that the children were sufficiently warmed up, she called her classes to order. The smallest children, Srolik among them, sat in the front. The rest of the children sat on benches according to age. Beyla, being twelve years old, sat on the bench furthest to the rear.

They began their day with the teacher teaching arithmetic to the older children. The smallest children were to draw pictures of their walk to school. All of the other children were told to read in their books. The teacher had taught the older children problems encountered in everyday life in the Soviet Union. These problems could be solved using mental arithmetic. After several examples were solved, she said, "Now I will give you the most difficult problem of the day. You may not write anything down, so pay close attention to what I say..."

"If seventy-five workers work harvesting wheat on a state farm, and each worker is paid three rubles for his labor, would the state farm have enough money to pay the workers and to get a threshing machine costing 150 rubles? The state farm has 400 rubles to spend."

Twelve-year old Natasha shot her hand in the air. She was called upon and she said, "Yes after the workers were paid, there would be enough money for the thresher."

"That is correct, Natasha. Now who can tell me how much the workers were paid altogether and how much money the state farm had left?"

The children were silent. Either they couldn't remember what each worker was paid (3 rubles) or how many workers there were (75) or the price for the thresher (150 rubles). There had been too much discussion and they had not been permitted to write any of the numbers down. Just as the teacher was ready to help them out, little Srolik raised his hand.

Srolik had a slight lisp. In Russian, if one wishes to tease a lisping young child in a derogatory manner, one calls him "*shepalaver*" (lisper).

"What does the little Jid-shepalaver have to say?" chuckled the teacher.

Srolik rose from his bench. "The state farm would have 175 rubles left after the workers were paid. Seventy-five workers getting three rubles each is 225 rubles. If you subtract 225 from the 400 rubles the state farm had, they would now have 175 rubles. If they spent 150 rubles for the thresher, they would have 25 rubles left," the young child lisped.

The children and the teacher were in awe of the little boy's memory and computation skills. The teacher smiled coldly, winked at the children, and said, "Watch out for that little Jid-shepalaver."

The Christian children laughed. The few Jewish children squirmed in their seats uncomfortably, but did not join in the laughter.

That night, Beyla and Srolik told the family about what had happened at school. "The teacher may have been smiling," said Sarah, "but she didn't like it that a small Jewish boy bested all of the other children. When it comes to Jews," continued Sarah, "you can never trust a Russian."

Sarah was still making her trips to Kiev. The city bustled with changes wrought by the Bolsheviks. Jewish children, in Kiev, went to Russian schools, just as Sarah's children did. Slogans and pictures of Bolshevik leaders decorated the city. But, by and large, the lives of the people of Kiev's large Jewish quarter remained the same.

Sarah still sold her goods and bought the items she needed to sell to her neighbors. But now, Sarah listened avidly to the political comments being made. The word "collectivization" kept cropping up. This frightening new Bolshevik program was bound to eventually affect Vashisht. It could turn all the farmland of Vashisht into one large state or collective farm. Her neighbors, and perhaps even she, would be forced to work on this large farm that would be owned by the government. The workers would be paid salaries for their labors. There would no longer be a need for Sarah's business or her services. Before any of this happened, Sarah wanted to leave Russia and go to America.

When Sarah was in Kiev, and the two younger children were at school, Fayge and Zushe looked after Zada. Zada was very frail. He ate very little and remained in bed most of the day. He no longer had the strength to make and repair shoes. He spent his time praying or talking to Beyla and beautiful eighteen-year old Fayge. Zushe, and even little Srolik, disappointed him. They were not interested in learning Hebrew or reading and discussing the Holy Books. To Zada, they would be failures as Jewish men.

Her father's failing health greatly troubled Sarah. Even though Zada was her greatest stumbling block in her plans for leaving Russia, she wanted him to be well and live many more years. Her wishes for his good health seemed to be in vain, however, because Zada's health continued to fail. Sarah knew that she needed to think seriously about possible travel plans.

Zada was growing weaker and weaker. He now rarely left his bed. Beyla and Fayge washed and combed his long, white beard several times during the week. They sang to him and talked to him for hours at a time. One of the two sisters always remained at Zada's bed side.

As Zada weakened, he could no longer feed himself. His granddaughters fed him and took over his complete care, while their brothers shied away more and more. The boys knew Zada's disappointment in them, but because of the anti-religious propaganda of the Bolsheviks, the boys felt vindicated in their avoidance of religion.

The girls had fewer religious obligations. Zada, therefore, did not consider them to be failures as Jews. Their loving care warmed the old man's failing heart and he never tired of their company. As Zada continued to weaken, it became difficult for him to speak. He would hold each girl's hand in his palsied, wrinkled hands, and whisper prayers and blessings upon them. He would then turn his face to the wall and sleep. On one such night, Zada whispered blessings on his granddaughters, but did not turn away. He continued to hold each girl's hands until his hands stopped shaking, loosened their grip, and were becoming quite cold. Zada had died.

––––––––––

Sarah and the children wrapped Zada's body in a blanket, in which it would be transported to Narovle in their wagon. In the bigger town, the women of the Jewish Burial Society would wash the body, dress it in a simple white shroud, put Zada's *tallit* (prayer shawl) around his neck, and place his body in a plain pine coffin. The coffin would rest in the synagogue until the next day, when it would be carried to the Jewish cemetery for a proper, traditional Jewish burial.

After Zada's funeral, Sarah and her four children stayed at Yossel's house. Yossel, Gittel, and Sarah were cordial once again. Over the years, they had patched up their differences. Therefore, Sarah and her children remained at Yossel's house during the _Shiva week_ (mourning week).

Many friends and relatives came to the Shiva house to express their condolences. There was much talk about Zada's good and long life, about conditions in Russia, about the consolidation of farmlands, and about immigration. Sarah learned that the Bolsheviks had made immigration very difficult. The wily Sarah knew that she needed a plan.

Passport Pictue, 1924

*Sarah shared her passport with Beyla and Srolik. Sarah was in
her mid-thirties. Beyla was sixteen years old, but was registered as
fifteen years old in order to share her mother's passport and come
to America for half of the fare. Srolik was thirteen years old.*

Chapter 2: Leaving

While she was in Narovle, Sarah made some discreet inquiries about which officials would take bribes in order to facilitate immigration. Armed with this information, she had Beyla write to Anna and Herschel, asking them to send money, if it proved to be necessary. Sarah did not know how much money she would need for the bribes, documents, train tickets, and passage on the ship. She informed her children in America, that when she knew what was needed, she would let them know. She assured them that she and their younger brothers and sisters would repay any money that was sent to them.

When Sarah returned to Vashisht, she dug up the bag of gold buried under the stove. The bag was heavy, but Sarah suspected that the costs of going to America would be heavier.

Sarah traveled to Narovle to see Zetomkin, the Bolshevik, now called "Soviet" official, in charge of immigration for the area in which she lived. He was gracious and unctuous to the lovely middle-aged widow, as he told her how difficult the Soviet immigration laws were. Getting passports and booking trips for five people would be very time-consuming and very expensive. He would have to consult with his superiors in Minsk, the provincial capitol. If he got the family clearance to leave Russia, they would have to board a ship in another country. That country needed to grant them permission to enter and to leave.

Zetomkin knew that Sarah faced a great obstacle because of her inability to read and write. "Most immigrants," he said, "go to America in Steerage Class. It is the least expensive passage you can get, but I have been told that all Steerage Class passengers are removed from the ship when it enters New York harbor, and are sent to an island in the harbor before the ship finally docks. At this island the steerage passengers are examined physically and often they are asked to read and write. If something is wrong physically or they are illiterate, they can be sent back to the country from which they sailed."

"The only way to avoid problems of possible deportation upon arrival in the United States is to travel in a higher class. I would suggest Second Class, which unfortunately, is very much more expensive than Steerage Class. But in Second Class, the passengers stay on board the ship until it docks in New York City. When they disembark there, they are never tested or examined."

Zetomkin offered to find out the cost of Second Class passage for Sarah and her family. He would also find out the cost of train fare, passports, and any other necessary legal documents they would require. "Of course," he said upon conclusion, "there will also be some charges from me. Do you think you can gather enough money for such a trip?" he asked.

"Yes," replied Sarah. She now knew that she and her four younger children would be paying Anna and Herschel money for a long, long time; but she also realized that this was definitely the time to leave Russia.

"But what if my children in America can't or won't help?" she pondered. "I will not worry about that until I know how much money I will need and how much help Anna and Herschel can give me."

———

When the letter from America came, Fayge read it aloud to the whole family. Anna wrote that she had just learned that she and her husband, Meyer, were going to have a baby. She said that they did not have large sums of money, but that she was prepared to send whatever was needed, even if she had to sell household belongings or pawn her engagement ring. She hoped that they would send her information about the amount of money they would need, very soon. It was her observation that in a very

32

short time, immigration would be getting more difficult. The American newspapers were reporting that the American Congress was working on a law that would halt most immigration from Russia. She wanted the family to be in America before this terrible law was enacted.

Zetomkin wanted them to leave for America quickly too. He had heard of the impending American ban on most immigration from Eastern Europe. It would dry up a lucrative source of bribery money for him, so he wanted to get as many big bribes as he could get, before "the well went dry." Consequently, Zetomkin got Sarah the information she needed, very quickly.

Sarah had enough money in her bag under the stove to pay for the stiff bribe for Zetomkin and for all of the documents needed for the family's trip. After she paid for these, the bag of gold was much thinner, but it wasn't empty.

Zetomkin told Sarah about a ship leaving from Riga, Latvia in five months. He asked if she would be able to get enough money together by that time to pay for the ocean passage and for train tickets for the long train ride to Riga. Sarah couldn't answer. She had not yet heard from Anna regarding amounts of money she could send.

––––––––––

Six weeks later, Anna's letter came. It contained as much money as Sarah had saved under the stove in all those years. Anna explained that she and Meyer owned a house, which they had re-mortgaged to obtain the needed money. They would have to pay the bank back in installments in a timely fashion or they could lose their house. Anna said that the money she sent was the entire loan on her house. She said she knew that when the family came to America, they would get jobs and pay Meyer and her back as quickly as possible. Herschel, she informed them, had just gotten married. His wife, Lily, had furnished their little apartment, and now they had no money left. Although Lily didn't believe that they were obliged to help, Herschel was deeply shamed because of his lack of contribution. His shame was keeping him from writing, but Anna assured them he would get over it and welcome the family with open arms.

After receiving Anna's letter, Sarah rushed to Narovle and finished her dealings with Zetomkin. Now she must await the documents from Minsk, the train tickets, and Second Class ocean liner tickets. All of these would be sent to her home in Vashisht. In the meantime, she and her children must dispose of most of their belongings and pack what they were bringing to America.

———

The family's two most difficult separations were from Basha, their cow, and Boris, their faithful old horse. Boris was sold, along with the wagon, to Peter Geshenko, a farmer who lived just outside of Vashisht. Basha was given as a gift to their beloved Christian friend, Masha, who had always been so good to the family and had saved them during the Polish pogrom.

A tearful Zushe delivered Boris to the Geshenko farm. When Zushe returned, he silently gave Sarah the money he had received for Boris. It was at this time that Sarah burst into tears, too. She wept for Boris a long time.

While Sarah was weeping, Beyla was in the lean-to with Basha. Beyla had cared for Basha when the cow was little more than a calf. She was more a pet to the girl than a farm animal who gave the family milk. Beyla was the one who milked Basha every morning, and every morning she talked to the cow about her plans for the day and her hopes and plans for the future. She would miss Basha dreadfully.

"Basha," Beyla said tearfully, "if cows were allowed on trains and ships, I'd take you with me to America. Because we can't, we're giving you to the nicest Christian in Vashisht. Masha will take such good care of you, that you'll probably forget me. But I- I'll remember you always I love you, Basha!" Beyla burst into tears and ran into the house.

———

Srolik often felt curious about his father. Sarah had told him that he had a different father from his brothers and sisters. She had told him that she and his father were deeply in love, but that when they married, his father had a hard time adjusting to her large family, and her children never became attached to him. Consequently, Sarah said, she believed it would be better for all concerned, if they were divorced. Sarah told Srolik that the divorce broke both their hearts. She said that she felt love for his father, even now. She assured Srolik that his father had not wanted to leave, but that she had forced him out. She even told him that his father wanted to take his baby son when he had left, but that she forbade it. She said she loved her baby too much to let even his own father have him.

———

Now that the family was making its final farewells, Sarah asked Srolik if he would like to meet his father before the family left for America. Srolik looked forward to doing so.

Srolik wrote a letter to Avroham in Kiev, in which he explained that his mother, he, and his brothers and sisters were leaving Russia (now the Soviet Union) for good. He asked if his father would like to see him before he left. "If so," he wrote, "send me a letter telling me when and where we should meet."

Avroham answered Srolik's letter very quickly. He indicated great joy at the prospect of finally meeting his oldest son. He told Srolik that he had married and he had three other children by his new wife. Srolik's siblings in Kiev ranged in age from infant to seven years old.

In a state of great excitement, Srolik traveled to Kiev with his mother. They took a room with two beds in an inn in Kiev, and Sarah accompanied Srolik, on the streetcar, to a street in the Jewish Quarter. There, Sarah directed Srolik to Avroham's house. She said she'd remain in a nearby coffee house for however long Srolik's visit lasted.

———

Srolik knocked on the door of his father's apartment. Loud children's laughter and voices could be heard at the door, as Srolik waited for his knock to be answered. A short, plump, red headed woman answered the door.

"You must be Srolik," she said smiling broadly, "I'm your stepmother. Come in! Come in!"

Srolik followed her into a dimly lit, small apartment. In the kitchen sat a man with blue eyes and a light brown, short beard. Srolik knew immediately that the smiling man was Avroham.

Avroham was stunned by how much the boy resembled him. He

rose and shook hands with Srolik saying, "How are your mother, your grandfather, and your brothers and sisters?"

"They're all fine," said Srolik, "but Zada is dead."

Conversation was difficult and stilted. Avroham and Srolik were two strangers that could not bridge the long years of separation. To make matters worse, Avroham's wife and children kept coming into the kitchen and interrupting Srolik and Avroham in their vain attempts at meaningful conversation.

"It is too bad that you are leaving the country," said Avroham. "With more visits, we could have gotten to know each other."

"Yes" concurred Srolik. "It is too bad." After a protracted silence, he said, "I must be going. My mother is waiting for me."

Avroham said, "Please send your mother my regards. Tell her I wish her and her children good luck in America."

"I have a gift for you," he continued. He opened a drawer and withdrew a small package, wrapped in tissue paper and tied with string. He gave the package to Srolik.

"Thank you," said the boy. He broke the string and unwrapped his present. His father had given him a blue woolen cap and a pair of blue woolen gloves. Srolik donned the cap and gloves and shook hands with the blue-eyed stranger. Both the boy and the man realized, sadly, that there would never be a relationship between them. The years had reduced their relationship to a blue woolen cap and blue woolen gloves.

Srolik ran to the coffee shop in which Sarah waited. He hugged and kissed his mother and showed her his gift. When Sarah asked Srolik how the visit with his father had gone, he said, "A nice man, who is a stranger, introduced me to his wife and children, who are also strangers. The nice man gave me a little gift. My visit didn't get me a father. It got me a cap and gloves."

A sad Sarah and an even sadder Srolik returned to the inn. On the following day they returned to their family in Vashisht. Srolik would never contact Avroham again.

Fayge was twenty-one years old and very beautiful. Her thick, long, honey blond braids crowned her head. Even in the thin winter sunshine, her beautiful hair shone. As she walked about the village, male eyes followed each determined step she took. Her attire was far more in keeping with Kiev than Vashisht. Her shiny black boots had been fashioned by Zada a year before he died. Her beautiful fur coat had been purchased by Sarah in Kiev, when Fayge was eighteen-years old. Not only did it keep Fayge warm during Vashisht's viciously cold winters, the fur coat, with its matching fur hat and fur muff made twenty-one year old Fayge look like a sophisticated young city-woman.

Fayge knew that she was lovely and she knew that she turned male heads. And being young, Fayge's head was turned too. She had set her sights on a young man whose father was a rabbi in Narovle. He and his father often came to Vashisht when a rabbi was needed by someone in the village's Jewish community. At these times, young David Cohen's eyes followed Fayge, and he spoke to her at every opportunity he could get.

Sarah warned Fayge, and Rabbi Cohen warned David, that a friendship between a girl from so humble a family and a rabbi's son was unsuitable. The infatuated Fayge believed that David would turn a deaf ear on his father. She was wrong. David did not choose to go against tradition, and he ended his friendship with the beautiful Fayge, by marrying his father's choice, the daughter of a rabbi from Mozyr.

Fayge's broken heart mended quickly. Her medicine was the exciting prospects and many preparations for the family's impending trip to America. Everything was happening too fast to brood about a lost love. Instead, Fayge made her farewells to friends, neighbors, and relatives in Vashisht and Narovle, and she never looked back. The only thing preventing Fayge from making a truly smooth departure from the home and people she had always known, was not the loss of David Cohen... It was the tenacity of Husmann.

Husmann was a love-sick young man of twenty-three. For four years, he had been pursuing Fayge. He pressed small gifts and poorly written poems upon her. In his poems he declared his undying love for her. His constant declarations of love gave her no peace.

For four years, Fayge had rebuffed Husmann. Early in his pursuit, she had tried to be kind to the infatuated young man, but kindness caused his persistence to increase. As Husmann's frantic courting persisted, Fayge's rebuffs became stronger and less sensitive. She no longer cared for the lovesick young man's feelings, and made it quite clear to him that she did not like his stalking, his gifts, or his poetry. She demanded that he stay away from her permanently; but to no avail! Husmann was always there, begging Fayge to reconsider.

On the day that Sarah's family boarded the hired wagon that would take them away from Vashisht to the train in Mozyr, a small weeping crowd of friends, neighbors, and relatives formed to bid Sarah and her family farewell. As the wagon slowly pulled away, a man on horseback joined it. It was Husmann. Husmann followed the wagon on its long trip to the train station in Mozyr. Throughout the trip he kept pleading his case with Fayge. He even tried to convince Sarah that she should make Fayge stay, because he loved her so much, that no other man would ever be as good to her as he would be.

Fayge was offended and annoyed. Her disrespect for Husmann and his humiliating pleas caused her to speak sharply and unkindly, "Go home, Husmann," she said, "You humiliate me and yourself with this wretched display. Make yourself a life! Marry some unlucky girl! But leave me alone!"

Husmann continued to follow them in silence. When they were close to the railway station, he spoke again. In an otherworldly, deep voice filled with anger and pain, the rejected suitor said, "Goodbye. May you arrive in America safely. But let me warn you…when you are there you shall not be safe from me. I'll get you! Remember…Husmann will get even…I will get you!" He then turned his horse and galloped away in the direction of Vashisht.

The family had very little time to discuss their encounter with the crazed Husmann. They had arrived at the railroad station and there was much to do.

————

The train ride was long and interesting. As they peered out of the windows, Russia and Latvia flew by before their eyes. The scenery, replete with lush forests, sleepy towns, and many farms, was so engaging that they often forgot hunger. The train made several stops to allow new passengers on and to allow passengers to leave at the small towns and cities on their route. At each station, local men and women boarded the train to sell food and beverages to the passengers who were remaining on board. Sarah and her family were *kosher* (followed Jewish dietary laws), so they bought only tea and fresh fruit from the food vendors, because their religion forbade them to eat non-kosher meat or use non-kosher eating utensils and plates.

The family did very well on the fresh fruit, the tea, and the beautiful and interesting landscape. When the conductor announced their imminent arrival in Riga, there wasn't one member of the family who could believe the train ride was over. They had been so mesmerized by the farms, towns, cities, and the great Russian and Latvian forests that had whizzed by, that they had lost all sense of time.

————

After showing their documents to the uniformed men at the station, they were passed through and found themselves on a sidewalk in front of the large train station.

Riga was incredible! They needed to remain in this bustling Latvian port city for two days, before they could board the ship that would take them to America; consequently, they needed transportation to a hotel or inn in the Jewish Quarter. This was not difficult, because dray wagons, horse drawn carriages, and automobiles that served as taxis lined the sidewalk. Sarah pointed out a dray wagon to which she, Zushe, and Srolik carried two suitcases each. Beyla and Fayge struggled with the weight of a small trunk that they both carried to the wagon together.

After being dropped off at a small inn in the Jewish Quarter, they arranged for their two-day stay in Riga. They dragged their luggage and their exhausted bodies to the room they had acquired. Zushe and Srolik removed only their shoes and fell into bed with their clothes on. The three females in the family tried to sleep in their undergarments, on the other of the room's two beds, which was barely wide enough for two of them. Because they were so exhausted, they managed anyhow. Indeed, all of the five weary travelers slept for six hours without any interruption or anyone awakening even once.

While the dawn crept over Riga, the family washed and used the communal toilet, located at the far end of the hall. As Beyla and Zushe left the bathroom, they each expressed their wonder at the pump that brought them ice-cold water with which to wash, and at the toilet that had water flushed into it when one pulled a chain suspended from a wooden box located near the ceiling. The water washed their wastes down a hole, about which each of them wondered, "To what the hole lead, and to where their wastes went?"

Sarah, Srolik, and Fayge laughed at their brother and sister. The three of them had been to Kiev and had seen the "wonders" of the modern plumbing of the early twentieth century.

The family found a small kosher restaurant not far from the inn, where they each ate a hearty breakfast. When they were finished, Sarah asked the proprietor where there was a reliable shop that sold watches. He directed them to a nearby main street on which they could take the streetcar that ran from there to City Central. He said there were several reputable watch shops located there.

Sarah was grateful that she and her children could speak Yiddish and Russian. Yiddish was useful in speaking to her fellow Jews in the Jewish Quarter of Riga, and Russian resembled many languages like Polish or Czech and would probably prove useful on this trip. To Sarah's great surprise, there was a resemblance to Yiddish in the Latvian language, because Yiddish and Latvian are Germanic languages. If it was necessary, they could probably get by even if they needed to talk to a Christian Latvian.

The two untraveled members of the family were awestricken by the streetcar clanging on the tracks in the middle of Riga's busy traffic; and they were thunderstruck by City Center! The sidewalk was crowded with people and lined with many, many shops. Never had they seen roads crowded with so many wagons, bicycles, and an occasional automobile or two. The volume of noise from the people and vehicles stunned them. Having been to Kiev, Sarah, Fayge, and Srolik found their wonderment very amusing. The whole family felt very happy to be in bustling Riga.

As they walked along, they gazed into shop windows showing every manner of fine clothing and jewelry. Then they came upon a shop that seemed to specialize in timepieces. Sarah liked the appearance of many of the watches in the shop's window. It was her intention to buy Anna and her new daughter-in-law, Lily, beautiful watches that hung on long gold chains. Sarah had seen such watches being worn by the most fashionable ladies in Kiev. She would also buy Herschel and her son-in-law, Meyer, pocket watches attached to gold chains.

The family entered the brightly lit shop. It's electric lighting dazzled all of them. Even Sarah, Fayge, and Srolik who had seen electric lights in Kiev, had never been in an establishment that was so brilliantly lighted. Speaking in Russian, Sarah inquired about the watches she sought for Anna and Lily. A clerk directed her to a case containing at least ten watches of the type Sarah was seeking. After selecting two of these, she inquired about watches for the men in her family in America. She was taken to an even larger case, containing at least thirty pocket watches.

Now the real work began. Sarah asked to speak to the owner of the shop. The clerk fearing he would lose his commission for the sale, assured Sarah that he could help her. He said that the owner of the shop wasn't in.

Sarah and her children turned to leave. The clerk hurried after them and mumbled, "Don't go, I'll try to find the owner." He disappeared through a door in the rear of the shop, and reemerged with an elderly, bearded Jewish man, whose ear locks almost reached his shoulders. The younger members of the family thought that this elderly Jew looked like Zada.

"*Landsmann* (Countryman)," Sarah said speaking in Yiddish, "I am going to America to join two of my children. I have not seen them since 1910. Fourteen years ago, I sent two children, in their teens, to America. Now they are both grown up and married."

"I am a poor woman, but I do not want to come to my children and the people that they have married, empty-handed. These four watches would surely show them how much they mean to me. I am prepared to purchase them with some of the little money I have accumulated to help me, and these, my remaining children, to settle in America, but I cannot spend everything I have."

"When you came through that back door, I was greatly surprised. I never expected to see a Jew, wealthy enough to own this fine establishment. I ask you with deep sincerity, to show understanding, and give me your lowest possible price."

The old man raised his eyes heavenward, emitted a long sigh, and said, "You have chosen my finest watches. Choose some of the cheaper ones. As much as I'd like to give you a reasonable price, these watches are so fine, that you will probably find my prices too expensive. Yet, my prices are so low, that I will write them in Russian rubles on a piece of paper, because I don't want anyone to know how foolhardy I am for a lovely woman's touching story."

The storeowner wrote four prices and showed them to Sarah.

"Preposterous!" Sarah exclaimed. Those prices are at least twice what these watches would be sold for in Kiev. Give me fair prices, or I will leave, and purchase watches at another store whose prices are better."

The elderly proprietor looked pained. "I am a religious man," he said. "It is a sin to cheat people. Are you accusing me of being a cheat?"

Sarah looked squarely into the man's small eyes. "There is lots of room to maneuver prices," she said. "A high price that is still an honest price is a long way from a low price that is fair to the buyer of your watches. As a truly religious man, you know that God expects us all to be both fair and compassionate. I understand your need to make a living and I am not asking you to give up all of your profit. I am asking you to show compassion to a widow who is being united with children she has not seen for fourteen years. I wish to come to my children with gifts that will show them how much I value them; yet, I will need money to get my other children and myself, settled in America. Can you not give me a price that would help me achieve both of my goals?"

"I am a good Jew," said the shop owner. "I would like to make a lovely widowed mother happy as she travels to America with her children. Therefore, I shall write my last price. As *Adenoi* (God) lives, I will not sell these watches for a kopek less."

The owner wrote his final prices on the piece of paper. He had greatly reduced his prices from the first bid, and Sarah now believed the new prices were fair. She had her children's and their spouses' names engraved on each person's watch and was extremely pleased with her purchase.

The family walked around Riga for the remainder of the day. As the sun was sinking in the sky, they boarded the trolley and traveled to the street nearest the restaurant in which they had eaten breakfast. They ate a fine, large kosher dinner at the restaurant, and then returned to the inn in complete darkness. They were grateful for the gas street lamps that lit their way. Riga was a marvelous city, indeed.

————

After a good second night's sleep at the inn in Riga, the family began to get itself together for the trip to the ship. Sarah was glad that the merchants in Riga accepted Russian currency, when she gave Zushe money and told him to go with Srolik to buy them food for breakfast. She reminded him that they had passed several shops selling food, just a block away.

The three females packed and dressed with care. They wanted to look nice when they boarded the ship. While they were still primping, the boys returned, bringing milk, apples, and bread for all of them. The fresh milk and bread were delicious, and the crunchy apples were a wonderful dessert.

Sarah paid the innkeeper, and she and the girls went out on the sidewalk with the luggage. The boys ran to the main thoroughfare, where they had taken the streetcars the day before. They stopped a dray wagon and directed the driver to the inn where he would pick up their mother, their sisters, and their luggage. They kept pace with the dray wagon until it arrived at where Sarah and her daughters were waiting. Once everybody and everything were ensconced in the wagon, the bouncing trip to the docks began. They bumped and pitched for almost an hour. Riga's traffic, a sluggish horse, and a long awaited destiny made the ride seem utterly interminable.

————

At the dock, the dray wagon dropped them very close to a long, rectangular one-story building in which their documents would be examined before they could board the ship. With great difficulty they carried, pushed, and pulled their luggage into a building, teaming with people scheduled to board the ship. Many of them were speaking Yiddish. Most of the Jews were in line, waiting to be processed for boarding in the steerage area. It seemed to Sarah and her family that the steerage passengers were being asked to read to the officials at a long table. If this were done to Sarah, she would fail! Sarah could read numbers, but she couldn't read words. Would Sarah be allowed to board the ship?

On a distant wall, Beyla spied a sign written in Russian. The sign hung behind another long table where fewer officials sat and where the line of people waiting was much shorter than the line for steerage. The sign read, "Second Class Passengers." The family hurried over.

Zushe presented his documents first. He was asked to read a small paragraph in either Russian or Yiddish. As he read the Yiddish, the family sweated in fear.

Fayge, who had already suffered the trauma of Husmann, was next to suffer the trauma of processing for admission to the ship. She presented her documents and smiled gently at the flat-faced Slavic official. He was totally oblivious to her charms, but was drawn to and seemed fascinated by the red rash which had appeared on Fayge's neck. "What is that?" he asked pointing at the rash.

"I always get a rash if I'm nervous or excited," the lovely young woman said. "This trip to America has excited me."

"We don't send Russians, Poles, Latvians, Jews or anyone else to America if they have rashes," sneered the Latvian official. "The Americans send such people back to us, and there's hell to pay when they land. We'll keep you here until you are less excited."

Sarah rushed up to the man and said, "Let her on the boat. The rash will be gone by the time we arrive in America. Besides, we are Second

Class passengers. We were assured that there would be no examinations of Second Class passengers when we get to America." Sarah's hand reached out. A ten-ruble note protruded from it.

The Latvian official snatched it. "I can get into big trouble for this," he said.

Another ten-ruble note appeared.

The Latvian official pocketed the second bill, and quickly stamped all of their documents. With great rapidity, he waved Sarah and her children through. They then nervously boarded the ship that would take them to America.

––––––––

The ship was filled with many wonders and was gargantuan in size. The family's two cabins seemed like palaces. Each cabin had its own little bathroom. There were enough bunks to allow each member of the family to sleep alone. Sarah's children could not remember ever having beds that they did not share with at least one sibling.

They stowed their belongings and went out on the deck. They stood at the rail and watched their fellow passengers walk up the gangway. What an array of people! Among them were many people who resembled the Jews of Vashisht and Narovle. Most of these were *shtetle* Jews (Jews coming from small Jewish towns). The vast majority of the Jews in Russia lived in shtetles. There were also people from Poland and the Baltic States. Most of the people were peasants, whether Jewish or Christian, going to America, where they would be peasants no more.

Interspersed with the horde of peasants were people, who appeared to Sarah, to be Russian gentry. Russia's gentry was being roughly treated in the Bolshevik's new order. Perhaps these were among the lucky members of the upper classes who had managed to leave Russia with some of their wealth, to start new lives elsewhere. This more refined group generally headed for the second and first class sections.

Most of the noisy peasant passengers walked in the direction of the steerage section. Sarah's children would have like to join them and talk to them, but Steerage Class was strictly separated from Second Class and

First Class. The passengers in steerage were not permitted leave, and the upper deck passengers could not go into the steerage section.

On the shore, a band was playing. The music and the noises of departure were very exciting. Suddenly the ship made a huge blast of sound. The gangplanks were lifted. They were leaving Europe and going to America!

———

For Sarah's family, life on the ship was unbelievably opulent. So great were the food choices, that they were easily able to maintain their kosher diets. Fruits, vegetables and eggs were available at every meal. Some of the foods were unknown to the family, so experimentation with new fruits and vegetables frequently occurred. Beyla developed a love for bananas. She had never seen a banana until she had boarded the ship, and after her first taste of this tropical fruit, she craved it constantly.

For two days, the sea was calm. It looked like beautiful green glass. The sun twinkled on a sea so quiet that even the sailors commented on it. The Baltic was not known for its friendliness to ships, but rather it was known to be rough much more than calm, and even when calm, to be somewhat choppy. This idyllic weather and exceptionally calm sea was a rarity that both passengers and crew were reveling in.

Sarah and her family spent most of their time on deck, observing the crew and their fellow passengers. They enjoyed watching the ship create foam as it cut through the lovely green water.

———

On their third day at sea, the ship came close enough to land for the people on board to see houses, trees, and a green rolling landscape. A sailor told Srolik that they were sailing in German waters and that the land they saw was Germany. He said that they would drop anchor at Hamburg, long enough to pick up a few new passengers and some supplies.

But before they were fully docked at Hamburg, they saw a dreadful sight....Boys and young men were diving into the murky water to retrieve some of the ship's garbage that was being dumped into the sea. As the family watched them go after the garbage, a horrified Srolik asked his big sister Fayge, why they were doing such a disgusting thing. Fayge shook her head and explained, "Just recently, Germany lost the Great War. Now the

German people are being heavily taxed to pay the victors for some of the damages caused by the war. This has caused great hardship for German businesses, and many Germans workers are now out of work. The people that you are seeing diving for the ship's garbage are hoping to retrieve something that can be either eaten or sold. The Germans are in a desperate state," Fayge explained sadly.

The stop at Hamburg was very short and soon the ship was at sea again. They were leaving the Baltic Sea and entering the North Sea. From there, Europe would soon be left behind, as they sailed westward, across the great Atlantic Ocean to America.

———

Beyla had just finished stuffing herself with two delicious bananas when she realized that tall waves were slapping against the sides of the ship. The ship rocked from side to side and soon was bouncing up and down. This trip through the North Sea was nothing like the gentle glide through the Baltic. The ship pitched precariously! With each pitch of the ship, Beyla felt her stomach lurch. Her mouth tasted very sour. Unable to contemplate food, she rushed out of the dining room, planning to get to her cabin to lie down. Before she even got near her cabin, she felt so nauseated, that she ran to the railing of the bouncing ship, hung her head over it, and vomited for a very long time. Finally, a desperately sick Beyla crept to her cabin and lay down in her bunk. For the rest of the stormy, bumpy trip to America, Beyla remained in her cabin, feeling dreadfully sick and being unable to eat very much at all.

Her mother and her siblings looked after Beyla and worried about her. While Zushe, Fayge, and Sarah had occasional bouts of seasickness too, none of them fared as poorly as the stricken Beyla.

In the rare moments when Beyla felt strong enough to speak, she kept blaming her condition on the bananas she had eaten. She vowed that she would never eat another banana again. When told that her illness was seasickness, caused by the ship's pitching on a very choppy sea, Beyla rejected the explanation. It would be several years before she would try to eat another banana.

———

The sea calmed down two days before their arrival in New York City. The sun shone and all of the family, except Beyla, promenaded the decks and ate the lovely food that was provided for them. Beyla remained in her bunk, feeling very weak from having been so violently seasick for so many days. She relished napping without the violent pitching that had been caused by the rough seas. She had also begun to eat most of the food brought to her by her family.

Beyla was lying in her bunk, enjoying a peaceful reverie about life in America, when the door of the cabin burst open and Srolik shouted, "Get dressed and come on deck quickly. We will soon be in New York!"

Bella, 17 years old   *Fanny, approximately 1927*

Bella and Irving, approximately 1929   Sol and Eva, approximately 1929

Family Portrait, 1929
Rear, l. to r. Irving, Murray, Meyer, Anna, Harry, Lily and Baby Erna, Sol.
Front l. to r. Bella, Fanny and Baby Millie, Sarah, Milton with Ida
seated in front of him, Max, Arthur, Eva (pregnant with Mel)

Chapter 3: New York

New York City's weather welcomed the family. The sun shone brightly on the water and the many ships in the busy bay leading to the harbor. As the family squinted in the bright sunshine, they saw a small island on which there was a very large green statue of a woman holding a torch aloft in one hand and a book in the other hand.

"That must be the Statute of Liberty!" exclaimed an excited Srolik. The book I read about America talks about this statue. The Americans placed it in their harbor to welcome people like us.... people who want to live in America and become Americans."

There were many people standing along the rail up and down the ship. Most of them stood in awe and said nothing. Sarah stood along the rail too. Her thoughts raced as tears poured out of her eyes. "I've done it!" she thought. "I brought my family to safety! We no longer will have to be afraid, because we are Jews."

Sarah's victorious thoughts were dashed by an announcement being made by the captain. "Ladies and Gentlemen...I am sure that all of you were aware of a law that would soon be passed by the United States Congress, establishing quotas for every European country. This law was designed to limit the numbers of immigrants the United States will permit to enter the country. This difficult law has now unfortunately been passed, and passengers with passports from countries in Eastern Europe will find that their countries' tiny quotas have already been filled for 1924. The authorities have informed me that no passenger from the Soviet Union, Lithuania, Latvia, Estonia, Romania, or Poland will be admitted to the United States. The small quotas for these eastern European countries are already filled."

"I am engaged in a discussion with these authorities, in the hopes that they will change their minds, but the situation looks very grim. It is very likely that I will have to turn the ship around and return to Riga with all of the passengers from Eastern Europe still on board. A launch will come to take the passengers from Germany to New York City. Germany has a large, unfilled quota."

"We will probably be allowed to stay in this bay until we have refueled and have taken on new provisions for the trip back to Latvia. Make yourselves comfortable until everything is resolved."

The vast majority of the passengers were, indeed, from eastern European countries whose quotas were filled. Gloom enveloped the ship. Dejected passengers wept quietly as they stared at the welcoming statue that now refused to welcome *them*.

Sarah's victory was short lived. She was devastated, because she would not get to be with Anna, Herschel, and her new son and daughter in-law. But even more devastating was the fact that she and four of her children were being returned to the hated land they had left.

———

Fayge dejectedly watched the German passengers board the launch that had come for them. In her misery, she mused, "Did that awful Husmann somehow wish this calamity on me?"

Suddenly, Fayge saw another launch pull alongside the ship. Four people were scrutinizing the passengers standing forlornly at the ship's rail. One of the men's eyes fell upon Sarah. "Mama!" he yelled. "Mama!"

Sarah had seen the launch too and had heard the man calling, "Mama," but no mental connection occurred until one of the women on the launch jumped up and shouted, "Mama, it's me Mama…Anna!" Sarah felt faint. The man and woman calling to her were her children, Anna and Herschel! Anna was big with child, but even from the height at which Sarah stood, she knew her daughter's face. Anna, in her late twenties, bore a remarkable resemblance to herself, at the time that she had bid her daughter and Herschel farewell when they left Russia.

Sarah called back to them as she burst into tears. Anna and even Herschel were crying. It seemed as if all of their hopes had been dashed. The family would be returned to Russia. They would never be reunited. Anna was so unhappy about the sad outcome of her family's trip, that she momentarily lost her powerful reasoning power.

"Pick up Baby Beyla," Anna shouted, tearfully. For her, the years had momentarily slipped away.

"This is Baby Beyla....all grown up," Sarah yelled down to them. She pointed to the very lovely, dark-haired teenager standing next to her. "Even Srolik, who was an infant when you left, is a big boy," she continued as she pointed to her darling, youngest son.

Anna shouted up to the family that the man with her was her husband, Meyer. She introduced them to Herschel's wife, Lily, too.

Suddenly Sarah remembered! She sent Zushe to run to her cabin to get the watches which were in a drawer in the cabin, tied tightly in a red scarf. If she kept these watches, the authorities would probably confiscate them upon their arrival in either Latvia or Russia, so as soon as Sarah had the watches in her hand, she shouted, "Herschel, I'm throwing down presents for all of you. Wear them in good health....Herschel, catch!"

Sarah flung the scarf containing the watches overboard toward where Herschel was standing in the launch. It was a brilliant pitch and an even more brilliant catch. Her children on the launch untied the scarf and shouted their surprise and thanks to Sarah.

They talked and talked until the captain of the launch reminded them that the launch was rented for only two hours, and their time would soon be up. Feeling great sorrow, Sarah's "American family" left in the launch. In tears, they bid their family farewell.

———

Waiting for the launch, as soon as it docked, were two Coast Guard officers and a New York City policeman. They were interested in speaking to Herschel. "Hand over the package that was thrown to you," said the taller of the Coast Guardsmen.

Herschel looked bewildered. "There was no package," he replied. "My mother wrapped some watches in a kerchief, and threw them to me. They were gifts for the four of us."

"Let me see the watches," ordered the man.

Herschel, Anna, Lily, and Meyer handed over the watches. The two Coast Guardsmen and the policeman examined each watch and quietly conferred with each other, as the four family members waited. The tall man was the spokesperson. "These watches look like they're made of gold. We think you've been involved in smuggling. We're taking you to the station, so that they can decide whether to charge you," he said. Herschel was handcuffed and put into a police car. Before the law enforcement officers got away, a very frightened Anna ran up to them and asked where the police station was located.

Having been told where Herschel was being taken, Meyer hailed a taxi, and a tearful Lily and very worried Anna and Meyer got in. The taxi took Herschel's three relatives to the police station.

In the station house, many people were milling around, but there didn't seem to be any sign of Herschel. Lily went to the police sergeant's desk and tearfully explained what had happened to her husband. The Irish policeman felt some pity for the young woman crying before him, and told her that Herschel would be all right, but would have to spend the night in jail. He would be held until his mother was taken from the ship, so that she could clarify exactly what had happened. The sergeant further stated that he was an immigrant, too, so he understood the excitement relatives feel when they are expecting to be reunited with their loved ones. He felt sorry for the disappointed people and told Lily not to worry. Everything would probably be straightened out in the morning.

Anna's husband Meyer did not wait until the next morning. His business, which was located in Manhattan, prospered because he kept the corrupt police and politicians of the area in Manhattan in which the business was located, "happy." Because he periodically "paid them off," they left him in peace. Now he wanted to "call-in" some of his favors.

He quickly placed a telephone call to the police precinct where his store was located. He asked that his brother-in-law be promptly released, with all charges dropped. He promised his contact a generous pay-off.

Meyer's contact assured Meyer that he would get Herschel off, if the morning's investigation went badly, but because the Coast Guard was involved, he wouldn't interfere before the investigation took place.

————

In the morning a Coast Guard launch pulled alongside the anchored ocean liner. Two Coast Guardsmen boarded the ship and went to see the captain. After a few minutes, two of the ship's sailors were dispatched to the Second Class area, and Sarah and her entire family were brought to the captain. The family's luggage was loaded onto the Coast Guard launch, followed by Sarah, her children, and the Coast Guardsmen. After a speedy ride to the wharf, the family and their luggage were jammed into two waiting police cars that sped off to the police station in which Herschel was being held.

At the police station, Anna was the spokesperson. In a trembling voice, she explained to the sergeant in charge, just how Herschel came into possession of the watches. She begged the sergeant to release him, and then turned to her newly arrived family and told them in Yiddish about the events that had transpired when their launch arrived at the dock. She explained that because of the watches, Herschel might be arraigned for smuggling.

"Tell the policeman that I have a receipt of purchase from the store in Riga where I bought the watches," said Sarah. "And tell him to look at your names that I had engraved on the back of each of the watches."

Anna did as she was told, and the policeman asked to see the receipt and the engravings. Sarah rummaged through her suitcase and presented the receipt from Riga.

Meyer realized that he would not need his police connections to get Herschel released. The receipt and the engravings would probably satisfy the policeman, as to the immigrant family's innocence.

Meyer was correct. In minutes, a very rumpled and tired Herschel was returned to his family. All charges were dropped, and Lily cried with relief.

On the other hand, Sarah and Anna's tears were tears of anguish. They both knew that the family was going to be returned to the ship and then to Europe. They were in anguish because they feared that they would never see each other again. The sympathetic Coast Guardsmen and New York City policemen looked away and gave the recently reunited family some time together. After a little over an hour, the senior Coast Guardsman called the captain of his launch to announce that he was returning the family to the ship. The captain of the launch replied, almost hysterically, "The goddamned ship set sail for Europe over an hour ago. We can't catch it or stop it! I'll call Immigration and ask them what we should do with the people you have," the captain of the Coast Guard launch said, angrily.

The young Coast Guardsman explained the problem to the police sergeant. The sergeant said that the family could visit at the police station while the disposition of their case was decided. "It's my guess," he said to Anna, "that your family will be taken to Ellis Island, and be kept there until they can get on the next ship to return them to where they had come from."

———

Meyer wanted nothing to do with Ellis Island. He believed that their ship having sailed was just his chance. He promptly telephoned a politician to whom he had been very "kind." Meyer explained the situation and asked the politician to do what he could to legalize his wife's family's immigration to the United States. The politician replied that he needed to contact the Department of Immigration, where he knew an official that could help Meyer's family.

In less than an hour, Sarah's family was released from the police station. A courier from the Department of Immigration had arrived with documents legalizing their entrance to the United States.

———

— Meyer knew he had a huge debt to pay. His new greenhorn relatives would pay this debt in addition to the debt they owed for their transportation to America.

— Sarah knew that what had transpired was the work of God! Only God could change a wretched fate into a fate with infinite possibilities.

— Superstitious Fayge knew that Husmann had not been instrumental in their American adventure. She was greatly relieved.

— Lily, Herschel's young wife, knew that her first encounter with Herschel's newly arrived family had been very unpleasant. The young woman seriously doubted that she would like these people who had just been reunited with her husband. She felt certain that she would have to work to put some distance between Herschel and his troublesome, greenhorn family.

— All of them knew that their arrival in the United States was providential. Now, more than ever, they believed that the opportunities in this marvelous new land would be endless.

————————

Anna took charge of the new arrivals. She hailed three taxis, and the entire family, plus luggage, was stuffed into them. The taxi drivers were told to go the nearest BMT subway station. Not counting their speedy ride to the police station, this was the family's first ride in an automobile. They were thrilled! But even more thrilling was the traffic and many pedestrians they saw on their five-minute ride to the subway. Compared to this crowded, bustling city, Riga was only a town. Even Kiev had very little motorized traffic. New York truly astounded the new arrivals.

Wonders continued! Anna directed the newcomers to a staircase going underground. A little apprehensively, they copied the New Yorkers walking down the mysterious stairs. Anna said that the stairs led them to a train station where they could catch a train to Brooklyn. She explained that New York City was extremely large and needed transportation above the ground and under the ground. The trains running under the ground were part of a subway system that connected four of New York City's boroughs. The borough they were leaving was called Manhattan. They were going to Brooklyn, the borough in which she and Meyer lived.

Anna also explained that Lily and Herschel had recently moved to a lovely apartment on Staten Island. Staten Island was the only borough of New York that was not part of the New York subway system. To get to

Staten Island, one had to take a ferry. She told them that the many fairly large red boats that they saw crisscrossing the bay in which their ship had been anchored, were Staten Island ferries.

The noise of the trains and the large number of people getting in and out at so many stations were immensely exciting to Sarah and her newly arrived family. Little did they know that the wonders of New York had just begun.

Beyla asked Srolik if he liked the sound of the English language that the people were speaking. With a large guffaw Srolik replied, "They sound like a lot of ducks quacking." Beyla was convulsed in giggles when she said, "The noise and darkness of these tunnels are not frightening. I guess it is because the subway cars are mostly so well lighted, and each time the lights go out, they go out for only a moment."

Just as Beyla was talking about the noise and darkness of the tunnel, the train blasted into daylight and continued to travel to a station that was elevated. Anna told the family that the streets they saw beneath them were the streets of Brooklyn. All talk stopped. The new arrivals were too busy ogling the Brooklyn streets and the people coming into and leaving the train at the various stations at which the train stopped.

————

Sightseeing was brought to an abrupt end when Anna announced that they were getting off at the train's next stop. They alighted onto an elevated train platform and then descended a long, steep staircase onto a busy Brooklyn street. Its sidewalks were crowded with pedestrians, and its wide roadway was congested with cars, buses, and trucks of all sorts. All of this was beneath, and in the shadow of the train station and tracks that ran high above their heads.

The honking traffic alongside them and the clattering trains above them caused a cacophony that made conversation difficult, if not impossible. Anna, therefore, shouted directions, and the family walked away from the train station to a quieter street devoid of trains and the large volume of traffic beneath the tracks. The street on which they were walking had mainly three and four story houses and many, many stores. The immigrants marveled at the height of these buildings, causing the four "American" family members to laugh.

"Didn't you see the tremendous height of the buildings in Manhattan?" asked Herschel.

"No," said Fayge, "Everything seemed big, but we couldn't see how tall they were from the taxi, and we had no time to dally before we were herded into the bowels of the earth to board a train that would drop us off above the earth!"

Herschel, Lily, Anna, and Meyer laughed heartily at Fayge's description. Then Herschel said, "What if I told you that your apartment, which is a few blocks from Anna's house, is four stories up? You will be living higher above the earth than the train was, higher than some of these trees."

Herschel was met with a stunned silence from the immigrants.

The street on which Anna and Meyer lived consisted entirely of two story brick houses. It was tree-lined, very quiet, relatively new, and quite pretty. A small number of people were on the street, and Anna seemed to know most of them. It seemed friendly — like Vashisht.

Anna's house was in the middle of the street. She explained that the two-story house belonged to her and Meyer. It consisted of four apartments. They lived in one of them and the other three apartments were rented to other families. The rent they collected from their tenants, was used to pay off the mortgage on the house. Once the mortgage was all paid, the house would be theirs - free and clear. Then the rent money they received could be used at their own discretion.

All of this was difficult for the new arrivals to understand. Where they had lived in Russia, Jews couldn't own houses or collect rent. They paid rent to a Christian landlord. Now, under the Soviets, all houses belonged to the government. Everyone paid rent to the government, who claimed that all of the people owned the property; but as Sarah saw it, only government officials benefited from the rents that people paid.

In the newcomers' eyes, Anna and Meyer lived in a wondrously large apartment. It had a kitchen, three bedrooms, a sitting room that was called a living room, and a bathroom that was theirs alone. The kitchen and the bathroom had hot and cold water running out of faucets in the sinks and in the bathtub. This awed Sarah's family, too.

Many windows brought in the daylight, but the apartment was ablaze with electric lights and lamps when darkness fell.

The stove was so different from their Russian stove, that Anna asked Lily to demonstrate how the burners and the oven worked. But the greatest wonder was the refrigerator. This large food-storage box made its own ice! Lots of food, wrapped in very interesting ways, lined the shelves of the refrigerator. Anna explained that most people in America still did not own refrigerators. They used iceboxes in which they stored their food. The ice was purchased every two or three days from an iceman.

Beyla asked if they would have these wonders in their apartment. Anna replied, "You will have some of them and not have others. I tried to get an inexpensive place for you, because Herschel and I will pay the first and perhaps the second month's rent; but you, Zushe, and Fayge will have to get jobs to support yourselves, Mama, and Srolik. Mama will keep house and Srolik will go to school".

"Won't I go to school too?" asked Beyla.

"No. You're grown up enough to go to work and help out. If you want to go to school, go at night. They'll teach you English."

Beyla was greatly disappointed. In Russia she was heading for the gymnasia. She even had hopes of going on to the university. But here in America, she would be uneducated. Being a young girl in her teens, however, her disappointment quickly evaporated, and was replaced by the excitement of seeing and hearing about all of the wonders of life in America.

———————

After eating a good meal, the family was taken to their new home, four blocks and a world away from Anna's lovely apartment. Their apartment was four stories up. They lugged themselves and their luggage up to their door. On the fourth floor, there were three other apartments and a communal toilet for the use of all of the residents on the floor. The toilet consisted of one flush toilet and lots of stench. Every member of the family grimaced as he or she passed the tiny odiferous room.

The apartment itself was far roomier than their cottage in Vashisht. It consisted of two bedrooms and a kitchen. It was sparsely furnished, but there was enough furniture to give them a good start. Anna showed them how to light the gas burners on their kitchen stove and in their oven. She explained once more about the iceman who delivered ice every other day. She also explained that their apartment was called a "cold water flat," which meant that it only had cold water running into its tub. It also had no heat in the winter. A pot bellied stove that burned coal was located in the kitchen. The family's warmth would come from that stove.

Sarah said, "I cannot imagine that so small a stove can warm this whole room; and what warms the bedrooms?"

Anna answered, "Many people live this way, but I doubt that you will be here more than one winter. When Fayge, Zushe, and Beyla earn money, you'll be able to move to better quarters. In the meantime, you'll have to wear heavy clothing when you're awake, and use lots of blankets and quilts when you're in bed."

"What about that tub?" said Fayge. "Is that our source of water?"

"Yes," said Anna. "It's better than buckets from the well, isn't it?"

Fayge nodded. "How will we communicate with the storekeepers when we buy food?" she asked.

"This is a Jewish neighborhood. Very few of the people living here are Christian. All of the storekeepers speak Yiddish and all of the food sold around here is kosher," answered her sister.

"How convenient," said Sarah. "We'll go downstairs and investigate some of these stores. Will you come with us and explain American money?" she asked Anna.

"Yes," replied Anna, "and when we unpack and store the food you buy, we'll set up a payment schedule for repaying your debt to Meyer and me."

———————

That night, her first night on American soil, as young Beyla lay in her new American bed, she reflected on how her family had arrived at this juncture....

— First: Mama's unlikely marriage to a much younger man, brought emotions in her family to such a pitch, that it resulted in Anna and Herschel being sent to America ahead of the rest of the family.

— Second: Zada died at a time that Sarah believed was a time still possible for emigration.

— Third: They were too late! The doors to America had slammed shut. They were to be returned to Russia, even though their ship was anchored in American waters.

— Fourth: Mama threw the watches to Herschel, because she wanted her children, and not the thieving guards at the border of Latvia or the border of Russia, to have them.

— Fifth: While they were in the American police station, the boat set sail for Latvia.

— Sixth: They got legal papers to enter the United States, because of Meyer's connections.

As she turned these events around and around in her sleepy mind, she marveled at the family's good luck. Only they, of the hundreds of eastern Europeans on the ship, would become Americans. The rest would return to their unknown destinies. Beyla believed that God's hand was in all of this. She wondered if He had a purpose in giving them this amazing gift.

——————

Two days after their arrival, Anna took Fayge and Beyla to Manhattan to start jobs. Both of the newcomers were frightened. Neither of them spoke nor read English. How could they possibly get along?

The crowded train ride took almost an hour. They got off at 34th Street and walked to 7th Avenue. The walk on 34th Street would have been extremely interesting, because they passed wonderful store windows and lots of hurrying people, but Anna made them hurry too. On 7th Avenue they dodged men pushing large clothing racks on wheels. They walked around trucks that had pulled their vans up to the large gray brick buildings, where the huge trucks were loaded with clothes. Anna had explained that New York was the clothing manufacturing capital of the world. This hustle and bustle went on for many hours, five days each week. She told her sisters that they too would be working in factories making clothes.

Their first stop was at a building whose entrance was clogged with men carrying out huge, fairly flat, heavy cardboard boxes. They allowed the men to pass, and Fayge and Anna entered the elevator. Beyla had been told to wait in the lobby for Anna's return.

Beyla didn't think she had waited very long, because she was fascinated by all of the traffic, human and motorized, that scurried past the open door. When Anna returned, Beyla was startled. Anna notified her that Fayge was now employed in a fine shirtwaist factory. The sewing skills that she had learned in Kiev impressed her employer, and she was hired at the "princely" salary of $18.00 per week. Anna assured Beyla that $18.00 was excellent pay.

"How did she communicate with people?" asked a tremulous Beyla.

"In Yiddish, of course. Most of the employers, designers, cutters, pattern makers, and operators in the garment industry are Jewish," Anna said.

"Pay attention to where we are walking," continued Anna "You will come back here at 5:00 o'clock and meet Fayge. The two of you will travel home together."

"What if I can't find my way?"

"I'll give you a slip of paper with directions. If you are lost, go up to someone who is speaking Yiddish, show him the slip of paper, and ask for help," Anna said.

When they had arrived at the building Anna had in mind, they entered a crowded elevator that creaked its way up to the ninth floor. On the ninth floor they entered a door and walked into an office right near the door. "This is my sixteen year old sister," said Anna. She has recently arrived here from Russia. Would you please direct us to an unoccupied machine, where I can get her started?"

The woman at the desk turned a sour face to Beyla and looked her over very carefully. She then stood up from her chair and told Anna, in English, to follow her.

Beyla was petrified! They walked through double swinging doors into a huge dusty room, where the noise of the many thundering sewing machines terrified Beyla even more. Sewing machine operators, both male and female, sat hunched over their machines, sewing rapidly. Each operator sewed one or two seams and laid the item aside where workers assigned to collect the work, picked it up and deposited it on someone else's machine for further sewing. Each operator sewed different seams on the garment. The garments appeared to be ladies' undergarments of a type with which Beyla was not familiar.

"What are they sewing?" asked Beyla.

"Brassieres for ladies' breasts," whispered Anna. "This is a factory that makes ladies' underwear. They call it "lingerie.""

The sour faced woman from the front office led Anna and Beyla to a corner in which a sewing machine and lots of scraps of cloth were kept. She told Anna that they could use that machine and the cloth. She then left them.

For two hours, Anna worked with Beyla. She showed her how to thread the bobbin of the machine, and how to sew a seam. While her young sister practiced, Anna explained how she would get paid. "This shop," she said, "is a piece-work shop. You will be paid by the piece. You will get very little money per piece, so it will be necessary for you to work fast and carefully, so that you complete many pieces. In that way, your money will add up and you may earn as much as $8 to $10 per week. If you're slow, you'll get so little money that it won't even pay to come to work. You are learning fast. Keep practicing, and when you feel confident enough, go to the man on the high stool in front of the machines and tell him that you're ready to work. Once he gives you a machine, you will start earning money for what you do."

"Pay attention to what the experienced workers are doing. I'm sure you'll do very well," Anna said. "I'm going to leave you now. I'll see you tonight, after supper. I'll want to hear how you made out." Anna left quickly.

Beyla was on her own!

———

Anna came to Sarah's apartment right after her supper. Her mother and brothers and sisters were just finishing theirs. She was invited to join them for tea. As they all sat around the large kitchen table, Anna questioned her sisters about their day in the city.

Fayge, who was an experienced seamstress, liked the garments she was making and the people she worked with. She didn't like the noise of the machines, but she said that she believed she'd get accustomed to it.

Beyla was on the verge of tears when she told her story. The man on the stool was called the "foreman." He was loud and nasty, and he was in charge. When he assigned Beyla to a machine and told her what to do, he laughed and called out to everyone that she was a little "greenhorn." Whatever that meant, she realized that it wasn't a compliment, because everyone in the factory laughed at her. She said that she worked very hard and seemed to have produced a decent volume of work, because the nasty foreman said that she was doing well for a little greenhorn. "Anna," Beyla asked, "what is a greenhorn?"

"A greenhorn is someone who is new to a place and usually makes lots of mistakes," said Anna. "Keep working well and you will leave your nasty foreman behind."

"What do you mean?" asked Beyla.

———

Anna then proceeded to tell them about the turns life had taken for her when she came to America. "Herschel and I lived with Tante Chinna and her family. Her apartment was so crowded, that I knew she wished that I would earn enough to get my own place. I was your age, Beyla. Herschel was going to school and working in a grocery store after school. I paid *Tante* (Aunt) Chinna a part of my salary, and saved money for our own apartment."

"In the meantime, I learned about taking bundles home." I longed for a place of my own, with a sewing machine of my own. I knew that, if I took bundles home, I could sew many garments, Herschel and I would then do very well."

"In a few months," Anna continued, "I got an apartment on the third floor of a tenement on the Lower East Side. After Herschel and I moved in, I saved even more money and I rented a sewing machine. Before long, I had paid for the first sewing machine and had bought two more. I hired two greenhorn girls like myself, and we sewed bundles all day long."

"Our little apartment got very crowded, so I rented a bigger apartment on the second floor of a nicer tenement. By the time I married Meyer, I had ten girls working for me."

"Was Sonia, the woman I met at your house, one of those girls?" asked Sarah.

"Yes," replied Anna. "She is now my dearest friend. She was a greenhorn when I was a greenhorn. She was the first girl to work for me. She worked for me until I stopped working, when Meyer and I moved into our house. It was then that Sonia took a job in a real factory. We didn't want to separate, so she moved in with us. She is our boarder and pays us rent, but I love her like a sister."

"Where is Sonia's family?" asked Fayge.

"Still in Poland," said Anna. "None of them have emigrated. Her parents are dead and all of her brothers and sisters are married and have families. They don't want to come to America."

"I hope my experience with working will be as good as yours," Beyla said to Anna. "And I hope that I'll make lots of friends."

"If that's what you want, that's what you'll get," replied Anna. "America is full of possibilities."

For the next five or six weeks, Beyla failed to see these possibilities. Her work exhausted her and the foreman seemed nastier than ever. Every few minutes he'd shout at the top of his voice, "Come on girls!" If he thought a girl was slacking off or malingering, he'd throw something at her. Beyla hated the foreman and feared him.

———

Other adjustments were much easier for the family. Sarah had set up the family's living routine. Srolik was enrolled in school. After school he worked in a neighborhood factory that sanitized old mattress fillings and sold them to mattress factories for reuse. His job was to remove the ticking from the mattresses. It was a dirty and physically trying job, and he was paid by the piece, but whatever small amount of money he made was badly needed by his family. Srolik did his schoolwork late at night, very often until eleven or twelve o'clock.

Zushe worked in the mattress factory, too, but Zushe was too old to go to school, so he worked all day.

Sarah's children gave their mother all of the money they earned. She kept a certain portion for household needs and doled back what she believed each child needed. Once again, she saved money. This time she was saving for a better place to live and for repayment of the family's loan to Anna and Meyer.

Only Beyla was dissatisfied with Sarah's monetary arrangements, because she received very much less money returned to her than her older sister Fayge received. Sarah explained that Fayge was of a marriageable age and needed nice clothes. "What is more," said Sarah. "Fayge earns much more than you do."

Beyla was not mollified. She was jealous of Fayge, and felt cheated. She wanted to look, talk, walk, and dress like an American. She needed money to do so.

———

Sarah was an attractive woman in her late forties. She was beginning to form friendships with women in her Brooklyn neighborhood and she often chatted with some of the storekeepers in the shops where she bought food. Sarah's closest friendship was with her neighbor, Tillie Goldstein, who lived in the apartment just under Sarah's apartment. The two women often drank tea together in the early afternoon, when most of their chores were done.

One afternoon, Sarah went downstairs to chat with Tillie. When Tillie asked her in, she introduced Sarah to a visitor, her cousin Max, who lived on the Lower East Side. Max had recently been widowed, and was visiting his cousin, because his shop had closed and he had not started working in a new job. Sarah, Tillie, and Max talked for several hours, and when Sarah got up to leave, Max said that he would visit Tillie again on the following weekend. He said he hoped that he would see Sarah again, too.

Max found work and began to visit Tillie every other Sunday. Often he'd go upstairs to Sarah's apartment and invite her to take a walk with him. This continued for about three months, when one Sunday, Max asked Sarah to have supper with him at a restaurant on the following Sunday. Sarah agreed. At the restaurant Max told Sarah about his daughter and his two sons. His sons were married, but his daughter, Eva, was still at home. She was two years younger than Beyla.

On the Sunday following their dinner at the restaurant on the Lower East Side, Sarah invited Tillie and Max to join her family for supper in her apartment. Now Max met Sarah's unmarried children.

Sarah's friendship with Max soon turned into a courtship. She had not been living in Brooklyn for a year, when Max proposed and Sarah accepted. They were married a month later and moved into an apartment on the Lower East Side. This apartment was a "hot water flat," that was heated in the winter by steam-heat. Unfortunately, they still shared a smelly bathroom with the four other families living on their floor. Their apartment was large. It consisted of three bedrooms, a very large kitchen, and a long hallway called a "foyer." Sarah and Max shared one bedroom. Fayge, who now called herself "Fanny," still slept in the same bed as Beyla, who now called herself "Bella." Eva, their stepsister, slept alone on a narrow bed in the same room. Zushe, who now called himself "Sol," and Srolik, who now called himself "Irving," shared a bed in the smallest bedroom. All of Sarah's children were glad that they had moved to Manhattan, because the Lower East Side was crowded with people, and the young adults in Sarah's family were prepared "to take on the town."

Sarah's daughters and sons still gave their salaries to their mother and received an allowance that Sarah deemed appropriate to their needs. Irving and Eva went to school, but only Irving worked after school.

Sol, Fanny, Bella, and Eva went to age appropriate clubs that proliferated in their crowded Jewish neighborhood. Fanny's club catered to people in their twenties. Sol, Bella and Eva's club catered to people from sixteen to twenty. Eva was not quite fifteen, but she tagged along with seventeen-year-old Bella.

Beautiful as Fanny was, she did not enjoy the club or the shallow attentions of the boys in the club. She began to stay at home reading novels that she borrowed from the library. Her ability to read English far surpassed her ability to speak it, so a whole new world of English literature opened up to her. Sarah began to worry that her beautiful blond daughter would not find a young man to love, but she had no such troubling thoughts about Bella or Eva. Bella had become an extremely good-looking brunette who loved to dance and go to the movies. Whatever Bella did, Eva seemed to follow. Sarah wondered if she had better keep a sharper eye on the two younger girls.

Sol had become a dashingly handsome, black-haired young man. He sometimes frequented the club for twenty year olds, but mostly he liked to play cards with his cronies.

Irving had very little time for his studies and his homework, because of his job in a mattress factory near his East Side home. He did little socializing with his friends, using what little spare time he had for schoolwork.

America was enveloping Sarah's children. All of them were speaking English outside of their home. They were losing much of their Russian accents, although, for all of them, their speech would forever broadcast the fact that their first spoken language was not English. Although they sounded foreign-born, the mores of the youth of America had caught and captured all of them. It was the "roaring twenties," and the twenties roared at the Lower East Side clubs. Fanny had bobbed her hair, keeping a heavy, long blond braid in her drawer, to remind her of her Russian hairdo. She and Bella wore short flapper skirts and rolled their stockings below their rouged knees. They frequented the movies, and stood in long lines to be admitted to Rudolph Valentino or Charley Chaplin movies. They both loved to dance the tango, but their favorite dance of all was the Charleston.

Sol admired his cousin Louis. Louis claimed to be a gambler, but Sarah suspected that he might be connected to "The Mob." Although Sarah spent most of her time at home and did not speak English, she remained sharp witted and astute. She was delighted that her sister Chinna lived only two blocks away and she loved visiting with Chinna, Chinna's husband Nachim, and Chinna's children. But, she was troubled by her handsome nephew, Louis. Chinna's youngest son Louis was not only handsome and debonair, he looked nothing like the other young men on the Lower East Side. He wore clothing that was like Rudolph Valentino's, his hair looked like patent leather, and even though his legs were healthy, he sported a cane. He wore spotless white spats over highly shined shoes and he bore no resemblance to the hard working young men of their neighborhood. Sol and Eva thought he was the "slickest guy" in the neighborhood. They also admired the fact that he always had lots of money in his pocket, and didn't hesitate to spend it. It was the money, even more than his manner of dressing, that aroused Sarah's suspicions. Was her nephew a thug or a bootlegger?

When Sarah tried to broach the subject to Chinna, her sister immediately became defensive. She lauded Louis' generosity to her and her family, maintaining that if he were a criminal type, he would not be so generous and loving. What is more, Chinna more than implied that Sarah was an unloving aunt who was meddling in their family's business.

Clever Sarah, not wanting to alienate her sister, gave up on Chinna, but became even more vociferous with Louis' admirers in her own home. To Sol, Bella, and Eva she spoke bluntly. She told them to stay away from Louis and his friends, and she told them why! Sol and Bella seemed to heed her warnings, but for Eva they fell on a "deaf ear." She was entranced by Louis' charms, good looks, and expansive spending. American-born Eva considered her stepmother to be a backward, hopeless greenhorn.

––––––––––

Although Eva was attracted to Louis, Louis was totally indifferent to her. His lovely dark haired, dark eyed, seventeen-year old cousin Bella, however, was quite a different thing. He and his friends often discussed his immigrant cousin's charms. One of his friends, a youth nicknamed "Peanut," because he was so tall and muscular, kept pressing Louis to "set him up" with his cousin Bella. Louis was protective of Bella, and didn't broach the subject to her until, during one of their conversations, when she expressed an interest in speakeasies. Louis suggested that she bring a friend, and Peanut and he would take them both to a very swinging speakeasy. Bella hesitated, but then told him that she'd let him know.

When fifteen-year old Eva heard about Louis' invitation, she gave Bella no peace. She begged Bella to accept Louis' invitation and to bring her along.

Bella was conflicted. On the one hand, she feared her mother's reaction if she accepted. On the other hand, seeing a speakeasy would be an exciting adventure, and her mother had no right to deny her a good time. After all, she was seventeen! Besides, she needed to be there in order to protect Eva, who was only fifteen!

Without discussing it with Sarah, Bella accepted Louis' invitation. When Sarah was finally told, she was very angry. "In America, children don't obey their parents," she thought. But, Sarah did not forbid the speakeasy outing. She feared a rift with her sister Chinna, so she allowed Bella and Eva to go with Louis and Peanut, admonishing all four of them about drinking; and emphatically ordering them to be home by midnight.

On the Saturday night of the big outing, both Eva and Bella were dressed in their very best. Their hair and makeup had been worked on for two hours, and both girls looked radiant. Louis and Peanut were all dressed up too. Sarah smiled inwardly when she beheld the beauty of the four young people.

The night at the speakeasy was wonderful. The glittering lights and even more glittering people astounded the teenaged girls. Louis introduced them to several young men who passed their table. He introduced both girls as his cousins. Their escorts drank and smoked, but Louis only allowed the girls one drink each and no cigarettes. Peanut followed Louis' dictums concerning his behavior to the girls, even though he didn't like to do so. He planned to ask Bella for a date, without Louis, at some future time. The entertainment, music, and dancing in the smoky, crowded club delighted the girls, but at 11:30 P.M., Louis announced that they must leave. He did not want to antagonize his Aunt Sarah.

Sarah was somewhat mollified by Louis' adherence to her orders, yet when the young men left she said, "So now you've been to a speakeasy. Just remember that they are against the law. If that speakeasy had been raided by the police, you and all of the other "fancy" people there, would have been arrested. This is the first and last time I will allow such an outing!"

Bella saw the virtue in Sarah's edict. Young Eva, however, considered her stepmother to be too strict and very mean. She was determined to disobey and do as she pleased.

———

Sarah did not prohibit the girls from going to the social club. She understood that young people needed to mingle and have fun. However, Bella didn't like her own club. She preferred the older men at the club that Fanny went to when she didn't have her nose in a book. On one such evening, she asked Fanny to take her to the older crowd's club, and Fanny agreed.

Both of Sarah's daughters stood in the doorway of the clubroom. Jazz blared from a phonograph, and most of the room's inhabitants stood around in small groups, talking. A young man named Charley introduced himself to the girls. From that point on, he never left Bella's side.

Unbeknown to Fanny, a young man who had been talking politics to some other young men, spotted her as she entered the room. His eyes remained on her for most of the evening, but he was too shy to approach her. Besides, she was very busy with two other young men who kept her dancing most of the night.

When the evening was over, both girls were escorted home by Charley. He told Bella that he'd call on her again.

Charley was true to his word. He came calling several days later. He brought a box of candy and impressed Sarah and Max with his good manners. He and Bella took a walk, and he invited her to a Charley Chaplin movie on the following Saturday night.

Bella had fun with Charley on their movie date, and several other dates followed.

One evening, Charley came over with the shy young man who had stared at Fanny all night at the club. He said that the young man was his cousin, Murray, who had recently arrived in America. He said he had brought his cousin so that Fanny and he might join them for a walk in a nearby park. The four young people enjoyed their walk, and Fanny agreed to see Murray again.

———

Bella's role model was her cousin Esther. They were the same age, but their lives were very different. Esther was the American-born daughter of Sarah's brother, Label, who had been the first of Sarah's siblings to emigrate to America. He was now a well established businessman, who owned a dry goods store in Brooklyn. When Bella visited her sister Anna and her baby nephew, she often dropped in at Uncle Label's beautiful apartment to visit with her cousin Esther. Esther was a high school student. There was even talk of her going to Hunter College, after she graduated from high school. Esther's beauty and advanced education caused her to be greatly admired by most, and greatly envied by Bella. Bella wished that she could be a student instead of a greenhorn sewing machine operator, but *she was* an immigrant sewing machine operator, and she had to make the best of it.

The family experienced Esther's first "shock wave" one evening, just as Bella was coming home from work. To her surprise, Bella found Uncle Label and Tante Ruchel sitting in Sarah's kitchen. Uncle Label's face was deep red and perspiration clung to his brow as he bellowed his heartache to his sister and her husband. Uncle Label's wife, Ruchel, just wept.

It seemed that the beautiful, accomplished Esther, was willing to throw everything away and run off with a man that she had never brought to her home. She had telephoned her parents to say that she would like them to meet this man before she married him, but unless they promised to be civil, she would not bring him home. She said she was in love with him and her mind was made up. Label said that he hung up on her!

"What does America do to children?" he cried. "I know nothing about this man, but I know he is unacceptable, because of the secretive way he and Esther have behaved. She is my child, and I'll forgive her, if she gets rid of this man, and begs my forgiveness."

Ruchel cried harder! Label shouted "Stop sniveling! We have to find out where she is. Beyla, you and Esther were friends as well as cousins. Do you know anything about this?"

"No," said Bella.

Sarah said, "Why did you hang up the phone before you knew where she was?"

"I was angry!" shouted Label.

The conversation continued in this vein until Label, exhausted from shouting, ordered Ruchel to leave. They would go home to Brooklyn and await further contact from Esther.

———————

On the Sunday after Label and Ruchel's visit, when Bella and Sarah visited Anna in Brooklyn, the three women decided to walk over to Label's house to find out what he had heard about Esther. To their horror, they found every mirror in Label's house covered. Label and Ruchel sat on low stools wearing their bedroom slippers. They were sitting Shiva!

"Who died?" the three women exclaimed. "Who are you mourning?"

"Esther is dead to us. She has married the man. It turns out he's a policeman and a *Goy* (non-Jew). She is dead to us," Label whispered in a weary voice.

Ruchel sobbed, "She wanted to bring him here so that we could meet him, but Label told her she wasn't his daughter. He said his daughter is dead!"

Label, Ruchel, Sarah, and Anna all cried together. Bella felt a terrible lump in her throat, and deep pity for Esther. When Esther's parents sat Shiva for her, to them she was really dead! They no longer had a daughter, and Esther no longer had parents.

An even greater tragedy occurred in Tante Chinna's family. Handsome, debonair Louis was gunned down in front of his house. It happened because the bootleggers were having a major territorial dispute. Rival gangs were engaged in a gang war that made the streets of the Lower East Side dangerous for their members. Louis was murdered in retaliation for the murder of a gangster in a rival gang.

Louis' funeral was as flashy as Louis had been in life. None of his family members had ever seen so opulent a funeral. Even though flowers were not customary at a Jewish funeral, the gang that had murdered Louis decked the chapel and his casket with gigantic arrangements of the most expensive and exotic blooms. Family members were both scandalized by the flowers and fascinated by the magnificent display.

Chinna and Nachim were almost prostrate in their grief. Louis had always been their joy. They simply did not accept that his largess and generosity came from money earned in criminal activities. His murder caused them to doubt his innocence, and the presence, at his funeral, of so many men who looked like gangsters, further shook their convictions about how their son had lived his life

During the Shiva week, a man named Tony Giardano visited Chinna and Nachim, ostensibly to extend his condolences. After he left, they discovered a large package of bills on their kitchen table. When they found the money, Louis' parents were greatly puzzled. They asked Louis' good friend Peanut why Mr. Giardano had come and why he had left so much money. They told Peanut that they had never seen Giardano before.

"Of course not," said Peanut. "Giardano belongs to the gang that shot Louis down. It is customary for the murderers, in a gang fight, to provide for their victim's family and to also provide a very expensive funeral. The money Giardano left, represents the money Louis' murderers believe he would have spent to take care of you, if he had lived."

Chinna and Nachim were repulsed by the package of money. Chinna threw it at the bottom of Louis' closet.

Several months after Louis' tragic death, Chinna came across the money when she was clearing out Louis' belongings. She knew that she would never fully recover from Louis' tragic death, but she began to question herself as to what Louis would have wanted her to do with the money.

While they loved the freer atmosphere of America, both Chinna and Nachim still greatly missed the forests and open spaces they had enjoyed when their home was in Vashisht. Living on the crowded Lower East Side had always been difficult for them. Louis used to promise them that someday he would buy them a large plot of land in the Catskill Mountains, north of New York City. Consequently, less than a year after Louis' death, his parents bought a large, old farm north of the city. Tragically, young and handsome Louis had paid for his parents' yearned for land, by losing his life.

In 1925, when Sarah's family had been in America for only a year, a letter from a relative in Vashisht told them that Husmann had died in a terrible accident. He had been repairing his parents' roof when he lost his footing on the ladder, fell off, and struck his head. He was unconscious for two days, and then he died.

The third tragedy to hit the family began with a bad dream about Husmann. Perhaps it was because she was so upset about her cousin Louis' death, or perhaps it was caused by the ice cream sundae she had eaten with Murray before he took her home on Saturday night, but whatever the cause, the hapless Husmann, who had both loved and threatened Fanny before she left Russia, came into her dream and leered at her. "I promised to get you and I will very soon. There will soon be a great tragedy in your immediate family!"

The dream really upset Fanny. Then she shrugged it off. A ghost from her past did not announce impending tragedy...or maybe he did.

Fanny shuddered!

———

Two days later Bella was meeting her friend Frieda on a busy street corner near Frieda's place of work. Both girls were going to eat supper together and then go to see the latest Rudolph Valentino film. It was rush hour. People were leaving work and hurrying to subways, buses, and taxis. Automobile horns were honking, cars backfired, and a huge double-decker bus pulled up along the curb of the sidewalk on which Bella was waiting for her friend. Crowds of people entered the bus, and as it was about to close its doors, a large man, running to catch the bus, pushed Bella and knocked the slim young girl off her feet. When she fell, one of her legs extended under the bus. The bus started, and its huge, rear, double wheels crushed Bella's leg. One moment of searing pain, and then, blessed darkness!

———

-- A great whiteness....nothing more.

--The whiteness was changing into bright, flashing light. Strange shadows occasionally undulated through the light.

--Total silence.....no sound at all.

--Uninterrupted buzzing broke the silence. The buzzing

76

metamorphisized into rustling movement and strange voices that quacked ....quacked quietly.

Over time, the sounds and shadows moving through the bright, white light combined. Both sight and sound then gained some definition....the sound was speech.... English speech, sometimes speaking to her and at other times speaking to other people lost in the whiteness. The rustling was the rustling of long, starched skirts. The skirts were the moving shadows, now becoming defined and blasting through the whiteness.....the whiteness dulled....it was dissipating....

Full consciousness finally overtook Bella's brain. She realized that she was in a strange white place. Women in long, white costumes bustled about. They handled her body and spoke to her in English.

Understanding eventually came. She was a patient in a hospital. The women were nurses, and they were also nuns; strange women who lived in female Christian communities that Bella did not understand at all. Bella had never seen a nun until she came to America. Christians in America were different from Christians in Russia. Both groups seemed to worship Jesus, but many of their actions and even the appearance of their churches were different. When Bella first saw nuns walking down a New York street, they were dressed in strange black costumes, with some white around their faces and long white skirts peeking out from under their long flowing black outer skirts. They were so strange looking, that Bella was a little afraid of them.

The nun/nurses in this hospital were different. They were dressed entirely in white, and they talked to her. Sometimes one of them sat alongside her bed and read quietly out of a small book or prayed with some black beads. Because Bella didn't have the strength to participate in her environment, she merely observed. Occasionally Mama, or one of her brothers or sisters sat by the bed. They often cried. She wanted to tell them that it was all right, but she couldn't speak...so she continued to observe.

One day, after the nun had left, Mama sat down in the nun's chair. Mama stroked Bella's head and pushed a stray strand of hair off her face.

Silent tears rushed out of Sarah's eyes as she gazed lovingly at her young and very sick daughter.

"Don't cry, Mama," whispered Bella. "Tell me what happened."

Mama gasped. A great smile broke across her face. "There was an accident," she said. "You have been very, very sick. You are in the hospital. Now that you can speak and can understand, I know you will get well. You've been in shock. You've been here for several weeks- in a coma. You've come back! You'll get well!"

––––––––––

It took a year and ten operations. It took therapy- lots of therapy. It took kindness, love, and care from nuns, doctors, family, and friends. Above all, it took courage and strength from Bella. She entered St. Vincent's Hospital a lovely, superficial teenager, with one foot still in Russia. She left St. Vincent's Hospital a mature, determined young woman who would labor to achieve normalcy and who had become more Americanized by the nuns in one year, than she would have been in three years among her own people on the Lower East Side.

The year at St. Vincent's was a year of searing pain, many surgeries, and loving, caring, kindness. Bella would always believe that nuns were superior people who had been chosen by God to bring peace to the lives of others. No matter what she heard in years to come about the human frailty of some nuns, she didn't believe it. To her they were her English language teachers, her caregivers, and the repositories of the great love that brought her back from near death to vibrant life. She loved and trusted them.

––––––––––

One of Bella's great surprises, during her year at St. Vincent's, was Charley's constancy. He visited her two and three times a week, always bringing flowers, candy, little gifts, or books written in English, Russian, or Yiddish. He openly declared his love for her, and caused her deep regret, because she was unable to love him in return. She liked him very much, but she found him to be without luster. She tried to discourage him kindly, but to no avail. Charley's devotion never wavered. He was madly in love with her.

Crucifixes hung on the walls of St. Vincent's. Her beloved nuns wore crucifixes on their habits. Yet, for Bella, the crucifixes weren't there. She had entered St. Vincent's with certain attitudes she had learned in Russia. She had learned that Jesus was the Christian God. She had learned that he was killed brutally by the Romans, but that many Christians believed that the Jews had killed him. On Good Friday, Christians *celebrated* Jesus' death. In Russia, anti-Semites often looked for Jews to punish for his death, and Good Friday was a day of pogroms. These pogroms took the lives of many innocent Jews. The attitudes, brought with her from Russia, had caused Bella to dislike effigies of Jesus hanging on the cross. They had been disquieting at best, and at worst, caused her to feel great fear. Along with her health, St. Vincent's cured Bella of this fear. She now understood that to good Christians like her nuns, Jesus' death on the cross was a sign of their god's love for humanity. God's love for humanity, caused the nuns to love humanity too. The nuns at St. Vincent's practiced this love in Jesus' name.

––––––––

While St. Vincent's did away with Bella's fears of Christian icons and the Christian religion, it did not do away with all of her pain nor with the disfigurement of her leg. All of the doctors who had worked on Bella's leg recommended amputation, but Bella had not accepted their recommendations. She threatened suicide every time the subject of amputation was brought up. Because Sarah feared that her highly emotional, very sick teenaged daughter would make good on her threat, she directed Bella's doctors to do what they could to save the leg.

What they could do required one operation after another, cutting away infected flesh from the knee to the ankle. They grafted skin onto the raw wounds, but there were always places that burst open and caused painful ulcers. The skin on the leg was blue in color, uneven, and very unsightly. The ulcers were prone to infection and needed very delicate and constant care. (Bella would eventually learn to provide this care by herself.)

Bella hated her ugly, discolored, and misshapen leg; but it was hers! She vowed to never let anyone but her doctor or nurse see it. She planned to wear several pairs of stockings and long skirts to hide it. But, she was determined that she would learn to use that hideous leg, and would walk again. The pain and disfigurement were secondary to her passionate wish for independence and physical viability. In Bella's mind, no prosthetic leg could provide this viability. She could only rely upon her own poor, disfigured leg to do so.

———

Bella left St. Vincent's in a wheelchair. Therapy and gigantic effort allowed her to discard the wheelchair- first for a walker- and then for two canes. Using the walker and the canes was emotionally taxing for Bella. The only way she could walk with them was when she wore high shoes laced 1/3 of the way up her calf. To the wounded, beautiful young woman, these high shoes were ugly, and a glaring symbol of her disfigurement.

Charley kept coming to her house to see her, but she refused to leave the house with him. When she was finally able to discard one of her canes, she acquiesced, and promised to go with him to the club. Both Charley and Sarah were thrilled that Bella was putting an end to her reclusiveness, and they hoped that she would once again join in the social life of the young adults of the Lower East Side.

Their hopes were dashed to nothingness! When Bella entered the club, the room was decorated with welcoming signs and everyone paid her great and loving attention. Bella was sure that this fuss was being made, because everyone felt sorry for her. She detested pity, and abhorred Charley's many gestures of kindness, because she believed that Charley pitied her even more than everyone else. She resolved to never go back to the club again, and she terminated her relationship with poor, broken hearted Charley.

———

Bella was determined to start a new life. She began to apply for jobs, wearing her detestable high shoes. After several unsuccessful attempts at getting a job in the garment industry, she applied at the Eagle Pencil Company. She thought she would be hired for a job on the line. Instead, she was hired as an inspector who sat at a table filled with boxes of pencils. She checked for flaws in the boxes, or in the way they were filled. Bella's job was boring, but not overtiring. With her high shoes tucked under the table, she felt a return of confidence, and soon formed friendships with several of her female co-workers. Young working men flirted with her and tried to make advances, but she fended them off.

Pearl, a homely girl, who read a great deal, lived with her mother in a ramshackle tenement, not too far from Bella's house. Because Pearl's conversation was interesting, Bella began to walk home from work with her. On the weekends, the two young women would often go to the movies or visit at each other's houses. Sarah was delighted to see that Bella had a friend and seemed to be re-entering the world.

———

Fanny and Murray were getting married. Anna would be the matron of honor and Murray's brother would be the best man. Bella, Eva, and two of Murray's female cousins served as bridesmaids. Unhappy Charley, served as a groomsman, along with Sol, Irving, and Herschel, now called "Harry."

The wedding was lovely. Bella's long dress covered her high shoes. She no longer needed a cane and usually walked without even a limp. Her excellent recovery was a result of good care, her youthful strength, but most of all, her determination to be completely viable.

———

Harry and Lily had a lovely apartment on Staten Island. It was far away from the pushcarts, crowds, and the stench of the Lower East Side. Few Jews lived on Staten Island, but Harry and Lily lived next door to a synagogue, and had become acquainted with many of its congregants. Lily also had two older sisters who lived on Staten Island. Her sisters each had children and now the aloof Lily had a baby boy too. Her sisters tried to reach out to her, but Lily mostly remained aloof.

Lily had been young when she came to the United States. She had gone to school in America and had lost all of her foreign ways. She disliked the foreign ways of Harry's family and of her own sisters. Family members from both families gave Lily "plenty of space." They realized that she looked down upon them, and they resented it. Her dealings with both families were tepid, at best.

Even though Lily was not friendly, certain members of Harry's family aspired to own property and do business on Staten Island. Irving and Sol both worked in a small mattress factory on the Lower East Side. Now that Anna and Meyer's loan was repaid, they hoped to accumulate enough funds to be able to start their own mattress factory, and they wished to do so on Staten Island, where property was less expensive than in the other four boroughs of New York City.

———

One morning when Bella had come home from work, she heard strident voices coming through the apartment door. She rushed in to find Eva and Sarah in a terrible argument. Eva was speaking very rudely to her stepmother, who slapped her when her language became vulgar. The young woman slapped her stepmother back, just as Bella entered the room. When Bella saw her mother being slapped, she shoved her stepsister away from her mother and began to pummel her. Sarah separated the two fighting young women, just as Irving and Sol returned home from work. When they heard what happened, they looked at Eva with great disdain. Sol said, "I don't care about the reason for the disagreement; anyone who strikes my mother is dead to me." Giving Eva a very dirty look, he turned on his heel and left the apartment, angrily slamming the door behind him. Eva, feeling terribly outnumbered, and in great distress, ran into her bedroom and wept. She did not join the family at dinner. When her father asked about her, he was told that she was sulking because she had had an argument with Sarah.

Sol never came home for dinner. No one knew where he had gone. Eva skipped dinner too, remaining in her bedroom alone, until Bella came in to go to bed. When Bella entered the bedroom, Eva left, slamming the apartment door behind her. Bella went to sleep, not caring where her stepsister had gone.

Bella was awakened by Sol's angry voice saying, "It's over!" She lay in bed after he slammed his bedroom door, and wondered what was "over?" As she lay in a twilight zone between being awake and sleeping, she heard moans coming from the kitchen. She rushed out to find eighteen-year old Eva doubled over and moaning.

Bella called Sarah, who very authoritatively demanded that Eva tell her what was wrong. Tearfully, Eva confessed that she and Sol had been secretly in love. Because she had slapped his mother, he had broken up with her, and declared that he would have nothing to do with her. The emotionally over-wrought young woman decided that life without Sol was not worth living. She took a swig of peroxide to end it all, but when the peroxide began to take its effect, she moaned and cried with pain, terror, and remorse. Sarah's anguished cries added to Eva's moans were heard by their neighbor, who had entered their apartment to help. When he discovered Eva's plight, he began to force raw eggs down her throat causing Eva to vomit violently. Another neighbor ran to a telephone to call for an ambulance. When the ambulance came, Sarah forced Sol into it, so that he would accompany Eva to the hospital. Her parting words to her son were, "You will not shame this family. As soon as Eva is well, the two of you will be married."

Bella and George, 1931

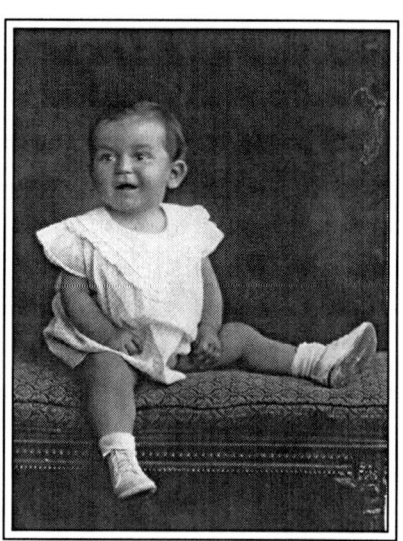

Isabelle, 1933

Bella and Isabelle, 1936

Isabelle, 1937

Chapter 4: Richmond Terrace

After Eva and Sol's marriage, family discussion about moving to Staten Island intensified. Fanny, who had been living on the Lower East Side with her husband Murray and a new baby girl, expressed interest in living on Staten Island. And now that they had accumulated some money, Irving and Sol accelerated their plans for going into their own business on Staten Island, too. They had seen a small building there that they would be able to rent cheaply. It could serve as their mattress factory. They would need to hire one man to help in the manufacturing and Bella would leave the pencil company and sew mattress ticking for a living. Sol would be their inside man and would also work with their paid employee on assembling the mattresses, while Irving would be their outside man who would sell mattresses to furniture stores and other places. He would also place orders for the materials they would need. Eva would act as the business's secretary and bookkeeper.

If their business was to be on Staten Island, they all needed housing there. In their quest for housing, they came upon a brick two-story building that consisted of three apartments and a store. Sol and Irving decided to borrow money from Anna and Meyer for a down payment on the building. Fanny, Murray, and their baby girl could be tenants in the back apartment. The front apartment could be for Eva and Sol. Bella could live there with them. The third apartment, located behind the store, could house Sarah, her husband Max, and Irving. Sarah and Bella would live rent-free.

For the time being, the brothers could make no permanent plans for the store. They would use it to warehouse mattresses. It was their hope that in the not too distant future, they could stock and maintain a furniture store there. For the present, however, they lacked the funds necessary to do so.

The family moved to Staten Island in early 1929, when, in the prosperous economy of that time, the brothers' new mattress business seemed to be humming along. The family never looked back at the Lower East Side. Life on Richmond Terrace in Staten Island was far more appealing than life in a tenement.

———

Sarah and Max joined a synagogue located about a mile from their new Staten Island home. Max had retired, and the two lived frugally on their meager savings.

A telephone was located in Eva's living room. All of the family who lived in the Richmond Terrace building, received their personal telephone calls on this phone. Because Eva and Sol paid the phone bill, only they placed calls on this telephone. The other family members placed calls only in emergencies.

———

In late 1929, two very important events that made huge impacts on Bella's life occurred. She discarded her high shoes and began to wear pumps and other flattering feminine shoe styles. Her joy, which was without bounds, was only mitigated by the fears she shared with the whole world. The stock market had crashed! While Sarah's children did not own securities and were not immediately touched by this economic disaster, they understood that things did not bode well for the American economy, and they waited apprehensively for the disaster to adversely affect their business and their lives.

———

One glorious Indian summer Saturday, in late October, Bella received a telephone call from her friend Pearl. Pearl said that on Sunday, she was going to visit her mother who was a patient at a rehabilitation hospital run by the city of New York. In this lovely, unexpected weather, the lawns of the city's rehabilitation center would probably be crowded with recovering patients and their visitors. Pearl suggested that she and Bella meet at the hospital, which was located on an island in the East River. They would visit Pearl's mother, who would greatly enjoy a visit from both young women. At the same time, they could enjoy the beautiful weather, and then have their dinner together in a restaurant, where they could catch up on the news in each other's lives. Bella liked Pearl's suggestion that they meet at 2 P.M. the next day, at the rehabilitation hospital.

Sunday was as magnificent a day as Saturday had been. The sun shone brightly and the breeze that blew was so gentle that very few of autumn's last leaves left their trees to fall to the ground. In well-treed areas, the ground blazed with color from many fallen red and yellow leaves. Being outdoors on such a day, made the hearts of the three women sing.

Bella looked as lovely as the beautiful autumn day. She wore a black, lightweight sweater over her long flowered blue dress, and her black hair shone in the sunlight. Bella's lovely face and figure caught the attention of most of the young men who saw her

The lawn of the rehabilitation hospital was crowded with recovering patients and their visitors. Pearl's mother was delighted to see the two girls, and thrilled that she could sit outdoors during their visit. Pearl and Bella sat on a bench located on a path that cut through a large lawn, while Mrs. Kahn was seated, facing them, in a wheelchair with a light blanket covering her legs.

On the bench, on the other side of the path, sat a young man who appeared to be a patient at the hospital. He sat alone, with his eyes riveted on Bella, who was feeling extremely uncomfortable because of his staring. The young man finally spoke. "I hope I'm not annoying you with my staring," he said.

"You are!" Bella replied, tartly.

"I'm staring because I cannot separate this glorious day from your glorious face. Is the day making you so beautiful or are you making the day this beautiful? Whichever it is, I'm dizzy with pleasure!"

"What is your name?" he asked.

"My name is Bella, and I thank-you for your extravagant compliment."

"My name is George," the young man said as he rose from the bench, crossed the path, and stood in front of Bella. Now it was Bella's turn to pay attention. The young man with the silver tongue was very handsome. He had thick, wavy black hair, too pale skin, and light hazel eyes. He had a thin, fashionable mustache that was slightly auburn in color. The unusually colored mustache added to, rather than detracted from the young man's good looks, by softening the intensity of his dark handsomeness. His pallor was not natural to him. It was clear to see that he was pale because he wasn't well.

George apologetically asked if he might share the bench with Pearl and Bella, because it was still difficult for him to stand for a long time. Bella and Pearl made room on the bench and introductions were made all around. Mrs. Kahn sat happily listening to their conversation. They discussed movies and the stock market crash, and spent a long time talking about how difficult it had become for people to find jobs. George said that he had been looking for work when he had collapsed on a New York City sidewalk. He had come to New York from Boston, where he had lived with his sister and her family. He had had a "falling out" with his sister's husband, which had caused him to leave the university and their home. He intended to make a new life for himself in New York City. "Instead of getting a job, I passed out on a New York street. I was barely conscious when I was taken to Bellevue Hospital, where I was diagnosed with acute appendicitis and was operated on that very day," George explained.

"Did you call your sister?" asked Mrs. Kahn.

"No," said George. "I left Boston on very bad terms with her as well as with my brother-in-law."

"What will you do when you leave here?" asked Bella.

"I'll find a job. I have some money, and I've rented a room in Manhattan," said George. "I'll get along."

The two girls and the two recuperating patients chatted until visiting hours were over. Pearl pushed her mother back to her room in her wheelchair, while George and Bella slowly walked back to his building together. They said their farewells at the door of the building, but just as

Bella turned to leave, George stopped her and said, "Will you come again soon? I'd really like to see you again."

Feeling very forward, Bella promised to be back the following Saturday. A very happy young man said that he would meet her in the building's lobby at 2:00 P.M. on Saturday. He then slowly walked to the elevator.

Bella rejoined Pearl, and the two girls spoke of George throughout their dinner at Chan's Pagoda. They decided that on the next Saturday, they would meet once again and they would have a dinner together at the end of visiting hours, but they agreed that it would be better if Bella visited with George by herself.

_____

For Bella, the week dragged by slowly. All she could think about was George. "Was he really as handsome as she remembered? Did he really have such a pleasing voice and appealing manner?" She found it hard to wait until Saturday, because she wanted desperately to check her memory against reality.

_____

While Bella mused about George, George's mind raced with recollections of the beautiful young woman he had met. He had been in a funk over where his life had taken him, but now he thought his luck had changed. Bella was not only beautiful, she exuded an unusual charm that had totally captivated him. All he could think about was their meeting again on Saturday. Meeting Bella made him feel as though his bad luck would be a thing of the past.

_____

Saturday finally came, and once more the weather cooperated. After dressing carefully in a long, slim black skirt and a fashionable red sweater, Bella once again enjoyed the sunshine on the ferry. For most of the trip, she stood on the prow of the boat and admired New York City's impressive skyline. She was unconscious of the stares of the young men who passed her. Instead, she was concentrated on the activities in the busy harbor. Was it only six years ago that she and her family sailed into this same harbor to start their new lives in America?

.At 1:50, Bella entered the hospital lobby that she and George had designated for their meeting place. George was not yet there, so Bella took a seat upon an easy chair, from which she could observe the elevator. No sooner was she seated, when the elevator doors parted, and a much stronger looking George emerged. He spotted her immediately and walked over quickly.

"You seem much stronger this week," said Bella.

"I am," he answered. "There is talk of my being discharged later this week."

"Oh, I'm so glad," said Bella. "But I'm sure you'll have to rest in your room for a few days, before you resume a normal routine."

"You're probably right," he replied. "But I'll worry about that when the time comes."

George's returning strength enabled them to slowly stroll the hospital's lawns. When fatigue overtook him, they sat on a bench and chatted about the music they liked and about some of their past experiences.

George told Bella about his home in Warsaw, Poland. He told her that his sister Sadie was his mother's oldest child. His mother and Sadie had been abandoned by Sadie's father when he went to America to establish himself in preparation for his family's immigration, because while in America, he met another woman with whom he fell in love. He divorced Sadie's mother and they never heard from him again.

Several years later, Sadie's mother remarried. The first child in her second marriage was George. George and Sadie were devoted to each other. Sadie doted on her little brother, but was otherwise, very unhappy. George's father, Sadie's step-father, was very strict and unloving to his step-daughter. By the time Sadie was eighteen, there were five more children in the family, and their mother was too busy, or perhaps not sensitive enough to be fully aware of her eldest daughter's misery. She was, therefore, greatly surprised when Sadie announced that she was immigrating to America.

George missed his big sister. Every letter she wrote from America was read and reread by the boy. Most of her letters were full of praise for life in Boston. She had a job in a shoe factory and had made many male and female friends.

90

When George was thirteen years old, Sadie had been married for three years. Her husband, Joe, whose leg had been seriously shrunken by polio, limped, and his shrunken leg tired easily. In spite of this, he was a dynamic young man and very clever. Working at a shoe factory during World War I, Joe believed that he understood the shoe business. Because economic times were good, he and a young partner started their own fledgling shoe manufacturing company, which succeeded very quickly. Sadie and Joe were married, and she found herself living in the lovely, upscale Boston suburb of Brookline, where she enjoyed a prosperity that she had never before known.

On George's thirteenth birthday, Sadie sent him a ticket to America. She begged her mother and step-father to allow George to visit her for a year. She convinced them that the trip would broaden her young brother and be both enjoyable and beneficial for him.

George arrived in Boston in 1919, where he enrolled in school in Brookline, and spent an idyllic year with his sister and brother-in-law. When the time came for him to return to Poland, letters flew from Sadie and from George, begging George's parents to allow him to extend his visit. They acquiesced and the visit grew into a permanent residency. George never went back to Poland.

In 1927, George entered the university. Sadie and Joe were very proud of him. Their little girl, Mona, was three years old, and they looked upon George, almost as a son. Therefore, from the time George became a college student, Joe liked him to stop in at the shoe company's office, during his summer vacations, to learn the workings of the factory.

When the stock market crashed in 1929, Joe lost a great deal of money. The shoe business was in a big slump, and financial conditions were very shaky. At that time, Joe insisted that George come to the shoe factory's office, to help out, every afternoon after his classes were over. Joe believed that George could save the business a clerical salary, by the work he would do.

George reluctantly complied. He had been spoiled by Sadie and Joe, and was unaccustomed to having demands placed upon him. Sometimes he skipped coming to the office because of his work at the university, and other times he shirked his office duties because of his busy collegiate social life. Most of his friends were the sons of very wealthy Bostonians and they had no financial responsibilities. George did not want to miss out on the fun he was accustomed to having with them.

————

On one particular Friday, in the spring, George did not come to work in the office, because some of his friends were going to Cape Cod for the weekend. George chose to join them in their partying at one of the boy's summer home. On Sunday night, after a wonderful weekend of fun, George returned to his home in Brookline.

Anger and recrimination met him at the door! Joe decried George's lack of responsibility. George protested that he had telephoned and left a message with the maid concerning his whereabouts. Joe angrily reminded him that he was no longer a little boy whose whereabouts were of importance to his family. He was a man whose work in the office could lessen some of the Depression's strain on the family's business. If he showed so little regard for the well being of the business, Joe railed, there was no need for the business to support him. Joe said that if George continued his "playboy" behavior, his tuition to school would be cut off.

Joe's threat made George feel uncomfortably dependent. He stormed up to his room, determined to be in charge of his own life.

Most of George's friends were away from Boston during the summer. School was over for him until September, so he was more diligent about his work at the shoe factory's office. The summer of 1930 passed peacefully.

When school started, George resumed his old habits. In late September, he once again, went to Cape Cod for a weekend of fun. When George came home, his argument with his brother-in-law was so vehement and so demeaning, that George impetuously packed his clothes, cleared his bank account, left a note for his sister, and took the train to New York City.

————

Looking for work in late 1930 was more than daunting. George had no success at all. To make matters worse, a nagging pain in his side was becoming more severe, but was never seen by a doctor, because George feared that his money was running low.

In mid October, George collapsed on the street. He was rushed to Bellevue Hospital, where they immediately performed an appendectomy. He was later sent to the rehabilitation hospital to complete his recuperation. Throughout all of this, he angrily never contacted Sadie and Joe. He was alone, in poor health, unemployed, and friendless.

George did not immediately share all of these details with Bella, but by the time she left him, she was aware that this young man was different from anyone she had ever known. He had been to college, was alienated from his family, was very handsome, and spoke in a manner that enchanted her. Therefore, when he asked her for her telephone number, she gave it to him immediately. He promised to call her as soon as he left the hospital and was settled.

———

Bella didn't hear from George until early December. She had already given up hope of ever hearing from him again, when he telephoned her. He said that he had waited this long, because he didn't want to call her until he was truly able to take care of himself.

Bella understood, and invited him to come to Staten Island to visit her. She suggested the next Saturday night. An embarrassed George told her that he had a job working as a waiter in a restaurant, because, he explained, it was the only job he could find. Saturday night was the restaurant's busiest night, so they would have to meet on a Monday or Tuesday, when he didn't have to work. A date was set for the following Monday, and a very excited Bella began counting the days and hours until she saw George again.

———

This meeting became the first of many. George and Bella couldn't seem to get enough of each other. When he spoke to her about the economic or political situation in America and the world, she listened with rapt attention. Bella had never met anyone as interesting or attractive as this young man.

George loved the melody of Bella's accent. Her accent shamed her and she tried very hard, without success, to speak like someone born in America. George believed that her manner of speech simply added to her overwhelming charm. He could not remember ever being so enchanted by a girl.

By winter's end, they were in love. Bella's family liked George, and they particularly liked the fact that poor, unfortunate Bella had met someone who was blind to her disfigured leg. And blind he was! Bella and George's dates became passionate and demanding. They knew that they must consummate soon, and in the moral climate of the 1930's, Bella would not consider consummation without marriage. Therefore, a date was set for a wedding in September.

Sarah wanted Bella's wedding to be the best one the family had ever seen. Frugal Sarah dipped deep into her savings, and began to plan a very grand affair. Bella prevailed upon George to reconcile with Sadie and Joe, and to invite them to the wedding. George also invited some of his college friends from Boston.

———

George's job as a waiter did not satisfy either George or Bella. Her brothers Sol and Irving, were doing passably well in the mattress business, when they had an idea that they thought would improve their business and also provide George with a better job. The plan was to increase mattress production and open a furniture store in their building on Richmond Terrace. They thought that an expanded business would have room for George, and they knew that Bella was able to invest some of the money needed for their business expansion. (Bella had several thousand dollars from the settlement made with the bus company whose bus had crushed her leg.)

Bella and George thought that the plan to expand the business was a good one, so in May of 1931, they became partners in the business. Bella continued to work for the business, sewing mattress tickings. George went to work as an owner/salesman. It was believed that he would be successful at sales because he had a "silver tongue."

———

George gave up his room in Manhattan and temporarily rented a small, furnished apartment on Staten Island. He quickly learned the business begun by his future brothers-in-law, and began to work as a mattress salesman. His work took him from the factory building to the furniture stores that were the factory's customers. Sol was freed of most of his sales duties, when George became the main salesman, so Sol became the business's delivery man, and helped Eva to man the furniture store.

Housing arrangements on Richmond Terrace changed. After they were married, George and Bella would live in the back apartment. Eva, Sol, and their newborn son would live in the apartment behind the store. Fanny, Murray, their baby girl, Sarah, and Max would share the largest apartment in the front. Irving would move in with Sol and Eva.

———

People talked about Bella and George's wedding for years. Who would believe that the marriage of a beautiful couple, married in a lavish and beautiful wedding, would end so ignominiously? Both the bride's and the groom's families seemed very happy with the match, George's college buddies were mesmerized by Bella's charms, and the bridal couple was visibly, deeply in love. When did the discord begin?

George seemed thrilled about his impending fatherhood, when three months after his marriage he learned that Bella was pregnant. Although business wasn't good, he believed that he was working very hard to make the business successful. Sol and Irving disagreed. They often had arguments with him, in which they told him that when he was dealing with customers, he must stick to the subject of mattresses and must not divert the conversation to the political and economic crisis in the United States. George believed that his brothers-in-law were bores possessing no knowledge of the subtleties of good salesmanship. Their constant criticism made George very unhappy at work. He wanted to leave the mattress business and find a job where he would be independent and appreciated. Bella reluctantly acquiesced to his doing so, but quite a few serious arguments occurred before she agreed.

Bella's brothers agreed to buy George and Bella out. They believed that George was lazy and a drain on the business. Bella continued to sew tickings for her brothers, because the only sure income in her household was the meager salary she received for her sewing. Her brothers made only small and unpredictable payments on the money she had contributed toward their business expansion, because in those dour days of 1932, their business was not doing well at all.

George spent most weekdays job hunting in Manhattan. He invested money in employment agencies that promised him work, but the precious money was lost and no jobs materialized. He and his weary pregnant wife often sniped at each other in their frustration over money and jobs. Their baby was due to be born in late July or early August. In the heat of June, Bella had stopped working, and no money at all was coming into their home.

One of the few pleasant activities of that dismal summer of 1932 was Bella and George's walks to the ferry terminal. On lovely summer mornings, before the pavement heated to the point that one's feet burned through one's shoes, Bella would accompany George to the ferry terminal. The one and a half mile walk in the refreshing morning breeze coming from the sea would rejuvenate the couple and rekindle their hopes for success. When they arrived at the terminal, they would kiss, George would enter the building, and Bella would slowly lumber home. These were their most compatible times. George would go off on his quest for employment and Bella would go home turning her hopes for his employment over and over again in her mind.

On one such early August morning, Bella suddenly felt a wetness between her legs. Her water had broken! George hailed a taxi and directed the driver to the Staten Island Hospital on Jersey Street. He told Bella he would bring her the suitcase she had packed for the hospital.

When they arrived at the hospital, Bella was whisked away. George went to a phone booth and called Eva. He told her to notify the family. He then called the family member he liked best, Harry's wife Lily. She was now the mother of two small children, so she couldn't come to the hospital, but she chatted with George. They discussed baby names, and when she learned that the baby would be named for Bella's father, whose name had been *Isroil Michal*, she asked him if he had any favorite names beginning with the letter "I." (It is customary for Jews whose forefathers came to America from central and eastern Europe, to name newborn infants after cherished deceased people. The baby's religious name carefully replicates the deceased's name, unless there is a difference in sex between the baby and the deceased. At such times, the English name usually uses the first letter of the name that is being honored.)

"I love the name *Isabelle* for a girl," said Lily. "My sister has a daughter with that name."

"I like it too," said George. "What do you think of *Ira* for a boy?"

"I like it," replied Lily. "They're both lovely names."

No one, least of all Lily, would have believed that George's tenure in Sarah's family was almost over.

———

In the early evening, Bella gave birth to a little girl. When Bella was fully conscious, a nurse carrying what looked like a bundle wrapped up in a small pink blanket, came to her bedside. "You have a beautiful baby girl," she said.

Inexperienced Bella lifted the blanket from the baby's face, so that she could examine her. What a shock! The baby's face was beet-red. She was grimacing and had her eyes squeezed tightly shut. Her nose had been flattened during delivery and her jet black hair stuck up in the air every which way. In short, she was ugly! Bella, who had expected a baby that would look like a doll, began to cry.

The smiling nurse said, "Why are you crying? Your baby has everything she needs- ten fingers- ten toes. You should be very happy."

"Happy!" shrieked Bella. "She's a girl. How can such an ugly girl have a happy life?"

The nurse laughed. "Her nose is only temporarily flattened. It will right itself. Her hair will settle down, and her skin will not be red. Wait until you see her tomorrow, her appearance will be much improved."

On the next day, Bella did see an improved appearance. She would have been happy, but she felt neglected because the baby's father only had come for a few minutes in the evening. He said that he had been looking for work all day. At that time they named the baby Isabelle, and with each of the baby's visits to her mother, Bella fell more deeply in love with her. To the new mother, hers had become the most beautiful baby in the world!

Throughout Bella's ten day stay at the hospital, George came to see her and the baby three times. He always apologized for his absence by saying that he had missed visiting hours, because he was job hunting in Manhattan. Then on her last day at the hospital, George declined Irving's invitation to join him when he went to the hospital to fetch his sister and his new niece. George said that if he accompanied Irving to the hospital, the car would be too crowded with people and baby paraphernalia. When Bella saw that only Irving had come to take her and Baby Isabelle home, she was deeply hurt, but she said nothing.

When Bella arrived at her home, she was introduced to a high school girl named Margaret, whom Irving had hired to help her during her first week at home from the hospital. Margaret was a capable girl, and with her help, Bella would probably be on her feet very soon.

At dinner, George dropped "his bomb!" He said that he believed he would never be able to find suitable work in New York. Because he was more familiar with Boston, and would be more likely to find work there, he proposed that he go to Boston the next day to begin a new job search.

Bella exploded! She angrily said that she didn't want him to leave her so soon after their baby's birth. She urged that he wait a month or two until she and the baby were strong enough to accompany him to Boston. She demanded that he wait until then, and tearfully added that she and the baby needed him.

George was adamant. He refused to wait. He informed her that he had been planning this trip throughout her stay at the hospital. He declared that he had been unemployed long enough and he would not be deterred. He was going to Boston the next day!

Bella and George didn't speak to each other for the rest of that night. Although they slept in the same bed, they slept like strangers. They did not even bid each other good night.

True to his word, when George awakened, he packed a rather large suitcase. He packed in silence, as Bella silently watched. He then picked up his suitcase and left. The new parents had not exchanged one word... not even "goodbye."

About six hours after George had left, he telephoned Bella. He told her that he would always love her and that he would commence his job search on the following day. Bella had said very little during George's phone call, because Eva was in the room and Bella didn't feel free to speak her mind.

Bella didn't hear from George for several days, and in shame, she secluded herself from her family as much as possible. It was clear that they desperately wanted to know what was happening, but Bella said nothing. Seven days after George left, he called again. This time he assured her that job hunting was going well and he would be home soon. After that call, once again, there was a long silence. Bella began to despair. She called Georges sister Sadie in Boston. Sadie said that she had not seen George and she didn't know where he was. Terrible suspicions danced in Bella's mind. "Had George had an accident?...Was there another woman?"

It was fortunate that Margaret, the girl they had hired to help out, was still with Bella, because after her phone call to Sadie, Bella's health seemed to decline. She did very little in the way of taking care of Baby Isabelle. It was necessary for Margaret to become the baby's main caregiver.

———

Several weeks had passed since George's last call and it wasn't until Isabelle was almost two months old, that the mystery of his whereabouts was solved. A registered package arrived for Bella, which she quickly signed for and opened. There were several legal documents inside the large envelope which was postmarked from Reno, Nevada. It announced that George had petitioned for divorce. Bella was invited by the Nevada court to contest the divorce, if she chose. When she read the contents of the envelope, Bella emitted a piercing shriek and collapsed on a chair near the kitchen table. Margaret ran for Sarah, and the two women put Bella to bed. Bella turned her head away and only said, "I will not contest the divorce. It's over!"

———

Bella descended into a severe depression. She rarely spoke, did nothing

toward the care of Baby Isabelle, and turned away from anyone who came
to talk to her. Her family was in despair. They summoned a doctor, who
couldn't seem to snap Bella out of her withdrawal from life. She ate very
little and began to waste away. Everyone was frantic with worry.

One day, Dr. Fine came to check on Bella. As usual, Bella turned
away and said nothing. The doctor told her that he understood her despair.
He said that anyone who had been deserted and was now faced with the
prospect of raising a baby alone, would be as depressed as she was, "But,"
he said, "I might have a solution to your problem. You are a lovely young
woman who can expect a fulfilling life, if you are free of some of your
gigantic burdens, – and probably the biggest burden you are facing is your
responsibility to your baby. I am acquainted with a wealthy Jewish couple
who have been trying for eight years to have a baby. They have been totally
unsuccessful, so I told them about you and your little baby girl. They have
expressed a keen interest in adopting Isabelle."

Bella turned to face Dr. Fine with fury in her eyes. As she reared up
out of bed she said, "Leave this house! Isabelle is my child and I'll raise her
with her own mother's love!"

The well-meaning doctor left quickly. He believed that he had found
just the medicine to cure his lovely young patient's depression.

Bella let Margaret go that very day. When Margaret left, Bella picked
the baby up from her crib, cradled her in her arms, and said, "Isabelle,
Isabelle – I'm your mommy, and as you grow up you will never feel the
need for anyone else's love. I'll love and care for you until I close my eyes
permanently; and I'll teach you about what to look for in a husband, so
that when my kind of love no longer suffices, you'll have the love of a friend
who will be with you for life. I promise you that you will be loved and
protected by me, until you can be on your own!" She kissed the baby and
called to Sarah to come in so that they could chat.

———

New living arrangements on Richmond Terrace were made once more.
Sarah and Max took over Bella and George's back apartment. Irving moved
in with them. Bella and Baby Isabelle shared the large front bedroom.
The rent for the front bedroom was much less than the rent for the back

apartment. Eva, Sol, and their small son shared the big apartment with Bella and her baby, while Fanny, Murray, and their little girl moved into the apartment behind the store.

———

Bella made arrangements to receive financial assistance from the city of New York. While being on Home Relief shamed her, leaving her baby while she went to work (if, indeed, she could find a job) shamed her even more. She couldn't work for her brothers, because the mattress factory was doing very poorly, as was the furniture store located in the Richmond Terrace house. What was even worse, because Sol and Irving's business was fairing so badly, it not only provided too little money for their own families, it made it impossible for them to repay their debt to Bella, reinforcing Bella's need for financial assistance.

———

As bad as the financial news was in the United States, political conditions in Germany put even greater fear into the hearts of Sarah's family. Hitler and the Nazis were ranting anti-Semitism of the worst kind. Jews in Germany were suffering serious discrimination and persecution. Many American Jews feared for the lives of the Jews in Germany, and…. Germany's anti-Semitism seemed to be becoming contagious! On the radio, Father Coughlin, an American Catholic priest, spewed a virulent hatred against Jews. Americans of German decent were joining *The Bund*, where they wore uniforms with swastikas. These Bundists paraded in several American cities and held a rally that filled Madison Square Garden in New York, where they screamed their anti-Semitic thoughts for the world to hear. Closet anti-Semites, who had silently harbored violent feelings against Jews, began to speak out and act out in communities all over America. Sarah's family saw this anti-Semitism first-hand, on Richmond Terrace.

A gang of disgruntled, unemployed school dropouts hung out in front of the drugstore across the street from the house in which Sarah's family lived. Because the boys were unable to find work, they could always be found loitering in front of the drugstore, where they harassed female passerbys or screamed insults at black people or Jews who happened to pass their way. One of their greatest frustrations was the "rich Jews" who owned the furniture store across the street from their hangout.

Sarah's family bore the young anti-Semites' insulting catcalls in silence. Hot-headed Sol wanted to do battle with the young hoodlums, but he was restrained from doing so by both Sarah and Eva, until one hot July afternoon in 1934. On this day, when everything was quiet around the house on Richmond Terrace, and two very small children napped in the front apartment, the anti-Semitic youths' hatred broke forth in earnest. Eva had put her four-year old little boy down for a nap, far away from his room's open window. Bella, on the other hand, had put her almost two-year old baby, to sleep in her crib, which was located directly opposite her room's open window. Suddenly, the quiet was shattered by virulent anti-Semitic catcalls being screamed by the hoodlums loitering across the street. A storm of rocks rained through Isabelle's open window. Two of them landed in the baby's crib, missing the sleeping baby by inches.

Bella grabbed her baby and went screaming down to the store to tell Sol. Sol ran up the stairs and when he saw the rocks in Isabelle's crib and the rocks on the floor of the bedroom in which his little son had slept through the whole commotion, a burning fury coursed through him. He returned to the store, pulled down a large steel mattress hook that had been impaled in one of the mattresses, and charged across the street. He grabbed the first hoodlum that he came upon and held the boy's neck in a choking hold. He placed the lethal steel hook against the young anti-Semite's Adam's apple, pressing slightly. "Repeat your insults against Jews," he shouted. "Let me hear them, and this piece of shit is dead!"

Eva and Sarah came running across the street. They begged the hot-headed Sol to let the boy go, but Sol ignored them.

"Your rocks landed in the crib of a baby, less than two years old. Fortunately the baby's not hurt. If she were hurt, this piece of shit would not be the only dead anti-Semite on Richmond Terrace. If I had to die doing it, I'd kill the bunch of you!" screamed Sol.

The hoodlums stood paralyzed with fear. They were afraid that if they moved, the furious young Jew would kill their buddy.

Eva screamed at Sol to let the boy go. Sol still ignored her.

"Find another place to hang out, because if I see you here, someone will die!" shouted Sol. He flung the boy he was holding to the sidewalk. Still menacing the group with the large steel hook he said, "Get the hell away from here. It's still not too late for me to kill one of you!"

The hoodlums ran away at full speed and the family never saw them again.

———————

Life on Richmond Terrace became peaceful once again, but the worsening economic climate of 1934, caused the entire family to suffer. Deprivation was rife in America, and a fact of life for Sarah's family. Sol and Irving's business went from bad to worse. Finally they were forced to close the mattress factory. There was very little business in the furniture store as well, but the brothers kept it open.

Bella had to live on her Home Relief checks. Her brothers did not have enough money to get along themselves, let alone to repay their debt to her.

Fanny had given birth to a little boy. She wanted to move back into the large front apartment. This satisfied Bella who was afraid of the return of the anti-Semitic hoodlums. Sarah asked Irving to move in with Bella. She felt better knowing that Bella and the baby had a man sleeping in their apartment. Irving did so for six months, but then decided that there was no future for him in New York. He had heard that employment opportunities were better in Florida, so he decided to drive down there to try his luck.

Sol, Eva, and their little boy moved behind the store again. Sol took a job with W.P.A. (Work Projects Administration). This was an organization established by the United States government to alleviate some of the country's massive unemployment. Unemployed men worked in construction or in repairing the infrastructure. They received very low salaries, but low pay was better than no pay.

Fanny's husband Murray was the only man living in the house on Richmond Terrace who had a job in private industry. While his income wasn't handsome, it was sufficient to the needs of his family. For them, the pain of the Depression came more from observing those around them doing without necessities, than from being deprived themselves.

While Sol was working for the W.P.A. repairing holes on New York City's streets, Eva manned the store. The little business done there, supplemented their tiny income. Now and then Sol was hired to do a moving job on the weekend. This was another small, but welcome, supplement to his family's meager income.

Sarah and Max lived very frugally on their tiny savings. Theirs was a family that knew how to handle financial adversity, but the peacefulness of their lives was none-the-less shattered by a collect telegram from Irving. It said that he was in jail in Georgia! He would be allowed to call the next morning and would explain everything at that time.

After a sleepless night for the family, Irving's phone call came. He spoke to Sol, telling him that while on his way to Florida, he had missed a sign that said that a Georgia chain gang was working on a road that motorists were prohibited from using. Not seeing the sign, he drove onto the road and was arrested. His car was impounded, his wallet and money taken, and he was thrown into a cell with two other prisoners who were notified by the arresting officer that he was a "New York City Jew Boy." His cellmates' greeting was to give Irving a terrible beating, which was the first and last communication Irving had with them. After the beating, Irving's cellmates totally ignored him.

The next morning, Irving was removed from his cell. He was told that his family could be notified about his whereabouts by telegram. They were to be told that he would call them on the following day when he could give them particulars as to whom and where they should send $1,000 for his release.

When Irving was returned to his cell, his mind went round and round trying to figure out where his family could quickly raise so vast a sum as $1,000. He would have to, somehow, communicate the urgency of his need. He must tell them that he no longer had a car or any money. Hopefully, they would take it from there.

The phone call was brief and to the point. When Irving was cut off, Sarah began to wail. She and Max had a few hundred dollars left. They said they would go on Home Relief and send all of their money to Georgia. Fanny and Murray had even smaller savings. However, they were willing to contribute all of it. While they all knew that Anna would be able to help, Bella insisted that getting the money from Anna, in Brooklyn, would take too long. She believed that Irving's plight required immediate attention, so Bella went into action immediately!

Bella's good friend, Minnie, lived behind her candy store, with her husband and four sons, just up the street from the house on Richmond Terrace. Bella knew that Minnie was a miser whose income was derived from her husband's low paying job in Manhattan and the candy store that Minnie manned. Bella knew that Minnie must have money squirreled away in her home, because she distrusted banks since the bank crash. Minnie lived as modestly as a Home Relief recipient, so Bella surmised that the money she didn't spend must be in her house and would therefore be immediately available. Consequently, Bella ran up the street to where Minnie lived and weeping heartbrokenly, told Minnie about Irving's plight. She assured Minnie that if she lent them the money, it would be paid back as soon as possible. At the conclusion of Bella's woeful tale, without saying a word, Minnie went into her bedroom and reemerged with the entire $1,000 for Irving's release.

The money was wired to Georgia, and Irving was released by his captors with only the clothes he was wearing and three dollars in his pocket. An exhausted Irving got home by stoking coal on a train that was run by steam and was heading to New York. When he learned how the money for his release had been procured, he vowed that someday he would repay Minnie for her trust and for her money with far more than she had lent him.

All was not grim on Richmond Terrace. Delivery of furniture purchased in the store, was often the opportunity for fun for the four children living in the Richmond Terrace house. The large, somewhat dilapidated moving van that was usually parked on the hill that ran along the side of the house was put into service to carry the newly purchased furniture. Either one or both of Sarah's sons were the deliverymen. Very often they invited any of the children who lived in the house to come along for a ride. Depending on which children were available, they could have from one to four young passengers.

Sol and Irving provided all sorts of adventures for the children when the little people joined them for a delivery. Sometimes it was just an ice cream party. At such times the children were taken to an ice cream parlor for unusual treats that were not pre-packaged like the ice cream they could purchase at the drug store across the street or at Minnie's candy store. At other times, the children were taken to lovely treed neighborhoods, almost devoid of traffic, where children played safely in the street. Sarah's grandchildren marveled at the beautiful suburban streets and wished that they too, could someday live in such a beautiful environment. Best of all, however, was when Sol and Irving told the children stories about Russia. Four little imaginations traveled back to Vashisht and the vast forest surrounding it. The children were made to feel as if they knew how their family had lived, before they had come to America.

Once, a table and chairs was being delivered to a house on a street that had few houses, but had a huge cemetery on one of its sides. It was 5:00 P.M. The December evening was cold and dark. Only two children had come for a ride, Sol's almost seven-year old son, Mel, and Bella's four and a half year old daughter, Isabelle. Isabelle was afraid of the encroaching darkness and of ghosts in the cemetery. Mel relished his little cousin's fear and added to it by making spooky noises and laughing at her frightened reaction. All of a sudden, Isabelle, who was really frightened, began to cry. Mel was undone! He put his arm around her and said, "I'll *always* protect you, Isabelle. Don't cry. There's nothing to be afraid of. There really are no ghosts." Isabelle felt comforted. Neither of the children realized that a lifelong bond was formed between them on that cold December night, in the moving van parked alongside a dark and spooky cemetery.

———————

When Irving returned from Georgia, he moved into the apartment with Bella and Isabelle once more. He doted on his beautiful, dark haired little niece. He constantly bought her toys, and when he was at home, enjoyed playing with her and teasing her. He wanted many things for her, but the shortage of money made extras extremely hard to come by.

One Sunday, when Isabelle was only four years old and was somersaulting all around his room, Irving said, "Bella, I want you to give Isabelle dancing lessons. She seems so agile, that I'm sure she'll be good at it and enjoy dancing. You know that I often play pinochle," he continued. "I am very lucky, most of the time. Dancing lessons are not so expensive, and I'm sure that if I gave you three dollars a week, it would cover the lesson, the carfare to the lesson, and maybe even a snack for the two of you. The money from my pinochle winnings will pay for the lessons and a pleasant Saturday for the two of you."

Bella protested. She didn't want Irving to give her so much money. His reopened mattress factory was only limping along, but Irving insisted, and finally wore Bella down. She decided to take Isabelle to a dancing school in Brooklyn, Miss Anne's School of Dance, which had an excellent reputation. Bella's niece Ida was taking lessons there too. Bella planned to bring the two children to her sister Anna's house after their lesson, and then have a nice, long visit with her sister.

On Saturdays, by the time Bella and Isabelle got back home from Brooklyn, it was eight o'clock. Isabelle was immediately put to bed, and Bella then spent a short, quiet evening at home. Her Saturday's were usually so full, that she couldn't even wait up for her younger brother, Irving. Irving usually came in very late, after spending the night carousing with other unmarried male and female friends.

Bella never referred to Isabelle's father as *Your Daddy* or *Your Father*. She referred to him as *George*. Isabelle knew that George was her missing father. Her mother called him *George* when she spoke of him, and she spoke of him quite often.

One day, Bella reminded Isabelle of her aunt who lived in Boston. She told Isabelle that Aunt Sadie was George's sister, and the mother of two daughters. Her oldest daughter, Mona, was a good deal older than Isabelle, but the younger daughter Monica, was only a year younger than Isabelle, and like Isabelle, did not yet go to school. Because Monica didn't go to school, Aunt Sadie was bringing Isabelle's little cousin with her to New

York. They planned to visit Isabelle and Bella, and Bella said that Isabelle would probably enjoy playing with her younger cousin from Boston.

Bella was bustling around the apartment, making things orderly and attractive, in preparation for her visitors. While she was preparing a luncheon for all of them, she told Isabelle that Aunt Sadie always said that she didn't know where George was, and that she insisted that George had never contacted her when he had left his family, nor had he contacted her since. Isabelle was too young to question Bella about whether she believed Sadie or not. In any event, the doorbell rang, interrupting their conversation.

Bella opened the door for Sadie and Baby Monica. Sadie was carrying a beautifully wrapped box which she gave to Isabelle, along with a big hug. She and Bella embraced, and Bella lifted Monica into her arms and kissed her cheek. While both women admired each other's little daughters, Monica followed Isabelle into the bedroom. In the bedroom, Isabelle unwrapped the contents of the box and exclaimed with pleasure over how pretty her gift was. In the box, there was a beautiful brown sunsuit and a bright yellow blouse that could be worn under it. A pair of white socks with a brown band around the cuffs completed Sadie's gift to Isabelle. After Isabelle examined her gift, she ran into the kitchen where her mother and Aunt Sadie were chatting. She loudly thanked her aunt for her gift. "I really love my new clothes," she enthusiastically exclaimed. "Thank you! Thank you!"

Bella served lunch, which the two little girls mostly ignored. When they were excused from the table, the two small children went into the bedroom once again. They played together for a short while, when "out of the blue," Monica picked up the gift box containing Isabelle's lovely gift, and flung it out of the open window. Little Monica thought that her joke was wonderful, and she laughed uproariously. Young Isabelle was horrified! She thought her cousin's actions were meaner than anything she had ever seen and for her, her cousin's laughter was untenable. In a rage, Isabelle eradicated her cousin's laughter by punching the mean little girl in the face. Isabelle then angrily knocked her cousin down and sat on her as she pummeled her screaming little visitor. Bella and Sadie came running into the room. Bella dragged Isabelle off her distressed cousin and whacked her small daughter's rump hard, several times. A weeping little Isabelle tried to justify herself and indict her cousin by pointing at her beautiful new clothes crumpled and scattered across the pavement below the open window, but to no avail. Bella angrily went downstairs, dragging little Isabelle with her. They both retrieved the lovely clothes that had caused the great commotion, and went upstairs, where Monica was sitting on her mother's lap, sporadically sobbing.

Bella commanded that Isabelle apologize, which Isabelle did. Sadie made no such demand of Monica. She and her daughter left soon after Bella and Isabelle had come back upstairs, and to Bella's distress, they left before the two little girls had made their peace.

———————

Three days later, Sadie's husband Joe called Bella. A terrible tragedy had occurred on the train ride back to Boston. Brokenheartedly, Joe told her that little Monica had choked on a peanut she had been eating and had died on her way back home. Sobbing, Joe said that Sadie was prostrate with grief.

Bella was overcome with sorrow for Monica and for Monica's family. Isabelle who had no understanding of death, asked her weeping mother if Monica would come back to visit them again. When Bella said, "No," immature little Isabelle thought that was just fine.

———————

About six months after Monica's death, Bella and Isabelle took the long train ride to Boston. They took a bus from the train station to Brookline, and they walked a few blocks to Sadie's house. Bella lugged a suitcase from the bus stop to the house. She was worn out when she rang the doorbell that was answered by a uniformed maid. Isabelle had only seen uniformed maids in the movies, so she was immediately in awe of her surroundings. When Sadie came to greet them, she and Bella burst into tears. This further discombobulated Isabelle. As they walked through the lovely house to a dinette off the kitchen, she couldn't keep her eyes from darting in all directions, as they encompassed the spaciousness and beauty of her aunt's house. In the dinette, a table was artfully set with inviting snacks for the three of them, but Isabelle's attention was immediately drawn to a small platform upon which a child-sized table with four child-sized chairs stood. On each chair was a doll, one doll being more beautiful than the next. In addition, alongside the enchanting table, was a small cabinet with glass doors. It was filled with books, puzzles, and games. Four and a half year old Isabelle went directly to the enticing toys, with every intention of playing with them. "No!" shouted her Aunt Sadie. "Monica was very selfish about her toys. She never shared them with anyone. Because she was like that, I follow her wishes and do not allow any other child to play with her toys."

Frightened and disappointed, Isabelle slinked back to where her mother sat. Bella, who had great sympathy for Sadie's loss, tried to understand her sister-in-law's behavior; but little Isabelle had no understanding of it at all. Isabelle thought, "George was a bad daddy. His sister is a bad aunt. And Monica was a bad cousin."

––––––––––––

If Isabelle did not like her Aunt Sadie, her dislike was more than balanced by her love for all of Bella's siblings – most of all her debonair, unmarried, handsome Uncle Irving. It was he who insisted upon her going to dancing school, where Miss Anne, the dancing teacher, constantly praised her ability. He often watched Isabelle prancing about the apartment, practicing her dance steps. He watched her with an adoring smile on his face. All of Uncle Irving's actions pointed to his complete enchantment with his black-haired little niece. She, in turn, thought her uncle was the best man in the world.

––––––––––––

It was the end of the session for Miss Anne's School of Dance. A recital was to be held in mid-June and excitement reigned. Isabelle, being the youngest child to perform at the recital, was slated to open the show. A beautiful, skimpy, pink satin costume, dotted with pink and silver sequins, adorned the four and a half year old girl. A pink feathery boa was carried throughout her song and discarded when she went into her tap dance, which ended with her rolling on the floor all around the stage.

During dress rehearsal, Isabelle "wowed" them! The little black haired girl belted her song out at the top of her voice. As she sang, she made appropriate motions to match the words….

"I wrap my troubles in bubbles

But that don't help my cause

BECAUSE

Pop goes the bubble

And I'm back in trouble

And soap gets in my eyes."

When the adorable little girl pointed vivaciously to her eyes, the spectators melted. At the dress rehearsal, Isabelle's silver tap shoes performed flawlessly. Miss Anne thought that the opening of the recital would be a hit.

———————

It was the night of the recital. Everyone was excited. Isabelle knew that Uncle Irving was in the audience with the pretty lady she had met about a week ago. Uncle Irving said that he was engaged to the pretty lady. They would be married in less than a year. Then the pretty lady would really be Isabelle's Aunt Ethel, but Isabelle was asked to call her "Aunt" Ethel now. Isabelle peeked through an opening in the curtains. The auditorium was dark, and she couldn't see any of the audience, but she knew that Aunt Ethel and Uncle Irving were there.

Miss Anne had finished her welcoming speech. She left the stage and the piano began to play the overture to Isabelle's song. Miss Anne gently nudged Isabelle onto the stage. The bright lights momentarily blinded the little girl. When she could see, she realized that she couldn't find Uncle Irving out there. Isabelle's overture was playing a second time. Terror welled up in the small girl's throat. Instead of singing, the frightened child turned and ran backstage, where both Miss Anne and Bella nudged her onto the stage again; each of them assuring the mite of a girl that she would do very well. When Isabelle once more found herself on stage, the audience burst into loud applause. Above the applause, Isabelle heard "Yay Isabelle! Knock 'em dead!" The voice was Uncle Irving's.

Isabelle did "knock 'em dead!" When she left the stage, the applause was deafening. Miss Anne and Bella hugged her and told her to go to the dressing room to await the Grand Finale.

At the beginning of the Grand Finale, Isabelle tapped danced out on the stage to the strains of her song and the loud applause of the audience.

When the recital was over, Bella and Isabelle went into the audience to find Irving and Ethel. They were there, smiling broadly, and Uncle Irving was carrying a dozen red roses. When he handed them to Isabelle he said, "You were a star and you'll always be my star. I'm so proud of you. These roses are your first roses, and I am your first boyfriend. When you're a big girl, there will be many flowers and many boyfriends....but I'm your first!"

Aunt Ethel told Isabelle that she too had a beautiful curly, black-haired niece. She said that she'd like Isabelle and her niece to be flower girls at their wedding. Isabelle was delighted. She felt like the luckiest girl in the world. She believed that she was loved by the best people in the world.

———

Bella had not yet begun to date men. Sarah and Fanny constantly urged her to do so, but Bella still did not feel up to going to dances and clubs where young adults met each other.

One Saturday, while Bella was visiting Anna, Meyer's sister-in-law, who was a tenant in Anna and Meyer's building, dropped in. Rivka joined in their conversation, which soon turned to the tragic death of a woman who had lived on their street. This young woman was run down by a car driven by a drunken driver and her poor widowed husband just sat at home and never remarried. "It's lucky that they never had children," mused Rivka. "His home is like a cave. I used to be friendly with his late wife, so I drop in to see him now and then. He just sits and reads the newspaper."

"I always urge him to find a wife, so that he can resume living. He just nods his head. You know, Bella, I'll bet the two of you would like each other. You're almost the same age. May I give him your telephone number? His name is Morris Levinson."

Bella agreed and gave Rivka her telephone number.

"What does Morris Levinson do for a living?" asked Bella.

"Oh, didn't I tell you?" answered Rivka. "He buys and sells real estate. He's very successful – owns a lot of Brooklyn and Bronx apartment houses."

When Bella went home, her mind was full of the possibilities of Morris Levinson. She hoped he'd call her soon. Then on Tuesday night of that same week, Morris Levinson did call Bella. He said that he was unfamiliar with Staten Island, but he would like to meet her that very weekend. When Bella suggested Saturday night, he said that their date would have to get a late start, because he was an observant Orthodox Jew, who didn't travel on the Sabbath. Bella fully understood, having been brought up in orthodoxy herself. She suggested Sunday, and a date was made.

Morris arrived late Sunday afternoon. He was prematurely gray and appeared to be in his late thirties. Twenty-nine year old Bella thought he looked old. Bella introduced Morris to her little daughter. The three of them sat around the kitchen table drinking tea and eating cookies. Morris drank his tea from a glass and used a kosher spoon that Bella had set aside for Sarah's use. The cookies were placed on a glass plate that was parev, (food and utensils that could be used with either dairy or meat products. Glass was considered non-porous. It could be washed kosher clean.) Morris declared that he would always have a kosher home. To Bella, who had lived in a kosher home until her marriage to George, keeping a kosher home would not be a hardship; but somehow Morris's adamant declaration annoyed her.

Morris paid no attention to four and a half year old Isabelle. Instead he spoke about the play they were going to see at the Yiddish theater on the Lower East Side. He said that they would have to leave soon.

Bella excused herself and took Isabelle next door to stay with her Aunt Fanny and her grandmother until morning.

The play was excellent. Menasha Skulnick was an outstanding actor, and he outdid himself that night. Bella had not had so lovely an experience for a long time. After the play, they ate a very late supper at a kosher delicatessen famous for its huge, delicious corned beef and pastrami sandwiches; so, even though Morris said very little, Bella thoroughly enjoyed the evening Consequently, when Morris asked to see her on the following Sunday, Bella immediately said, "Yes."

———

Bella and Morris went on exciting dates for two months. After two months, Bella finally invited him to spend Sunday evening on Staten Island with her and certain members of her family. The dinner would be cooked and eaten next door, in her mother's kosher kitchen.

Morris arrived punctually at 5:30 P.M. He, Bella, and Isabelle went to the next-door apartment where introductions were made. Fanny sent the three children to another room to play, while in the living room, the adults were served wonderful chopped chicken liver on crackers. They ate and drank tea as they discussed the worsening conditions for Jews in Nazi Germany and the improving economy of the US.S.R. Fanny's husband Murray was clearly a communist sympathizer. His political comments visibly annoyed Morris, who finally couldn't restrain himself and blurted out angrily, "Are you a communist?"

"I'm not a card carrying member yet," answered Murray, "but I'm seriously contemplating it."

"I consider government ownership of everything only one step better than Fascism!" blasted Morris. "The communists own all the property and the fascists own their people's souls."

Murray became red in the face. "The communists own everything and distribute it fairly to their people," he declared.

"You're naïve," said Morris angrily. "The communists…"

———

Morris was interrupted by Sarah who requested that everyone come into the kitchen to eat dinner. The children were seated around a small table near the open doorway to the kitchen. The six adults sat at the kitchen table. It was clear that both Murray and Morris Levinson were still agitated, but the talk shifted to how delicious the food was, and tempers cooled.

After dinner the adults talked for a while and the children played. The talk had shifted to religious observance. Morris staunchly proclaimed his orthodoxy. Sarah and Max applauded it, stating that they too were orthodox. The other adults said nothing. Fanny's kosher kitchen was for her mother's benefit, and Bella had completely lapsed from orthodoxy when she was married to George.

When Morris escorted Bella and Isabelle to their apartment, he announced that he would wait until Isabelle was put to bed, because he had important things he wanted to discuss with Bella. When Bella returned to her kitchen, Morris told her that since the death of his wife, he had been very lonely. He said that he had thought that he could never have strong feelings for another woman, but strong feelings had returned. He told Bella that he loved her and he wanted to marry her. Morris did not know that Bella had some strong reservations about marrying him, so he went on with his proposal. He told her that in order for them to be properly married in the orthodox tradition, she would need a *get* (a Jewish religious divorce). Only a husband could grant a wife a *get*, so a rabbi would have to contact George, to convince him to grant Bella her freedom. Morris suggested that he knew a rabbi who could do the work from New York. This New York rabbi would contact a rabbi in the location in which her ex-husband lived and the two rabbis would work together.

Bella said that she would see the rabbi in New York. Even if she didn't marry Morris, she thought, a *get* was a good thing to have.

George was living in San Diego, California. The New York rabbi, Rabbi Golder, contacted Rabbi Fisher in San Diego. Rabbi Fisher got in touch with George. Rabbi Fisher told George that unless he wanted reconciliation with Bella, he should give her the *get* and set her free. George asked if there was someone else she wished to marry. The rabbi said that he didn't know, but that usually was the case. George became agitated and said that he didn't even have a picture of his daughter. Without a picture, he refused to grant the *get*. Rabbi Fisher gave this information to Rabbi Golder who relayed it to Bella. Bella was furious. She couldn't believe that George had feelings for the baby he'd abandoned, but then a vicious vindictiveness overpowered her. If he had feelings, she'd give him something to choke on!

Bella selected the most appealing picture of Isabelle that she had. The little black-haired girl was dressed in a skimpy, gypsy dancing costume. A tambourine was held at her hip. She was smiling and her eyes sparkled.

The picture had been taken on the day of Isabelle's most recent dance recital, and it was completely enchanting. "He'll really choke on this one," Bella thought.

When George beheld the picture, he wept. He said that he could not give Bella or his child up and he would not grant Bella a *get*.

Ordinarily this would have come as a blow to Bella, but well before George's refusal of the *get*, she had decided to break off relations with Morris, because he always seemed very cold to Isabelle. What is more, he had never brought the little girl a trinket or a toy when he came to her house to fetch her mother. Bella was sure that he would have made a very unsatisfactory stepfather for her daughter. This made it impossible for Bella to even consider Morris as a marriage prospect.

————

During the time Morris was courting Bella, a tragedy befell Sarah. It occurred at a place that the family called *Die Boimer* (the Trees). Die Boimer was almost a mile away from their house, not too far from the ferry terminal. It was a clearing, which consisted of two benches facing the water and Bayonne, New Jersey. Large, leafy trees grew in this clearing, providing lovely shade for anyone sitting on the benches.

Sarah and Max loved to walk up to Die Boimer to watch the ships and to smell the pungent sea air. On one such occasion, Sarah dozed off as she and Max were watching the ships. When she awoke, she saw Max dozing beside her. She tapped him gently on his shoulder, but he didn't move. She then shook him more vigorously, and he fell over without a sound. Max had died as he slept next to the dozing Sarah, both of them facing the sea that they loved so much.

————

Richmond Terrace was a long street. The children in Sarah's family did not know where it began or where it ended. Jersey Street was another long street that intersected Richmond Terrace right at the place where Sarah's family lived. The children didn't know where Jersey Street began either, but they certainly knew where it ended, because Jersey Street ended with a very steep hill that ran alongside their house, and ran right into the railroad tracks at the bottom of the hill on which their house stood. Beyond the railroad tracks was the narrow arm of the sea that separated Staten Island from Bayonne, New Jersey.

The hill was used as the parking place for the store's moving van and Irving and Sol's cars. It was also used as a playground by the neighborhood children, because it only had the traffic of the moving van, which unfortunately moved very rarely, and Sarah's sons' two cars. Most of the store's few customers came on foot or on the bus, but occasionally a customer driving a car, parked on the hill too.

One cold winter day in 1936, no cars moved on the Jersey Street Hill, because the day before, snow had fallen, and the hill was too slippery for motor vehicles. Yet, the hill was buzzing with happy, noisy activity. Many neighborhood children had come to the hill to slide down it on their sleds. If, as was the case with some of them, a child had no sled, a large cardboard or corrugated box would do nicely as a sled-substitute.

Sol's son Mel and Fanny's daughter Millie were among the fortunate sledders who owned real sleds. Several of the children who lived in the dilapidated wooden shacks on a tiny dead-end street that intersected Jersey Street had come with large corrugated boxes that had been cut down to their sizes. These children, from *Shantytown*, found that their improvised *sleds* worked quite well. A child could slide down the snow covered, slippery, steep hill very rapidly on a corrugated *sled*.

Another child who came from across the street on Richmond Terrace also used a corrugated *sled*. His name was Bobby, and he and his family lived in an apartment above the drugstore. This quiet African-American family had moved onto Richmond Terrace a year before. Bobby, their eldest son, played with the Jewish children across the street and the Irish children from *Shantytown*. Since Sol had routed the bigoted teenage hoodlums who used to hang out at the drugstore, all of the children in the neighborhood played together without a trace of prejudice.

Isabelle and Marty, Fanny's younger son, were very unhappy, because their mothers had summoned them home for their afternoon naps. They were very angry that they had to leave the sledding on the hill. Just as sleep was beginning to overtake the two unhappy children, everyone was greatly startled by the screeching and clanging of a rapidly braking train.

The people inside the house were not aware of what had happened until Millie and Mel came flying home, crying at the top of their lungs that Bobby had been run over by a train!

Bobby's death plunged the entire neighborhood into mourning. Very quickly, thereafter, Bobby's family moved away. Bobby's terrible death became a part of neighborhood lore, but it didn't stop the children who lived in the neighborhood from using the hill as their playground. Bobby's accident, however, caused the railroad company to erect a concrete barrier at the foot of the hill. This barrier completely blocked pedestrian and vehicular access from Jersey Street to the tracks.

During the time that the concrete barrier to the tracks was being erected, the workmen on the hill would often smile at the playing children or comment about a game being played. But on one sunny, but chilly spring day, the game devised by three and a half year old Marty and his four and a half year old cousin, Isabelle, would not have gained them any adult smiles. The two toddlers had discovered that tumbling from the back of Uncle Sol's car to the front of Uncle Sol's car was lots of fun. They did this repeatedly, until one of them accidentally released the car's hand brake, causing the car to roll forward in the direction of the men building the barrier.

One workman saw the car moving down the hill without a driver. As the car gained momentum, the workman jumped on the running board, reached into the rolling vehicle through an open window, and pulled on the hand brake. The car stopped and the workman set everything right mechanically. He then turned his angry attention to the little dark haired girl and the little blond boy cowering in the back of the automobile.

"Where do you live?" he growled.

They both pointed at the house.

"Whose car is this?" he snapped.

The frightened children stammered, "Uncle Sol's."

"Get out of the car," he ordered gruffly.

They both obeyed immediately. The workman pulled one child out on his right and the other child out on his left. He continued to pull them rapidly into the hallway and up the stairs. Fanny, Bella, and Sarah hearing heavy footsteps on the stairs, came out on the landing.

The workman having already dragged both little children upstairs, angrily admonished the women for allowing such young children to play in a car alone. Both mothers stated ashamedly that they weren't aware of what the children were doing, and they assured the workman that it would never happen again. They then both thanked him sincerely, while Sarah silently thanked God for sparing her grandchildren.

Both of the children were spanked, lectured about safety, and put to bed.

———

Every Saturday a group of children from *Shantytown* came down to Richmond Terrace to hang out on the hill or around the emergency exit door of the Star Theater, located across the street from the furniture store. The children who lived on Richmond Terrace joined them. On the luckiest Saturdays some of the children had the ten-cent admission to the movies. Isabelle, who loved going to dancing school and seeing her Aunt Anna's three children, disliked missing the fun of going to the movies or hanging out with the neighborhood children. When her summer dance recital was over, she happily joined them when they all hung out near The Star. She was able to do this because dancing school was closed from early June through early October.

During the summer of 1938, Isabelle turned six years old. She thoroughly enjoyed going to the movies at The Star with other children from the neighborhood. Isabelle even liked the newsreels that showed important events taking place in the world. It was from the newsreels that she had learned about the Spanish Civil War, the Nazi's horrible treatment of Jews, the Japanese invasion of China, the kidnapping of the Lindbergh baby, and the terrible Hindenburg disaster. She and her mother spent lots of time together, and she was able to talk to Bella about anything, so she often brought up what she had seen in the newsreel. Bella would generally elaborate on the subject. Because of these conversations, Isabelle became very well-informed for a child of her age.

When Isabelle did not have a dime for the Saturday movie, and she hung out with the children who had gathered at The Star's exit. Kathleen, a year younger than she, was Isabelle's favorite friend there. Kathleen came down to Richmond Terrace with one of her older sisters or brothers, from *Shantytown* where they lived. There were six children in her family, and Kathleen was the youngest of her family to come down to The Star. She had a baby brother, but he stayed at home with Kathleen's mother. Kathleen often came down to The Star exit carrying a large orange. She loved oranges, but her family could only afford them on Saturday and Sunday. One of Kathleen's brothers or sisters would peel the orange for her and Kathleen would bite into it, causing orange juice to spray and spurt all over the delighted little girl. Kathleen would laugh at the mess she was making and continue to devour the orange, with gusto, making an even bigger mess. Isabelle loved to watch Kathleen's joy as she destroyed her orange. After the orange was eaten, the sticky little girl and Isabelle would play together until one of them had to go home.

When someone lives near the sea, its smell becomes a part of his life. When he goes farther inland and loses the sea's smell, he knows that he is far away from home. When he travels home and encounters the pungent, delicious sea scent, he knows that he is home, even before he is actually at his residence. The sea's smell is part of home to those who live near it.

Sarah's four grandchildren, who lived on Richmond Terrace, were sea babies. All of them fell asleep listening to the music of the buoys. Buoys, boat whistles, and sea smells gave them comfort. Never did they expect to see the sea turn on them and become evil. Never did they expect the sea to become an enemy. But it did!

On a Sunday in the summer of 1938, there was a huge storm in the Atlantic. The weatherman on the radio warned that the storm was a hurricane that could be expected to do damage to some New York land areas located close to the sea. Richmond Terrace and Jersey Street were both New York land areas located close to the sea.

The predicted hurricane did not come all at once. In the early hours of the morning it started with gentle rain. It being Sunday, everyone who lived in the brick house on the corner of Richmond Terrace and Jersey

Street was at home. In *Shantytown* most of the people were at home too. Very soon, the rain began to come down with such force that most of *Shantytown's* devout Irish Catholics decided to skip church and stay home, even though it was Sunday. It rained without let up. By eleven o'clock, the wind started to blow very hard. Soon it was blowing so hard that the windowpanes in the house on Richmond Terrace rattled noisily. The sound of the wind was so loud that it drowned out the sound of the driving rain. Sarah, her children, and her grandchildren felt a great unease, but everyone still went about his or her business. Sarah was knitting. Fanny, Bella, and Eva were preparing lunch in each of their apartments. The men were reading newspapers and magazines, and the children were either reading or playing with toys.

In *Shantytown* the houses shook. No one cooked or read or knitted or played. Everyone was terrified! The wind and rain were so forceful that *Shantytown's* inhabitants did not dare to leave their houses; yet to remain in their houses seemed to place them in peril, too.

By the time Sarah's family sat down to eat lunch at their various tables, the wind was at its strongest. It was difficult to eat without thinking about the terrific noise and force of the wind.

As the people in Sarah's family ate, the houses in *Shantytown* were being washed away. They had been blown down by the ferocious hurricane winds that had caused them to collapse. Four families perished. Kathleen's oldest sister had been visiting relatives, so she was the only survivor in her family. Isabelle would never again be able to take delight in watching Kathleen sloppily eat an orange. Indeed, some of the children who usually came to The Star, would come there no more. The Hurricane of 1938 did damage in many places, but it did more than merely damage the shacks on the little street off Jersey Street in Staten Island. The shacks were obliterated, and everyone in them perished.

On Monday, when the sun once more was shining brightly, Sarah's family heard the news about *Shantytown*. As they picked up debris and cleaned up and repaired hurricane damage, they mourned their impoverished Irish neighbors. They also thanked God for the deliverance of their own family.

Several days later there was a large funeral at the church where the hurricane victims from *Shantytown* had worshipped. Bella decided that she and Isabelle should pay their final respects to their deceased neighbors, by attending the funeral.

The sun was very bright and the day quite warm, when Bella and Isabelle went to the church. Much to Bella's surprise, the large church was so crowded that they and many other mourners could not get in. They joined this large crowd of mourners and spectators who stood on both sides of the street. Only the roped off area for the hearses was devoid of spectators.

When the church service was over, the caskets began to be carried out – large, flower covered, brown wooden boxes – one to a hearse. The somber crowd was completely silent, until the silence was suddenly broken by a woman's sob and the cry, "The children!"

Bella and Isabelle were standing across the street from the church's entrance. They were among the first to see the smaller, white, flower covered caskets being carried out. Isabelle whispered, "Is Kathleen in one of those smaller white boxes, Mommy?"

"Yes," answered Bella.

Isabelle loved playing with her cousins and the other children in the neighborhood. She also loved her teasing uncles, loving aunts, and her grandmother. But best of all she loved to both play and to talk seriously with her mother.

Bella was captivated by her lovely dark haired daughter, but she never babied her. When Isabelle asked about her missing daddy, Bella hid none of the details concerning both George's good qualities and his bad ones; but, after Isabelle learned about George's desertion, it seemed as if she lost interest in him altogether. It was as if she thought, "He didn't want me, and I don't need him!"

When Isabelle was five, George's first letter came. In it, George told Isabelle that he always thought about her. He enclosed $5 as a gift for her, and declared that he would always love her.

Bella had just terminated her relationship with Morris, at that time. When she had discussed that doomed relationship with Isabelle, she had told her that she didn't think Morris was prepared to be a good enough daddy to her, because he had never paid enough attention to her, nor brought her any gifts. "A good daddy, like a good mommy, loves his child more than anything in the world, and tries to be there for his child in every way," said Bella.

Having experienced Bella's reaction to Morris, little Isabelle understood her mother's bitter mirth over George's letter. For someone who "always loved" his child, he had put great distance between them in every way. Although $5 was not a small amount of money in the Depression, his gift was too little, too late.

Bella and Isabelle didn't feel that they truly needed anyone else. In the winter, they often played together in the snow, and one time when Isabelle had overslept and had missed her ride to kindergarten, Bella had pulled her to school on her sled. When Bella had come home after leaving her daughter at school, Sarah scolded her, saying that she put too much strain on her sick leg walking the long distance to Isabelle's school. Bella just laughed and said that she genuinely enjoyed the long walk in the snow with her little girl.

Mother and daughter sang together and played together. Bella often read to Isabelle, and best of all, they always talked. They each filled up the other's life.

George's second letter, a few months later, was truly a surprise. It was addressed to Bella. In it, he apologized for having left her and their baby, and he asked for Bella's forgiveness. He said that he had never stopped loving them and begged Bella to allow him to come home. George said that he had been unable to accumulate any money, because the jobs he had had were all low paying. He begged her to please send him a one-way ticket to New York, so that the three of them could be reunited.

To Bella's immense surprise, Sarah spoke in favor of George's return. She offered to buy the ticket that would bring him home to be Isabelle's father and Bella's husband. Bella categorically refused Sarah's offer! She told her mother that she didn't trust George, and she said that she feared that if he came back he would make her pregnant with another child and then leave again.

Bella answered George's letter with a short note. It read, "If you wish to come home, come home the same way that you left!" She signed it "Bella."

George answered Bella's note with a letter accusing her of being vindictive. He said there was no hope for their reconciliation.

Bella felt little regret. She and Isabelle continued to live their lives, filled with love for one another and reasonable contentment.

———

A very special movie was playing in the big theater near the ferry terminal. It was *Snow White*, an animated full-length film, made by Walt Disney. Such a movie had never been made before, and the four children on Richmond Terrace and their mothers were going to see it after lunch. Everyone was excited about the movie, because people they knew who had already seen it, had raved about it. This was going to be a great day.

Isabelle and Marty were playing ball with Millie and Mel on the Jersey Street hill. Actually, the two younger children were, as usual, being exploited by the two older children. Millie and Mel threw the ball to each other. If one of them failed to catch it, the ball usually rolled down the steep hill and was stopped at the concrete barrier. Isabelle and Marty ran for the errant ball, and when one of them retrieved it, it was thrown to one of the bigger children. The two younger children knew they were being exploited, but they continued to shag the ball anyway. They were grateful that the older children allowed them to play at all. Marty left the game only because he needed to go to the bathroom. He ran to Aunt Eva's bathroom, behind the store, but never got there. A shelf holding rolled up mattresses was on fire. The little boy began to scream, "Fire! Fire!" in the direction of Aunt Eva's apartment and she came running out. She ran past the burning mattresses, and into the hallway leading to the upstairs apartments. She began to yell at the top of her lungs, "Fire, fire...everyone get out!"

Bella heard her cry. She came to the landing and yelled, "Where is the fire?"

"The mattresses in the store are on fire!" yelled Eva.

Bella ran across the landing and began banging on Fanny's door. No one in the front apartment had heard Eva's cry, because Fanny was using a noisy vacuum cleaner. She did, however, hear Bella hammering at her door. Fanny quickly alerted Sarah, and the three women ran down the stairs.

Eva ran across the street to the telephone pole that held a fire alarm box. She pulled the alarm.

The fire trucks came quickly, but not quickly enough. The store and Eva's apartment were ablaze. Large flames licked the store's ceiling and entered the apartment above it. The firemen had their work cut out for them!

A large crowd had gathered on the sidewalk. All vehicular traffic on Richmond Terrace was stopped. The crowd was quiet as they watched the firemen work. Sarah, Fanny, and Eva stoically watched their homes and their belongings go up in flames. Any emotional reaction to the fire would come from them later.

Not so with Bella. Unlike her silent depression when George had abandoned her, the fire caused Bella to become hysterical! "Everything I own is in there!" she screamed, and then she wept loud and long. She had never reacted to adversity this way. It was as if the sum of all that had afflicted her in her thirty-one years, had come to a head with this fire. She wept! She screamed! She paced! She even ran up and down! Sarah feared for her, and little Isabelle was ashamed of her. Isabelle began to cry too. She begged her mother to compose herself, but an inner demon was in charge of Bella's behavior.

A policeman, carrying a glass of water, put his arm around Bella. "No one is hurt in there," he said. "Everyone will be all right.....here, take a drink of water."

Bella took the water. She took a sip and started to sputter. The hysterics began again.

Little Isabelle approached her mother. "Mommy, Mommy, I'm scared," cried the little girl. "You've lost all of your things, but I've lost my Mommy," she wailed. "Please talk to me....I'm afraid!"

Something broke through Bella's fit of hysteria. She became aware of her acutely distressed little girl. She stooped down, kissed Isabelle, and then said, "Mommy is all right. Please don't be scared. Even if we have lost everything else, we've got each other." She remained quiet for the rest of the time that the fire was being fought.

––––––––

When the fire was out, the family assessed the damage. Bella's hysteria had been misplaced. Bella's apartment in the upper rear, only sustained smoke damage. The store and Fanny, Murray and Sarah's front apartment above the store were a total loss!

Those whose homes had been destroyed, spent the night in a hotel and began making plans for the future. Bella insisted that she and Isabelle would spend the night in their smoky apartment and protect their belongings. She was immovable about this, so Irving elected to spend the night there too. He wanted to protect his sister and his little niece.

The next morning, the entire family conferred about how and where everyone would live. Insurance would certainly cover all of the expenses for the repair and replacement of the contents of the store, and for Sol and Eva's apartment. During the building and repair period, Sol's family would temporarily rent a furnished apartment elsewhere on Staten Island. Fanny's family had fire insurance, too. They would also receive money for the contents of the room in which Sarah lived. Their plan was to stay in the hotel until they found a new apartment and bought new furniture and clothing. Fanny now wanted to live in a neighborhood that was predominantly Jewish. Sarah wanted to be able to see and smell the sea. Coney Island, a small peninsula off Brooklyn, seemed to serve all their needs. They decided that Fanny would begin apartment hunting that very day.

Bella said that she too, would move to Coney Island. The idea of a

Jewish neighborhood appealed to her, as well, and she didn't want to be too far away from Fanny, who was more than a sister to her...she and Fanny were best friends.

Ethel, Irving's fiancé, had been born in America. She was pretty and had a very pleasant disposition. Everyone in the family liked her. With the advent of the fire, Irving sped up their plans for their wedding. He and Ethel found a beautiful apartment on Staten Island and began to furnish it. Irving moved in, but Ethel would move in in four months, after they had been married. She and her family were planning a lavish wedding in Brooklyn.

For the first time in their lives, the entire family was spread out. Not one of Sarah's children lived next door to another. Her three sons lived miles apart on Staten Island. Irving and Sol saw each other daily, only because they were business partners.

Chapter 5: Coney Island

Anna now lived only half an hour away by subway, from her sisters and her mother. Bella and Fanny could walk to each other's apartments in Coney Island, but it was a daunting walk….no longer a walk across the hallway of the same building.

Fanny had found a lovely apartment in Coney Island, located on 25th Street, quite close to Neptune Avenue. Her children would be living very close to the school they would be attending. The school was located on Neptune Avenue and 25th Street. The buildings on 25th Street, near Neptune Avenue, were all relatively new. They were two family houses, containing an apartment on ground level and an apartment one floor up. Fanny and her family lived one flight up, and Sarah lived in a sunny room in their apartment.

Bella's apartment was in an old, two-story building that was one of a row of such buildings on 30th Street, between Surf Avenue and Railroad Avenue. Bella's apartment was one of three apartments on the second floor. One bathroom served the occupants of the three apartments on the floor. Bella was greatly concerned about the bathroom. She took it upon herself to keep it sparkling clean. It was used by the Epstein family, her next-door neighbors, and by an unmarried middle-aged man who looked very sickly. The sickly man was rarely seen, but Bella worried that his germs could infect Isabelle. What is more, Rose Epstein, who was a jolly, friendly neighbor, was also an abysmal housekeeper. Her three children trashed their apartment, and Rose was defeated by their mess. Consequently, Bella took it upon herself to see to it that the bathroom they all shared was very clean. It was almost comic to watch her when either she or Isabelle needed to use the bathroom. Armed with a bottle of Lysol disinfectant and Babo scouring powder, and wearing elbow-length rubber gloves, Bella scrubbed the toilet or the tub before either she or her daughter used them.

On 30th Street, there was a small, very busy grocery store. It was owned by a family named Friedman. Almost immediately, the Friedman's six-year old daughter, Annie, became Isabelle's dearest friend. Not only did Annie and Isabelle play together after school, they were in the same class in the big school on Neptune Avenue and 25th Street. In the second half of 1938, the two little girls were in Miss Goodman's 1B class. (The New York City Public Schools divided all elementary and Junior high school grades into two parts. The first part of the grade was the "A" part. The second part of the grade was the "B" part.) Miss Goodman, Isabelle's and Annie's teacher, was a rigid, uncompromising old maid. The children feared and disliked her.

Miss Goodman seated her class according to each child's academic achievement, with the best students sitting in row one, and the second best students in row two, and so on. There were five stationary rows of desks and a lot of pupil movement, from one row to another, always based on the whims of the wicked Miss Goodman. Most of the children did not care too much about which row they were ordered to sit in, so long as they sat at a desk. No one wanted to sit past the stationary desks, near the windows, in the sixth row. The sixth row consisted of three oblong tables, laid end-to-end. It was called *The Tables*, and to sit there was considered a great disgrace.

Generally *The Tables* had only one inhabitant. In a kinder world, the children and the teacher would have felt impelled to come to the aid of this little boy. He was clearly developmentally impaired, and was in need of special attention. In Miss Goodman's world, the special attention he received was special cruelty. Jerry was either teased, ignored, or scolded for being unable to do what he was incapable of doing. Most of the time, staring vacantly into space, Jerry picked his nose and then put his "harvest" into his mouth. Both Miss Goodman and the children in her class were disgusted by his behavior, and if Jerry was not being scolded by his teacher, he was certainly being ostracized by his classmates.

Isabelle sat in the first row in her class. Annie traveled back and forth between the second and third rows. Both girls were satisfied with their seats, and tolerated Miss Goodman's tyranny until the wicked teacher made her terrible threat….

Because Annie's parents needed to work in their grocery store every morning, Annie was left alone to dress, get her breakfast, and get to school on time. Annie had a tendency to dawdle and often wore garish clothes that she chose herself, ignoring those that her mother had set out for her. Bella would never have involved herself in dawdling or mismatched clothes, but she became involved because she worried about Annie's safety. The walk to school was a long one. Many small streets and two heavily trafficked streets needed to be crossed to get to the school. Bella decided that she and Isabelle would wait until Annie was ready, and Annie would walk to school with them. Bella feared for the little girl if she crossed busy Mermaid Avenue and even busier Neptune Avenue by herself. Very often, because Annie dawdled, both little girls got to school late. Miss Goodman was not amused. Each time the girls arrived after the bell had rung, Miss Goodman scolded them roundly. They were both unhappy about it, yet Annie continued to dawdle.

Once Isabelle suggested to her mother, that she and Bella leave. "Let Annie go to school by herself. Let her be late," said Isabelle, "not me."

Bella answered, "It is important to get to school on time, but it is also important to get to school safely. Isabelle, which do you think is more important?"

"Getting to school safely," Isabelle muttered.

"In the morning, Annie's parents have to work in their store. She is left on her own and she wastes time…. She's just a little girl," said Bella. "We are going to the school, anyway," she continued. "Aren't you glad we can take Annie across those terribly busy streets?"

"Yes," answered Isabelle unconvincingly.

One day, after several other days of late arrivals, Miss Goodman warned that Annie and Isabelle would be seated with Jerry at *The Tables*, if they were late again.

It didn't take too long for "the axe to fall." Two days later, two quaking little girls entered Miss Goodman's classroom. They were late.

"You're late again!" scolded Miss Goodman. "Collect your belongings and move to *The Tables*!" she commanded. Two very humiliated little girls complied.

Moving to *The Tables* caused the last of Isabelle's compliance with Miss Goodman. As if a demon had possessed her, she decided that she would not cooperate with the hated teacher anymore. If Miss Goodman put her at *The Tables* with Jerry, she'd read like Jerry… (Jerry couldn't read at all. Miss Goodman just passed over him when the class was doing a reading lesson.)

A very important part of Miss Goodman's reading program, was the use of flashcards. She used these cards as a vehicle for teaching the phonetic aspects of reading English. For Isabelle, they were pure boredom. She was a very strong reader, who had already mastered the phonics taught in first grade.

On Isabelle's first day at *The Tables*, Miss Goodman flashed a card at her and awaited her response. Isabelle looked blank. Miss Goodman supplied the answer and went on to the other children. Then Miss Goodman presented a card reading *oo* as in *food,* and she called on Isabelle again. Once more Isabelle looked at her teacher blankly.

"Are you feeling all right, Isabelle?" asked Miss Goodman.

Isabelle replied in a whisper, "Yes."

A perplexed Miss Goodman went on with the lesson and didn't call on Isabelle again that day.

For three more days, a blank faced Isabelle remained silent when called upon to read flashcards. Miss Goodman, who was aware of Isabelle's fine reading ability, called her up to her desk, while the class was working in their reading workbooks. Selecting a very easy primer, much below

Isabelle's reading level, Miss Goodman said, "Isabelle, please read this page to me."

Isabelle assumed her blank face and stared at her teacher.

The teacher, recognizing that Isabelle was being extremely disobedient, said, "I want to see your mother tomorrow, right after school. If you do not bring her the message that I want to see her, I'll write her a letter telling her that you have disobeyed me."

Isabelle was trapped. She knew that she must comply, so when Bella and Isabelle got home, after their walk from school, Isabelle did not even wait to remove her coat, when she blurted, "Miss Goodman wants to see you tomorrow, right after school."

"Why?" asked Bella.

"I don't know," mumbled Isabelle.

That night and the next day at school were very difficult for Isabelle. All she could think about was the meeting between Miss Goodman and her mother at 3:00 P.M.

When Bella arrived, Annie was told to wait for them in the schoolyard. When Annie left, the meeting began.

"Mrs. Brodsky," said Miss Goodman. "Isabelle used to be one of the strongest readers in the class. Something has happened to her, and now she cannot read at all."

"Really," said Bella, turning to her daughter. "Have you forgotten how to read?" she asked.

"No," whispered Isabelle. "I sit where the dumb people sit, so I'm acting like a dumb person."

"Miss Goodman," said a scandalized Bella, "I assure you that Isabelle will read again. If she could read last week, she'll read again tomorrow."

When Bella and Isabelle got home, Bella put her little girl on her lap and said, "It is sad to be a person who is unable to do things. It is worse to be a person who can do things and pretends that she is unlucky and can't! A person who is lucky enough to be able to do things, not only should do them, but should see if she can help the unfortunate person who cannot do them."

"I am embarrassed that your teacher had to call me to school, because you decided to defy her. You have shamed both of us," Bella said solemnly.

Isabelle began to cry.

Bella let her cry for a short while and then said, "Tell me why you are sitting in a seat that you hate so much."

Isabelle told Bella the whole story, including Jerry's disgusting habit.

"Jerry is an unfortunate little boy. You should be very kind to him," her mother said. "Miss Goodman is not kind to him, and it makes me sad," said Bella. "She also was unkind to Annie and you when she changed your seats, but neither of you explained why you were late, so she didn't know."

"I didn't want to tattle on Annie for dawdling," said Isabelle.

"That was good; and you were right," replied Bella. "Tomorrow I expect you to read and do all of your work. A pupil can learn from anywhere in the room," Bella continued. "Miss Goodman's unkindness may have come from not knowing why the two of you were late so often. But regardless of where it came from, you may not be disobedient to a teacher. Even the worst teacher teaches you something. She gives you much more than you give her; therefore, you must always show teachers respect," said Bella.

"But what if a teacher is really mean?" asked Isabelle.

"Discuss it with me. If I must, I'll take care of it," said Bella, "but you must never be disrespectful to a teacher. Do you understand?"

Bella didn't wait for an answer. She kissed her daughter, put her off her lap, and began to cook their dinner.

For the rest of the school year Isabelle tried her best and never showed Miss Goodman disrespect or defiance. Although Annie continued to dawdle, Miss Goodman finally changed both girls' seats to rows that had desks.

During Isabelle's travails with Miss Goodman, Sarah was making her own adjustments to living in Coney Island. She was not happy with the location of the apartment she shared with Fanny and her family. The apartment was too far away from the beach and the boardwalk. It was on 25th Street, while all of the activities Sarah enjoyed were in and around a pavilion on the boardwalk at 29th Street. To get to these activities required a very long walk, which tired Sarah and sometimes caused her arthritic pain.

————

In America, Sarah was no longer able to earn money. She now required financial assistance, and proud Sarah abhorred the very idea of Home Relief. Bella was being supported by Home Relief, but Bella had no other alternative. Sarah did – her alternative was her own grown children. Her children shared Sarah's belief in their obligation to their mother, so arrangements were made for Sarah's upkeep. Anna, Harry, Sol, and Irving each contributed a small amount of money toward their mother's support. Because Murray only earned enough to support himself, Fanny, and their two children; Fanny was not asked to contribute. Of course, Bella, on Home Relief, was exempted from contributing, as well. With her children's assistance, Sarah had enough money to live very frugally on her own, but she was not content to be alone, and she abhorred taking money from her more affluent children. She knew that the Depression was hurting them badly, and even the small amount of money they contributed to her, was a hardship. Sarah, therefore, hatched a plan.

At the pavilion on 29th Street and the boardwalk, from fifty to seventy-five elderly, Yiddish-speaking Jews came to socialize every day. Some of them were married couples. Most, however, were widowed men and women, who lived alone or lived with their children. They spent their time at the pavilion, singing Yiddish songs, discussing politics and the news, critiquing the Yiddish theater, and lamenting over the persecution of the Jews in Germany. Sarah was an active participant in the singing, and soon became a social leader among the elderly people who congregated there. She found the singing enjoyable and the discussions interesting, and now that most of them knew her, Sarah started to work on her plan.

Sarah began to closely observe the single men in the pavilion. She sought to form a liaison with a man who looked like he needed and could afford a woman's care. Such a man would give her financial independence and she would give him a clean home, meals, clean clothes, and companionship if they found themselves to be compatible. "It would be a business arrangement for the two of them," Sarah thought.

It took Sarah several weeks to light upon the proper prospect. His name was Jacob Appleman, and he was a small, bent-over man who was not repulsive, but was also not attractive. He was supported by the rents collected from his properties in the Bronx, and he lived very frugally. In actuality, however, Jacob Appleman was a wealthy man who could well afford to improve his living conditions. He had been widowed just the year before and his only daughter lived in Chicago. Appleman rarely saw her, so a woman like Sarah could possibly improve his life. Therefore, Sarah and Appleman came to an agreement. He would give her thirty-five dollars per week, to take care of all of their bills, supply them both with food and a clean home, and pay the rent. In 1938, this was a handsome amount of money, so a deal was struck and Sarah became Mrs. Jacob Appleman.

––––––––

Sarah and Appleman were legally married, but were never man and wife. They never even became friends. If Sarah had depended on the quiet Appleman for companionship, she would have gone mad. So Sarah continued to frequent the pavilion, especially since she now lived very close to it. Sarah's and Appleman's apartment was located in a sturdy, reasonably attractive brick apartment house, located on 29 Street and Surf Avenue – just one short block from the boardwalk and the beach. The apartment was small, but sufficient to their needs. It consisted of a living room with a small eating area near the pullman kitchen and a large bedroom. At the time that they moved in, the bathroom provided hot and cold New York City water and also provided salt water piped in from the nearby Atlantic Ocean. Sarah valued the ocean's salt water, because she believed it contributed to good health.

In the pavilion, Sarah and her cronies enjoyed each other's companionship every night. They congregated during all four seasons. During balmy days, many of them sat on the boardwalk and enjoyed the good weather. In the summertime, most of them deserted the boardwalk and spent their days on the beach.

Appleman sometimes joined them and sometimes went off to places unknown. Sarah didn't question him and he didn't supply information. Their union, as it existed, satisfied both of them and lasted for many years.

———

Bella's first friend in Coney Island was her neighbor, Rose Epstein. Rose really liked the good-looking young woman with the pretty little girl. They often drank coffee together after all of the children had gone off to school. On one such morning, Bella told Rose about George and her abandonment. Rose informed Bella that she had a widowed brother that Bella was sure to like.

Rose was right. Her brother definitely appealed to Bella, and for Hymie, it was love at first sight. Bella was beautiful. Bella was interesting. Bella was something he had only dreamed of.

The enchanted Hymie did present certain problems for Bella. He was in his early forties and she was barely thirty. He looked young and very strong, but there certainly was a big age difference between them. Hymie had two teen aged sons, who were being raised in an orphanage. Bella needed to know why.

Suddenly Isabelle found herself being sent either to Aunt Fanny's or to *Bubby's* (Grandma's) for the night. "Uncle" Hymie and Mommy were "going out." This happened a lot, but Isabelle didn't mind. She liked Uncle Hymie and she liked how he looked. She thought he looked like a handsome Indian. His face was red and his hair was very straight and very black. He never failed to bring Isabelle a new toy or new book when he came to get her mommy, and he always took Isabelle for a ride in his car before he and her mommy dropped her off for the night.

"Uncle" Hymie's car was special too. It was a shiny black Pontiac with a rumble seat. Bella and Hymie sat inside the car that had room for only two people. In the back of the car, where other cars had their trunks, "Uncle" Hymie's car had a rumble seat for Isabelle to sit in. When Isabelle was sitting in the rumble seat, she was outside the car. The wind blew her hair and whipped her face as she rode. Isabelle loved it! The best thing about Uncle Hymie wasn't his car, though. It was the way Bella was when she came to pick Isabelle up from Aunt Fanny's or Bubby's house. Bella was happy! "Uncle" Hymie made Bella happy!

———————

Miss Goodman did one more nasty thing to Isabelle. It happened on Promotion Day. Before Miss Goodman passed out the children's report cards, she explained that everyone had been promoted to 2A except for a few extremely good students who would be in a special class with other good students from the other 1B classes. These students would see that their report cards would read that they had been promoted to 2A/2B. This was a class that would do the entire second grade work in the first half of the year. In the second half, the children in this class would go on to 3A. No one was allowed to look inside the report card envelope until the last child had received his. The great suspense was broken when the children pulled their report cards out.

Isabelle could not believe her eyes. She knew that she was one of the stronger students in the class, yet her report card said, "promoted to 2A." Several children who were weaker students than she, were loudly jubilant, because of their report cards which read "promoted to 2A/2B." In Isabelle's envelope there was also a small note. It said, "Please see me before you leave school." It was signed "Miss Goodman." While the other children and Miss Goodman wished each other a happy summer, Isabelle dawdled at her desk. When the last child left, she went up to see Miss Goodman. Miss Goodman smiled a broad, very false smile and said, "I didn't want you to go off on your summer vacation thinking that I had made a mistake about your promotion. I know you are wondering why a good student like you is not going into the 2A/2B class. You are right to wonder. But being a good student is not enough for entrance into the 2A/2B class. In order to go into a special class, a student should always follow her teacher's orders. She should never be so headstrong as to defy her teacher. Such a headstrong child should not be given special privileges or be put into special classes," the nasty teacher declared.

137

"Have a nice summer and remember what I said," Miss Goodman concluded with a false and wicked smile.

Two large tears coursed down Isabelle's face. She said nothing to her teacher, nor did she make a sound. She simply walked out the door and didn't turn around.

————

When Isabelle reached the street, she leaned against the school building and cried for a long time. After a while, she stopped crying, dried her eyes, and walked to the corner. The school guard escorted her across busy Neptune Avenue.

Isabelle had been told to go to Aunt Fanny's house and wait for her mother there. When she got there, Bella and "Uncle" Hymie were standing in front of the house. Bella smiled and said, "Uncle" Hymie is no longer "Uncle" Hymie. He and I were married in Connecticut yesterday. Now he is your daddy and you should call him "Daddy."

Isabelle was flabbergasted, but very happy. She may have lost the 2A/2B class, but she had gained a great daddy! She was even more surprised when she learned that they would be moving away from Coney Island to White Plains, a town quite far away. They would be living near her new daddy's business, a Richfield gas station; and they would be moving in only five days!

Chapter 6: New Family

Tarrytown Road in White Plains was like no other place Isabelle had ever seen. It was a very long street running from the town of White Plains, out to Hymie's yellow Richfield gas station, and to areas beyond it. There were almost no houses on Tarrytown Road, but a block away from the gas station there was a red brick two-story house, surrounded on one side and in the rear by a magical garden. This house and garden belonged to Mr. Marino. He and his family lived on the first floor. On the second floor, in a large sunny apartment, lived Bella, Hymie, Isabelle, and Hymie's two sons, Sidney and Stanley. Right next door to Mr. Marino's red brick house was a saloon. A street intersected Tarrytown Road in front of the saloon, interrupting its straight, almost totally empty march out of the town of White Plains into places unknown to Isabelle.

Isabelle now had two *brothers* as well as a *father*. The two teenagers had spent most of their lives in a Jewish orphanage. They had been living with their father for less than a year. Fifteen-year old Stanley was four years old when his young mother died. His brother Sidney was barely two. Hymie had had no offers of help from anyone, and very little money. He, therefore, went to the United Jewish Charities and asked them for assistance. The social worker suggested the orphanage for the boys.

The orphanage was an unloving place. Most of the aides were there only for their paychecks. They were uninterested and unloving to the children in their care. Even though Hymie visited the boys almost every Sunday, and they were kept clean and well fed, an essential element was missing in their upbringing. No one had given them warmth, and consequently, they expected and gave no warmth to anyone. No one had cared about the boys' schooling either. Stanley, who was naturally brighter then Sidney, was more successful at his studies than his younger brother. Neither of the boys, however, were stellar students. What they were good at was stealth. In order to get along at the orphanage, "one had to do what one had to do;" and the trick was not to get caught. Once more Stanley surpassed Sidney. He was far more devious than his younger brother.

———

Bella determined to be kind and loving to the boys. She was enthralled with Stanley's good looks and glib tongue. Sidney, however, puzzled her. While he was not as handsome as his older brother, his appearance was appealing. The problem was his communication. Sidney barely spoke. He answered questions in monosyllables and contributed nothing of himself to conversations. In addition, he suffered from an embarrassing and serious problem. Sidney wet his bed at night!

Hymie said that Sidney was shy and had suffered greatly in the orphanage. Sidney's brother had tyrannized him and his caregivers had ignored him. "But," said Hymie, "when you have been exposed to both of my boys for a while, you will see that Sidney has the bigger heart and is far more dependable than his older brother. Stanley is for Stanley. Be careful of him. He really needs to be taught about respecting other people's rights."

Young and inexperienced Bella believed that with love she would win over both boys and set them both on the right path. She chose Sydney's bed wetting as her first undertaking.

———

Every night, Bella made Sidney void just before he went to bed. She would then set her alarm clock for every three hours. When the alarm clock woke her, she would go to the boys' room and gently awaken Sidney. She would quietly guide her half-asleep, stepson to the bathroom. Sidney soon became continent to the point where Bella could awaken him every four hours. Then when he showed that he could be continent for six or seven hours, Bella set her alarm clock accordingly. In time, Sidney was able to wake himself. He had achieved continence and was deliriously happy about it.

Bella's attention and his success at remaining dry at night caused Sidney to fall in love with his young and pretty stepmother. Even when he had an occasional accident and did wet his bed, she only asked him to help her clean and turn his mattress. She never scolded, and permitted no one in the family to make fun of him. To Sidney, Bella was an angel, brought into his life by his father.

———————

Both boys liked Isabelle. She was an independent little girl who seemed to grow to look more like her mother every day. Sidney befriended her. He gave her the comic books he had finished reading, and he often took her for walks in the woods near their house. Stanley only bothered with her if he was asked to look after her for a few hours. At those times, he'd park her in front of the radio with him. She'd be forced to listen to whatever program he was listening to, or he would allow her to read a book. Isabelle didn't mind. She loved to read.

———————

Isabelle really liked the apartment in which they lived. For the first time in her life, she had a room of her own. Bella and Hymie shared the master bedroom. Isabelle's two new brothers slept in twin beds in the third bedroom. All of the rooms in the apartment were larger than any in the apartments that Isabelle had lived in, in the past. She loved the spaciousness and particularly liked the artificial fireplace in the living room. It looked almost real, and Isabelle wished that it really was real.

———————

When they encountered Isabelle, the landlord and his wife always stopped to chat with her. They had funny Italian accents that sounded, to Isabelle, almost as if they were singing when they spoke. She was often invited into their apartment by Mrs. Marino to sample something she had cooked or baked. Mrs. Marino's cooking and baking were very different from the food to which Isabelle was accustomed, and surprisingly tasted very, very good to the "picky" little girl.

One afternoon, when Isabelle had been invited by Mrs. Marino to eat some wonderful Italian cookies, she saw a large picture of a fat man in a uniform, hanging on the Marino's living room wall. It seemed to Isabelle that she once had seen this man in a newsreel at the movies. She thought she had seen him with Hitler, and that the commentator for the newsreel said that they were friends. She didn't trust her memory, so she interrupted Eleanora, the Marino's thirteen-year old daughter who, as usual, was reading a book.

"Eleanora, who is that man in the picture on the wall?" Isabelle queried, pointing at the fat man.

"Mussolini," answered Eleanora. "He's the president of Italy. My dad thinks he has saved Italy and can save the world."

"Do you think so?" asked Isabelle.

"No," answered Eleanora curtly.

"Why?" asked Isabelle.

"I don't want to discuss this with you," said Eleanora. "You're too young; and I want to read. Go out and play." Eleanora returned to her book.

Mr. Marino liked to show Isabelle things in his wonderful garden. He showed her the beautiful flowers and the fruits and vegetables he grew, and he often gave her some fruits and vegetables to give to her mother. One day Mr. Marino took Isabelle to a distant place in his garden. Several grape arbors, heavy with grapes, had been erected there. Mr. Marino said that he and his wife made delicious wine from the grapes they grew. He promised that he would give Isabelle and her family several bottles of the wine they would make for Christmas.

Isabelle was very confused. She really liked the Marinos very much. They were kind and friendly people. "Could it be possible that Mr. Marino admired a person who believed the same things that Hitler believed?" Isabelle pondered.

"No," she decided. "Only hateful people admired hateful people. Then why would a wonderful man like Mr. Marino hang a hateful man's picture on the wall?"

Isabelle could make no headway with her thoughts, so she dismissed them. She decided that she had probably seen someone else's picture in the newsreel.

———

The house in which the family lived was one block and across the street from Hymie's gas station. Hymie and Jack, his African-American mechanic, were the only two people who worked the gas station. Sometimes Isabelle and the two boys came down to see them, but Isabelle never came alone. There was a lot of traffic on Tarrytown Road and Isabelle was not allowed to cross the big street alone. Sometimes Isabelle came to the gas station with her mother. Bella often brought Hymie and Jack some lunch. When she did, she and Isabelle ate with them.

———

Their lives' in White Plains in 1939 would have been wonderful, except for the fact that the gas station was not doing well. An Esso station that was newer and shinier than their old Richfield station, opened across the street from Hymie's station. The Esso station started to slash prices, causing a price war with the Richfield Station. Hymie could not sustain the price war very long. He had nowhere near the money that a company-owned Esso station had. Nevertheless, he hung on.

———

School had started. For Sidney it was a disaster! When he had entered, he was found to be so far behind, that he was put back a grade. Stanley was able to limp along. His grades were poor, but he managed to pass. Socially, however, Stanley was a star at the White Plains High School! All of the girls loved Hymie's handsome son.

Isabelle's elementary school was located a long way from where she lived, but Isabelle didn't mind. It was fun to walk through the woods to get to school. Isabelle had heard her mother's stories about walking through Vashisht's woods to get to her Russian school, and Isabelle used to pretend that she was in Russia. When Isabelle got to school, however, her pretence abruptly ended. Hers was not a one-room schoolhouse. Children of Isabelle's age were all in 2A, and children of other ages were in other age-appropriate classes. But there was one way in which her school was like the Russian school….there were few Jewish children, and nobody cared about the Jewish children's feelings. This indifference was shown frequently during *Bible Study* classes.

Every Wednesday morning, the entire second grade (two 2A classes and two 2B classes) were taken to the gym. The children were seated on the floor and each child was given a large, beautifully illustrated children's Bible. When the stories from the Old Testament were read, Isabelle felt at ease. She loved these stories and already knew some of them. But, some of the stories from the New Testament made Isabelle afraid. Sometimes they said bad things about Jews. Other times the stories talked about Jesus bringing the truth to the Jews, but the Jews rejected what Jesus said. Often, Jesus was referred to as *God* or the *Son of God*. Isabelle believed none of these things and felt a need to talk to someone about it. She knew that her classmate Eileen Ackerman was Jewish too, because both girls had talked about their religion. They had both agreed that they were the only Jewish children in 2A. Therefore, one day, after a Bible Study class, when the children were sent to the playground for recess, Isabelle brought up her grave doubts about what they had been taught.

Eileen angrily replied, "The Bible is right! Everything they said in the Bible Study class is right! And anyway, why are you talking to me about it? I'm not Jewish!" Isabelle walked away shocked and hurt.

At home, she recounted the incident to Bella. Bella said, "Eileen is afraid, but this is America, and in America she doesn't have to be afraid. Eileen wants everyone to like her, and she thinks that if they know that she is Jewish, they will not like her."

Bella then proceeded to tell Isabelle the story about picking pears in the Ukraine. She told her about how she had denied that she was Jewish. "It's all right to say almost anything to save yourself from harm," said Bella, "so it was right for me to save myself by denying my Jewishness, when I was in danger in the Ukraine. But," continued Bella, "it is not all right to deny your Jewishness so that people who are not Jewish will like you. If they don't like you, knowing who you really are, they don't have to like you. You're a wonderful girl and being Jewish is a wonderful part of you. If they cannot accept you because of your religion, you don't need them. They're not nice!" Bella, then, kissed her little girl and returned to mending a pair of Sidney's pants.

———————

Right next door to the house in which Isabelle lived was a saloon. Often, when she was roller skating or jumping rope, she could see men going into and coming out of the saloon. To Isabelle, most of the men looked like bums. They were usually dressed like working men, but somehow they didn't look like the working men Isabelle was used to seeing.

On one particular Saturday, when everyone in the family believed Hymie was working at the gas station, Isabelle, who was jumping rope, saw him stagger down the two steps in front of the saloon. In great shock she asked, "Were you in the saloon, Daddy?" He didn't answer. Instead, he staggered past her and continued down the street, past their house, and on to the gas station. Isabelle remained rooted to one spot, and watched him until he entered the station. When he was out of sight, she ran up the stairs to their apartment, and in an excited and disturbed voice, told her mother about her encounter with Hymie.

A very worried-looking Bella told her daughter that she would speak to Daddy and ask him to explain everything to her. She told Isabelle that if she learned something that Isabelle should know, she would tell her. "In the meantime," Bella continued, "don't worry about a thing. Mommy is here, and she'll never let anything bad happen to you. Go out and play," she told her daughter. "Everything is all right."

Her mother's words were good, but there were creases in her mother's forehead. Isabelle knew that something bad was worrying her.

———————

Hymie did not come home for dinner. At eleven o'clock that night, when even the boys were asleep, he tiptoed in. He entered his dark bedroom and began to undress, when suddenly the lamp on Bella's side of the bed switched on. Bella sat up in bed, fully awake.

"Where have you been?" she hissed angrily.

He sat down on the bedroom chair and despondently began to remove his shoes and socks.

Again, Bella hissed, "Where have you been?"

"At the gas station," he answered. "I was sleeping off a drunk!"

"What?" Bella asked, totally confused.

"I've been trying to hide it," he said "but today the kid saw me and I decided to talk things over with you."

Bella remained silent.

"I've had a drinking problem since two years after I got out of the army. Prohibition was passed a year after I got out. I went up to the country to work for my father. My father and his brothers owned a resort that began to boom in the 1920's. Along with it being high up in the Catskill Mountains, it was clean and comfortable, had good food, great sporting facilities, and above all a still that made illegal liquor. Our guests could defy Prohibition and drink all the liquor they could pay for. It was like one gigantic speakeasy."

"My father and his brothers divided the labor and the revenue of the hotel. One of them was in charge of food, another in charge of the building and grounds, another in charge of sports and entertainment, and my father was in charge of the stable and the still. He turned the working of the still over to his three sons: Willie, the youngest, Sam, the middle son, and me, the eldest. We learned the recipe for the liquor and the workings of the machinery. When the liquor was made, it had to be tasted and approved before we bottled it."

"My brothers and I made it, and did the tasting. All of us began to like the taste of the liquor very much, but Sam and I more than liked it. We loved the buzz it gave us; in fact after awhile, we craved that buzz. Willie never craved it the way Sam and I did."

"Both Sam and I knew we had gotten into great trouble. We had become drunks! We needed to get away from that still and stop drinking liquor. Our family's hotel was doing very well and my father had made quite a lot of money. He also understood that Sam and I needed to get away, so he gave us each enough money to buy New York City taxi shields. Owning our own cabs would make us enough money to live comfortably."

"We left the Catskills in 1922. I was already married to the boys' mother. I didn't know she had a heart condition when I married her, and she didn't know that I had a drinking problem. When we moved to the city, we already had two children. Each birth had made her weaker and I'm sure that my drinking hadn't contributed to her good health, either."

"I drove my cab for ten hours a day, and when I came home I worked for four or five more hours, doing housework and caring for the boys. My life was miserable, so it only made me want to drink more."

———————

"My brother Sam was killed by liquor quickly. After we got settled in New York City, Sam lived the high life. He was single, made a good living, and spent most of his money in speakeasies. Six months after we arrived in New York, Sam was killed in an automobile accident. Fortunately, he had no passengers in the cab. He was drunk when he died."

"You would think that Sam's death would have stopped my drinking, but it didn't. In fact, after his death, I went on a year-long binge. In my drunken state, I didn't notice how very sick my wife was, but I did know that she wasn't well. That's why I did so much of the work around the house."

"My wife's death shocked me into instant sobriety. It didn't last long, though. When I put the boys into the orphanage, I felt free to drink again."

"Driving a cab wasn't a good idea for a drunk, so I sold my taxi shield, and used the money I got for it to buy the Richfield Station. It was a good move for me. When I was drunk and unable to run the station, Jack took over. There's never been a better guy than Jack. I'm lucky to have him as my employee and my friend. Now the station is failing, and as with all drunks, I hide my fears and misery in the bottle."

"Bella, I love you and I love little Isabelle. I felt sure that married to you, I could control my drinking. I'm so sorry! I've failed you, the three kids, and myself." Big, strong Hymie began to cry.

Bella was completely shocked. She had been totally ignorant of Hymie's drinking problem. She had been married to him for five months, and until now, knew nothing of his terrible secret. She was frightfully conflicted.

147

She had no idea of how to help Hymie. No one close to her had any such problem. Could she, with her ignorance, be of help? Or, should she take Isabelle and go away?

"I don't know how to help you Hymie," Bella said. "It seems to me as if this is the kind of problem where you have to help yourself. I would leave you tomorrow if I thought you would always be a drunkard. But before I left I'd still have to tell you my thoughts about your problem…."

"Your drinking did not just betray your first, very sick wife, it betrayed the boys and now it is betraying Isabelle and me. I know that the possible loss of the gas station drives you to drink more, but we could get by without the gas station. We cannot get by with your drinking! And, if you agree that your drinking harms me, Isabelle, and the boys, add a new baby to the group. I think I'm pregnant! Do you have it in you to become sober for all of us?"

Hymie looked at Bella with eyes red from weeping. "I'd give my life to stop drinking, just for you Bella. Add the kids and a possible new baby, and I'd even try to learn to fly. What I'm afraid of," he said, "is failure. I've failed so many times before. Would you give me a chance to try again, Bella?" he pleaded.

"I have no other choice," she said. "I love you and I feel a responsibility to your two neglected boys. I'll do everything I can to help you, but I am afraid the job is really yours. You'll have to stop drinking on your own."

———

By the end of March, 1940, the family, including certifiably pregnant Bella, moved from the lovely White Plains apartment to Coney Island. They now lived in a second floor, three-bedroom apartment located in a dingy brick house that was one of a fairly long row of identical dingy brick houses located on 36th Street, between Mermaid Avenue and Railroad Avenue. The apartment completely lacked charm. It was strictly utilitarian, but it did, however, have a few valuable assets. First and foremost, the rent was low. Secondly, Isabelle had a very short, safe walk to P.S. 188, the elementary school in which she would be enrolled in a 2B class. (Her step-brothers went to two different schools that were not close to home; but they were old enough and could manage.) The apartment's third asset was its proximity to Mermaid Avenue, Coney Island's main shopping street. Bella's severely injured leg and ponderous pregnant body didn't allow for a lot of walking. She was grateful that Mermaid Avenue was close by, because it made shopping for food for the family easier.

For Bella, the apartment's greatest asset was that she now lived next door to her sister Fanny. Fanny and she could enjoy seeing each other daily.

Bella's new apartment did not have a bathroom of its own. The family was supposed to share a bathroom with another apartment on their floor, but the other apartment was never rented. Consequently, Bella's and Hymie's family had the use of the bathroom in the hall for themselves.

In addition to the loss of their lovely White Plains home, Hymie lost contact with a very valued friend. When the gas station was closed, Hymie had to let Jack go. Jack and his family moved back to North Carolina. Both men were devastated over the Richfield Station's demise and about their separation from each other.

Jobs were almost impossible to find, but Bella's brother Irving was able to obtain a job for Hymie with their cousin Izzy Rosenkranz. (The job was to be temporary, but it proved to be the job Hymie kept until his death, many years later.) Irving and his cousin Izzy Rosenkranz had been friends even when they were young boys in Vashisht. Izzy's family left for America in 1919. When Irving came to the United States, five years later, the friendship continued as if it had never been interrupted.

In 1940, the cousins were still good friends. Izzy Rosenkranz owned a small business in Jersey City, New Jersey. His factory cleaned cotton that was sent north from the south, and packed it into large bales. Cousin Izzy's factory sold the cleansed cotton to mattress manufacturers and furniture upholsterers in the New York City area. Irving was one of Izzy's customers. He bought the cotton he used in the manufacturing of mattresses from his cousin.

When Hymie lost the Richfield Station, he took a job as a truck driver for Izzy. He picked up the cotton bales containing unleansed cotton from the train that came up from the south. He would also deliver cleaned cotton to Izzy's customers. It was hard, dirty work, and Hymie was paid only $21.50 per week. Hymie took the job, because he was desperate. Bella was pregnant, they had no money, and there were five, soon to be six, mouths to be fed.

Izzy told Hymie that conditions would soon improve. He said that even though times were bad, his business was growing. He would soon be looking for a bigger plant in the Bronx. When he found it, he promised Hymie to put him in charge of the truck drivers, and he promised to give him a raise.

Hymie hoped that the move to the Bronx would come soon. Even though Bella liked living near Fanny and Sarah in Coney Island, the Bronx was very nice, and if the plant was located there, it would be convenient for the family to move there too. In the meantime, Hymie, who no longer owned a car, traveled two hours each way to Jersey City. After the expense of carfare, there was only $19 left of his tiny salary. The family was desperate for more money.

———

Sidney took a job delivering groceries after school, to Sea Gate, an upscale, gated community not far from where they lived. He delivered the groceries on a bicycle with an oversized front basket and two side baskets. He kept most of his tiny salary and his tips for his own use, but contributed three dollars per week to the household.

———

Finding a job seemed to be very difficult for Stanley. If he got one, he couldn't seem to keep it. What is more, he was agitating to quit school. He had turned sixteen and considered school boring and a waste of time. Hymie finally was worn down and consented to Stanley's quitting. Stanley promptly went to Manhattan on a job search, but a month after he had quit school, he was still unemployed. Although things were bad for Stanley, no one's attention was focused on him at this time. The summer was brutally hot, and Bella was greatly weakened by the ferocious heat, hard work, and her pregnancy.

———

Hymie had been controlling his drinking by limiting his occasional binges to the weekends, when he was at home. Many Saturdays and Sundays would find him in the living room on an easy chair, out cold, in a drunken stupor. At these times, Bella, the boys, and Isabelle ignored him. Bella, who ran the house, and took care of all of the family's needs, fell into an exhausted sleep after she put Isabelle to bed. There was little companionship between her and her husband. Fatigue distanced both of them, but Bella was made even more distant by Hymie's despised alcohol addiction.

Early on one warm July day, Sarah came to visit Bella. When she saw her daughter, she became alarmed at Bella's pallor and apparent fatigue. She suggested that Bella take a nap and that Isabelle spend the day with her. She said she'd bring Isabelle home for supper. Bella gratefully accepted her mother's offer and Isabelle and Sarah started the long walk to Sarah's house.

While walking, Sarah asked Isabelle if she would prefer a little brother or a little sister. Isabelle, who hadn't a clue about the impending birth, was puzzled by her grandmother's seemingly irrelevant question. (The prevailing prudish and straight-laced attitudes concerning pregnancy and birth were "alive and well" in Bella's household. She had filled Isabelle's head with the lies and nonsense about birth commonly fed to young children in Jewish immigrant families in 1940.)

Isabelle answered her grandmother passionately. "If my mommy were going to buy a baby, I'd want her to buy me a sister."

"What if she got you a brother?" asked her grandmother.

Isabelle thought her grandmother's question was so foolish, that she decided to answer more foolishly. "I'd flush a brother down the toilet!" Isabelle exclaimed. "Everyone knows that I don't want another brother."

Sarah had never told her children anything about sex and birth. Living in a country hamlet in Russia, they saw animals copulating and reproducing all of the time. What is more, she and the other women of Vashisht were almost always at some stage of pregnancy during their child-bearing years. Here in America people seemed to have children only when they wanted to have them, but this American phenomenon hadn't happened in Vashisht.

Sarah wondered what Isabelle knew about the baby that would be born to Bella in a month's time. It was Sarah's observation that Isabelle knew little or nothing about the impending birth, and Sarah's observation was entirely correct. Isabelle had been told that babies were purchased at the hospital. The child totally believed this far-fetched story. In fact, she had never really paid attention, nor noticed that her mother's body had undergone changes. Furthermore, she had never heard any discussion about a baby, nor had she seen any preparations for the arrival of a baby. Therefore, Isabelle was in a state of total ignorance about the arrival of the baby who would soon be part of her family.

———

Isabelle may have been ignorant of an important family event, but she was far from ignorant about current events. She was aware of the impending presidential election and she wore electioneering pins (called *buttons*) saying "Vote for F.D.R." and "4 More Years – FDR." She was also very much aware of the war in Europe. Everyone in Isabelle's world hated Germany, Hitler, and the Nazis. They were the *bad guys* in the war that was going on in Europe, and in addition, the Nazis hated and persecuted Jews. They were also dropping bombs on England and they had made a pact with Russia that had divided Poland between the two of them. When they made this pact, Isabelle's Uncle Murray felt betrayed.

Uncle Murray was still a Communist sympathizer. Aunt Fanny ridiculed him, because she, like her mother, trusted nothing that was Russian. Nonetheless, Uncle Murray often made impassioned speeches supporting the Communist government of Russia. But in 1939, when Russia and Germany signed a pact of friendship and carved up Poland between them, Isabelle's Uncle Murray lost all faith in his Communist *heroes*. His faith was never completely restored, even when Germany disregarded its friendship with Russia and invaded the U.S.S.R in 1941.

———

One sunny morning in late July 1940, Fanny woke Isabelle. She said, "Wake up Isabelle, you have to go to your grandma's house. You have a new baby sister and your mother is in the hospital. She will stay there for ten days. During that time you will stay with Bubbie." (*Bubbie* is a pet name derived from the Yiddish word *bubbe* meaning grandmother.) "I'll come around every day to see how you're both doing."

Isabelle's Aunt Fanny gave Isabelle breakfast and then walked over to Bubbie's house with her and Marty, her son who was a year younger than Isabelle. The two women talked a lot about Bella and the baby's health. It seemed that Bella was quite healthy, but the baby was too small, weighing 3 lbs. 4 oz. at birth. The baby was being kept in an incubator to keep her warm. Sarah and Fanny were worried about the baby, but both of them had great faith in the wonderful American hospitals and felt optimistic about the baby's well-being.

Isabelle could not understand how a whole, large suitcase of her clothes was at Bubbie's house. Her Aunt Fanny told her that her mother knew that she was going to the hospital to get a new baby, so she prepared the suitcase, knowing that Isabelle would stay with her grandmother while she was gone.

Staying with Bubbie was fun! There was no bedtime! Her grandmother's food was gruesome, so Isabelle would be given money to buy hot dogs, hamburgers, ice cream, frozen custard, malts, and all other forms of goodies to slake her hunger. In the evening, when Bubbie was singing Yiddish songs with her cronies, Isabelle was given money to see silent films at an open-air, silent film theater that was located on the boardwalk, just opposite the pavilion where the old people sang. Isabelle went to these movies every night of her stay with Bubbie. The movie was over at about 11:30 P.M. At that time, a very, very tired Isabelle was taken home to Bubbie's house, where they both slept until about 10:00 A.M. After breakfast, they went to the beach for another day of fun. Isabelle rarely missed her mother, because life with Bubbie was such "a blast!"

When Isabelle had been with Bubbie for nine days, her grandmother took her shopping at a little basement shop on Mermaid Avenue. She was going to get a new dress and new socks in honor of her mother's homecoming. Bubbie was buying Isabelle's new clothes, so that her little granddaughter would look nice when Bella and the new baby came home.

The shop was not well lighted, but although it was very small, it was crammed with clothes for women, girls, boys, men, and babies. Bubbie told Isabelle to select a dress she liked and to try it on to see if it fit. Isabelle saw a bright red, dotted swiss dress that she thought was beautiful. It fit her perfectly and she matched bright red socks to it. When Bubbie bought her selections for her, Isabelle was ecstatic.

They then went to Woolworth's and bought red satin ribbon for Isabelle's hair, which they both knew was in an unacceptable condition for Bella's return. They could not replicate Bella's hairdo, because it was Bella's practice to make Shirley Temple curls all over her daughter's head. She would wash Isabelle's hair every night, when she gave Isabelle her bath. In the morning she twisted the clean, shiny black hair into a mass of curls that bobbed charmingly whenever the little girl moved her head.

Baths were rare events at Bubbie's house. Because Isabelle swam in the ocean every day, Sarah saw to it that she was bathed in fresh water at the end of the week to wash off the ocean's salt that had deposited on her skin and hair. Isabelle was delighted and deliberately refrained from enlightening her grandmother to the fact that baths and hair washing were a nightly ritual at Bella's house.

On the evening of the ninth day, Hymie came over and told them that Bella and the baby were staying at the hospital an extra day. Baby Phyllis needed to weigh a little more before she would be allowed to go home. Bubbie decided that Isabelle's second bathtub bath at her house should be moved up to Day Ten. Isabelle's wild and bushy hair would be washed that day too.

On the eleventh day, Fanny came over to her mother's house to help carry Isabelle's belongings back to her home. Bella was expected home sometime after lunch, so Fanny got to Sarah's house about 10:30 P.M. It would take them a while to make the long walk to 36th Street and, in

154

addition, Fanny was planning to give her mother and her niece some lunch at her house.

When Fanny looked at almost eight-year old Isabelle, she squealed, "Bella will kill you! What have you done to her beautiful little girl?"

A very insulted Sarah said, "What do you mean? She's bathed, her hair is washed, and she's wearing a brand new outfit she selected herself!"

"Her hair is horrible! You've put her short curly hair into two braids loaded down with garish red ribbons. The braids stick out on either side of her head, like they're growing out of her ears! And the dress....the dress belongs on a gypsy with a tambourine. Bella will kill you! That little girl is her pride and joy. She keeps her looking like a doll...."

Sarah interrupted angrily, "Bella has greater concerns than whether her daughter's dress is stylish or her hair is beautiful. I did the best I could. I never worried about how my girls looked until they were almost grown. I tried to do more than is necessary to satisfy my fussy daughter, and before she even has a chance to berate me, my other daughter does it for her! You've said enough! Let's go to your house for lunch and then to Bella's house to see her and the new baby."

The three of them said very little on the long walk to 36th Street. Fanny would sometimes glance at Isabelle in her ridiculous hairdo and dress and stifle a laugh. Isabelle, deeply wounded, couldn't understand her aunt's reaction to her appearance. She thought she looked wonderful, and she was sure her mother would think so too.

After a quick lunch at Fanny's apartment, the three of them went next door to Bella's apartment. Sidney and Stanley were there waiting to see their new little sister. There was a new crib and lots of baby paraphernalia in the house, too.

At 2:30 Bella and Hymie slowly came up the stairs. In Bella's arms was a bundle wrapped in a pretty pink blanket. She deposited the bundle in the waiting crib and turned to Isabelle, not even noticing her garish appearance. She took her older daughter in her arms and hugged her, kissed her, and petted her for a long time. Then she said, "Mommy is so glad to see you. I've missed you very much."

Isabelle couldn't understand why her mother looked so much prettier than she remembered her. Was it her pink and black dress? Isabelle didn't realize that over the past months Bella's appearance had undergone great, though gradual change, because of her pregnancy. The eight year old didn't realize that her mother's greatly improved appearance was due to her no longer being pregnant and to having had a good rest at the hospital.

"Come," said Bella. "I want you to see your little sister."

Isabelle peered into the crib. The baby's eyes were squeezed shut. When Bella unwrapped her, she kicked her tiny feet and flailed her balled-up fists. Her skin was quite red, and she was very skinny.

A very disappointed Isabelle had expected the baby to look like a doll. This baby was ugly! Isabelle turned to her mother angrily and said, "Why did you go to the hospital and buy a baby now. You knew we didn't have enough money for a pretty baby. You bought a cheap baby and she's ugly! Why didn't you wait until you saved up more money?"

Isabelle couldn't understand why everyone laughed. But Bella, seeing her older daughter's distress, did not laugh. Instead she said, "All brand new babies look like this. They need a mommy and daddy to take care of them and love them, and then they grow into beautiful alive dolls. Baby Phyllis will be beautiful, because she has a whole family that will love her."

Bella was right. Within one month, the scrawny baby was no longer scrawny. Within another month, she looked like a live doll with soft, fuzzy blond hair and large black eyes that looked like shiny buttons. But best of all, she smiled a lot, because her mother, father, brothers, and sister gave her lots of attention and loved her.

———

Isabelle was in 3A at P.S.188. She liked everything about school. She liked to read, write, play with her friends, and even do arithmetic. Her best friend, June, was in her class and they did everything together.

One afternoon when June and Isabelle were walking home from school, they decided that on Sunday, they would put up a comic book stand. They would collect all the comic books in their houses and earn money by selling them. They would set up their stand, on a wooden crate, in front of the bank on Mermaid Avenue. Lots of people passed by there and they would probably do a brisk business.

On Sunday morning they executed their plan. There were lots of people on the avenue, but their business was not brisk. They had sold only three comic books for four cents each. Twelve cents wasn't much for a whole morning's work, and now they needed to go home for lunch.

Just as they were beginning to collect their gear, Sarah came along, heading for Isabelle's house to see Bella, Fanny, and most of all, the new baby. She stopped at the comic book stand and said to Isabelle, "What are you two doing here?"

June, who didn't speak or understand Yiddish, didn't understand the conversation between Isabelle and her grandmother. She could see, however, that Isabelle's grandmother was angry.

"We're selling comic books that we've already read," said Isabelle. "We've made only twelve cents all morning."

"Finish packing up your books and come home," said Bubbie. "I'm going to your house. I'll talk to you there."

When Isabelle left June, she went upstairs to her apartment. Sarah, who had preceded her, immediately assaulted Bella with an angry lecture. Bella when Isabelle came in. She had said very little when she walked home with the two little girls, but whatever speech she had saved up on the walk home, came rolling out now. "Even in Vashisht," she said, "we were never so poor that an eight year old child was put to work selling household possessions for a few pennies," Sarah railed. "You can't possibly be so poor as to need that!"

Bella stared at her angry mother in bewilderment. "I don't know what you're talking about," she declared.

"You don't know that Isabelle and another little girl were selling books in front of the bank on Mermaid Avenue?" Sarah asked.

"No," said Bella, as both women turned to the child for an explanation.

"Mommy," explained Isabelle, "June and I were selling the old comic books that we had in our houses. All of the kids do it. Kids can buy comic books they have missed for a few cents, and the sellers make money for new comic books. I have loads of old ones, because Sidney always uses the money he earns to buy comic books. After he reads them and I read them, no one else wants them. It would have been very good to sell them all, but we didn't sell very many. Between June and me we only made 12 cents."

Sarah, who could not speak English, understood the language quite well. She and Bella burst out laughing when Isabelle was finished with her explanation. "I'll never fully understand America," Sarah declared. "I judged Isabelle's activity by Russian standards. In Russia, if a child was selling books, she would be doing so to augment the family's income."

––––––––––

Isabelle found 3A to be very interesting. Mrs. Dubenage not only taught the usual reading, writing, and arithmetic, there were many discussions about current events. Most of these were about the evil Nazis who were heavily bombing British cities, especially London. The children were horrified by the stories of homes, schools, hospitals, and factories being bombed. Thoughts of the many fires in those cities were frightening. Worst of all, however, were the pictures of crowds of people sleeping on the platforms of London's subway stations. The children knew that these platforms were cold and damp. Mrs. Dubenage's 3A class decided to do something about it.

It was decided that the class would knit an afghan to keep an English child warm. Both boys and girls would knit 6" by 6" squares. Mrs. Dubenage would crochet them all together to make the afghan. Several of the girls in the class already knew how to knit. The boys and the girls who didn't know how to knit would receive instruction from Mrs. Dubenage. Isabelle was among those needing knitting instruction.

Isabelle was an excellent student in all of her academic areas, but in knitting, she was a dismal failure. Mrs. Dubenage gave up on her when Isabelle presented a triangular piece, that was knotted in several places. An almost tearful Isabelle asked her teacher why her square had become a sloppy, unacceptable triangle. Her teacher replied that most of the damage was done because Isabelle kept dropping stitches.

While Isabelle struggled unsuccessfully to knit a 6" by 6" square, many of the boys and girls were able to produce perfect squares. Soon

Mrs. Dubenage had enough squares to crochet together to form an afghan. Knowing that Isabelle could write poetry, she asked her to compose a poem that would come from her class, and would be enclosed with the afghan when it was sent to London. Isabelle did not fail at this task. When the afghan was put in a box for mailing, placed on the top of it was the poem, written by Isabelle:

"We're American children – eight years old
We'd like to save you from the cold
A wooly afghan we have made
And for your safety, we have prayed
We're sorry that you have to sleep
Down in the subway – very deep
We wish you'd win the war real fast
So your discomfort doesn't last
And so the Nazis, cruel and bad
Will stop making people feel so sad."

———

On the day they sent the afghan, a new pupil entered their class. Her name was Martha Rosen, and she had come all the way from London. She and Isabelle became friends almost immediately. Martha had come to America, because of the *Blitz*. The *Blitz* was the name the English gave to the Nazi bombing of British cities. In London, where Martha had lived with her mother, father, and four year old brother, thousands of children were sent to live in the countryside to escape the bombing. Martha's younger brother was among these children.

Martha's father was now in the army fighting somewhere in Belgium. Her mother worked in a factory making guns. It was decided that Martha would be better off, living with her father's sister in America until the war was over. Martha's aunt lived only one block away from where Isabelle lived, so the girls enjoyed playing together a lot.

Isabelle loved Martha's English accent. She wished that she could speak that way too, but when she tried, she sounded "fake." She also loved to hear Martha's stories about her home in London. The stories about the Blitz, air raid shelters, burning houses, and dead people were very scary, but very interesting. To Isabelle, the worst thing of all was Martha's little brother living in the country with strangers. Isabelle would have hated to see her adorable baby sister, Phyllis, sent away from their family.

Martha always wore a beautiful gold bracelet. A gold tab on the bracelet was engraved with Martha's name, her London address, her birthdate, and even her blood type. Isabelle thought that Martha's bracelet was the most wonderful piece of jewelry she had ever seen. She wished she had a bracelet just like it.

One day Isabelle asked Martha about how she had gotten the bracelet. Martha said, "All of the children in London wear identification bracelets or necklaces. Identification is worn in case a child dies or is badly wounded. It would tell the medical authorities whom they should notify."

"When I was making the crossing on the huge ocean liner, there were hundreds of other British children on the boat. Our ship was in a convoy of many ships. The other ships were protecting our large ocean liner. Suddenly a large group of German planes attacked the convoy. We were on a choppy sea, and the bouncing ship and attacking planes frightened all of us very badly. Lots of children screamed and cried."

"Some of our protecting ships opened fire on the German planes. We saw some of the planes plunge into the sea. Finally all of the German planes turned and flew away. I guess the anti-aircraft guns on the convoy's ships were too much for them."

"No one on our ship was hurt. We were just badly frightened. I was glad that I was wearing my bracelet. If something had happened to me, I'd want my mother to know," Martha concluded.

Isabelle remained silent. Martha's experience was overwhelming. Isabelle no longer envied Martha's bracelet.

Chapter 7: The Bronx

No one in the family had a crystal ball, so they could not foresee the fate of the street they moved onto in January of 1941. The street bore a lovely female name, so Isabelle hoped it would have green front yards and trees. It didn't! It consisted of two blocks of unrelieved, brick or stone, four or five story walk-up apartment buildings. The "front lawns" of these buildings were the wide concrete sidewalks. The nearest tree was in Crotona Park, three long blocks away.

In thirty years, this street, *Charlotte Street*, would become a slum so grim, that a future president would speak of it as a prototype of urban blight. President Jimmy Carter would pledge that Charlotte Street would have a rebirth as a lovely spot for people's homes. In 1941, when Bella's family moved to Charlotte Street, it was not blighted, but was typical of many New York City lower middle class neighborhoods; and it needed no rehabilitation.

Moving onto Charlotte Street, for Isabelle it was an adventure. The family had a five-room apartment, facing front. The building's entry hall had highly shined brass mailboxes in which one could see one's face. All of the apartments were occupied by families, most of whom had children. Isabelle felt sure she could make many new friends.

For the second time in her life, Isabelle had her own bedroom. There were three bedrooms in their apartment. Bella, Hymie, and Baby Phyllis slept in the large front bedroom. Sidney and Stanley shared a medium sized bedroom. The tiny front bedroom was Isabelle's. Isabelle didn't care that her bedroom was small. It was hers alone and she loved it.

Theirs was the first house on Charlotte Street. It was located at the bottom of the Charlotte Street hill where it intersected with Jennings Street. Jennings Street was a long street consisting of stores of all types. In the neighborhood, people referred to Jennings Street as *The Market*.

When Bella's family moved onto Charlotte Street, it was wintertime. The heat was turned on and the windows were kept tightly shut. By springtime, however, the windows were flung open to bring in the fresh air. Along with the fresh air, the open front window brought in the noises of The Market. Isabelle's bedroom was one of the front bedrooms, and she awakened, each spring morning, to the sounds of people speaking in so many languages that it was difficult to realize that the Bronx was a part of the United States. The language that seemed to be used the least was English. Many of the adults in this East Bronx (today called *South Bronx*) neighborhood were European immigrants, so many of Europe's languages were being spoken. These foreign sounds wafted into Isabelle's open window. Eight-year old Isabelle had learned to distinguish between many of these languages. While Yiddish, which Isabelle spoke fluently, was the most prevalent language Isabelle heard, sounds of Russian, Polish, and Czech came into her window. These three languages were sometimes difficult to tell apart, because they were all Slavic languages and sounded somewhat similar. The second most prevalent language floating into Isabelle's bedroom was German, because German and Austrian immigrants had recently moved into Isabelle's new Bronx neighborhood. Isabelle also heard Romanian and Hungarian spoken outside of her window too.

Bella usually did the food shopping for the family, but sometimes Isabelle was sent to buy one or two items. Fruits and vegetables were sold in most of the outdoor stalls that lined Jennings Street. The long rows of these produce stalls were occasionally interrupted by a stall selling candy or by a clothing shop. The *Pickle Man's* alley was located between two of the produce stalls. A store that sold notions, some toys, kitchen gadgets, cutlery, and dishes was also located on Jennings Street. The *Banana Man* and the *Soup Greens Man* had their own small stalls as well, and behind all of the big and small stalls were buildings that contained such shops as: kosher butcher shops, fresh fish shops, poultry shops, and dairy stores. The dairy stores sold: milk, packaged butter, tub butter, sour cream, sweet cream, cheeses from all over the world, and eggs. They also sold such American packaged products as: sliced bread, Twinkies, Hostess Cupcakes, pretzels, and potato chips. Two shops that smelled like paradise were the bakery and the appetizing store. The appetizing store had barrels of different varieties of herring, olives, pickled vegetables, tasty jarred products, and a vast variety of smoked fish and freshly made salads. The appetizing stores aroma was topped only by the smells wafting from the bakery. Freshly baked breads of many types, bagels, rolls, pies, a great variety of cakes, and cookies made the bakery smell so good that sometimes Isabelle just stood near the doorway and sniffed.

Often, Isabelle was given money so that she could buy a charlotte russe at the bakery. A charlotte russe was sold in a paper cup. The bottom layer of a charlotte russe was sponge cake. The cake was covered with a mass of fresh whipped cream topped with a maraschino cherry. This delicious confection was eaten, as one walked through the streets.

———

Isabelle went to school at P.S. 61. Her school was just two blocks away from home, so she walked to school with friends. Her best friend on Charlotte Street was Luba, whose real name was Corrine. She was called "Luba," because of her brother's corruption of the Yiddish word *libbe* (beloved). Her brother heard his mother calling Baby Corrine *libbe* and he called her *Luba*, which became the nickname everyone called her for the rest of her life.

Another good friend of Isabelle's was Jeannie. Isabelle thought that Jeannie, who was ten, and had been born in Germany, was very wise. Foreign children and children who were older than she, seemed very wise to Isabelle.

One day, just after *Rosh Hashana* (Jewish New Year) had passed, Isabelle and Jeannie were walking to school together. Isabelle said that in a little more than a week they would stay home from school again, because it would be *Yom Kippur* (the Jewish Day of Atonement). Isabelle said with a giggle, "I wonder what the gentile teachers and kids do on Rosh Hashana and Yom Kippur when so many kids and teachers are absent to celebrate the High Holy Days. I don't think there's a class at our school with more than two or three Christian kids."

"I guess they put the gentile kids from several classes with one of the Christian teachers," said the wise Jeannie. "I'm sure they don't do any work. They must read, see movies, and draw pictures all day long."

"In Germany we had a better system," continued Jeannie. "Jewish kids went to Jewish schools and Christian kids went to Christian schools. In Hamburg, where I come from, the Jewish schools closed on the Jewish holidays, because everyone, even the teachers, were Jewish."

"That does sound like a good system," said Isabelle.

————

When Isabelle came home for lunch, she told her mother about her conversation with Jeannie.

Bella shook her head and replied, "Jeannie was a small child when she lived in Germany. She was kept unaware of the horrible and dangerous conditions of life being imposed upon Jews there. Her parents were trying to protect her from this knowledge, so they didn't explain the bad law that kept Jewish children out of the public schools. Jeannie went to a Jewish school, because the Nazis no longer allowed Jewish children to be educated in the regular public schools. When Jewish children were expelled from the public schools, the Jewish community opened its own schools."

"The schools are only a small part of the Nazi persecution of the Jews. They do many bad things to our people. Jeannie and her family came to America to escape this persecution," said Bella, sadly.

"But, I don't want you to repeat our conversation to Jeannie. If her parents don't want her to know all of the reasons for their coming to America, don't you be the one to tell her."

Isabelle answered solemnly, "I won't, Mommy."

————

While Jeannie did not fully understand the tyranny she and her family had faced in Germany, she and all of the girls in 4A, 4B, and 5A at P.S. 61, understood the petty tyranny they faced from Carolyn! Carolyn was small in stature, but loud in volume. She looked like a normal member of Luba's 4B class, but she screamed, yelled, and threatened every fourth grade and 5A girl to such an extent, that her evil manner and nasty threats made all of the girls forget that she was small. They trembled at her loud voice, and relinquished control of the hopscotch game they played before school began. The hopscotch game was a game in which the participants dropped their books or school bags in a line, leaving a narrow space between each set of books. Then the participants in the game lined up to take their turns. Each girl hopped around the books, by going through the narrow spaces between them. If a girl's shoe touched a book or a school bag she was "out." She was also "out" if she put both feet on the ground. The last girl left standing on one foot was the winner of the game. Carolyn always decided who could play. If an unfortunate girl was not chosen by Carolyn, she didn't get to play. Nobody knew when Carolyn attained this power, but everyone knew why. All of the girls were afraid of her!

Isabelle was no exception. Because of her fear of Carolyn, Isabelle often boycotted the beloved hopscotch game and just hung around with others who had done the same, or those few unfortunates that Carolyn had verbally abused before banning them from the game.

Except for Carolyn's frightening yelling, school was fun for Isabelle. She liked all of her subjects, her teacher, and most of her classmates. She left home for school feeling happy and returned home feeling happy, too.

———

Isabelle did not feel this way about the Yiddish school she had to attend for an hour after school, Monday through Thursday. On Sunday, the Yiddish school had a music session from 9:00AM to 12:00 Noon. Isabelle was expected to attend on Sunday, too, but sometimes Bella took pity on her and let her sleep in and skip the Yiddish music on Sunday.

The Yiddish school was a Sholem Alechem school that was part of a chain of Yiddish schools spread throughout the Bronx, Brooklyn, and in parts of Manhattan and Queens. These schools were secular schools located in areas of New York City in which large numbers of Yiddish speaking immigrants lived. They emphasized reading, writing, and speaking Yiddish. Indeed, they were named for one of the most famous Yiddish writers, Sholem Alechem.

While mastering Yiddish was not the only objective of the Sholem Alechem schools, it was their most important objective. Their curriculum also emphasized the reading of Yiddish literature, because in the second half of the nineteenth century, continuing on into the twentieth century, a rich literature had been and still was being written in Yiddish. The Sholem Alechem schools exposed their young students to this literature, in the hope that as they grew older they would continue to peruse the excellent works of these Yiddish writers.

Along with literature, the Yiddish schools taught Bible stories and some of the religious tenets of Judaism. The Bible stories were taught merely as stories, emphasizing none of their religious significance. Where appropriate, their moral significance might be discussed, but the religious rules of Judaism were taught as, "some of the things that some Jewish people chose to do." No stigma was attached to those who had left these rules and lived more secular lives. The Ten Commandments' type of morality was the only morality strongly emphasized in these schools.

Because of the events occurring in Europe in early 1941, Nazi anti-Semitism was also discussed at the Sholem Alechem schools. The Jews of the United States were aware of the atrocities being committed on the Jews in Europe. The Sholem Alechem schools wanted their students to be aware, too. In this vein, they also taught Zionism. While few of their staff were active Zionists, a strong surge toward Zionism appeared in their curriculum. It was the belief of most Jews that Palestine should be opened as a refuge for the dreadfully persecuted Jews of Europe.

Isabelle should have loved Yiddish school. The Sholem Alechem schools' curriculum was filled with subjects that peaked her interest. But Isabelle did not love Yiddish school. She hated it!

————————

The Yiddish school that Isabelle attended was on Wilkins Avenue, less than two long blocks from Isabelle's home on Charlotte Street. If Isabelle had the time, she would go there by way of The Market. She would examine the outdoor stalls, as she sauntered through the shopping crowds. Then she would make a stop at the Pickle Man's alley, where the Pickle Man's barrels were lined in a row. The Pickle Man was fun to watch and hilarious to listen to. He spoke mostly in Yiddish. His pickle barrels were loaded with sour or half-sour pickled tomatoes and sauerkraut. Many customers brought their own jars, which he filled with sauerkraut, tomatoes, or pickles in brine. Other customers took their purchases home in the same kinds of boxes that, today, are associated with "carry-out" at Chinese restaurants. Still other customers were like Isabelle. They would stop at the "Pickle Man's" and buy one or two pickles to eat as a snack as they went about their business. In warm weather, when Isabelle stopped at the Pickle Man's alley, this large, burley, loud-voiced man would be dressed in a short-sleeved shirt with a stained apron wrapped around his ponderous middle. First he would tease Isabelle about whether she had been a good student at school. Then he would take her order for a two cent half sour pickle. He would plunge his very hairy arm deep into the pickle brine and retrieve a large, perfectly shaped, delicious half-sour pickle for Isabelle. The whole transaction was conducted in Yiddish, after which, eating her pickle, Isabelle would happily skip away toward the Yiddish school she hated so much.

<hr>

Yiddish school was hated, because Isabelle's Yiddish school teacher was a tyrant! Chaver (Friend) Levine brooked no lateness nor any mistakes in reading, writing, or answering his questions. Any child who committed one of these "sins" was publicly humiliated by the cruel teacher. If the class became noisy, for any reason whatsoever, Chaver Levine banged a huge wooden block on his desk and screamed vilifications at his students. Nobody wanted to get into trouble with Chaver Levine, and Isabelle was no exception.

<hr>

When Isabelle did not have much time to spare, she took a route to Yiddish school that was less crowded and less interesting than The Market. She went by way of Stebbins Avenue, a small street connecting Charlotte Street to Wilkins Avenue. On one side of Stebbins Avenue stood a church and a small apartment house. On the other side were apartment houses.

Because of its lack of distractions, Isabelle got to Yiddish school very quickly when she used the Stebbins Avenue route.

One frigid Monday, after a heavy snowfall had fallen on Friday, Isabelle, carrying her Yiddish books, was walking on Stebbins Avenue, on her way to Yiddish school. Suddenly, the dreaded Carolyn, who had just left the church, bellowed, "Why are you walking in front of my church?"

Gathering all of her courage Isabelle answered in a tremulous voice, "This is not your street. It belongs to everyone."

In answer, Carolyn jumped off the church's bottom step, lunged at Isabelle, and pushed her into the frozen, dirty snow that had been made into a long hill alongside the road when the sidewalks had been shoveled three days earlier. Isabelle's Yiddish books flew out of her hand and were strewn all over the hard, wet, icy mound of snow. Bella had paid for these books with great difficulty, and expected her daughter to take good care of them. They were probably ruined, and Isabelle expected to be in big trouble at home. But what distressed Isabelle the most was the icy mound's affect on her hands and legs. Not only was the mound of snow very cold, but the snow had frozen into sharp, small, pointy hills of ice, at most of its surfaces. These icy peaks cut and scratched the little girl's bare legs and hands unmercifully.

Isabelle's pain dispelled her fear of Carolyn. She sprang forward from the icy mound with "blood in her eyes!" She lunged at Carolyn, knocking her onto the hill of ice. She was much taller than Carolyn and very much angrier, so she pummeled the little bully as Carolyn lay on the ice, until the bully began to cry.

Isabelle pulled the weeping Carolyn off the icy hill, and holding the smaller girl's coat tightly, she said, "You're a miserable person! I'm not afraid of you anymore. If I see you hit or holler at anyone at the school or on the playground, I'll beat you up worse than I did today!" Isabelle let go of the little bully's coat, and Carolyn, wailing loudly, ran away.

Isabelle gathered up her wet Yiddish schoolbooks. While a mild fear of Chaver Levine remained, Isabelle was determined to face him down. If she did not succeed, she planned to ask her mother to help her.

The Yiddish school was located, one flight up, in a rickety old building. When Isabelle entered the hallway of the building, she could hear the children reciting in unison. Class had already begun! She tip-toed into the large classroom with trepidation. When he saw Isabelle, Chaver Levine stopped the recitation by banging loudly on his desk with the huge block of wood he kept specifically for this purpose. He achieved immediate silence, and then turned his venomous attention to the trembling little girl.

"You are very late, Madam," he said sarcastically. "Did you enjoy your day in the snow?"

"Chaver Levine, I was not playing in the snow. I was pushed into a frozen, snowy hill at the side of the road, by a terrible girl who frightens everyone. My coat was covered with snow and my hands and feet are all cut up by the ice. I should have gone home so that my mother could treat the bleeding cuts on my legs and hands, but I was afraid to miss your class. In a way, I feel just as bullied by you as I felt by that awful girl who bullies everyone!"

Isabelle had rendered Chaver Levine speechless. He silently gestured to her to take her seat, and the lesson continued. As Isabelle opened her damp and battered Yiddish reader, she marveled at her own courage in speaking up to the hated Chaver Levine. She also wondered about what her mother's reaction would be to her story and her badly damaged Yiddish books.

———

Bella's reaction to her story astounded Isabelle. Instead of being angry, Bella hugged her little girl and said she was proud of her. She said that Isabelle should never tolerate a bully, unless the bully is so powerful, that Isabelle knows she can't win. She continued, "Chaver Levine is a grown-up bully. While I don't like your speaking disrespectfully to an adult, at any time, you were seriously agitated by your encounter with Carolyn. I think that maybe you made Chaver Levine stop and think about his behavior, too. If you did, it was good."

"As for your wet, dirty books and their bent pages, we can dry them and flatten the pages as much as possible. You can still read from them this year."

"Your *heft* (writing book) seems to be irreparable. Hefts are not so expensive. I'll give you money to buy a new one from Chaver Levine." (Yiddish writing books differed from the notebooks used when writing English. Each space contained a narrower space within it. The Yiddish was written in the narrower space. Because of this difference, Isabelle needed to purchase her writing book from her Yiddish teacher.) "In the meantime," Bella said, "let's clean the scratches and scrapes on your legs and hands, and put some Mercurochrome on them."

Isabelle knew for sure that she had the best mother in the whole world!

———————

On the following day, Isabelle got to school early. The hopscotch game was just starting. Each game allowed for ten girls to play. There was no sign of Carolyn, and the girls were in their second game.

Suddenly, Carolyn appeared. She slinked into line silently, preparing to participate in the third game of hopscotch. Isabelle roared, "Carolyn, get out of line. You can't play hopscotch anymore. You're too bossy and you make everyone feel bad!"

To everyone's surprise, a downcast Carolyn quietly left the line.

"What did you do to her, Isabelle?" asked one of the girls.

"I beat her up," answered Isabelle, without relaying any of the details. "Now let's play hopscotch."

Carolyn was never a bully again. Isabelle did not replace her as boss of 4A, 4B, and 5A. Isabelle didn't care to be a boss, even if she could. All she wanted was to go about her own business without harassment.

Chapter 8: War

It was a cold Sunday in December. Luba's family ate supper very early, so Luba was called home at 4:30 and could not come out to play again until 5:30. Isabelle did not have to be home for supper until 6:30. That gave the girls an hour to play together again. Therefore, Isabelle was waiting for Luba in front of the building in which Luba lived. She was bouncing a ball and chanting the rhymes or words that went with New York City children's ball-bouncing games, but she hoped that Luba would finish her supper quickly and come out to join her. It was more fun to play with another person than to play alone.

Suddenly Luba's kitchen window flew open. Luba lived on the ground floor and her window was not too far above Isabelle's head.

"The Japs have bombed Pearl Harbor," Luba screamed. "My brother Carl says that means the United States is in the war!"

"Where is Pearl Harbor?" Isabelle asked. She had never heard of that place before.

"I'll ask Carl," answered Luba. Luba returned to the window in a moment. "Carl says it's somewhere in the Pacific Ocean. He said he never heard of it before either, so he doesn't know exactly where it is."

"Go home," Luba said. "There's lots of news coming over the radio. Tell your parents to listen, too."

Isabelle ran home, flung open the door, and yelled, "The Japs have bombed Pearl Harbor. We're in the war! Put on the radio. Let's listen to the news," she screamed.

Sidney, Stanley, and Bella joined Isabelle in the living room. Only Hymie, who was in a deep alcoholic stupor, ignored Isabelle's announcement. He slept in a chair in the living room and Baby Phyllis played in her playpen, while the rest of the family hovered around the radio.

The news was not good. The Japanese had inflicted great damage on the American fleet that was docked at Pearl Harbor, in Hawaii. They did this while Japanese diplomats were in Washington D.C., discussing peace with President Roosevelt. No one doubted that America would be at war with Japan by the next day.

Everyone's predictions proved correct. Congress declared war on Japan on the very next day.

———

On that day, Isabelle returned to school. There was no hopscotch game. Everyone was talking about Japan's sneak attack on Pearl Harbor. When the children were called to line up in the schoolyard, they did so by classes, standing in straight lines. Just as they all became settled, so that they could start an orderly assent to their classrooms in the six-story school building, a plane flew overhead. All eyes turned to the sky…Were they going to be bombed?

Of course the Japanese were too far away to bomb New York, but would our country go to war with Germany? The Germans weren't as far away as the Japanese. Could they bring the blitz to New York City? These were the thoughts and fears of the children and teachers standing in P.S. 61's concrete schoolyard.

———

In a few days, the United States did go to war with Germany. America began a great mobilization. Factories stopped making cars, pleasure boats, and even tools and kitchen gadgets for the people at home (called the "*Home Front*"). America's factories were converted to the manufacture of military supplies, weapons, and military vehicles. They never shut down, working around the clock, twenty-four hours a day. There was a shortage of manpower, because young men were entering the armed services in gigantic numbers. The factories needed more workers than ever to cover their extra shifts, so they hired women. Women were praised for becoming workers for the war effort.

Some women even joined the armed forces. They were used for work in offices and military hospitals. Women in the armed forces were kept behind the front lines. By taking men's jobs in the armed services, women released the men to fight America's enemies. America was like a sleeping giant that had been awakened by the attack on Pearl Harbor. Within months, America's factories were supplying needed materials, not only to her own armed forces, but to the armed forces of her allies, especially England, the Soviet Union, and China.

Even children Isabelle's age were helping the war effort. Tin cans, newspapers, and used cooking oil were collected by children and delivered to depots where they were distributed to the proper places that would turn them into useful objects to help fight America's enemies. Women and girls knitted warm sweaters and socks for America's fighting men. Americans learned to "make do" when shortages and rationing greatly diminished the civilian supplies of products to which the American public was accustomed. Almost no one complained. Everyone was united in the fight against the Axis – Germany, Japan, and Italy.

———

Even though almost everyone was doing things to help the war effort, family life continued. In Bella's family, there was a crisis with Sidney, who was playing hooky from school almost every day. He was sixteen years old and he wanted to quit school. Hymie, who was never sober enough to face family problems, expected .Bella to take care of them, so Bella had to attend the conference held with Sidney's teachers and with the principal of Sidney's school. All of them agreed that Sidney was completely turned off of school. They urged Bella to sign the papers that would allow him to quit school and get a job. Bella reluctantly acquiesced. Sidney was no longer a student. He now needed to find a job

———

Bella's cousin Bertha owned a large candy store and newsstand near the subway station at Freeman Street. The newsstand was open until 2:00 A.M., and it was difficult to get help to man it in its later hours. Bella suggested Sidney for the job. Bertha's husband Nate was delighted to hire the boy, and Sidney began working at the candy store immediately.

Sidney came home from work in the wee hours of the morning. He grabbed a bite to eat, got in his bed with a new comic book, and when he finished reading it, went to sleep. The comic book was thrown between Sidney's bed and the wall. If Sidney was still sleeping when Isabelle came home from school, she climbed over her sleeping step-brother and retrieved the comic book. If he wasn't sleeping, she just helped herself to the book. Generous, good-natured Sidney didn't mind at all. Isabelle was delighted to have so many comic books accessible to her.

Sidney contributed ten dollars a week for his room and board. That was a little less than half of his salary, but his needs were few and he was happy to help out.

Stanley couldn't seem to keep a job. He was very handsome, had a glib tongue, and was quite active socially. He had developed a relationship with a girl who lived across the street from their house and constantly spent his time with her.

One day when Bella was going through her drawers, she spied the box that contained her only valuable piece of jewelry. It was an exquisite cameo pin with a diamond on a fine gold chain, hanging on the lovely silhouetted woman's neck. Bella rarely wore the cameo, because she lacked the occasions for such finery. But occasionally, she opened the box and gazed at the brooch. It brought back the carefree days of the twenties, when her younger brother Irving gave it to her as a gift. In those days she had many occasions to wear the cameo, and on this day of rummaging through her drawers, she wanted to look at it again.

When she opened the black leather box in which the cameo was stored, to her horror she found it empty. She immediately suspected Stanley, but she would not confront him until she was certain.

Bella did not have long to wait. One Saturday evening, a neighbor who lived on their floor, was walking out of the building, all dressed up. On the lapel of her suit jacket was Bella's cameo pin. Bella immediately confronted her. "Where did you get that pin?" she demanded.

Her neighbor, completely taken aback, replied, "Your step-son Stanley said that you were having hard times, with your husband drinking and your big family. He said he was selling the pin to get you some money for your family. He asked me for $15 for the pin, and I paid him."

A flabbergasted Bella said, "I wish you had discussed it with me. You know $15 is a ridiculously low price for so fine a cameo."

"I didn't know! Your family problems are your own! I bought the pin, believing Stanley. The pin is mine!"

Bella didn't pursue the subject any further. Instead she planned to confront eighteen-year-old Stanley as soon as he came home. No doubt he was dallying with his girlfriend, upon whom he had probably spent the money he had received for her cameo.

In the meantime, an infuriated Bella stormed into her apartment. She shook Hymie violently, waking him from his drunken sleep on the easy chair in the living room. She ordered him to wash his face, douse his hair with cold water, and come back to her.

When Hymie came back, she told him the story of her cameo. Hymie's judgment returned, instantaneously. He said that Stanley was always a leach and a cheat. He had tyrannized his younger brother in the orphanage and he never "pulled his own weight" in the family. He rarely worked, and even more rarely made contributions to the family's well-being. Stanley was always irresponsible, and now he was a thief as well. Hymie wanted Stanley out of the house.

Sorrowfully, Bella reluctantly agreed. Stanley was a grown man. There was talk of soon drafting eighteen-year-old men into the armed services. Stanley was already eighteen and if he was old enough for the armed services, he could certainly take care of himself.

At midnight, when Stanley came home, both Hymie and Bella confronted him with the facts about the cameo, and about his no longer being welcome in the house. The handsome thief's face crumbled. He began to weep and begged for another chance. Hymie was adamant.

"Go out and become a man," said Hymie. "Come back when you have something to show for yourself."

A dejected Stanley moved out the next day.

One day Bella, Isabelle, and Baby Phyllis went on the long subway trip to Coney Island to see Sarah and Fanny. Isabelle was thrilled to be going, because she would see her idol, Fanny's older daughter, Millie, and her playmate since infancy, Fanny's son, Marty. Little did they know that both Fanny and Sarah would have good news.

They stopped at Sarah's house first. As usual, Sarah was not at home. They went to the pavilion on the boardwalk to find her; and there she was, singing her heart out with her Yiddish-speaking cronies. As soon as Sarah saw Bella and her girls, she quickly walked over to them, hugged and kissed all three of them, and then directed them to a bench that was some distance from the noisy pavilion. As she faced her beloved sea she began.

"On the Yiddish station on the radio, I hear about horrible things happening to our people in Europe. On WEVD they constantly exhort us to support America's war effort. In this way the Nazis will be defeated and our people will end their suffering. They suggest that we buy war bonds, which will mature in ten years. The money from these bonds will go to the American government to support the war effort. In the meantime, the bonds will gain more value, through interest, so that if I spend $500 on bonds, in ten years they will be worth much more.

"I want to support the war effort, but even more, I want to help Isabelle go to college, when she is of age to do so. I know Hymie loves her, but he is not her own father and he may balk at college bills. My other grandchildren have their own fathers. Because Isabelle does not, and because I think she is as bright as any of my other grandchildren, I am going to put $500 worth of war bonds into Isabelle's name. I'm sure it will help her to get a college education when the time comes."

"I have only saved $150, so far. The rest of the money will come. Consider it like our bag of gold under the stove in Vashisht."

Bella and Isabelle laughed. Isabelle thought the idea of chickens roosting on top of a bag of gold was hilarious. She was really glad that her mother and grandmother kept telling her stories about Vashisht. She was even happier to be so well-loved by her grandma and her mother. It never ceased to amaze Isabelle, that Sarah, who was illiterate herself, had such a burning desire to see her grandchildren become well educated.

———

After some more, rather mundane conversation, the three generations of females started the long walk to 36 Street to see Fanny and her family. When they arrived at Fanny's apartment, they were all quite tired. Bella, however, was completely exhausted, because she had to carry her chubby, adorable, blond toddler most of the very long way.

Fanny immediately served them lunch. As they ate, she told them her big news. She and Murray had been looking for an apartment in the East Bronx. She wanted an apartment that was within walking distance of Bella's apartment. They had found a place in the beautiful building in which Murray's brother lived. The building had an elevator, so apartments that were on high floors were easily accessible. They had rented a small apartment on the sixth floor. Their children would sleep on folding beds in the living room. Fanny was sure that they would manage quite nicely.

"Where is the building located?" Bella asked.

"It's on Longfellow Avenue, near 174 Street," Fanny replied.

"That's a very long walk to my house," said Bella.

"Don't worry. I'll be the one walking over to your house most of the time. I can get exercise, walk my dog, and do my shopping on Jennings Street, when I come to see you," Fanny said good-naturedly. "I know it's a difficult walk for you with your bad leg, but I can come quite often."

———

Bella's delight over her sister's news was so apparent, that she left Fanny grinning with delight too. She and Sarah decided to take the streetcar back to 29 Street. Sarah could get off there, but Bella and her daughters would continue on to Stillwell Avenue, where they would take the subway to the Bronx.

When Sarah left Bella and her daughters and walked home from the trolley, she thought, "I will not like having not even one of my children living on Coney Island, but perhaps it is better that Bella and Fanny live near each other. Both of these daughters of mine are very close. They will be very happy seeing each other several times a week."

––––––––

Bella had been brooding about the whole episode with Chaver Levine. She saw very little difference between a child bully and an adult bully. She kept turning the problem over in her mind, and finally decided on a solution. She would withdraw Isabelle from the Sholem Alechem School and enroll her in the *Arbiter Ring* (Workmen's Circle) School on Hoe Avenue and 171 Street. Her only misgiving was that she had heard that the Arbiter Ring Schools were socialist in their political leanings. She preferred that Isabelle arrive at political decisions without others proselytizing her. She determined that she would carefully observe Isabelle's Jewish education, and take appropriate action, if it proved necessary.

––––––––

Chaverte (*friend*) Tapatchnick, Isabelle's new Yiddish teacher, was a slight woman, possessing a highly intellectual demeanor. She took an immediate liking to Isabelle, and often talked to her about subjects outside of the Yiddish curriculum. When Chaverte Tapatchnick learned that Isabelle read mostly mystery stories, she believed them to be beneath Isabelle's intellectual ability. She, therefore, brought her a book called *The Mysteries of Paris* , and told Isabelle that her daughter, who had read only mysteries too, changed after she read this book. Her daughter no longer wanted to read mysteries, and instead turned to many other kinds of books. After Isabelle read the "magical book," she too lost her obsession with mysteries and followed Chaverte Tapatchnick's suggestions, which included many fine books of literary merit. Isabelle read them all.

One of Isabelle's favorite hours at Yiddish School was the Bible Story Hour on Monday. Chaverte Tapatchnick would read an Old Testament Bible story and the four children that made up Isabelle's small class would discuss it with her. Very often, the discussion boiled down to a conversation between only Isabelle and Chaverte Tapatchnick.

On one such day, when Chaverte Tapatchnick had concluded the Cain and Abel story, Isabelle's hand shot into the air. "If Cain lived in the Land of Nod and was married to a woman who came from there, how did the people from the Land of Nod get there? I thought that God had only created Adam and Eve and that they were the parents of Cain and Abel. I thought that they were the only people on earth," said Isabelle.

Chaverte Tapatchnick formed her small hands into a tent-shape. After a rather long and thoughtful pause, she said, "I can only give you my opinion when I answer your question. In my opinion, when ancient Jewish scholars wrote the Adam and Eve story to explain the creation of the human race, they were not very careful with some of the details."

"Modern science has cast some doubt on the ancient creation story," she continued. Isabelle you might want to go to the library and take out some children's books on the subject of Darwin's theories of evolution. I'd be happy to talk to you about them, if you would like me to."

"Chaverte Tapatchnick was wonderful!" thought Isabelle. "She left all subjects open to discussion."

On another Bible Study day, the subject was Noah. All of the students, including Isabelle, speculated outrageously about the size of Noah's ark. To them it was hilarious to contemplate an ark so huge that it would accommodate all of the animals that Noah had collected. Chaverte Tapatchnick drew their attention away from their ludicrous musings about the size of the ark. Instead she asked them why they thought that God destroyed the earth and all living creatures upon it.

Chaim's hand flew up. "Mankind was bad and had corrupted everything," he said. "God destroyed mankind and the earth as a punishment".

Then Chaverte Tapatchnick asked the more thought provoking question. "Do you believe that God's punishment was just?"

A lively thirty-minute discussion ensued. The consensus was that a merciful god would have chosen some other way.

"So," asked Chaverte Tapatchnick, "you do not believe that the God of the Bible is merciful?"

"No," blurted out Isabelle. "He was an idea made up by ancient Jews who were more cruel than people are today."

"You are probably right about His being created by ancient Jews, but I'm not so sure that they were more cruel than people are today. Just look at what is going on in Europe right now," said Chaverte Tapatchnick sadly.

The children left class that day with serious and sad thoughts assaulting their brains.

A third Bible story that engendered a lively discussion was Abraham's imminent sacrifice of his only son Isaac. After the discussion, the consensus was that Abraham's test was too cruel, and God's need for that kind of loyalty was unnecessary.

Chaverte Tapatchnick not only didn't discourage these sacrilegious discussions, she encouraged them. She believed that the children were enlarging their intellects by analyzing these biblical situations.

———

A very sad discussion came as a result of a story in the Yiddish anthology that the children were using as their Yiddish reading book. The anthology was a fine mixture of stories by Peretz, Sholem Alechem, and other giants of Yiddish literature. It also contained some poetry and some stories of current interest. The story the class was reading was about an elderly widow in the Warsaw Ghetto, who on the first night of Chanukah, placed a candle in her window. As she did so, a passing Nazi soldier shot and killed her.

The children in the class were horrified by the story. It resulted in a long discussion about the atrocities being committed against the Jews of Europe. Everyone left the class feeling depressed and helpless.

———

However, everyone was not paralyzed with helplessness. A gigantic rally had been organized to protest the world's seeming indifference to the Nazi assault on the Jews of Europe. Even more importantly, the rally called for the opening of Palestine to fleeing Jewish refugees. It was held in Madison Square Garden, New York City's giant, indoor sports arena. Jewish children from every denomination of Judaism packed the gigantic building. Thousands upon thousands of Jewish children, from the Ultra Orthodox to Reform, called for a land of refuge for their beleaguered co-religionists. The rally was publicized in the media. For many people in the United States, this was their first knowledge of the Jewish tragedy occurring in Europe.

Isabelle, who was a participant in the rally, was acutely aware of the peril in which Bella's birthplace, Vashisht, had been placed. She thanked

God that her family had escaped, but she was worried about her mother's aunts, uncles, and cousins who were still in Russia. She sometimes tried to imagine, with terror in her heart, what it could have been like if her grandmother had not thrown the watches overboard when their ship was anchored in New York's harbor approximately twenty years before.

———

The war required great amounts of manpower for the armed services. At the beginning of hostilities, only men over twenty-one years of age were drafted into the armed forces. But, as the fighting intensified, it was clear that the United States needed to dip into its younger male population. Young men, eighteen to twenty-one years of age, would now be drafted into the military.

The prospect of being drafted into the Army was not a pleasant one for Sidney. He, far and away, preferred the Navy; so on his eighteenth birthday, he enlisted in that branch of service. Bella was devastated. She had grown to love the quiet, dependable boy and didn't want to see him leave home or be in harm's way.

As soon as Sidney was posted on a ship, he was sent to the Pacific theater to fight against the Japanese. His ship was L.S.T. 609. It participated in many invasions that were part of the United States' strategy of "island hopping" in the war in the Pacific. The most notable two invasions in which L.S.T. 609 participated were the invasion of Leyte in the Philippines and the invasion of Iwo Jima.

When Sidney enlisted in the Navy, he designated Bella as recipient of his allotment check. Even though he meant for her to use the money to make life easier for her and the family, Bella deposited every single check sent to her in the bank. She wanted Sidney to have the money to fall back upon when he returned to civilian life.

Every night, when Bella had cleaned up the kitchen after dinner and put her girls to bed, she sat down at the kitchen table and wrote a *V Mail* letter to Sidney. (These letters were less bulky and were delivered to the servicemen overseas more quickly than regular mail.) Her letters were always cheerful, full of family news, and very affectionate. She never neglected to tell her stepson how much she loved him, how proud they all were of him, and how much he was missed by everyone.

Even though Phyllis was less than four years old, because the family talked about her brother Sidney and because he had given her her favorite doll when he left for the Navy, little Phyllis thought of her big brother with a lot love. Phyllis had coveted the doll for a long time, but Bella wouldn't buy it for her, because she thought it was too expensive. When Sidney gave Phyllis her wished-for doll, his little sister dubbed it "Sidney Doll." Because she was so young when she named the doll, she mispronounced its name, calling it "Sinny Doll." Phyllis cherished Sinny Doll. Young as she was, she valued the doll to such an extent that she didn't drag it around as she usually dragged and abused her other dolls. Instead, she played with it gently and kept it only within the confines of her home.

After Sidney was in the navy for six months, Phyllis decided that she could play with Sinny Doll on the "porch." The "porch" was not really a porch. It was a small concrete ledge outside the front window. It was built to hold plants, and was large enough to hold them or a very small girl and her toys. The "porch" was surrounded by a tall wrought iron fence designed to protect the plants. The wrought iron fence extended about two feet above Phyllis's head, and Bella, believing that it was a very safe outdoor place for Phyllis to play, often put her tiny daughter out there along with some of her favorite toys. The small girl would play there happily for over an hour, giving Bella time to do other things.

One lovely late spring day, when Phyllis had been playing on the "porch" for more than an hour, Bella heard the tiny girl cry out in anguish. She ran to the window to see what was causing Phyllis such distress. Phyllis pointed to the pavement, one story beneath her. She tearfully explained that she was playing with Sinny Doll when two big girls came along and saw her. They asked her what she was doing and she replied that she was playing with her Sinny Doll. They requested that she hold the doll up near the iron fence, so that they could see it better; and Phyllis did so. They then requested that Phyllis jump up and throw her doll down to them, so that they could see it even better. When Phyllis complied, the doll hit the pavement and shattered into many pieces. The big girls ran away.

Bella retrieved the pieces of Sinny Doll and quietly threw them away. She sadly realized that Sinny Doll was Phyllis's first great loss.

———————

About the same time as Sinny Doll's tragedy, Bella had an unexpected guest. Fanny was visiting, but she was Bella's expected guest. True to her word, Fanny generally visited her sister three or four times a week. She enjoyed the long walk from Longfellow Avenue accompanied by her little Pomeranian dog, Chi Chi. She would visit with her sister and then the two of them would buy some groceries on Jennings Street. On the day in question, as the sisters sat in Bella's living room gossiping, the doorbell rang. When Bella answered the door, she gasped, "Stanley." Her handsome stepson stood in the doorway looking more handsome than ever.

Stanley regaled Bella and Fanny with tales of his happy successes. He said he was employed as a sales manager in the garment industry. He told them that he had many friends and was very happy.

Fanny asked him why he was not in the Army.

He replied that he had been rejected, because he had a heart condition.

Bella immediately began to worry about his health and his heredity. His mother had died at a very young age of a heart condition. "Are you careful of your health, Stanley?" she asked. "Did you go to a doctor to check your heart?"

"Oh yeah," he replied. "I feel as fit as a fiddle, and the doctor said I have nothing to worry about."

After some more small talk, Bella served lunch for the three of them. She then informed Fanny that her leg was bothering her and she wouldn't be able to go shopping. When Fanny started to put herself together to leave, Bella said, "Today is June 1. I'm a little short in my rent money. Hymie gets paid tomorrow, but I don't want to be late." Bella said that she had twenty dollars, but was short the twelve dollars she needed for the $32 per month rent. She asked Fanny if she could borrow the twelve dollars for two days.

Fanny immediately pulled out her coin purse and counted out twelve dollars. After she handed the money to Bella, she rose to leave. She and Stanley bid each other goodbye.

Stanley jumped up and cleared the table. He told Bella to rest her leg. He also asked her if she needed any shopping to be done. He said he'd be glad to do it for her.

Bella thanked him, but refused his offer. When Stanley started to prepare to leave, he said to his stepmother, "If you like I can go to the *Super* (building superintendent) for you. You can keep your leg up and rest. I'll pay the rent and come back with the receipt."

———

Bella, remembering only her affection for Hymie's older son, handed him the money. Stanley departed and he never returned. After half an hour had passed, an anguished Bella limped downstairs to the Super. The Super said that he had never seen Stanley.

———

Fortunately, Hymie was cold sober when he came home. When Bella told him what had happened, he insisted that they immediately go to the police station. He wanted Stanley apprehended. At the police station, they were told that the police would gladly apprehend Stanley, but that first Bella and Hymie would have to press charges against him. Hymie was willing to do so, but Bella stayed his hand. "If Stanley gets into serious trouble, and goes to jail," she said, "let him be the one to have put himself there. He is your son and my stepson. I don't want us to lift our hands against him."

"He needs to learn a lesson," said an embittered Hymie.

"Not this kind of a lesson," replied Bella. "We cannot be the ones to destroy his future."

No charges were brought against Stanley.

———

While the world was at war, the East Bronx was at peace, and on a beautiful late spring day in 1943, its streets were crowded with playing children and strolling people of all ages. Bella, almost eleven-year old Isabelle, and almost three-year old Phyllis were among the happy spring strollers. They were only a block away from where they lived, when they were forced to walk around a group of boys, who were and eight and nine years old, and who were huddled around something in the middle of the sidewalk. As they skirted the huddled boys, Isabelle thought she heard a whimper. She listened more closely and then became certain that she heard the pained whimper of a small animal. Impulsively, Isabelle angrily chased the smaller boys away. Her pitying eyes saw a trembling, soot-covered, tiny puppy. She swept the little dog into her arms and continued her walk toward home.

Phyllis had always been petrified of dogs. If she saw a tethered dog thirty feet away from her, she ran into a nearby building shaking and sobbing in terror. The poor little dirty puppy that had so recently been tortured by the bad boys did not terrify Phyllis, but immediately put pity into the little girl's heart. She petted the filthy, trembling, little dog nestled in her sister's arms, and she cooed to him, "It's all right little doggie. You can come and live with us. We'll play with you and you can be our very own little doggie."

Isabelle and Bella looked at each other in complete wonder, as little Phyllis continued to pet the frightened puppy.

When they arrived at home, Bella said, "We cannot have a filthy dog like this in our house. We'll have to give him a good bath. Isabelle, put him right into the bathroom sink."

The bathroom sink was filled with warm water and the tiny, shivering puppy was put into it. The dog whimpered throughout her ordeal, which lasted a long time, because the soot and dirt on the poor animal kept turning the water black. This necessitated many frequent changes of water. To Bella's dismay, she saw many miniscule bugs floating in the water as it went down the drain.

"This dog has fleas!" exclaimed Bella in alarm and disgust. "We have to get rid of them!"

In 1943, the most popular insecticide for the extermination of cockroaches in New York City's infested apartments was a product called *Flit*. Flit was potent and had an evil smell. It did a fair job on cockroaches, but when Bella brought the can of Flit into the bathroom, Isabelle protested loudly.

"Don't use that strong stuff on the puppy....you'll kill him!" she shouted.

"Don't kill my doggie!" Phyllis bawled.

Undeterred, a determined Bella advanced on the still trembling puppy, whose fur, because of its repeated washings, had gone from black to light gray. She poured Flit over the little dog's entire body, only shielding the puppy's mouth, nose, and eyes from her onslaught. The puppy cried, and shivered even more violently than before. Her fur, which was now as white as snow, separated into wet tufts, exposing irritated pink skin. After Bella allowed the Flit to remain on the dog's body for a few minutes, she thoroughly rinsed the little animal in warm water. Myriad numbers of insects and gallons of dirty water flowed down the drain. The little puppy was terrified and its skin was surely irritated, but it was now immaculately clean.

Bella gently dried the little dog, cooing to it as one would coo to a baby. She filled a saucer with milk and offered it to the puppy. The little animal shakily walked up to the saucer, smelled the milk, and then wolfed it down.

An old pillow was placed in a large corrugated box. The little puppy, that Isabelle had discovered was a female, was placed on the pillow. She promptly fell asleep. Phyllis said, "Mommy, my puppy is sleeping! Oh Mommy I love her so much. She'll be my puppy for the rest of my life!"

Bella looked at Isabelle and shrugged. "I guess we now have a dog living with all of us in this tiny one bedroom apartment!"

Isabelle said, "Oh Mama, I'm so glad. She's such an adorable puppy, and Phyllis is not afraid of her. Perhaps this little dog will cure Phyllis of her fear of dogs."

"Perhaps," said Bella. "Well girls, what shall we name our new little dog?"

"Flitty," said Isabelle, "in remembrance of her first and nastiest bath!"

Everyone agreed, and Flitty remained the family's dog for many, many

years. She lived with Bella's family until long after Isabelle was married
and had moved away to her own home. In the many years of Flitty's life
with the family, she gave them joy and protection. The lovely white dog
did however manage, on one occasion, to break away from Bella while
she was being walked. It was her time to be in heat, so her escape caused
her to give Bella's family her one and only litter of puppies. Flitty's five
puppies were delivered by Flitty under Bella and Hymie's bed. She tended
the babies in the family's only bathroom, making the use of the bathroom
more crowded, but a place of fun to watch canine maternal love. When the
puppies were old enough, they were reluctantly given to a neighborhood
pet shop that sold them to other families.

Flitty died when Phyllis was eighteen years old. From the day Flitty
joined the family, she gave them joy. The only grief she gave them was her
death.

———————

Coney Island had only one very tall building, the Half Moon Hotel,
located at the boardwalk and 29 Street. The Half Moon Hotel was built to
provide upscale beach vacations, and was far more elegant than any other
edifice on Coney Island. It was also emptier. Building the Half Moon
Hotel had been a big mistake, because Coney Island had developed into a
lower middle class vacation spot, and lower middle class people could not
afford to pay the rates needed to stay at this lovely hotel. The hotel was
usually badly underbooked.

———————

For the hotel's owners, World War II proved to be an economic boon.
A profitable deal was made with the government to turn the Half Moon
Hotel into a Naval Rehabilitation center. Sailors were sent there for rest,
recuperation, and rehabilitation. A large section of the beach, at 29 Street,
was roped off for the use of the recuperating sailors. To the delight of
onlookers, in the spring, summer, and fall, volleyball games were constantly
being played there. Onlookers rooted the players on. During the summer,
the players and other sailor-onlookers, spent lots of time, ogled the girls
on the beach, as well.

Among the girls being ogled were two of Sarah's granddaughters.

Ida, Anna's lovely sixteen year old daughter and Millie, Fanny's beautiful fourteen year old daughter certainly came into their share of naval admiration. Both Ida and Millie were tall and slender. Ida was dark-eyed and brown haired and Millie was dark eyed and blond. Every weekend when the girls came to visit their grandmother, they sat on a blanket together, under their grandmother's blue beach umbrella with a white stripe. The umbrella was not far from the volleyball game, and the eyes of the Navy were often upon the two comely teenaged girls who lent such grace to their swimsuits.

Alas, a third granddaughter of Sarah's also shared her cousins' blanket. Isabelle was growing fairly tall too, but a pre-pubic plumpness made all onlookers aware that she was not in her cousins' league. She showed promise of becoming svelte and lovely, but in 1943 and 1944, she was clearly still a chubby child. Ida and Millie were kind to Isabelle, and she loved to listen to their grown-up conversation. But even more, she craved the stares her cousins so easily drew from all the young males on the beach. Thus, as the war in Europe soaked the ground of that continent with the blood of millions, and the war in the Pacific took human life as if human life had no worth at all, in Coney Island, normalcy was still the rule. Young men ogled lovely girls, and gawky pre-teens envied the loveliness that would soon be theirs too.

———

By the summer of 1940, France had capitulated and was out of the war. The Low Countries and Scandinavia were under German control, as well. Even the Soviet Union seemed to be on its "last leg." This vast country's European area had been largely overrun by German troops, who stood poised to enter Moscow. Bloody house-to-house fighting destroyed the city of Stalingrad, and was causing horrific loss of life to both the Nazis and the Russians. Besieged Leningrad was gripped in so deadly a siege that gigantic numbers of Russian lives were lost due to starvation and deprivation. To complete the dismal picture, a scorched earth policy was commanded by the Soviets, so that the invading Germans would not be able to live off the Russian land. This policy destroyed huge tracts of the Russian countryside.

Great Britain had suffered a terrible defeat at Dunkirk and was almost collapsing under the frightful battering its cities were taking from German bombs. Yet, only this badly wounded island democracy, in all of Western Europe, remained sufficiently on its feet to join the United States and the small contingent of Free French in a large counter attack against seemingly invincible Nazis. The counter attack began in 1942 with a joint Allied invasion of North Africa from which the invading armies slowly routed the Nazis. The Allies then invaded Sicily, and, with massive casualties, fought their way up most of the Italian boot.

While the fighting was bloody in both Africa and Italy, it was the bloodiest in the U.S.S.R. The Soviet forces very slowly, and with tremendous loss of life, pushed the Nazis from the gates of Moscow. The Nazis were also routed out of Stalingrad and westward across Russia's vast and endless European plain. The U.S.S.R. needed some relief, and kept agitating for a "Second Front" to relieve the pressure on them caused by Germany's gigantic army fighting in Russia.

The Second Front came in June of 1944. A joint American, British, and Free French force invaded Normandy, in France. Germany was forced to greatly reduce its army in the U.S.S.R., in order to fight the invaders in the west. A slow push from three sides ensued. Allied forces were pressing hard from the south in Italy and from the west in France. Russian forces were pressing hard from the east. In addition, American and British bombers were leveling Germany's cities. Yet, the seemingly doomed Nazi's, fought on.

———

As the Allied armies advanced across Europe, they came upon atrocities that transcended human belief. They found many camps to which Jews had been transported to be gassed to death and then burned in huge furnaces. Many other Jews lost their lives through the Nazi's deliberate policies of starvation, subjecting them to excessive exposure, torture, and to bogus, painful medical experiments, using healthy people as human guinea pigs. In Russia and Eastern Europe, gigantic pits filled with thousands of corpses were unearthed by the advancing Soviet army. The Nazis had emptied whole towns of Jews by brutally driving them to nearby forests, shooting them, and burying their bodies in massive pits.

Atrocities abounded in World War II, but the Nazi genocide against European Jews was without equal. Almost as brutal, however, were Nazi policies against gypsies, homosexuals, and the Nazi's political enemies. Eleven million innocent civilians were murdered by the Nazis during World War II. Six million or more of these were Jewish men, women and children. Hitler's government was fighting two wars – one was against the Allies and the other against the Jews.

The bombing of Pearl Harbor had caused the United States to lose most of its Pacific fleet. The United States also suffered some stinging defeats when the Japanese invaded and captured most of America's island possessions in the Pacific.

In order to turn the war in the Pacific around, the United States used a strategy called *island hopping*. Pacific islands, in Japanese hands, were invaded by American troops, one at a time. The battles that ensued during *island hopping* were usually very bloody. The Japanese were vicious and tenacious fighters, who usually fought to the death. It was their belief that to surrender to one's enemy was a terrible disgrace. Even after Germany's defeat in April of 1945, when the Americans were able to release many more troops to fight the Japanese, and the Japanese clearly understood that they couldn't win the war, they doggedly fought on.

Even though Japanese cities were being leveled by American bombers, the Japanese did not surrender until August of 1945, after the United States was forced to drop atomic bombs on the cities of Hiroshima and Nagasaki. America had been dropping leaflets on Japanese cities, warning that the United States was in possession of a terrible, new secret weapon that would be unleashed against them, if they did not surrender. The Japanese government didn't believe the warnings and Japan continued to fight on. Because of the Japanese practice of fighting to the death, American casualties were very high and would become even more astronomical if the United States' forces were forced to invade the Japanese home islands.

Therefore, a difficult decision was made. President Truman ordered the newly developed atomic bomb to be used against Japan. It was used in order to save American lives. When America had dropped the first atomic bomb on Hiroshima, the newspapers had reported it with gigantic headlines. Most Americans had never heard of Hiroshima, nor stopped to think of the suffering, pain, death and destruction that had been leveled against innocent men, women, and children on the ground. America and her allies rejoiced over the bombings and felt sure that the end of the war was at hand. Yet, the Japanese did not surrender. The second atomic bomb, dropped on Nagasaki, finished the job. The Japanese finally surrendered, and because the atomic bombs caused the war to be ended sooner, thousands of American lives were spared.

Isabelle rejoiced with everyone else when the atomic bombings took place. Until the pictures of the devastation and the severely wounded survivors were printed in the newspapers, very few people thought in terms of nuclear war's horrors. The world was now in a new era. With nuclear power, warfare had changed. The way was now clear for the next more frightening conflict, the Cold War. Now military giants would face off against each other threatening the use of nuclear weapons. Would these giant countries, who had been allies in World War II, live responsibly, or would all of humanity perish in a nuclear holocaust, caused by Communist countries and capitalist countries fighting against each other?

The Cold War ended and humanity did not! Yet the fear of nuclear holocaust remains. Today, many countries, some of them rogue nations, possess the means to destroy all of us. The threat is real and the future is unknown.

When World War II ended, few people fully understood what the attack on Hiroshima had unleashed. Would a doomed mankind find out, or would humanity possess the restraint to never again use nuclear weapons? People didn't ponder these apocalyptic questions at the war's end. In the victorious countries, there was too much to celebrate. And celebrate they did!

Chapter 9: The Aftermath

In August 1945, when the war ended, Coney Island was packed with vacationers, permanent residents, and sailors. Everyone celebrated. Everyone partied. Everyone rejoiced! The strict social mores of the time fell by the wayside. Teenage boys, sailors, and men of every stripe kissed girls they didn't even know; and it was all right. Old ladies sitting in the pavilion shook their heads at the sight of this joyous, but promiscuous hugging and kissing, and then they smiled. There was so much to celebrate.

Isabelle was sharing the blanket near the blue umbrella with the white stripe with her lovely older cousins, Ida and Millie. Three sailors walked up to them and each sailor lifted a girl up from the blanket and kissed her. Then they laughed and walked away. Isabelle was flabbergasted. A sailor had kissed her! Was she a grown-up now?

———

Another common celebration at the war's end was the block party. Bella took Isabelle and five year old Phyllis to Brooklyn to visit Anna and her family. The war had been over for four weeks, and Bristol Street, where Anna lived, was having a block party. Food and drink were being served in the roped off street. All traffic was re-routed, and people were dancing in the middle of the street to music blaring from a loud speaker.

Bristol Street was several blocks and many worlds away from the avenue on which the elevated train ran. The avenue covered by the elevated train tracks, was flanked by grey, tall, dismal apartment houses whose occupant's windows could see into the racing trains' lighted windows. These buildings housed *colored* (African-American) families, most of whom had emigrated from southern states to New York City during the war. The lure of the many available jobs in New York, and the wish for relief from the South's vicious practices of Jim Crow, had drawn thousands of colored people to many northern cities.

Because Bristol Street was so close to where they lived, several colored young men came to "scope out" the block party. Among them were two colored soldiers, wearing their uniforms and proudly displaying their overseas combat ribbons. One colored soldier approached mature-looking, thirteen year old Isabelle, and asked her to dance. (Isabelle was no stranger to colored people. Joan Underwood and Betty Braithwait were colored school friends that she liked very much.) Yet, when the young, colored soldier asked her to dance, she promptly refused him. She knew, instinctively, that in her world, in 1945, a white girl dancing with a colored boy was strictly taboo.

Isabelle had a lot of growing up to do. It would take her quite a few years to sort out what was and what was not bigotry; and to reject bigotry, regardless of whether it was leveled against colored people, Jews, women, or any other group persecuted without justification. She still needed to gain the courage to detach herself from the bigoted behavior so prevalent in the society in which she lived. She needed to gain the courage to follow her own heart and learn the bitter lessons taught by World War II.

As soon as the war ended, Jewish people in America who had left loved ones in what had been Nazi occupied Europe, contacted Jewish and non-sectarian relief agencies to help them find their relatives. In most cases, their searches were in vain. Their relatives were usually among the six million Jews who had perished at the hands of the Nazis.

Sonia, Anna's dearest friend, made this hapless, tragic search, only to find out that all of her brothers, sisters, their spouses, and their children had been murdered by the Germans. Her grief knew no bounds, but when she finally recovered sufficiently to return to an almost normal existence, Sonia felt impelled to put her affairs in order.

Sonia was a very good friend of Anna's, and an extremely hardworking woman. She never earned a great deal of money, because she was a lowly sewing machine operator in the garment industry; but no matter what she earned, it was more than enough to cover her needs, because her needs were less than modest. Sonia's rent was the pittance she forced Anna to accept. Her food needs were of the most modest kinds, because she hated spending any money unnecessarily. In addition, her desire for clothing was almost non-existent and she lacked clothing that most people would call "bare necessities." (One winter, in the midst of the Depression, when Bella was living on Home Relief, she took pity on Sonia and gave her a shabby, old coat that even impoverished Bella wore very infrequently because of its disreputable appearance. Bella did this, because on a visit to Anna's house, she had seen Sonia come home from work, on a bitterly cold winter evening, wearing only three disreputable-looking sweaters in which to fight the cold.)

In short, Sonia was a miser! She spent no money on pleasures, and denied herself many of the necessities that people ordinarily considered to be their due. Her only enjoyment was derived from her dear friend Anna's company and the pleasures she took in observing the development and growth of Anna's three children. To her immense delight, Anna's third child was born late in Anna's life, so Sonia was able to enjoy him as a toddler and as a young child, just at the time when she was extremely worried about her family in Poland.

By the time the news of her family's destruction came to Sonia, her miserly habits had permitted her to save the princely sum of $65,000. She decided to leave it all to Anna's youngest son, the little boy who had always given her so much pleasure.

Chapter 10: Summer, 1946

J ust before Isabelle entered High School, she met Collette. It was summer and Isabelle was staying at her grandmother's house. She planned to stay with Sarah until her mother collected herself and found a summer place for the family in Coney Island. In the meantime, Isabelle did not want to hang around in the Bronx. As soon as school let out, she packed two suitcases, took the long subway ride to Coney Island, and descended upon her surprised and completely delighted grandmother.

On the very next day, Isabelle went to the beach. There, on the first day at the beach in the summer of 1946, she ran into Irene, a girl she knew from her junior high school. Irene's family was spending the summer in Coney Island, but in Isabelle's estimation, Irene was barely tolerable, because she had a horrible tendency to lie and gossip. Isabelle would have kept her conversation with Irene very brief, but accompanying Irene was Irene's cousin from France. Isabelle found sixteen-year-old Collette, two years older than Isabelle and Irene, to be extremely interesting. Besides, on this first day at the beach, finding people to hang out with was a very important matter to Isabelle.

Collette was charming, soft-spoken, and quite pretty. Because she had come from France only six months before, Collette's English was weak; but she could make herself understood, as she "limped along" speaking English with a fetching French accent. Isabelle was enchanted.

Irene could see that Isabelle was attracted to her cousin, and it rankled her. Collette innocently turned much of her attention to Isabelle, causing Irene to snap curtly, "We have to go Collette. My brother is waiting for us."

Collette dutifully left with her cousin, but one could clearly see that the lovely French girl was not happy. Collette found life with Irene's family to be stifling. Not only did Irene control her social life, but living with her American relatives was stressful and noisy. Her cousins constantly argued with each other and could be counted upon to argue with their parents over almost everything. Adding even more noise, was the radio, which blared loud music all of the time. Collette, who had grown accustomed to the quiet of a convent, found the noise of her aunt's household very disconcerting. While the young French girl charmed most of her American acquaintances, she was not at all charmed by the environment in which she found herself.

Irene was very possessive, not allowing Collette to form friendships of her own. Isabelle had hoped that she and Collette could become friends, but Irene blocked any of Isabelle's friendly overtures. Isabelle finally gave up and turned elsewhere. As usual, Collette was forced to share only Irene's company, which did not satisfy her need for friends, at all.

———————

One evening, when Isabelle had come to the boardwalk to find some teenaged cronies, she stopped to chat with her grandmother, who was sitting on the bench just outside of the pavilion. Several elderly Jewish ladies sat with Sarah, and they vociferously praised her granddaughter's beauty. Isabelle was glad that this embarrassing praise was interrupted by a woman who was accompanied by a pre-teen girl.

"Hello Tante (Aunt)," the woman said to Sarah. She was more than plump, but her face and black hair were very beautiful. "How are you doing?" inquired the woman.

With a broad smile, Sarah said, "Oh my God! It's Esther! It has been a very long time since I've seen you." The two women embraced, kissed, and wept.

Speaking Yiddish, Esther said, "This is my daughter, Linda." In unaccented English, she said, "Linda, this is your great aunt, Sarah."

Sarah remarked that Linda was a pretty child. She then introduced Isabelle to Esther by saying, "This is Bella's daughter, Isabelle." And turning to Isabelle she said, "This is your second cousin, Esther, and her daughter, Linda."

Esther wore a large Star of David hanging on a gold chain around her neck. Tearfully she said, "Tante, I've never stopped being Jewish!"

Sarah replied, "Of course not. You are Jewish for life. Every member of our family is Jewish. But enough of this serious talk," Sarah continued. "What brings you to the boardwalk this evening?"

"We're taking a walk. I left my two boys at home with their father. We live only three blocks from here," answered Esther.

"Well," said Sarah, "when you go to the beach on Sundays, be sure to come to 29 Street. Most of my children and many of my grandchildren come to see me on Sunday. I sit under my blue umbrella with a white stripe. You can't miss us, and I'm sure your cousins would love to see you again and meet your children."

"Thank you Tante! Thank you! Thank you!" a very tearful Esther replied. When she walked away she was still weeping.

Mrs. Jessenou was the first of Sarah's scandalized cronies to pounce. "How could you?" she demanded. "Isn't that your niece who married a Christian?" she spit out. "Didn't your brother sit Shiva for her?" she continued venomously. "Isn't she dead to your family?"

"Does she look dead?" asked Sarah, through almost closed teeth. "Yes, she is my niece. She has been my niece since she was born, and will always be my niece, whether I like her behavior or not! My foolish brother sat Shiva for a child who is alive. To me, that is a bigger sin than marrying a gentile," continued Sarah. "I do not like to see Jewish children marry out of their religion. In fact, I hate it; so it hurt my heart when my brother's child did just that. But, she married a human being. She bore him three human children. And she and her children will always be members of my family!"

Sarah's cronies were fearful of Sarah's wrath, so their criticism immediately ceased.

———

The encounter with Esther bore fruit. On many Sundays that summer and in summers to come, Esther and her children visited with Sarah's children and grandchildren and any of the other family members who so often came to visit Sarah. Eventually, even Esther's siblings came, and they all were reconciled. Only Esther's parents remained estranged. To them, Esther was dead!

———

The summer of 1946 was the summer Isabelle's wish to be like her lovely cousins seemed to come true. It was impossible for the tall, black-haired, fourteen year old to walk on the beach without young male eyes following her. The bolder males made their presences known; and in the summer if 1946 Isabelle began to date.

Isabelle's first date was with Ira. Ira was a tall, blonde, handsome teenager, three years older than Isabelle. He asked her to come to a beach party on 30 Street, the street on which his family was staying for the summer. At the beach party, the teen-aged boys had made a fire in a metal garbage pail, where they cooked hot dogs. The evening was quite cool, so most of the teen-aged couples lying on their blankets covered themselves with other blankets, in order to stay warm. Ira and Isabelle did so to.

For a while, everything was alright. Ira's allergies were bothering him, so he was too busy sneezing and blowing his irritated nose, to bother Isabelle. All around them, couples were snuggling and kissing under their blankets, making fourteen year old Isabelle feel extremely uncomfortable. Ira, however, did not bother Isabelle, because his nose kept him otherwise occupied.

But then Ira's nose-blowing ceased and he turned his attention and his sore nose in Isabelle's direction. He tried to take her in his arms, causing the 14-year-old girl to panic. She jumped out from under the blanket and walked rapidly to the fire burning in the metal garbage pail. She studiously observed the activities around the fire – anything that would keep her out of Ira's reach!

Ira joined her and tried to coax her back under the blanket. Isabelle refused to budge. After the longest hour of her life, Ira took his frightened young date home – and that was the end of Isabelle's relationship with handsome, blonde Ira.

————

Isabelle never dreamt that the next boy she'd meet that summer would someday become very important to her. She met him in what she considered to be a very undignified way; and she was not personally impressed by him at all.

One cloudy summer day, that was too cool for the beach, Bella, Phyllis, and Isabelle decided to spend time with Sarah on the boardwalk. Six-year-old Phyllis and fourteen year old Isabelle were wearing identical red and white gingham skirts that their mother, in a rare spell of sewing creativity, had made for her two daughters. The girls looked nothing alike, and only because they were wearing identical skirts could anyone surmise that they were related to each other. Phyllis was a plump, adorable little girl, who wore her honey-blonde hair in long thick pigtails hanging down her back. Isabelle was a teenager, just emerging into mature, feminine beauty. Her long, wavy, black hair hung loosely down her back, stopping at her shoulder blades. She was slim, but curvaceous, and rather tall. Both lovely girls caught the attention of passerby's, who smiled as the girls enjoyed throwing a ball to one another.

Neither girl realized that they were being observed by a young man behind the counter of a concession stand in the building across the boardwalk from where they were playing. They might never have known, if Phyllis hadn't developed a sudden thirst and desire for a malt (called a *malted* in New York.) Phyllis ran to Bella, who was deeply involved in an interesting conversation, and rudely interrupted her. She asked her mother for money to buy a malted. Bella, not liking to be interrupted, quickly gave Phyllis the money, and returned to her conversation. Phyllis skipped happily to the concession stand to buy her drink.

"I'd like a chocolate malted with vanilla ice cream, please," the little girl told the young man behind the counter.

"Is that your sister you were playing with?" asked the young man.

"Yes," Phyllis answered.

"If you bring your sister over," he told the plump little girl, "I'll give you an extra scoop of ice cream."

In a flash, the excited Phyllis was at her sister's side. "That man over there," she said, excitedly pointing to the concession stand, "says he'll give me an extra scoop of ice cream if you come over."

"What are you crazy?" Isabelle retorted angrily. "Go get your malted and don't bother me! I don't go over to strange boys because they offer you some ice cream!"

Phyllis proceeded to "pitch a fit." She cried and carried on until it attracted Bella's attention. Bella, who was still embroiled in a lively conversation, didn't like being distracted, and didn't like hearing Phyllis's anguished pleas.

"What does she want?" asked the annoyed Bella. "Make her happy," she commanded.

Isabelle obediently, but reluctantly, walked over to the concession stand with Phyllis. The young man smiled at her broadly, while he concocted Phyllis's malted. He then said, "I've been watching the two of you play ball. You both look very pretty."

Isabelle remained silent.

He handed Phyllis her malted in a very large paper cup. She paid him, took the cup, and sauntered off toward the other side of the boardwalk. Before Isabelle could follow her, the young man asked, "Where do you sit on the beach?"

Isabelle, who thought the young man was presumptuous, answered saucily, "On the sand!"

"Come on," said the young man, his blue eyes twinkling, "I only wanted to join you on the beach. I have a portable radio, and I thought we'd both enjoy listening to *The Make-Believe Ballroom* together."

The young man had struck a chord! Avaricious Isabelle longed for a portable radio, but such radios were very expensive in post-war America, and not commonly owned in her circles. She looked at the young man and decided that even though he was pushy, she liked his smile and his beautiful blue eyes. While his nose and Adam's apple were large, his wavy dark hair was beautiful. All-in-all, Isabelle decided, he was really a good-looking boy.

"I sit at the blue umbrella with the white stripe," Isabelle said. "Come there tomorrow, if the weather is nice."

"I'll be there right after I get off," he said. "By the way, my name is Al."

"Mine is Isabelle," she said, and she turned away and walked back to her sister at the other side of the boardwalk.

———

On the following day, Al appeared with a huge, tan, imitation-leather portable radio. The two teenagers listened to popular music together and chatted. They talked about music, movies, and themselves. It turned out that during the school year, they both lived in the East Bronx, albeit quite a distance from each other. Al was sixteen and went to James Monroe High School, the school to which most of Isabelle's Jr. High School friends had gone. Both Al and Isabelle aspired to go to college when they graduated from high school.

When the two teenagers ran into the sea to swim, to their delight, they discovered that they were both strong swimmers. They swam and horse-played in the water for a long time.

The afternoon sped away and it was time for them to go home. Al walked home with Isabelle, helping her to carry the beach paraphernalia that she and Sarah had lugged to the beach earlier in the day. At her door, Al told her that Thursday was his day off. He asked Isabelle if she would join him for dinner at Nathan's hot dog stand and for a movie at the R.K.O. Theater.

Isabelle accepted his invitation, and they set a time for Al to pick her up.

———

On Thursday, everything started out well. Al and Isabelle chatted happily as they walked to Nathan's. They ate a delicious dinner of hot dogs, French fries, corn on the cob, and fruit drinks. Afterwards, they walked to a movie theater where they saw Ingrid Bergman in *Saratoga Trunk*.

In the darkened movie theater the whole tenor of the date changed for

Isabelle. Al put his arm around her shoulders. It made her nervous, but she didn't know how to free herself. In her mind, he was being very pushy, and she didn't like it at all.

After they left the movie theater, and all through the long walk home, Isabelle talked to Al in monosyllables. To her great distress, he still continued to keep his arm around her, this time around her waist. She couldn't wait until he dropped her off at her door. When he asked if she'd like to go to the movies with him on the following Thursday, she answered with a curt "No."

Al's feelings were visibly hurt. He bid her goodnight, turned and left.

––––––––––

If the date with Al was a disaster, the date with David was a delight! Isabelle met David in late July, when she encountered Irene and Collette walking on the boardwalk with three boys. One boy was Irene's brother and the other two were boys from New Jersey, whose families had spent the month of July vacationing in Coney Island. Both of their families were going back to New Jersey at the end of the month.

Irene introduced the two New Jersey boys to Isabelle. One of them was an incredibly handsome, green-eyed boy, who obviously found Isabelle as attractive as she found him. Isabelle, who had been strolling on the boardwalk with her friend Elaine, joined the other five teenagers. Isabelle immediately fell into an interesting conversation with David. At 27 Street, where Isabelle and Elaine lived, the two girls and David broke away from the group, and continued their conversation as they sat on a bench facing the sea. The other teenagers continued their stroll. Two hours later, the girls realized that it was 11:30 P.M., and they needed to go home. David offered to walk them to where they lived, but they both assured him that they would be alright without an escort. As they parted ways, David promised to see Isabelle at the blue umbrella with white strip on the following day. She said that she would look forward to it, and the three teenagers bid each other good night.

To Isabelle's distress, it rained relentlessly for the next two days. David and Isabelle, not knowing where the other lived, were unable to see each other while the rain fell.. On the third day, the sun shone brilliantly, so although the sand on the beach was still damp from the previous two days of rain, beach diehards started trekking back to the beach. Isabelle was among them, and she carried the blue umbrella with the white stripe.

When she arrived at the beach, Isabelle proceeded to put up the beach umbrella. As she was working, David came along and finished the job for her. Seventeen-year-old David looked and sounded wonderful to Isabelle; while David thought that, Isabelle was one of the prettiest girls he had ever seen.

David told Isabelle that he had a big problem. His family was returning to their home in northern New Jersey on Saturday night. If she would go out with him on Saturday night, he would probably have to stay at a hotel and then go home on Sunday. He planned to run this plan by his mother, but he didn't know if she would approve. He told Isabelle that he'd meet her that evening and tell her whether he had succeeded.

At 7:30 P.M., David and Isabelle met on the boardwalk. It was Friday night and the boardwalk was crowded with walkers. David and Isabelle didn't join them. They sat on a bench facing the ocean and talked. The first thing David told Isabelle was that he had made arrangements for Saturday night. The boy with whom he had been walking when he had met Isabelle was a friend of his from school. His family, too, had planned to leave Coney Island on Saturday night, but at the last minute, decided to stay another week. David said that he could sleep at their place on Saturday night and go home on Sunday. He hoped that Isabelle would spend most of Saturday afternoon and evening with him. Isabelle quickly agreed, and gave David her Coney Island address. She said that she would be looking forward to their time together on Saturday.

The gang of teenagers with whom Isabelle hung out, were sitting on the benches at 30 Street. David dropped her off there, where she joined her friend Elaine, with whom she planned to walk home later that night. David bid her a reluctant goodnight and went home to finish his packing. A very infatuated Isabelle couldn't wait for 1 P.M. on the next day, when David would pick her up for their long Saturday date.

At 1 P.M. David arrived at Isabelle's family's summer place on 27 Street.

The two teenagers took the subway to midtown Manhattan, chatting all the way. Their first stop was the Museum of Science and Industry. Both of them found the exhibits immensely interesting and had a particularly good time at the Bell Telephone exhibit. The Bell Telephone Company had rigged a device with which a person could pick up a telephone receiver, talk into it, and hear his own voice recorded just as he sounded on the telephone. In 1946, hearing one's own voice as it sounded on the telephone was unheard of. David enjoyed hearing his voice, but Isabelle was unpleasantly surprised when she heard hers. It sounded very different from the way she heard herself speak, and to her, her voice sounded tinny. It made her laugh, causing David to laugh too. They left the museum deep in conversation about why one's ears heard one's voice differently from how others heard it

The two teenagers had their dinner at a Chinese restaurant close by and then strolled over to Rockefeller Center. They had decided to see the film *Anna and the King of Siam*, playing at Radio City Music Hall. Both David and Isabelle had been to Radio City Music Hall and Rockefeller Center before, but they still were enchanted and commented on the beauty and vibrance of both places. On this magical night, everything looked bigger and better than it had ever appeared before.

After the movie, which they both enjoyed very much, they boarded the subway for the long ride to Coney Island. During a lull in conversation, Isabelle, who had had a full and glorious day, started to nod off. She forced herself awake, but David put his arm around her, laying her head upon his shoulder. In this manner, they traveled back to the Coney Island stop.

David escorted Isabelle to her door, kissed her cheek, bid her good night, and left. Isabelle, totally enraptured, was sure that she was in love with the handsome young man from New Jersey.

———

When Isabelle awoke on Sunday morning, she was stricken! She realized that David didn't have her winter address or even know her last name. With deep sadness, she donned her swimsuit to go to the beach, thinking that the most wonderful boy she had ever met was lost to her. Isabelle dejectedly went down the stairs to go to Elaine's house, so that the two of them could go to the beach together. To her surprise, as she passed the bank of mailboxes near the outer door, she spied an envelope stuck in the outside mounting of the boxes. It was addressed to:

"Isabelle

Second Floor Front Apartment"

Then the address on Twenty –Seventh Street in Coney Island. The return address was to David at his home in New Jersey.

A jubilant Isabelle tore open the envelope and read David's note. He told her how much he had enjoyed their day together and that he sincerely hoped she'd write back to him.

———————

Isabelle wrote back immediately, and a lively correspondence ensued. The correspondence, which continued over a two-year period, showed both young people that what could begin so propitiously could fade into nothingness.

In his letters, David would often comment negatively on something Isabelle had written. She would often think that a comment he made was arrogant or unkind. When he entered college, while she was still a "mere" high school student, she thought his letters had become condescending. Obviously, his remarks, and her negative reaction to them, were clear signs of their dissatisfaction with each other, and the correspondence ceased. With its end, the relationship between Isabelle and David died.

Chapter 11: Bigotry

High School was a terrible experience for Isabelle. Although she had no personal knowledge of the New York City Board of Education's practice of gerrymandering school districts to maintain de-facto segregation, Isabelle became a victim of the practice. Just as political gerrymandering is done to assure that certain populations will vote for the political party that has done the redistricting, school district gerrymandering was commonly done to assure that certain ethnic groups, especially African-Americans, remained mostly in separate schools. By making changes in the districts, the New York City Public Schools could effectively continue their de-facto segregation of most African-American students, even though housing patterns were changing and many African-Americans should have been going to predominantly "white" schools.

Students from Isabelle's area of the East Bronx had always gone to James Monroe High School. Because Isabelle aspired to be enrolled in the Honor School of James Monroe High School and follow in the footsteps of her idol, Millie, Fanny's daughter, Isabelle didn't even bother to take any of the tests open to students for enrollment in the special high schools New York City provided for students with special abilities. Her homeroom teacher had urged her to take the tests for Hunter High School and for the Bronx High School of Science. Both of these schools were for academically talented students. Isabelle did not consider herself academically talented, and she had already made up her mind. It was her wish to do as Millie had done. Little did she know that her plan would be dashed by the Board of Education's plans to redistrict her area of the Bronx, as part of their program of de-facto segregation of African-American students.

––––––––––

In the past several years, African-Americans had been moving up Boston Road and onto the streets surrounding Boston Road. They had not yet reached 170 Street, but were already filling in the streets in the 160's. As African-American families moved onto a street, most of the white families who lived there fled. Isabelle lived between 172 and 173 Streets. The redistricting encompassed the streets in the 170's, even though these were white neighborhoods, because by doing so, future redistricting would probably be precluded. Because of this redistricting, Isabelle found herself assigned to Theodore Roosevelt High School, while the vast majority of her friends were assigned to James Monroe High School. Isabelle was devastated!

––––––––––

One of the few friends who was forced to go to Roosevelt High School along with Isabelle, was her friend Sheila. Sheila lived around the corner from Isabelle on 172 Street. During the war, Bella had moved the family a block away from Charlotte Street to a lovely building with a courtyard at its entrance. In late 1944, she had rented an apartment that was very small, erroneously thinking that when the war ended, and Sidney returned from the Navy, the very severe housing shortage would abate, and she would be able to rent a larger apartment. This new little apartment was a miraculous find, because during World War II, New York, and indeed the nation, was suffering from an acute housing shortage. In New York, at this time, if an apartment became available, it was usually rented in an hour or less.

The new apartment on Minford Place consisted of one large bedroom, a living room, and a kitchen. The entrance foyer led to an area opposite the kitchen that was the size of a small bedroom, but afforded no privacy. Isabelle slept in the living room on a folding bed that was opened every night and closed every morning. Phyllis slept on a cot in her parents' bedroom. When Sidney returned from his service in the Navy, he slept on the same kind of folding bed that Isabelle used. His bed was opened in the area opposite the kitchen. If anyone wanted to access the kitchen from the bedroom, he would have to walk through the sleeping spaces of both Isabelle and Sidney. Privacy was an unknown entity in the tiny apartment on Minford Place.

If privacy was unknown during the night, neatness and aesthetic appeal were unknown in the bedroom, during the day. The bedroom set used by Bella and Hymie was quite nice looking, but its charm was totally lost during waking hours. During the day, Sidney's and Isabelle's folding beds were stored in the bedroom. Phyllis's cot was closed and stored there too.

Yet, as Isabelle grew older and learned about sexual abuse within other families, she realized how scrupulously careful she and the other members of her family had been to protect each other's privacy in all sexual matters. Hymie and Sidney never showed themselves without wearing either pajamas or trousers. At that time, the only naked males that Isabelle had ever seen were babies or very young little boys. The females in Bella's family were equally fastidious about covering their private parts. In Bella's family there may have been a lack of privacy and an exceedingly cluttered bedroom, but never a lack of dignity or decency.

————

Sheila and Isabelle often traveled together to and from Theodore Roosevelt High School. Sheila not only was pretty, she was very intelligent. She earned stellar grades, and she and Isabelle spoke about going to college together. When they became high school students, in the winter semester of 1947, they found it difficult to adjust to Theodore Roosevelt High School. It was a huge school with *Up* staircases and *Down* staircases. Students came from the neighborhood in which the girls lived, and from Little Italy. There were even some students who came from the more affluent Grand Concourse neighborhoods. Isabelle and Sheila had hoped to cling to each other in this huge land of strangers, but to their dismay, discovered that they were in few classes together and had no lunch periods scheduled at the same time. They were mostly in the company of the many strangers, from disparate parts of the Bronx, who attended Roosevelt High School with them.

Isabelle soon began to form opinions and became quite curious about some of her fellow students. When she realized that the quiet, sandy-haired girl who sat next to her in math class was also in her English class, she struck up several conversations with her in the hope that they would like each other and possibly become friends. She learned that Edith lived on the other side of Crotona Park. They lived a long, but doable walk from each other, so they decided to meet on the following Saturday to go to see a movie at a movie theater located almost between where they each lived.

On Saturday, after meeting as planned, the girls went to the movies and then bought ice cream sundaes at a nearby candy store. As they ate their sundaes, Edith asked Isabelle if she was born in New York City. When Isabelle answered in the affirmative, Edith told her that she was born in Munich, Germany. In 1935, when Edith was only four years old, her parents were deeply worried about her safety and the safety of her father, and her one-year-old baby brother. Her father was Jewish and quite wealthy. Because he had been a highly decorated soldier in World War I, he and Edith's mother decided to "tough-out" the Nazis and their anti-Semitic policies. Edith's father transferred most of his property and wealth to his Catholic wife, and tried to keep a low, personal profile. It was her parents' fervent hope that a wealthy war hero, married to a Catholic woman, would escape molestation from the Nazis. Even though Edith's father suffered occasional insults for being Jewish, and his wife was treated rudely for having been married to a Jew, they both tried to ignore their tormentors and lead normal lives. Through connections that he had, Edith's father even was able to enroll little Edith in a Nazi sponsored nursery school.

Four-year-old Edith kept hearing the terrible talk against Jews. It made her very uncomfortable, because she knew that her father was Jewish and that she was half-Jewish. Young as she was, however, she said nothing and participated in everything her school required of its pupils.

One day, the children were told that a very important Nazi official was planning to pay their school a visit. The children began to work diligently at making decorations for his visit. At the teacher's direction, most of the decorations had Nazi motifs.

When the awaited day arrived, the classroom and halls were decorated with the children's Nazi inspired artwork. As usual, the teacher and the children began the school day by raising their right arms in the Nazi salute. The teacher then introduced their uniformed guest, who greeted the small children, and then proceeded to tell them how lucky they were that the Fuehrer cared about children and the purity of German blood. He assured them that, in the not-too-distant future, all pure Germans like themselves, would no longer need to worry about the preservation of the German race. Racial inferiors, like the Jews, would soon be driven out of Germany.

Little Edith was in acute distress. She didn't want this evil man to drive her father away. And what about herself? Did this nasty Nazi wish to drive her out of Germany too? Was she, like her father, impure?

Their guest began to wander around the tables occupied by the young children. Periodically, he would stop and comment on a picture a child was drawing, or comment on the child herself. When he got to Edith's table he said, "What is this pretty girl drawing today?" He picked up her picture to examine it. It was a picture of a house with trees and flowers around it. A bright yellow sun hung in the sky.

"This is a pretty picture drawn by a pretty Aryan girl," said the Nazi.

Edith knew she wasn't an Aryan, and she hated the Nazi with all of her heart. She never did know what possessed her to behave as she did, but as the man returned her drawing to her table, she grabbed his hand and bit it with all of the strength she could put into her little teeth.

The Nazi guest yelped in pain!

The teacher yanked Edith out of her seat and marched her to the school's office. Her mother was called on the telephone and told to come and get her daughter immediately. Within minutes her mother arrived and took Edith home.

That night, an Aryan friend who had gone to school with Edith's father, and with whom Edith's father had served in the Kaiser's army, stealthily arrived at the kitchen door, located in the back of the house.

He told Edith's father that he and his daughter must leave Germany immediately. He said that both of their lives were in great danger.

Being a very wealthy man, Edith's father was able to give the proper bribes to the proper people. Father and daughter left Germany within four days. Edith's father was unable to bring very much money with them, but he could take himself and his daughter to the safety of Denmark, and from there, in five months, to the United States. In the United States, Edith's father had cousins who had fled Germany too. His cousins promised to help him raise his little girl.

Edith's mother was left in their large house in Munich. Although all of the family's wealth had been transferred to her, as time passed, it didn't keep her or her little boy from being deeply humiliated, almost daily. Even though she had divorced Edith's father, people treated her like a wanton woman, because she had been married to a Jew. Her little boy was attacked when he went outdoors, and he was not permitted to go to any school, but a school established by Jews for Jewish children. This was unacceptable to his mother. She got around this dilemma by asking her priest to come to their home to teach her son.

In time, having no ration books for her half-Jewish son, Edith's mother was forced to do what the few remaining Jews in Munich did to survive – buy food and clothing on the Black Market. (Most of the Jews in Munich had already emigrated or had been deported to the east.)

When the Allied bombings began, life became fraught with even more danger. Edith's half-Jewish brother was not permitted to seek safety in a bomb shelter. Consequently, his Catholic mother didn't seek safety in a shelter either. Both of them, petrified with fright, sat in their basement during the interminable air raids. Edith's mother constantly prayed to the Virgin Mary to protect them and get them through the war.

Before the war ended, the Nazis confiscated their house, along with most of their wealth. From January 1945 until the Nazis surrendered in May of 1945, the two pariahs suffered more than ever before. The relentless bombings and the scarcity of funds made housing and food even less accessible. Edith's mother prayed for the war's end, but feared that she and her son would not live to see it.

Yet somehow they did. Furtively living in a bombed-out crater that had once been a building, they were barely existing. They emerged from the crater filled with deep bitterness and an even deeper anti-Semitism, that Edith's mother had successfully imparted to her pre-adolescent son. She wished to be reunited with Edith and her father, but she was determined to make some serious changes in all of their lives.

————

Edith's mother and brother arrived in New York City in 1946. Edith, who was completely Americanized, felt strange in the presence of her curt, very German mother. While her father tried hard to embrace the new arrivals and make them feel loved and comfortable, he had difficulty relating to the trauma that they had endured in Nazi Germany. He wanted a fresh and happy start for all of them. His wife wanted immediate conversion to Catholicism for her son, her daughter, and her husband. When Edith and her father tried to convince her that they loved their Judaism and that it presented no danger in the United States, their pleas for understanding only evoked tirades that sounded like the speeches at Nazi rallies. Consequently, no affection grew between Edith's parents or her brother or herself. The constant discord made it clear that they needed distance between them. The family split, leaving Edith motherless and without a brother, and leaving her brother filled with hate, without a sister and without a father.

Edith's tragic story broke Isabelle's heart. In Isabelle's mind, Edith's entire family were victims of the Nazis. Even though they all survived, young as Isabelle was, she realized that every member of that family was deeply scarred for life.

————

Isabelle continued to be friendly with Edith, but her closest high school friend was still Sheila. When spring came, Isabelle and Sheila often went to the playground in Crotona Park and played on the apparatus or played ping-pong. At that time, there were several older boys at the playground that neither Sheila nor Isabelle had seen before. Their English was quite poor and they spoke it only when they spoke to Americans. When they spoke to each other, they spoke in a Slavic language that Isabelle couldn't identify.

After a few visits to the park, the boys began to smile at Sheila and Isabelle and make occasional comments on each other's activities. After several more days, they began to chat with each other, easily. The girls learned that the boys were survivors of Nazi concentration camps. Three of them were from Czechoslovakia and one of them was from Poland. Only one boy, Marty Bernowitz, lived nearby. He had come to America in 1946, to live with his mother's sister who lived on Charlotte Street. The other boys traveled to Crotona Park from other parts of the Bronx. All four boys had met in a displaced person's camp after the war had ended and had emigrated to the United States at the same time.

Marty Bernowitz was nineteen years old. He and his friends were very muscular, because they constantly worked out on the playground's apparatus. They were all beautifully built and very proud of their bodies. They told the girls that when they were liberated they were little more than sick, walking skeletons. After their stay in the displaced person's camp they were still scrawny, and they were still too thin even when they arrived in America. They maintained that their beautiful bodies were a result of good American food and working out in the park.

Marty was the most talkative of the survivors. He seemed to have really taken a shine to Sheila. It was clear that he felt a need to tell her his story. Isabelle and Sheila listened avidly to the handsome boy's stories and empathized greatly with his sadness.

Marty had come from a family that consisted of his mother, father, brother, baby sister and himself. They had lived in Prague, Czechoslovakia and were deported to Theresienstadt, just forty miles away from the city in which they had lived. Theresienstadt was disguised, by the Nazi's, as a "model ghetto." Families often lived together, but death from disease and malnutrition proliferated. In 1942, when deportations to Auschwitz began, Marty's father was deported and never seen again. A year later, Marty's mother and her three children were deported. When they arrived at Auschwitz, Marty was sixteen years old, his brother was nineteen, and his baby sister was four.

Marty's baby sister was a very pretty blond, blue-eyed little girl. When she and her family arrived at the Auschwitz train platform, the S.S. doctor making selections took time from his labors to appreciate her beauty and to talk to her kindly. After declaring that she was "as pretty as an angel," he directed her and her mother to the left. Marty and his brother went to the right. Those people directed to the left were put into the backs of trucks and immediately taken to the gas chambers and murdered. Marty's last sight of his mother and little sister was of them forlornly waving goodbye, as the trucks pulled away.

At Auschwitz, Marty and his brother did everything possible to remain together. They slept in the same bunk, tended each others' frequently inflicted wounds resulting from the vicious guards' beatings, and tried to be together as much as possible in order to be assigned to the same work details. But as the war was coming closer to its end, the two brothers found themselves separated from each other at their work assignments. Marty's brother was placed on a work detail that sorted the clothing of the new arrivals to Auschwitz. Marty was assigned to the job of shaving off the hair of those new arrivals that had not been gassed immediately.

For a while, Auschwitz was a busier place than ever. Trains from Hungary were transporting thousands upon thousands of hapless Hungarian Jews to their doom. Marty and his brother had lots of work to do.

As the Russian army came nearer to the death camp, huge marches of prisoners were organized according to sex. The thousands of emaciated, debilitated prisoners were marched in the direction of Germany. Marty and his brother became aware of the fact that they were participants in a *death march*, from which few, if any, of the marchers would survive. They were being forced to maintain a lively pace, far beyond their capacity to endure. If a prisoner dropped to the icy road because of injury or fatigue, he was shot immediately. Although the prisoners were mostly denied food and water, they were expected to keep walking. If they were unable to do so, they were executed.

Marty and his brother understood that few, if any, of the prisoners would survive the freezing march, so they stealthily made plans to try to escape. Their opportunity presented itself, when they came upon a trench at the side of the road, just at a time when their guard was otherwise occupied. They both rolled into the trench and lay there without movement until the marchers had all passed their inert bodies. Anyone seeing their bodies in the trench would have concluded that they were marchers who had died.

When the marchers had all passed, a very cold, ragged pair of emaciated young men picked their way across the fields, until they came to a farmhouse. They knocked, and to their delight, the farmer's wife spoke kindly to them and gave them each a blanket and a pair of socks. She fed them several bowls of hot soup and then directed them to the barn. She said that they could sleep in the hayloft that night.

Totally exhausted, the two brothers wrapped themselves in the blankets and collapsed in the hayloft. They slept until the cock crowed. They were just getting ready to leave, when the farmer's wife arrived. Speaking Slovakian, she wished them well and gave them each a loaf of bread, and four cooked potatoes. They answered her in Czech, thanking her profusely for her kindness.

After they ate one of the loaves of bread and one potato each, they started on their way. They found the road where they had previously been marching, and then proceeded to guide themselves by using the sun to keep them going west. They hoped to cross the border to the Czech part of their country, where their intention was to find some help to get them to Prague.

The boys had not walked more than four miles, when they heard a loud rumbling. They flung themselves to the ground in an area of tall dead grass, and trembling with fear, waited to see what was making the noise. They did not have long to wait. Coming toward them on the road, were three tanks, several armored trucks, an automobile carrying two highly ranking officers, and a long line of foot soldiers. It was clear to the brothers that these were not Germans. When the soldiers were passing, they could catch snatches of conversation. The soldiers seemed to be speaking Russian! The Russians had come! The brothers were free!

The two skeletal young men staggered out to the road with their hands held high. They kept shouting in Czech, "Welcome Liberators. Welcome!" Several Russian soldiers surrounded them, guns drawn. "We were prisoners in a concentration camp....we escaped a forced march....we're Jews," they tried to explain.

One of the Russian soldiers broke rank and ran over to the two brothers. In Yiddish, he said, "Did I hear you correctly? Did you say that you're Jews?"

"Yes," answered Marty's brother. We stole away from a forced march from Auschwitz Concentration Camp. We'd like to go to Prague, the city we come from." He too was speaking Yiddish, albeit poorly.

"We are an advance unit of the Soviet Army," the soldier said. "Prague is still in Nazi hands. Let me see if I can get you a ride back to Ruzomberok, which is now in our hands. It is not far from here, and you should be able to stay there in safety until you can go home to Prague."

With that, the Yiddish-speaking Russian soldier ran up to the car inching slowly behind the tanks. He saluted the officers within, and proceeded to tell them about the two escaped prisoners. The Russian officers looked Marty and his brother over, and then detailed one of the trucks to take them on a very fast trip to Ruzomberok, explain their situation at headquarters there, and quickly catch up with their unit again.

———

Marty and his brother were whisked to Ruzomberok, where they remained until Prague was out of German hands. The brothers immediately returned to the newly liberated Prague, but found none of their Jewish family or friends there. Very saddened, but pressed by necessity, they quickly sought living quarters and jobs to sustain themselves in their native city.

Both brothers found work in a large restaurant located in a very busy area of Prague. Marty was hired as a dishwasher and his brother took a job as a waiter. His brother instructed Marty not to tell anyone that they were Jews. He suggested that they keep their true identities a secret until they were sure of conditions in the recently liberated city.

The boys worked hard, ate decently, and rested....causing them to regain some of their strength. They even began to socialize with some of their younger co-workers. Marty's brother was becoming involved with the restaurant's pretty, young hostess. The two of them often went off together after they finished their work in the restaurant.

———

In time, Marty was becoming restless. Unlike his brother, he had formed no important relationships in Prague. In fact, he was "spooked" by the city in which he had grown up as a beloved member of a family that had perished as if they had never existed. The absence of the life and the people he had known and loved, made Prague seem like a huge graveyard, causing Marty to wish to move on. Marty had heard of large displaced persons camps that had been established in Germany, where the inhabitants were mostly Jews, who had somehow managed to survive the Nazi genocide. Other people, in smaller numbers, from all over what had been Nazi occupied Europe, were in these camps too. Most of them had been deported to Germany to be used as slave laborers, or had been deported to Nazi concentration camps for a myriad of political, racial, or sexual reasons. All of these people found themselves in the displaced persons' camps, where many waited for repatriation to their native lands.

Unlike gentile displaced persons, those Jews who followed the course of repatriation to their native lands, often found their ex-neighbors to be inhospitable. In Poland, the country from which the largest number of Jewish survivors came, their "countrymen" not only hindered their return, but often instituted bloody pogroms, attacking and killing many Polish Jews who had survived Nazi anti-Semitism.

Seeing the calamities visited on the remnant of Europe's Jewry in their original homelands, Jewish organizations tried, wherever possible, to reunite survivors with relatives living outside of Europe. If such relatives existed, the Jewish philanthropic organizations, worked hard to unite them with their surviving relatives who had suffered so much in Europe. The more Marty thought of the displaced person's camps and the help of Jewish organizations, the more he wanted to try his luck in one of them. His brother, however, had different aspirations. He wanted to marry the restaurant's pretty hostess, become a Catholic, and forget that he was ever a Jew. Living in Prague suited him, and he did not want to embark on an adventure that might reunite him with the beleaguered Jewish community.

The brothers could not agree. finally, Marty decided to go to Germany alone. He wanted to get himself situated in a displaced persons' camp, where he could be helped to reestablish his life among his fellow Jews. He sadly bid his brother farewell, knowing that his brother's desertion of Judaism would probably cause an irreparable rift between them.

Marty was in the displaced persons' camp for a little more than a month, when *HIAS* (Hebrew Immigrant Aid Society) located his aunt who lived on Charlotte Street. She had been searching for members of her family since the war's end.

Letters began to fly between Marty and his aunt. She invited Marty to come to the United States and live with her and her family. When Marty agreed, she started working with HIAS, and in the spring of 1946, Marty immigrated to America, where he went to night school to become more proficient in English. He worked in a super market and gave half of his small salary to his aunt for his room and board. His major plan was to own his own business and continue his education which had been stolen from him by the Nazis.

In his spare time, Marty and his friends worked out in Crotona Park. Along with working out, he had met Sheila in the park. Although she was barely fifteen, and a very protected American girl, Marty thought that she was mature, and he developed a serious interest in her.

Sheila's parents absolutely forbade their daughter to have anything to do with the survivors who worked out in the park, because her mother believed that a survivor's experiences and losses at the hands of the Nazis would have probably altered his personality in such a negative way, that a protected and deeply loved American girl would be unable to deal with him or his bitter past. Right or wrong, Sheila was forbidden to go to the park. She obeyed, and along with her, Isabelle stayed away from the park too.

Sheila's absence from the park deeply hurt Marty. Just as he was once again feeling affection for another human being, she disappeared. Marty's losses seemed unendurable, but he endured them and was sadly determined to continue to work and to learn.

Isabelle was once again struck by the cruelty of bigotry. Even though Marty had survived the war, he had lost his family, his brother, his education, and even the country in which he grew up. She knew that in order to overcome these devastating losses and develop a good life in America, he would have to possess tremendous strength and determination. He was on his own in a strange country, oppressed by very bitter memories. Would his personal strength help him to endure his pain and make a happy life for himself; or would he never fully integrate into his new life, and become a depressed, permanent casualty of the bigotry that he had endured?

———

Tante Chiriva was Bella's aunt on her father's side. Unlike Sarah she was literate, and up until the outbreak of World War II, had maintained a correspondence with some relatives and friends that she had left behind in Russia when she had immigrated to America in 1910. When World War II ended, she sought to resume the correspondence that the war had interrupted, but to no avail. All of her letters remained unanswered, and were returned to her marked "person unknown."

Chiriva went to her sister-in-law Sarah, her late brother Michel's wife, and asked her if she had heard from any of her family or friends. Sarah said that she had lost touch with the Russian branch of the family many years before. However, she added, only six of her eleven siblings had immigrated to the United States, so certainly some of her remaining five siblings and their children should still be in or around Vashisht or Narovle. Being unable to write, she gave Chiriva their names and the places where they had lived when she was in touch with them, and Chiriva said that she would try to contact them.

Many months passed, and to everyone's relief, in the summer of 1946, Chiriva excitedly told Sarah that she had heard from Sarah's youngest sister, Chaya. Chaya wrote that everyone in both of their large families had perished at the hands of the Nazis, except for Sarah's sister Leah, Leah's eldest daughter, Chaya's youngest daughter, and Chaya herself. She said that they were in great need of bedding and warm clothing. She also asked for information about her American brothers and sisters and their offspring.

Upon reading the letter, Sarah and Chiriva wailed loudly. The wailing then turned into terrible, unrelieved crying. Finally the crying was replaced with a long period of moaning and deep sighs, as the two women dwelt on their terrible losses. But, in a few days, with great difficulty, they put their mourning aside and turned their concentration upon their living relatives, still in Russia. Sarah began to fill a huge box with bedding, blankets, and clothing that she hoped would fit her surviving sisters and her two nieces. Chiriva enclosed a long, newsy letter about the family members living in America.

A letter arrived from Chaya almost six months later. She thanked her sister for the useful package and she thanked Chiriva for the news she had sent about her American family. She then informed Sarah and all of her other American relatives that she no longer wanted any mail from them. "It is better," she said, "for Soviet citizens and Americans to have nothing to do with each other."

Both Chiriva and Sarah understood that Chaya was terminating all correspondence between them, because she feared her own government. After some tearfulness and many sighs, Sarah said, "I guess because the American government and the Russian government disagree on many issues, it is unsafe for Soviet citizens to correspond with their relatives in America. Nothing much changes in Russia. The government in power now, just like the government of the Czar, terrifies its own people. No one ever feels safe in Russia. If it isn't murderous foreigners killing innocent people, the people's own government can be vicious and murderous. I always said that you can't trust Russians!"

Isabelle hated Theodore Roosevelt High School. She knew that she was sent there because of the bigotry of the New York City Board of Education. She also knew, however, that she would have to endure the hated school, if she were to achieve her goal of going to college; so endure she did! She entered High School in the tenth grade, having completed ninth grade in Junior High School. She needed to complete the tenth, eleventh, and twelfth grades in order to graduate. She decided to increase the number of major subjects she took each semester, thereby accumulating enough credits to graduate and still be able to skip one semester of high school. Through this device, she shortened her stay at the hated school, and graduated from high school in June of 1949, when she was not quite seventeen years old. In September of 1949, Isabelle became a student at Hunter College, in New York City. She had just turned seventeen when she entered college.

In her upper freshman semester at Hunter College, Isabelle ran into Irene, whom she had not seen since the summer of 1946. Unlike Isabelle, Irene had gone to James Monroe High School. Irene told her that she and her French cousin Collette couldn't get along, so two years earlier, when Collette was eighteen years old, she went off on her own. Within six months she had married a soldier, and no one had heard from her since.

That night, Isabelle couldn't get lovely Collette out of her mind. The pretty, quiet, unhappy French girl never found a family in the United States. Bigotry had taken her own family and country away from her. Her childhood had been full of insecurity and fear. Collette, along with Marty, Edith, Edith's German family, and Isabelle's unknown Russian family had suffered the ultimate bigotry at the hands of the Nazis. Yet, Isabelle sadly realized, bigotry was still alive and well throughout the world and in the United States too.

Isabelle, 16 years old, on the boardwalk of Coney Island, on a cold winter day in 1948

Sarah and Isabelle, winter, 1948

Sarah and Isabelle on the beach, 1948

Sarah and Al on the beach, 1948

*Isabelle, Coney Island,
New York, 1949*

*Isabelle on the beach at Coney
Island, New York with the Pavilion
in the background, 1949*

*Isabelle, Coney Island,
New York 1950*

*Al on the Boardwalk, Coney
Island, New York 1950*

Chapter 12: Teenage Years

When school let out in June of 1947, Isabelle did not have the patience to wait for her mother to collect herself and find a place for the family to live in Coney Island for the summer. She, therefore, did what she had done at the beginning of the summer, the year before. As soon as school was out, she descended on her grandmother in Coney Island. As expected, Sarah was delighted to have Isabelle, and on Isabelle's first night there, arm-in-arm, grandmother and granddaughter walked to the boardwalk together. When they arrived on the boardwalk, Sarah joined her singing friends in the pavilion, leaving Isabelle to her own devices.

Isabelle felt lost. She did not see anyone she knew, and was about to go back to Sarah's house to read, when she saw Al. Al was at the other side of the boardwalk with a fairly large group of teenagers, talking and horsing around. Even though Isabelle was not particularly fond of Al, she wanted to be part of the teenage group, so she walked up to Al, greeted him with a big smile, and struck up a conversation with him. A very pleased young man introduced Isabelle to the other boys and girls and then commenced to turn away from them and converse only with Isabelle.

Al told Isabelle that he had graduated from James Monroe High School and would be attending City College in the fall. Isabelle knew that only bright people, who passed a difficult entrance examination, were admitted to C.C.N.Y. In her mind, this was a plus for Al. He also mentioned that he still worked at Moore's Concession Stand until 4:00 P.M., and he asked her if he could see her on the beach. She acquiesced, because he had been so gracious when he introduced her to his friends. She believed that the young man with the lovely blue eyes deserved a second chance.

Isabelle saw Al on the beach or on the boardwalk for four consecutive days. They had fun together, swimming and talking. Al was a fabulous joke teller. He had a joke for every situation, but some of his jokes were off color. Fifteen year old, still prudish Isabelle was not sure she liked these dirty jokes. Having memories of the previous summer, and just having been regaled with Al's dirty jokes, Isabelle agreed to go to the movies with Al with some trepidation.

On Thursday, Al picked Isabelle up at her grandmother's house. Once more they walked to Nathan's and ate its delicious fare until they were stuffed. They then went to the movies, where once again Al put his arm around Isabelle. She was a year older and a year bolder, so Isabelle removed his arm. For the next thirty or thirty-five minutes they watched the movie in silence. When Al put his arm around her again, she removed it and hissed, "Keep your arm to yourself." The rest of the movie was viewed in silence, and the generally loquacious pair walked back to Sarah's house saying almost nothing to each other.

There were no more dates with Al. Isabelle, however, now had a circle of friends at the beach, and had become acquainted with quite a few boys who asked her out on dates. Her summer was full of good times, except for three incidents…two of them with a boy named Vic.

Isabelle's friend Elaine was back at Coney Island for the summer. On one evening's walk the two girls met three older boys from Bayridge, Brooklyn. All three of the boys had just been discharged from the army and had very interesting tales to tell of their experiences in the Army of Occupation in Japan. They walked the girl's home and left them with promises of seeing them the next day, on the beach.

On the following day, two of the Brooklyn ex-soldiers appeared at the blue umbrella with the white stripe. One of them, called Vic, plopped down on the blanket next to Isabelle and Elaine and began to talk to them about his plans. In September he would be entering the University of Wisconsin to begin his work toward a degree in either Chemistry or Physics. He didn't know what he would do with a degree in science, but he knew that science was certainly his main interest.

Isabelle told him that she still had two more years in high school, hoping that he would assume that she was sixteen years old. Vic did make that assumption, and he was aghast! He had thought that Isabelle was young, but certainly not as young as sixteen. He quietly informed her that he was twenty years old, and sixteen was really too young for him. Both ex-soldiers stayed for a short while, and then left. Disappointed, Isabelle was sure that she would never see Vic again.

That evening, when Isabelle was "hanging out" with the bunch of teenagers who "hung out" on the boardwalk between 29 Street and 30 Street, Vic suddenly appeared. He asked her to leave the group and take a walk with him; and she did. As they walked, Vic told her why he had come back to see her. He said, "I have a twin sister who has always been my favorite person in the whole world. She looks nothing like me. She is as dark, as I am fair. When we were little, we played together, and even though, as we grew older, we went our separate ways with our different friends, if there was anything important on our minds, we shared it with one another. While I was in Japan, my sister met a guy with whom she fell in love. They're engaged and will be married in a year and a half, when Vicky graduates from Brooklyn College."

"That first night when I saw you on the boardwalk, you stopped me in my tracks. You look enough like Vicky, to be her younger sister; but you're even prettier than she is. When you meet Vicky, don't tell her I said that. I really felt that I needed to know you, but when I learned that you were sixteen and would graduate from high school in two years, I felt that I was "robbing the cradle"…yet, when I walked away, I knew that I wanted to come back and see you again. That's why I'm here tonight."

Isabelle was touched by Vic's story, but very nervous about their age difference. If he learned that she was only fifteen, would he leave and never come back? And if he did come back, Isabelle was sure that Bella would absolutely forbid her to date a boy who was five years older than she.

226

"Vic," Isabelle replied, "you assumed that I'm sixteen, because I'm graduating in two years. You think sixteen is very young….Well, I'm not sixteen….I'm fifteen! But I really will be graduating in two years. If my age doesn't scare *you*, then *your* age will surely scare my mother!"

"This is truly a problem," said Vic. "I met your mother at the beach and she seemed very nice. Let me come to see you at the beach and let's see how awful our age difference really is. I really like talking to you, and I can get to know your mother at the beach, too."

"Okay," said Isabelle. "Come see me at my grandmother's blue and white umbrella."

For three weeks, Vic did come to the beach two or three times a week. He met Sarah and spoke Yiddish with her. He also met several of Isabelle's cousins who had spread their blankets on the sand around the blue umbrella with the white stripe. Everyone liked Vic, even Bella. But, as expected, Bella didn't like the five-year age difference between him and her daughter. As his visits increased, however, when Vic asked Isabelle if she would go out with him and some friends who lived in Rockaway, Bella reluctantly gave her permission, because she liked the young man. The stage was now set for two more of Isabelle's bad experiences in the summer of 1947.

––––––––

On Saturday night, Vic drove up to Isabelle's Coney Island home. He was dressed nicely and his blonde hair was slicked down. An excited, happy Isabelle left with him; but her mother, was left with misgivings.

First Vic drove to his friend Burt's house in Far Rockaway. After Burt entered the car, they drove about ten blocks to Carla's house. Carla was a small, feisty girl who had just graduated from high school. She and Burt promptly got into the back seat and began to "make out." Isabelle and Vic could hear the very recognizable sounds they were making, and Isabelle became completely uncomfortable.

"Cool it," Vic told them. "You're not alone." But the couple in the back of the car continued the noises and gyrations that rocked the automobile.

The behavior in the back of the car, struck young Isabelle dumb!

All she wanted to do was go home. Gathering all of her courage, she demanded, "Where are you taking us?"

Vic, speaking in a good-natured voice, and sounding unperturbed, answered, "I thought we'd go to Bayridge, where I live. Bayridge is on the water and we can park the car and see the boats and the lights of the city."

Isabelle courageously whispered, "I will not stay in a car with such carrying on! I want to go home!"

"I respect you Isabelle and I would never do anything you didn't approve of," Vic whispered. "We can leave them in the car and walk along the ocean walkway. On a lovely night like this, there will be lots of people around."

Isabelle's silence was taken as her agreement, and Vic drove the car to a lovely place facing the water. There were many cars parked there, pedestrians walking, and people sitting on benches facing the sea. True to his word, Vic parked the car, and he and Isabelle left it.

They strolled in silence for about ten minutes, when Vic said, "I have three more weeks at home, and then I go to Wisconsin until Thanksgiving. I hope that you don't hold me responsible for Burt's and Carla's behavior. I truly respect you, and would have never put you in the position you're in tonight. I would like to see more of you in what's left of the summer, and I'd like us to write to one another while I'm at school. How do you feel about it?"

Isabelle was moved by the beauty of the night and Vic's seeming sincerity. She promised to write to him.

When they returned to the car, a very disheveled pair sat on a bench close by. Burt and Carla must have finished whatever "business" they were conducting in the back seat, and then left the car for a cleaner breath of fresh air.

Vic harshly told them that he was taking them home. The trip to Far Rockaway was mostly silent, and when Vic finally dropped them off at Carla's house, Isabelle breathed a sigh of relief. (Her first bad experience was over.)

Vic heard Isabelle's sigh, and once again apologized. They chatted contently all the way back to Coney Island.

Vic found a parking spot about a block from where Isabelle lived. He said that he was sorry for their terrible evening and that if she would go out with him again, he promised that there would be no other couple with them. They'd go to Sheepshead Bay for a wonderful seafood dinner and just really enjoy each other's company. He then took Isabelle in his arms and kissed her.

The young couple got out of the car and began to walk the block to Isabelle's house, when they encountered Isabelle's second bad experience, in the guise of frantic Hymie. He rudely yanked Isabelle away from Vic and said to him, "Get going! You've kept her out too late, and her mother is undone!"

Isabelle quickly interjected, "Come to the beach tomorrow. I'll straighten this out."

When Vic rapidly walked away, Isabelle angrily confronted Hymie. "It's only 12:30. I'm humiliated! I'll never forgive you!"

Hymie explained gently, "Your mother is very upset. She said you were with an older man who has been discharged from the Army. She imagined him taking advantage of you. She said that she didn't even know your date's last name or where he lives!"

Isabelle knew that although she usually discussed everything with her mother, she would not tell her about this night. Instead, she stomped into the house and confronted Bella with her outrage and humiliation.

Bella did not even apologize. She said that if Vic was a nice boy, he wouldn't mind that they were protective of their daughter. She told Isabelle to go to bed, and she predicted that Vic would be on the beach the following day.

Bella's prediction was correct. Vic came to the beach several days a week until he went to Wisconsin. Isabelle and he went on several pleasant dates together and he always behaved like a respectful gentleman. The two of them corresponded in the autumn, and Isabelle invited Vic to have

Thanksgiving dinner with her and her family in their home in the Bronx. Isabelle looked forward to seeing Vic again on Thanksgiving.

———

One very hot and sunny Sunday afternoon, in late August, 1947, a large number of relatives were clustered around the blue umbrella with the white stripe. Several of them were complaining of thirst. One of them craved a hot dog. Fifteen-year-old Isabelle seemed the best one to send for the food and drink. She was given money and dispatched to Moore's to buy the drinks and snacks her relatives craved.

Heads turned as the slender, shapely teenager wearing a two-piece, pink bathing suit with white polka dots, danced gingerly across the hot sand on her way to the boardwalk. Her lovely figure, pretty face, deeply tanned skin, and long, thick, wavy, black hair caught the attention of most of the sunbathers. Oblivious to the stares, Isabelle approached Moore's on feet that had been cooked by the scorching sand. As she placed her order with her acquaintance, Al, she worried about her return trip over the blazing sand. She asked Al not to fill the drinks all the way, because she knew that she would need to hop and prance over the "sandy oven" to get to where her family was sitting.

Unbeknown to Isabelle, a man standing near Moore's counter, overheard her conversation with Al, and was greatly taken by her appearance. He walked over to her and said, "I promise you that I'm not being fresh, but I've been standing here for several minutes looking at you, and you'd be a perfect subject for my new colored film." (Film capable of taking colored photographs was brand new at that time. Black and white photographs were the prevalent mode. Colored pictures were extremely rare.) "Your black hair, suntan, and pink and white bathing suit are both colorful and beautiful," the young man continued. "May I take your picture?"

"Sure," answered the flattered Isabelle. "Go right ahead."

The photographer posed Isabelle and snapped two pictures. He told her that he would be glad to send her copies, if she would give him her address.

Being only fifteen years old, Isabelle was naïve in many ways, but she was still a savvy New York teenager, so she replied, "I don't give my address to strange men."

Al immediately interjected, "I'll give you my address. I promise I'll get the pictures to her."

The photographer copied Al's Bronx winter address and promised to send copies of the photographs to him. He then walked away.

Al told Isabelle that if the man ever sent them, he would bring the pictures to her house, in the Bronx. He said, "I doubt that he'll send them, though. He was probably just coming on to you."

Isabelle nodded. She then said goodbye to Al and returned to her relatives on the beach. For the rest of the summer of 1947, Isabelle saw Al only on those rare occasions when she went to Moore's to buy something to eat or drink.

On the beach, one day early in the summer of 1947, a very handsome boy struck up a conversation with Isabelle. She found his conversation interesting and not forward. The boy was a year round resident on Coney Island, who lived very near her grandmother. He had just graduated from high school and would begin his studies at the University of Pennsylvania in the late summer. His name was George.

Isabelle was quite taken by George. The only thing she didn't like about him was that he shared his name with the father she loathed. That not withstanding, she wished that he would ask her out on a date. But he didn't. Instead, on most of the days that Vic was not with her on the beach, George would appear. It almost seemed as if he watched to see if Isabelle was with another boy, and joined her only if she was alone.

One day George met Isabelle on the street, as she was walking to the beach. He was wearing street clothes when he saw her. He told her that he was taking a short ride to a shop in Brooklyn that had just about any phonograph record a person could wish for. He asked her if she'd like to come along for the ride.

Isabelle was dressed in her pink and white polka dot bathing suit and a sheer, skimpy beach cover-up. She said that she was not dressed properly to go to Brooklyn.

While the excuse she gave George was true, it masked the real reason for Isabelle's refusal....Bella had always warned about going into a boy's car unless Isabelle was very sure that she knew the boy very well and could trust him. Her mother pointed out, as a case in point, a very severely crippled young woman who had lived in their apartment house on Charlotte Street. This unfortunate young woman had become crippled because she had entered a young man's car after a dance, was raped by him, and then was thrown out of his car when it sped away, leaving the injured girl at the side of the road. Having heard Bella's cautionary remarks many times, and being acquainted with the rape victim, Isabelle had no intention of going into George's car.

George said, "You don't have to get out of the car. I'd love to have your company on the trip."

Isabelle didn't know George well, but he was, by far, her favorite male acquaintance that summer. She really didn't believe that he was untrustworthy, and because she realized that he would soon be leaving for college, she was hopeful that he would suggest that they correspond during the school year. She also didn't want him to think that she was a baby who was afraid to ride in his car.

Mustering all of her courage, Isabelle said, "Okay, I guess I don't have to get out of the car. Let me go to the beach to tell my mother and my grandmother that I'm going with you."

George said, "I have to be back home by noon. I don't have time to wait. Come on, let's go now. It's already ten o'clock."

With some trepidation, Isabelle accompanied George to his car. They drove to Brighton, where they should have gotten on the expressway, but just a few blocks away from the expressway entrance, George veered off course and rode two blocks in the opposite direction. George pulled up to a corner where a young man stood. The young man got into the car with Isabelle and George, and was introduced as Sonny. George said that Sonny wanted to shop for records too. Then, although they were only two blocks from the expressway entrance, George drove the car to a stretch of totally deserted land not too far from another expressway entrance. Sonny laughed evilly as they approached this area, and sneering at Isabelle said, "What if we told you to put out or get out?"

"I'd get out!" exclaimed Isabelle, tearfully. "George, stop the car and let me out!" she screamed.

"Don't be silly," laughed George. "Sonny was just kidding. I'd never let you out in this deserted place. Sonny just has a stupid sense of humor. Don't worry, no one will hurt you."

The three of them rode in silence for about five minutes. Then George and Sonny began to talk about music and records. Isabelle did not join in the conversation. She felt miserable and frightened, causing her to remain completely silent for the rest of the trip.

Their destination was a busy Brooklyn neighborhood. When they arrived, both boys left the car, leaving Isabelle. At first Isabelle contemplated getting out and seeking help, but being immature, she allowed the mores of 1947 and her fear of Bella's anger, to keep her in the car. She was ashamed to step out on a crowded Brooklyn street clad only in a skimpy bathing suit and sheer cover up. What is more, if she sought aid from the police, they would probably take her home. The prospect of seeing her mother's anger and distress over her disobedience was something Isabelle couldn't face. Consequently, when the boys returned to the car with their purchases, they found Isabelle where they had left her. The ride home was a silent one for Isabelle, but the boys spoke happily about music all the way to Sonny's house.

After Sonny left the car, George apologized to Isabelle. He maintained that Sonny had a "warped sense of humor," and really meant no harm. He then changed the subject to his imminent trip to Philadelphia to begin his life as a student at the University of Pennsylvania. He would be leaving in one week, and he asked Isabelle if she'd write to him.

Isabelle said she'd write and continued to pleasantly converse with George until he dropped her off at her grandmother's house. He got out of the car to continue his conversation with her, but as soon as they were face-to-face, Isabelle lashed out, "Whether Sonny was kidding or not, you're both dead, in my book! Nothing and nobody ever frightened me as badly as your creepy friend Sonny, who should have never been in the car while I was there, in the first place. The ride in your car was the worst, most horrifying experience of my life!"

"Isabelle," said George, "cool off. I'm sorry you got scared, but it was just a joke. Please give me your address," he continued, "I want to write you."

Isabelle glared at him venomously and hissed, "Go to hell!" She then turned on her heel and entered the building leaving the handsome boy standing on the hot pavement.

When she went upstairs to Sarah's apartment, Isabelle was surprised to see her Uncle Irving and her mother. He usually visited Sarah on Sunday, bringing his wife and two sons with him. During the day, Bella usually visited with her mother at the beach, not at her house. They were all there together, because Uncle Irving had been telling his sister and mother about Bella's old friend Minnie. Minnie's husband had died in 1945, and Minnie had come into some money from his life insurance. She also had some savings, because she had always been very frugal. After her husband's death, Minnie had been thinking of going into the furniture business. The housing market was booming, and the veterans of World War II were buying furniture for their newly purchased homes and newly rented apartments. Staten Island, where both Minnie and Irving lived, was one of the places experiencing a tremendous housing boom.

Minnie called Irving in 1946, and asked him if he could advise her on how to begin a furniture business. Remembering Minnie's kindness to him when he was in jail in Georgia, Irving felt he owed her a deep debt of gratitude. He agreed to help her as much as he could.

He not only helped her to understand the furniture market, he suggested a suitable site for her business, introduced her to furniture manufacturers, advised her on how to deal with them, and helped her get very beneficial treatment at his bank. With Irving's help and her seed money, Minnie's business took off to such an extent that by the end of 1946, Minnie was a wealthy woman. Now, as 1947 was drawing to a close, she was contemplating taking over a three-story building that could be turned into a three story furniture store. It would be the biggest, and probably, the most successful furniture store on Staten Island.

Irving finished his tale by saying, "If it were not for Minnie, God knows what would have been done to me at the hands of those prejudiced crackers in Georgia. I can never repay her enough."

Both Sarah and Bella were proud of Irving. Sarah was proud that her youngest child and the child of her greatest love was successful, and understood gratitude. Bella was proud of the little brother that she had guided through the snow-covered Russian forest to the school, where his fine brain bested all of the older children. Minnie, unlike his anti-Semitic Russian teacher, greatly appreciated his intelligence. His mother and sister were glad that he had been able to make good on his promise to pay Minnie back.

Isabelle and Vic had written several letters to each other that autumn. Isabelle so disliked Theodore Roosevelt High School, that her letters to Vic and David, and her outings with her girlfriends were what kept her happy until her Thanksgiving break. At that time, she would thankfully, have a four-day holiday from her hated school.

Vic had been invited for Thanksgiving dinner, and he arrived punctually. Bella had prepared a duck for dinner, and everyone ate on a table that she put in the living room. The five family members and Vic were somewhat crowded around the table, but the food was good and the company convivial. The conviviality was interrupted by the doorbell ringing.

"Who can that be?" asked Isabelle.

Isabelle answered the doorbell. Totally flabbergasted, she saw Al, the boy from Moore's, standing in her doorway. "Hello," she said, "this is certainly a surprise."

Al said, "It's a holiday, and I didn't have to work or go to school. That fellow who had taken your picture with color film really surprised me. He sent this picture for you to my house, and I wanted to bring it to you, in person, as I had promised. Al reached into the big patch pocket of his overcoat and withdrew a lovely colored snapshot of Isabelle standing in front of Moore's concession stand. As the photographer had predicted her tanned skin, black hair, and pink and white polka dotted swimsuit showed up beautifully in the colored print.

"Would you like to have this picture?" asked Al.

"No," said Isabelle, "you can keep it. You know Al, I really appreciate your visit, and ordinarily I'd ask you to come in, but its Thanksgiving, and I have a boy visiting me. He's home from an out-of-town college and he's come here all the way from Brooklyn. If you'd like to call me, I'll give you my telephone number. I truly appreciate your visit, and I'd like to see you again," said Isabelle.

Al wrote down the number and said he understood. He promised to call her soon.

Isabelle returned to the Thanksgiving table, and making no explanation to anyone, continued to eat her less than hot food.

Vic left at about 8:30, saying that he had a long ride home.

Isabelle sensed that Vic was dissatisfied with something about the day. Was their small, crowded apartment too modest for him? Did he dislike her family? Or the most probable of all, did he find a high school girl too young, or not as exciting as the co-eds in Wisconsin?

Isabelle didn't really care. She had not found Vic's visit particularly appealing. If he called or wrote to her, she planned to end her friendship with him. She conjectured, however, that she would never hear from Vic again. She conjectured correctly.

Another guess that Isabelle made was that Al would call her soon. Again, she had guessed correctly. Al called the very next day and asked Isabelle if she would like to have dinner with him on Saturday night. Isabelle immediately accepted his invitation.

They ate in a Chinese restaurant near the Freeman Street subway stop. The food was good and the conversation was even better. Al told Isabelle about his family and about the neighborhood in which he lived. He had gone to the same Jr. High School to which Isabelle had gone. It was located in Isabelle's neighborhood, so Al had needed to take two trolley cars to get there. The trolley cars had since been replaced by buses, but it was still a half hour trip, on two buses, to come to the neighborhood. Isabelle was touched that Al had come all that way to deliver a photograph. She was also touched by his story about his family.

Al lived with his grandparents, his mother, and his older brother in an apartment in the Parkchester area if the Bronx. His father had died in an industrial accident when Al was only nine years old. This made Al feel a great sense of responsibility for maintaining himself. Money was always tight in his family, so Al worked at many kinds of jobs since he was a small boy. He expected very little or no financial help from his family. He bought almost all of his own clothing and supplied his own pocket money. He had been doing so from the time his father had died. Thankfully, City College, the college he attended, was a full scholarship college. Entrance was based on a competitive exam and students only needed to buy their textbooks. Al had no room, nor board to pay, because he commuted to school from home.

Isabelle was greatly impressed with Al. His sense of responsibility and his industriousness seemed to be just the opposite of her no-count, biological father. She couldn't believe that she had disliked this boy for two previous summers. She was glad that he lived at home, near her home, and not at some distant out-of-town college. She hoped to see more of him.

They walked back to Isabelle's house, holding hands. Al did not kiss her good night, but he did promise to call her again, very soon.

Al remained an important boy in Isabelle's life from the fall of 1947, and for several years thereafter. On their dates they usually went to the movies or free concerts. Some dates did not include eating together, and other dates included meals at inexpensive restaurants. Isabelle met all of Al's friends and she and Al often dated with one or more of them.

Although most of their dating behaviors were wholesome, Al was already smoking when Isabelle met him. He gave Isabelle her first cigarette to smoke in the spring of 1948. They both smoked until the late 1970's, when with great difficulty, they both quit the loathsome habit. They were among the fortunate people who were not seriously impaired or killed by the evil habit.

––––––––

Al's best friend was a nice looking boy named Artie. He lived in a run-down neighborhood in lower Manhattan; but the location of his home was misleading. Artie was the pampered, only child of two people who had very good jobs and enjoyed indulging their only son in most of his wishes. Unlike Al, Artie didn't have to work. He was a student at Long Island University and had a steady girlfriend named Jackie. Isabelle and Al often spent time with Artie and Jackie.

Because neither Isabelle nor Al had made a commitment to each other, they both dated other people. Al often dated a girl he had met in Coney Island, who lived in Newark, New Jersey. The only way he could get to Newark was by taking the subway to Manhattan, then taking the train, called *The Tubes,* into Newark. In Newark, he boarded a city bus which took him to his date's home.

Isabelle knew of Al's dates in Newark. She surmised that if he was willing to make such a long trip, he probably liked the New Jersey girl quite a lot. Isabelle didn't mind, because while she liked Al, she was still quite interested in dating other boys.

––––––––

One day, after a date in Newark, Al was strolling on Broadway on his way home from The Tubes to the Bronx subway line. He passed a photographer's studio, whose window was adorned with several photographs. He was drawn up sharply, when a beautifully framed miniature of Isabelle caught his eye. The miniature was extremely unusual because in those days of mostly black and white photographs, Isabelle's picture was softly colored. The photographer had painted it, and to Al, the picture was sultry and beautiful.

Al entered the photographer's shop and said, "You have a picture of my girlfriend in your window. It's beautiful, and I would like to buy it." The photographer and Al haggled a little over the price Al should pay, but then they came to an agreement, and Al purchased the picture. As he left, the photographer congratulated Al on his choice of girlfriends.

When Al saw Isabelle on the following Saturday night, he presented the miniature to her. She was greatly surprised that her picture had been prominently displayed, in a tinted form, in the photographer's window. She explained to Al that she had taken glossy, black and white pictures to present to prospective employers in her search for modeling jobs. The modeling agency that she and her cousin Millie belonged to had suggested that she use that particular photographer for her glossies.

Al asked Isabelle if she'd like to have the lovely, colored, framed miniature. She agreed that it was a lovely picture, but she said that if Al wanted it, he should keep it. Al was glad to do so, because he really did want the picture for himself.

After Isabelle's last day of school, in June 1948, she once again packed two heavy suitcases and prepared for her, almost two hour, subway ride to Coney Island. Just as she was bidding her family good-bye, the doorbell rang. Eight-year-old Phyllis ran to the door. Much to everyone's surprise, Al stood there. He had come to help Isabelle with the suitcases she was carrying to her grandmother's house. He and his family were already living in Coney Island for the summer, and he had made the long trip to Isabelle's house from Coney Island to facilitate Isabelle's arrival at the beach. Al had had an extremely long and hard day, before he had come to Isabelle's house, because he had attended his summer school classes at City College in the morning. (He was going to summer school classes so that he could graduate early and begin to earn some meaningful money.) In the afternoon he had worked at Moore's, and then taken the long subway ride to the Bronx, in order to help Isabelle move to her grandmother's house. Isabelle was deeply touched. The sweetness and helpfulness of this blue-eyed boy was making a tremendously good impression upon her.

During the summer of 1948, Al and Isabelle really got to know each other. Very few of Isabelle's friends or any other boys were allowed to enter Isabelle's life, because of a strategy that Al had put into place. Al had arranged that his friend Artie, whose family also came to the beach for the summer, be Isabelle's constant companion until Al left his job at Moores at 4:00P.M. At that time, Al joined the two of them on the beach, and remained with them until he walked Isabelle home at dinnertime. After dinner, the two teenagers strolled on the boardwalk or went to a movie together. Later in the summer, they might go to the park on Neptune Avenue to whisper and "neck" in the sultry darkness.

Sarah laughed at what was going on. She understood that Al had put her granddaughter under siege, but she liked the young man and considered his strategies to be both clever and amusing.

At 11:00A.M., every weekday morning, Artie appeared at Sarah's door. He had finished his classes at Long Island University much earlier than Al would finish his classes. Artie had no after-school job, so when he got back to Coney Island, teenaged Isabelle was usually still asleep. Artie would dump his books and don a swimsuit before arriving at Sarah's house. He came there with the intention of waking Isabelle and going to the beach with her.

A chuckling Sarah sent Artie into the bedroom to awaken her granddaughter. Isabelle, with sleep still in her eyes, would rapidly don her swimsuit and gobble a quick breakfast. Then, she and Artie would go to the beach, carrying the blue umbrella with the white stripe. They would remain there until Al arrived at 4:00P.M.

Artie and Isabelle spent their days at the beach playing cards and talking about books, movies, and music. They also swam in the ocean together. Although Al believed that Isabelle was the most beautiful girl on the beach, he never worried about her friendship with Artie. Artie was a truly steadfast friend; and besides, he was "going steady" with Jackie. (Because Jackie lived far away in the Bronx and was employed as a secretary in an office in Manhattan, Artie and Jackie were only able to see each other on weekends.) All of these contributed to the success of Al's strategy. With Artie occupying Isabelle's time at the beach, the many young men who would have liked to become acquainted with the black-haired girl, stayed away. Al was able to go to school and work at Moore's without worrying that some other boy was stealing the girl to whom he was becoming more and more attached.

Having seen Isabelle's reaction to his "forward" behavior in the summers of 1946 and 1947, Al did things very slowly in 1948. But late in the summer of 1948, the two teenagers began to regularly stroll in the park. During their strolls they either held hands or Al would put his arm around Isabelle's shoulder or waist. Sixteen-year-old Isabelle did not object. When they eventually tired of strolling, they would sit down on a bench and chat. Al would put his arm around Isabelle, but he never did more than stroke her arm or squeeze her body closer to his.

One night, Al took Isabelle in his arms and kissed her on the lips. That beautiful, moonlit night in the park was the beginning of their deepening relationship. From then on, both of their bodies craved more and more of each other, but both young people, in keeping with the mores of 1948, abstained from heavy foreplay or sexual intercourse. In 1948, they *necked*, often *petted*, but never sexually consummated their relationship.

Isabelle on Minford Place in the Bronx, 1950

Chapter 13: Senior Year

The beautiful summer ended. Sixteen-year-old Isabelle had to return to her hated high school for her last year there.

On the first day of Isabelle's last semester at Theodore Roosevelt High School, as her homeroom class was receiving schedules, instructions, and several forms to fill out, Isabelle felt a gentle poke on her shoulder. She turned to face a stocky, dark-haired girl, who spoke to Isabelle in a halted, heavy foreign accent. She asked Isabelle to explain one of the forms they were supposed to fill out. She apologetically explained that she was insecure in her understanding of what was required of her.

Isabelle explained the form to the girl, and when the bell rang, walked with her to the next class. She learned that Nadia was from Lebanon and that she and her family had returned to the United States after her father's death, a few months before. Nadia had been born in America, but her family had returned to Lebanon when she was three years old. This was her first year back in America and her first year at Theodore Roosevelt High School.

Because Isabelle had never before met anyone from Lebanon, when she and Nadia met to eat lunch together, Isabelle asked Nadia a lot of questions. She learned that Nadia had been born in the United States, because her parents had been living in America from 1925 to 1935. Her father had represented his Lebanese company in America, so two of his four children were born there, but the rest of the family did not have American citizenship.

"I would like to see some of the famous sights of New York," Nadia said. "Would you consider going with me?"

Isabelle was charmed by this girl who had been raised in an exotic land and wished to see the sights of Isabelle's native city. Consequently, she "hung out" with Nadia at school whenever she could, and accepted an invitation to Nadia's house for dinner on a Wednesday night, several weeks after they met.

The neighborhood in which Nadia and her family lived was no better than Isabelle's neighborhood. Isabelle immediately came to the conclusion that they did not have a lot of money, but they had a lot of charm Nadia's mother greeted Isabelle by kissing her on both cheeks. She was warm and talkative and explained many things to her daughter's American friend.

"In Beruit, where we lived, there were three religious groups. The two largest groups were the Muslims and the Christians. We are Coptic Christians. What is your religion?" she asked.

"I'm Jewish," answered Isabelle.

"Jews are the third, and smallest religious group in Beruit," said Nadia's mother. "Christians and Jews get along very well. Our family has many Jewish friends in Beruit. When we lived there, we often shopped in Jewish shops and we had a Jewish doctor and a Jewish lawyer. But, both Jews and Christians have a hard time co-existing with Muslims. Muslim beliefs and the Muslim ways of living are quite difficult for both of our religious groups to contend with."

Conversation continued to be interesting throughout the delicious dinner. Nadia's mother served meat kabobs and wonderful herbal rice, both of which were totally unfamiliar to Isabelle. Isabelle was surprised to learn that Nadia's mother purchased her meat at a kosher butcher shop, because she believed that kosher meat was fresher than non-kosher meat. (Isabelle was embarrassed to tell her that Bella often bought non-kosher meat.)

When the girls went sight seeing, their expeditions were scheduled for several different weekends. Some of the places that Nadia and Isabelle visited were: The Statue of Liberty, St. Patrick's Cathedral, where much to Isabelle's surprise her Coptic Christian companion genuflected and prayed for a long time. (St. Patrick's is New York City's main Roman Catholic cathedral. Isabelle did not think that Coptic Christians would pray there.) The girls went to several museums, the Cloisters, and Temple Emanuel, New York City's main Reform Jewish Temple. They ate in China Town and perused China Town's interesting shops. They had lots of fun together and were well into the process of developing a warm friendship.

Then one day when Isabelle came to Nadia's house, she found the entire family huddled excitedly around their small television set. (In early1949, the U.N. General Assembly's important meetings were broadcast on New York City television.) Nadia explained that her sister was married to an assistant attaché to the Lebanese delegation to the U.N. That day was the first time that her brother-in-law would be televised. He was to represent Lebanon, and address the General Assembly. Isabelle immediately joined his excited family at the television set.

Nadia's brother-in-law's speech was shocking! He virulently denounced Israel and expressed the Lebanese government's enmity to the Jewish state. His speech made it difficult for Isabelle to remain in the same room with Nadia and her family. Nadia's mother switched off the television set in the midst of his terrible tirade and explained that her son-in-law was forced to espouse the Lebanese government's policy, but that he did not really share their viewpoint.

Isabelle was not mollified. She left their home immediately and ended her friendship with Nadia. Her experience with Nadia and her family made Isabelle realize how strongly Jewish she really was. If there was even a possibility that someone did not wish the Jewish people well, she was incapable of enjoying any positive relationship with that person.

One evening in the early spring of 1949, Al telephoned Isabelle to invite her on a date to see the Broadway smash hit, *Brigadoon*, and to have dinner with him. She readily accepted and looked forward to the wonderful time they would have in two weeks.

When the greatly anticipated day arrived, Isabelle and Al marveled at the warm, sunny weather. The beautiful weather and the prospect of seeing a hit musical put a lilt in their walk as they strolled to the subway station, holding hands. They chatted about inconsequential things during the long train ride. When they emerged onto the sunny, crowded pavement of New York's theater district, their happy mood intensified. Al steered them to an Italian restaurant that was one of his favorites. The restaurant was located one flight up, where the hostess seated the young couple at a window awash with sunshine. From this vantage point, they could observe the rushing pedestrian traffic and the congested, slow-moving motor traffic on Broadway. The view, the sunshine, and their happiness with each other caused a sense of contentment and joy to envelope them, as they chatted and ate their dinner.

After dinner the young couple walked along Broadway. They peered into shop windows and stared at the freakish speakers haranguing small audiences at almost every street corner. Mostly, however, they walked hand-in-hand in silent contentment. Something was very right in their lives.

Brigadoon's first act was extremely entertaining. At intermission, they left their seats to go to a smoking area. They found a lovely little outdoor balcony, big enough for only the two of them. They smoked and chatted until Al suddenly said, "Do you have an address book, Isabelle?"

"Yes," she answered.

"Throw it away," he said. "You won't be needing it. I'd like you to go steady with me. Will you, Isabelle?"

Even though they had been seeing a great deal of each other, both Al and Isabelle had still been dating others. Going steady was a serious step, so Isabelle, said, "Let me turn this over in my mind. I'll give you an answer when I've straightened out my thoughts."

Just then, the bell rang for the next act of *Brigadoon*. A disappointed Al and a befuddled Isabelle returned to their seats.

Isabelle was unable to concentrate on the second act of *Brigadoon*. All she could do was mull over Al's proposal that they "go steady." Did she really want Al to be her only boyfriend? She certainly liked him a lot, but there were aspects of his personality that irked her. For example, he didn't know how to dance, and refused to learn, even though he knew that his lack of dancing made her very unhappy. She was an excellent dancer, who detested sitting out all of the dances others were enjoying. In addition, Isabelle disliked some of Al's jokes because they were too raunchy. Worst of all, he sometimes said very unflattering things to her. Some of these were meant to be funny, and others were said in seriousness.

Al once joked that Isabelle's eyes reminded him of someone he had known in the country. When Isabelle asked who it was, he laughingly replied, "Bossie the Cow." Isabelle failed to appreciate Al's humor and was hurt. She believed that he rarely said flattering things to her, but managed to give her a verbal jab quite often.

When Isabelle met Anita, on a City College boat ride, Al told her that Anita was his oldest friend. The red headed girl had gone to kindergarten and all through school with Al. Now they were going to college together. Isabelle had chatted with Anita, but had not been particularly attracted to her. Isabelle had no interest at all in Anita's assessment of her, yet Al seemed to need to tell Isabelle what Anita thought.

"Anita thinks you'd be beautiful if your nose wasn't so long," Al told Isabelle. Isabelle, who personally didn't think she was beautiful, had nevertheless only heard very positive things about her appearance. She was only hurt by Al's disclosure of Anita's negative opinion, and wondered why he had repeated it to her. Did he think her nose was too long? Isabelle didn't think so. She thought he told her Anita's opinion to make her feel bad.

As Isabelle mused over the aspects of Al's personality that she didn't like, a small inner voice reminded her of his many, many more excellent personality traits that she valued greatly. He was bright, hardworking, dependable, and truthful. She found most of his conversation very interesting, and she shared most of his opinions about what was moral and what was not. They were in tune politically, and enjoyed the same movies and plays. She loved *most* of his jokes and liked most of his friends. Above all, she believed that if she went steady with Al, he would be steadfast and always be faithful to her.

When they left *Brigadoon*, Isabelle, suffering from some misgivings, told Al that she would go steady with him. A deliriously happy Al kissed her right on crowded Broadway.

———————

Isabelle did not know what educational path to follow. In her view, in the early fall of 1948, there were only two possibilities open to her. She could train to be a nurse, or she could go to one of New York City's free colleges and train to be a teacher. Because she was female, she didn't believe that any other options were viable.

Around this time, Isabelle got into the biggest trouble she had ever faced at school. It was caused by her name being on the same pass to the lavatory as her old friend, Natalie, with whom she had gone to elementary and junior high school. Natalie was a beautiful, well-behaved, very bright girl, who, like the vast majority of girls at this time, would be finished with her formal education when she graduated from high school. Like so many other female graduating seniors, Natalie's parents were unwilling to support her through four more years of school.

Isabelle and Natalie were in the same history class. Natalie needed to go to the restroom, so following the school's rule which required that all female students travel in pairs outside of their classrooms, Natalie put Isabelle's name on the pass. The history teacher signed the pass and the two girls left the room. When the girls entered the lavatory, they were greeted by a cloud of smoke. Six other girls were there, most of them egregiously breaking the school rule against smoking. Both Isabelle and Natalie ignored the group of smokers and entered the stalls. When they emerged Isabelle whipped out the huge black comb she used to comb her very thick, long, black hair. As she combed her hair, Natalie lit a cigarette. Isabelle did not join her, because she had vowed to never smoke in the school building.

Suddenly the outer door and then the inner door flew open. In stomped Mrs. Casey, the Dean of Girls. She angrily collected all of the passes, lined up all of the girls who were smoking, and sent the few non-smoking girls to their classes. Isabelle was among this group, but she didn't escape soon enough to avoid Mrs. Casey's sarcastic remark about her comb.

"That comb looks as if it is fit for a horse's mane," the dean sneered. "If you kept your hair shorter and thinner, you would not have to get herniated carrying that enormous, ridiculous comb."

Accepting the dean's nasty insult, Isabelle fled the bathroom. When she returned to her class, she explained to her history teacher why Natalie was detained.

Mrs. Casey gave a long and thorough tongue lashing to the errant girls. Each smoker received a pink slip, which was a disgraceful reminder to anyone seeking her record, that she had committed a serious transgression.

Two weeks later, Isabelle received a notice about a pink slip being put in her records. Natalie received no such notice. It was clear that there had been a mix-up in the dean's office. So, as soon as the mistake was discovered, both Isabelle and Natalie went to Mrs. Casey's office to have it corrected. Mrs. Casey, leering at the girls, heard their story and said, "You girls must really think I'm a fool! I do not mix-up names of smokers. Natalie, who is in the Commercial Tract, is not planning to go to college. What a good friend she is to you, Isabelle. She's ready to accept your pink slip as her own, because she knows that a pink slip can hurt your acceptance to some colleges. But I won't accept Natalie's lies or her sacrifice. I remember clearly, that you, Isabelle, were smoking in the bathroom!"

"Be on your way girls. I will not punish you for this latest fiasco; but don't depend on my good nature to last forever. Keep clear of me! I don't like liars!"

Isabelle and Natalie left the dean's office feeling terribly dejected. Isabelle decided that she would wait until she submitted applications to schools. If she saw that the pink slip would be detrimental to her applications for higher education, she would enlist Bella's help in getting herself exonerated.

Isabelle did not have long to wait. When she was in her civics class, a runner came into the room with an announcement. He said that Cornell University was allowing one girl from each New York City high school to compete for one of three scholarships to Cornell's School of Nursing.

The three winners would receive free tuition and board, and finish their education as Cornell graduates with a Bachelors degree and simultaneously be awarded their certification as R.N's. The girl who took Cornell's exam from each New York City High School, would have to be the applicant with the highest grade average from her school, and would have to have the endorsement of her school's administration.

Isabelle, along with several other senior girls, filed an application for a Cornell scholarship. To her complete delight, she was the highest applicant from her school. Now she needed to get the school administration's endorsement, and take a test at Governor's Island with the winners from other high schools. Isabelle went to the school office to get the endorsement. The school secretary pulled Isabelle's records, flipped through them, and then stood up and went into Mrs. Casey's office. Mrs. Casey emerged with an evil leer on her face and said, "You have a pink slip for smoking on the school's premises. It renders you ineligible for the Cornell scholarship. The second highest girl at Theodore Roosevelt High School will take the test on Governor's Island." Isabelle spun around and left the office without a word, but she cried all the way home on the bus.

When Isabelle got home, she told the whole story to Bella. Bella admonished her for waiting so long to tell her the story, but then cut her scolding short to call the school to see if she could get a quick appointment to see Mrs. Casey. She was in luck. Hearing the urgency in Bella's voice, the secretary, who was still at the school, double booked Mrs. Casey for the following morning. She told Bella that she would probably have to wait until Mrs. Casey had some spare time, but she assured Bella that she would get her in to speak to the dean.

On the next morning, Bella and Isabelle darted through a terrible downpour to get to the bus stop. The wind was very strong, rendering their umbrellas useless. Isabelle was pleased to be wearing her stylish, beautiful, new brown plaid raincoat with a matching military peaked-cap. Only her long hair got wet, but the rest of her was snug and dry. Bella was not so lucky. The rain had even soaked her heavy coat. It was damp, and Bella felt chilled.

The trip to Theodore Roosevelt High School took half an hour on two buses. The rain had changed to a gentle patter, so the mother and daughter felt more comfortable when they entered the school and took their seats on the outer office bench to wait for Mrs. Casey to be available to see them. From the vantage point of their wooden bench, they were able to decipher what was going on in the dean's office. Through the wide open door they could see the girl in the office weeping and hear Mrs. Casey's vitriolic remarks to her. The pitiless meeting lasted only about ten minutes, after which the student who had been in the dean's office emerged with her mother. Both of them were crying and speaking Italian. Bella and Isabelle had heard the dean's harsh remarks to them and then had heard her hand down her decree. Mrs. Casey had suspended the Italian girl for two weeks.

———————

The secretary now invited Isabelle and Bella to enter Mrs. Casey's office.

"Oh, it's you, Isabelle," said Mrs. Casey, showing her huge yellow teeth as she flashed them a false smile. "I thought you and I had our talk."

"We did, Mrs. Casey, but I wanted you, my mother and me to go over everything one more time, so that you really understand everything that is at stake."

"I'm glad to meet your mother," said the dean. "I'd like to hear a thing or two from the mother whose bright daughter, throws away every opportunity by breaking the school rules and smoking. Perhaps I can give her some pointers on how to improve matters for her daughter."

"I would like to hear your advice," said Bella, "but in my view my daughter needs very little changing."

"Oh you parents," chuckled Mrs. Casey, falsely, "if your children's grades are good, you think you've done your job. Just look at Isabelle in that elegant, expensive raincoat. What message have you given her? She believes that she is entitled to do and have everything her heart desires."

Bella's eyes narrowed. "You don't know my daughter or the price of the raincoat she is wearing," she answered, trying to stifle her anger. "Why do you focus on the clothing of my well-dressed daughter and not on the lack of proper clothing on that poor, rain soaked Italian child you just suspended from school? How will her suspension hurt her education? Are you not tampering with her future ability to earn money and improve her life?"

"But I am not here to discuss that unfortunate child with you," Bella continued. "I'm here to tell you that your office mistakenly gave Isabelle a pink slip. I know my daughter and Natalie both have integrity. When both girls, good students with good previous records, give their word about the matter, you should believe them."

"I've been at this high school too long to believe stories like theirs. What is more, my office is very careful. We don't make mistakes," said Mrs. Casey.

Bella angrily retorted, "I may take this matter up higher. Your pettiness will not be allowed to hurt Isabelle's future!" With that, Isabelle and her mother angrily left Mrs. Casey's office.

Bella's bravado went no further than Mrs. Casey's office. It did not get Isabelle qualified to take the test for the Cornell School of Nursing either, but Isabelle was not deterred. She planned to enter a school of nursing, anyway. She had heard that the three-year course in nursing at Brooklyn Jewish Hospital was a good one. If she entered their program, which cost a small sum of money, she could graduate as a registered nurse in three years.

Isabelle took the national nursing school exam and "aced" it! She put in her order for student nurse's uniforms, and only had to get her recommendations signed to be all set for her career in nursing.

In her senior year at Theodore Roosevelt High School, Isabelle had an excellent English teacher, named Mr. Mannes, who made literature and writing come alive. He told Isabelle to major in English at college and to "write, write, write!" He said she had a gift for writing and would find work doing it.

Isabelle didn't believe that Mr. Mannes was correct. Following the mores of 1948, she was convinced that a career in nursing was the way to go, but Mr. Mannes refused to give her his recommendation for her career in nursing. He reiterated that Isabelle should go to college and be an English major. Al never met Mr. Mannes, but he agreed with him completely. The prospect of *Nurse Isabelle* in a hospital surrounded by medical residents haunted Al. He certainly did not want Isabelle to become a nurse. Several other people in Isabelle's life cautioned her against becoming a nurse, too. They talked of nurses working long, exhausting hours for very little money, and emphasized many of the dirty, unpleasant aspects of the job. These negative comments against nursing finally changed Isabelle's mind, and she decided that college was a better place for her. Al begged her not to consider City College. He said that her presence there would be a terrible distraction for him. He suggested that she apply to Hunter College, a highly rated all female school in the New York City's system of colleges. Pliable Isabelle, following his suggestion, was accepted at Hunter College for the fall semester of 1949.

While Isabelle followed Al's suggestion in her school selection, she was sorely suspicious of his motives. Could he have suggested Hunter College, a school for only women, for the same reason that she had "enjoyed" Artie's company all summer? She felt reasonably certain of similar motives, but personally liked the idea of attending Hunter College, so she applied there and didn't apply to C.C.N.Y. When Isabelle measured her options without any distractions, college seemed to be the better course to follow, so she cancelled her application and her order for uniforms at the Brooklyn Jewish Hospital School of Nursing. Instead, she prepared to be a freshman at Hunter College in the fall.

Before Isabelle had graduated from high school, when she was only sixteen years old, Sarah viewed her as grown-up and thought she was beautiful. Because she would graduate from high school in June, and become a college student the following September, Sarah firmly believed that Isabelle should now own a fur coat. To Sarah, a female's "rite of passage" was possession of a fur coat. Sarah's parents had gotten her a fur coat when she was a teenager in Vashisht. She had seen to it that Fanny had a fur coat in Vashisht, too. Bella's accident and the Depression had kept Sarah from buying her a fur coat when she was single, but just a few years before, she had purchased a black Persian lamb coat for her youngest daughter, because she believed that every woman should have a fur coat.

Sarah's older granddaughters had been given fur coats by their parents. Anna's daughter, Ida, sported a lovely gray Persian lamb coat, while, Millie, Fanny's daughter, was wearing a brown mouton lamb. Sarah feared that with Hymie's drinking and his small salary, Bella would be unable to give Isabelle a fur coat. Consequently, Isabelle was given two hundred dollars by her grandmother and told to purchase a coat.

The delighted Isabelle did not have enough money for the grey Persian lamb that was so fashionable, so she chose a sheared mouton lamb, of extremely good quality. Her coat greatly resembled sheared beaver, and Isabelle felt like a queen when she wore it. However, Isabelle did not look like a queen when she wore her fur coat. When she was adorned in her fur coat and matching fur hat, Isabelle looked like a pampered, fashionable, and beautiful New York City teenager.

———————

It was around the time of the purchase of the fur coat that Bella received a telephone call from Sadie. Bella had not heard from George's sister very often, after she and Isabelle had visited Boston, shortly following Sadie's little girl's untimely death. In fact, two years had passed after the little girl's death, before the sisters-in-law got in touch again. By this time, Isabelle was six years old, and Sadie heard that Isabelle was taking dancing lessons, so she sent her niece a pair of tap shoes that were manufactured in Joe's shoe factory. Then in her last telephone call to Eva's telephone number, Sadie learned that Bella no longer lived on Staten Island and that she had remarried. At that time, Eva gave Sadie Bella's address in White Plains.

Sadie must have been in touch with her brother, because shortly after her phone call to Eva, George wrote a letter to Isabelle. In his letter he told Isabelle that he always thought about her. He further told his eight-year-old daughter that she had a daddy who "dearly loved her." He instructed her to respect "the man" her mother had married, but to never let anyone displace him as her father. This letter, like the only other letter Isabelle had received from George, lacked a return address and was post marked San

Diego, California. In the first letter, George had enclosed a five-dollar bill for Isabelle's fourth birthday. In this latest letter, Isabelle's "loving father" enclosed nothing.

From the time Isabelle was eight years old, she had heard nothing from either George or Sadie. Then one day, when she was sixteen years old, Sadie called. When Bella told Isabelle that Sadie wanted to see her, Isabelle was truly conflicted. On the one hand, Isabelle relished the idea of insulting George's sister by just completely ignoring her. On the other hand, she was burning with curiosity to see these phantom "relatives" with whom she shared her genes.

Isabelle's curiosity won out. She telephoned Sadie and made a date for Friday night. Al would accompany her to the hotel, in which her Boston relatives were staying. She would visit with them, while Al waited in the lobby, and then she and Al would spend what was left of the evening together.

Isabelle dressed with extreme care on the night she was to see Sadie. She wore a lovely green woolen dress and high-heeled pumps. She wanted to show her Boston "family" how well she had fared without them; but at the same time she wondered just how her prosperous Boston aunt would receive her.

Little did Isabelle know that if Sadie had gone to school to study which remarks would be most likely to irritate a sixteen and a half year old girl, she couldn't have done a better job. Virtually every comment Sadie made "raised the hackles on Isabelle's neck."

It started when Sadie opened the door and exclaimed with great pleasure, "Hello Isabelle. I'm so glad to see you. Why, you're beautiful! You look just like your father!"

Isabelle knew that she bore an extremely strong resemblance to her mother. Being compared to the "monster" who was her father was beyond irritating for her. She, therefore, replied softly, "Everyone says that I look exactly like my mother. I think you're looking for a resemblance that does not exist."

The short, dumpy woman said, "How can you say that? You don't even know what your father looked like. He was extremely handsome. He may have behaved badly, but he certainly was handsome." Sadie then quickly let Isabelle know that she strongly disapproved of her brother's behavior and that she had always thought that Bella was a lovely woman whom George had mistreated. She insisted that she hadn't heard from her brother for a very long time and that when she tried to trace him, she was told that he had become seriously ill with spinal meningitis. She said that she believed he may have died of the dread disease.

"Good!" said Isabelle. "If he is dead, the world has lost nothing and has gained some more space!"

"You may think that you don't resemble your father," said Sadie, narrowing her eyes, "but you have the same nasty, cutting mouth that he had!"

"Look," said Sadie trying to change the subject, "The wedding we came to New York to attend is a wedding of your distant cousin. It's on Sunday. I told a number of relatives that you might come, and they're looking forward to meeting you. I thought that you might like to meet them too. Instead of us sparring over resemblances, let's enjoy this weekend together. Will you go shopping with your cousin Mona and me tomorrow? We can have lunch together, too."

"Okay," said a somewhat reluctant Isabelle. On the one hand, she really wasn't impressed with these people. On the other hand, she was curious about the people she would meet at the wedding. After all, they were her relatives.

They chatted about Isabelle's college plans and Bella's present family. Sadie kept assuring Isabelle that she held Bella in very high regard. After about an hour together, Isabelle informed Sadie, Joe, and Mona that her boyfriend was waiting in the lobby. She told them that he was taking her home, and that she had to leave. Consequently, they made plans to meet at noon on the following day. Then Isabelle took her leave of them with a cold "goodbye."

———

On the following afternoon, although the weather was chilly, the sun shone in a cloudless sky. It was a perfect winter day for walking, or as Sadie had suggested, for shopping. When Isabelle arrived at the hotel, she called them from the lobby, and Joe said, "Sadie is on her way."

To Isabelle's surprise, only Sadie alighted from the elevator. Sadie greeted Isabelle with a kiss on her cheek, and said, "Mona has a terrible cold. She asked me to apologize for her, but she doesn't feel up to a shopping spree. She said that judging from your appearance your taste is so good that she's bound to like whatever you select for her. The way she feels, she would rather rest than go shopping in New York. Do you mind going shopping with only your old aunt?" asked Sadie coyly.

"Oh no," said Isabelle. "I've come to spend the afternoon with you. It doesn't matter where we do it, so long as we get to know each other."

With that, Sadie and Isabelle assaulted New York's Fifth Avenue. Sadie seemed to prefer the expensive small specialty shops to the expensive large department stores that lined the avenue. Isabelle had never shopped at these elegant shops, so their shopping spree started out as great fun. They bought several things in those small shops, and with each purchase, Isabelle realized that there was a huge chasm between this aunt and her much poorer aunts and uncles on her mother's side of the family. In each store, Sadie was presented with merchandise she had requested to see. Each time she asked Isabelle for her preference, stating that Mona would prefer Isabelle's youthful taste to her mother's mature taste. Sadie always purchased the item of Isabelle's choice in each of the many exclusive specialty shops they visited.

At 3:15 P.M. Sadie exclaimed, "Oh my goodness, we haven't even eaten lunch and its 3:15. Let's just go into this lovely purse store and buy Mona a purse. Then we can go to a restaurant for a very late lunch."

The décor and merchandise in the purse shop were the most beautiful that Isabelle had ever seen. Knowing that Sadie had purchased nothing for her, Isabelle felt sure that it was Sadie's intention to buy her a gift in this elegant, exclusive shop.

Sadie informed the clerk that she was looking for a black purse for a young person. The clerk brought them a vast array of purses whose astronomical prices paralyzed Isabelle's thinking processes. Sadie had purchased very expensive items in the other shops they had visited, but none of them could compare to the prices in this shop.

Sadie asked Isabelle for her preference.

"What is your price limit?" asked Isabelle.

"Forget that for the moment," said Sadie, "just pick what you like."

Not wanting to be piggish, Isabelle selected one of the lower priced purses, but still had major misgivings about the prices of every one of the purses they had seen.

"Do you really like this one best?" asked Sadie.

"Yes," said Isabelle, feeling tremendous elation over the purse she was sure was to be hers.

———

Sadie purchased the purse, and the two women, laden with packages, went to Schraffts. They ordered sandwiches and drinks, and then Sadie left her seat to go to the candy counter. She purchased a box of candy and had it gift-wrapped. When she returned to the table, she handed Isabelle the gift-wrapped box of candy, saying, "This is for your lovely mother. I always liked her."

Isabelle almost choked on her sandwich! There was nothing for her. This "aunt," unlike her aunts and uncles from Vashisht, had titillated her with the finest merchandise in New York City, but had sent her home with a box of candy for her mother. Her aunts and uncles on her mother's side of the family never took her shopping at all. Instead, they frequently gave her money saying, "Go buy something for yourself." Even though they were poor, unlike Sadie, they were generous and rich in their love for her.

Isabelle fumed on the subway trip to the Bronx. The only reason that she had agreed to see Sadie on the following day, was that she wanted to see the people at the wedding. This woman from Boston did not behave like an aunt and could never really be considered her aunt or be loved by her.

———

On Sunday, Isabelle arrived at 2:00 P.M. to share a late lunch with Sadie and her family. At lunch, Sadie told Isabelle about the fate of her family in Warsaw....Everyone who was in Warsaw was murdered by the Nazis. Three generations of their family were annihilated....Sadie's mother and step-father (Isabelle's grandparents), four of their seven children, and all of their grandchildren, except the two in America (Mona and Isabelle). There was also one little boy in Israel. Sadie said that she and her youngest sister, now living in Israel were the only living children of her parents, because Sadie said she truly believed that George was dead.

After this tragic tally, Sadie handed Isabelle a picture of her aunt in Israel. The black and white photo showed a lovely young woman in her mid twenties, sitting on the grass with a small boy, two or three years old. Sadie told Isabelle that her grandfather had been a teacher, but his true passion was Zionism. Consequently, he had sent his sixteen-year-old daughter to a kibbutz that ran a camp for non-Israeli teenagers. When the Nazis invaded Poland, all Polish teenagers remained in Palestine, Isabelle's teenaged aunt among them.

Isabelle's young aunt now lived in Tel Aviv. Her husband was a Sabra (a Jew born in Israel). He was a banker, and they had one little son.

A letter, written in Yiddish, by Isabelle's Israeli aunt, had been sent to Sadie. Isabelle was able to read the letter herself. In it, her young aunt asked about what had become of Yossel (George) and his daughter. Sadie, very much impressed with Isabelle's ability to read Yiddish, asked the sixteen year old if she would like to write to her aunt.

Isabelle, having been disappointed in Sadie, felt negative about her young aunt as well. She said, "No," and she regretted her teenaged negativity for the rest of her life.

In the taxi taking them to the wedding, Joe pointed out several stores that were customers of his shoe factory. Sadie, however, wanted to return to a more important topic. She wanted to convince the sixteen-year-old girl she had just met, that filial obligation out-weighs all past offenses. She said, "You know Isabelle, I understand your anger toward my brother. You have a stepfather who is apparently a very good man, so that makes being angry with your father even easier."

"When I came to America, I was your age. I left home to escape a stepfather, your grandfather, who was making my life miserable. I, therefore, was very interested in being reunited with my own father who had gone to America many years before. I believed, as you believe, that what was between my father and my mother had little to do with me. Even though my father had deserted my mother and married another woman, I felt sure that he would welcome me and understand his obligations to me, but I couldn't have been more mistaken. My father made it quite clear that he wanted nothing to do with his old life, and I was a part of that old life."

"I was devastated, but I had to make a life for myself. I did it without any assistance or love from my father. Yet, when I learned of my father's death, eleven years ago, I sat Shiva for him out of respect for the fact that he was my father."

"You know Isabelle," Sadie announced smugly, "I have every reason to believe that George is dead. As I told you, we searched for him in San Diego, and the final thing we heard, was that he had been hospitalized with spinal meningitis. We heard nothing of his being discharged from the hospital. We truly think he died."

Isabelle replied vindictively, "We do not share the same feelings. You're right when you say that whatever happened between my mother and George did not free him of his obligations to me. But I am not as forgiving as you are. If you can prove that George died, I won't sit Shiva, I'll throw a party! I'll even invite you to come!"

A shocked silence enveloped the taxi. Sadie despaired of ever convincing the angry teenager to see life her way.

Prior to the wedding ceremony, Sadie, with a heavy heart, introduced Isabelle to many of her distant cousins. She introduced her as George's daughter. None of her newfound relatives gained Isabelle's admiration or interest. Her only remaining curiosity was to see if she had more affinity to the bride than to the groom. Neither of them were to be seen, so Isabelle waited for the ceremony to see what they looked like and to whom she was related.

The groom was tall and blond. His face was made unattractive, because of a severe acne condition. Isabelle felt sure that she was not related to this unattractive man, because she was accustomed to very good looking cousins on Bella's side; and because she had always heard that George was very good looking. She felt sure that her newfound cousin would prove to be attractive.

The tall, slim, black-haired bride was quite lovely. Isabelle's guess was that she was her distant cousin, because both the bride and she had black hair and were tall and slender. Isabelle whispered to Mona, "The bride is our cousin, isn't she?"

"No, the groom is," answered the aloof Mona. "I thought you knew."

When the ceremony was over, everyone was milling around, waiting for the reception line to be formed. Isabelle excused herself, saying that if she attended the reception that would follow the ceremony, she would be traveling home too late. She said that Bella didn't like her to travel alone after dark.

Sadie and her family understood. Besides, the angry teenager would not be missed by any of them.

On the day after the wedding, Sadie telephoned Bella. She said, "Your daughter is beautiful and quite bright, but she does not have your lovely disposition. Her tongue, like the tongue of her father, is sharp as a knife. I hope at some future time she will reconcile with me and stop blaming me for George's shortcomings. If that day comes, perhaps we'll develop a relationship."

When Bella reported the telephone conversation to Isabelle, Isabelle said that she had no interest in a selfish, self-serving aunt, or in a boring cousin. She said that she was quite satisfied with the aunts and cousins she had.

Isabelle's disdain for Sadie and her family was really proven at the time Isabelle was to be married. Bella asked Isabelle if they should invite her Boston relatives to the wedding. Isabelle's answer showed her true feelings where they were concerned. "Even if I liked Sadie, Mona, or Joe, I would strongly consider not inviting them to my wedding. Their presence at the wedding would be a slap in the face to my *real* father – your husband! He has been my father all these years. George has been less than nothing.

Anyway," Isabelle continued. "I don't like the Boston, so-called relatives. So there's absolutely no loss in excluding them from my wedding."

———

When Isabelle and Sheila began their senior year at Theodore Roosevelt High School, the baseball season was going hot and heavy in New York. The city was embroiled in a "subway series" with the Bronx Bombers, better known as the Yankees, facing off against the Brooklyn Dodgers. Even tepid fans like Isabelle and Sheila were affected by the excitement of this World Series.

Isabelle and Sheila did something neither of them had even dreamt of doing before. On a beautiful fall day on which the Series would be played at Yankee Stadium, in the Bronx, the two girls decided to cut their afternoon classes and go to the ball game. "How would anyone know?" they conjectured. "Everyone would be in school."

The two-hookie players took the elevated train to the Yankee Stadium. They were early, so they bought their bleacher tickets, and then walked to a kosher delicatessen for a delicious lunch. When they returned to the stadium, the ball game was about to begin, so the crowds outside the stadium had thinned. The two pretty high school girls hurried to take their seats in the bleachers. When they got there, the girls couldn't believe their horrified eyes. The bleachers were packed! Sitting on the benches of the bleachers, practically on top of each other, were crowds of mostly Negro spectators. (The bleachers did not have assigned seats. They were the cheapest seats sold, and the spectators in them often sat crowded together.) The reason for the preponderance of male Negro spectators was that the Brooklyn Dodgers had lowered the color bar that had strangled organized baseball since its beginnings. They had hired Jackie Robinson, the first major league player who was a Negro, and now he was playing in the World Series.

Isabelle and Sheila thought that they would have to stand to watch the game, when one of the Negro spectators yelled, "Come on. Make room for the pretty girls. We can all squeeze together a little more." A whole long bench-load of male Negro spectators moved and squeezed until there was just enough room in the center of their bench for the two girls to squeeze in.

The game began. Jackie Robinson acquitted himself fabulously. The Negro spectators in the bleachers went wild, along with Isabelle and Sheila who were completely infected by the excitement. Probably very few of the spectators realized that they were watching a change in sport's history, indeed, in American history. Jackie Robinson was the beginning. In the future, many super-great African-American athletes would enter American professional sports, and eventually they would dominate it.

But, in the fall of 1948, when Isabelle and Sheila were playing hookie, only the thrill of the moment enveloped them. Then, just as they were screaming about a hit, Isabelle felt someone poke her shoulder from behind. She turned to see who it was, and almost fell off the bench.

"Isabelle, I thought it was you. And Sheila, you too. What a coincidence! I don't see you girls and you don't see me!" said Mr. Eddey, the girl's Civics teacher. Laughing uproariously, a pact was formed between the hookie playing teacher and his hookie playing students.

Sheila and Isabelle's dream of going to college together never materialized. Sheila's brother Paul was enrolled at N.Y.U. Her family firmly believed that Paul, a male, required a good college education. Sheila, although she was exceptionally bright, in their estimation did not require a degree. They believed that her future husband was required to "take care" of her. What she needed was an acceptable way to earn a living in the period between graduating from high school and getting married.

Sheila accommodated them. She won a scholarship to a comptometer operator's school. (Comptometers were early machines that computed addition, subtraction, multiplication, and division. Comptometers later were replaced by the computer.) Comptometer operators were well paid compared to most office workers. Their training took from eight to ten months after graduation from high school. When Sheila entered the work place, she was considered to be a successful young woman.

Isabelle's and Sheila's friendship faded quickly after graduation.

Isabelle's life was enveloped with college and Al. Sheila was a busy working-woman with an even busier social life.

Isabelle had been in college for two-and-a-half years, when Bella ran into Sheila's mother at The Market. Sheila's mother had just left the hairdresser and looked very pretty. They inquired about each other's daughters and Sheila's mother learned that Isabelle was married, but was living back home, because her husband was serving in the Army, and Isabelle was completing her college education. Sheila's mother told Bella that Sheila was in Colorado, where her husband, who was also in the Army, was stationed. They would be returning to New York in three months, when her husband would be discharged from the Army. Sheila, who was pregnant, planned to stay at home. Her husband would re-enter his family's business, operating an appetizing store, where, no doubt, he would work for the rest of his working years. Both he and his brother had entered the family business right out of high school and left it only to fulfill their military obligations.

"It's wonderful," boasted Sheila's mother, smugly. "My daughter stopped being a financial burden upon us right after she graduated from high school, and things are so much better, that I'm even able to afford to have my hair done weekly."

"My hair doesn't look as good as yours," retorted Bella, "but my daughter is no burden. I am proud that she will be as educated as your son. I see no difference between a girl's need for an education and a boy's need for an education. Every one of us benefits greatly from what we learn, and in the case of women, better educated women need no one to "take care" of them. They can "take care" of themselves!"

Both women parted ways, each more confirmed in her beliefs than she had been before their encounter.

Isabelle, 1950

Chapter 14: Hunter College

Isabelle was going to a wedding in Al's family. She wanted a very special dress for the occasion. She also planned to wear her dress under her gown when she graduated from Theodore Roosevelt High School.

Bella and Isabelle discussed the purchase of the dress, and Bella agreed when Isabelle said that for her two special occasions she wanted to buy the dress in a fairly expensive dress shop on the Grand Concourse, near Fordham Road. The shop had particularly lovely dresses, and Isabelle decided to make this the first purchase she would make, using the small college fund Sarah had given to her during the war.

Isabelle and her mother spent very little time in the elegant dress shop, because they were suited very quickly. Isabelle selected a lovely blue print, silk dress that draped beautifully over her slender body. It needed some slight alteration of the hemline, but otherwise, it was perfect. When Isabelle purchased the dress, she left it at the shop for the necessary alteration, and said that she would pick it up on Saturday.

On Saturday, Isabelle took the bus to Fordham Road and the Grand Concourse. She did some shopping at Alexanders, one of the first discount stores in the United States. At Alexanders, she bought hosiery and some lovely underwear at very reasonable prices. Packages in hand, she crossed Fordham Road and then the Grand Concourse. She entered the elegant dress shop and went to a fitting room to try on the beautiful dress she had purchased a few days before. When she emerged, several sales women and their customers observed her. They all lavished great praise on her about how lovely she looked and how beautiful her new dress was.

Just as the women in the store were "ooing" and "aahing" about how Isabelle looked, Mrs. Casey, the dean of Theodore Roosevelt High School entered the store. She glanced at Isabelle and her admirers and said, "Isn't it wonderful to be young and lovely. I work at the high school down the road, and I always enjoy the fresh good looks of the students. I love to see them in pretty clothes, looking young and lovely like this pretty girl." She then flashed Isabelle a big yellow-toothed smile.

Isabelle was amazed at Mrs. Casey's lack of recognition. She did not edify the hated dean as to who she was, and she did not remind her of her recent negative comments about her "fashionable raincoat."

The purchase of the dress, however, clarified an important aspect of Mrs. Casey's character for Isabelle. Mrs. Casey didn't recognize her when they were away from the school building. Apparently, Mrs. Casey viewed the students as something other than full-fledged human beings. They were part of the school, and it was Mrs. Casey's job to make the school operate properly. It was not her job to deal with the students sensitively or compassionately. Mrs. Casey believed that she only needed to make Theodore Roosevelt High School operate smoothly. Consequently, she could lie and "run over" people and it was alright....just so long as the school ran smoothly.

––––––––––

Isabelle loved the silk print dress that she had purchased on the Grand Concourse. She wore it to every important dress-up occasion she could. She planned to wear it to a wedding of one of Al's second cousins. It was the first wedding in Al's family to which Isabelle was invited. She really wanted to look her best there.

On the day of the big event, Isabelle was to be picked up by Al at 6:30 P.M. It being the month of June, nightfall came quite late. Orthodox Jews and Orthodox rabbis did not participate in weddings or any other events until the Sabbath had ended at sundown, so the wedding invitation was for an 8:45 arrival for the wedding ceremony, followed by a very late dinner. When Isabelle was picked up by Al, she knew none of these particulars.

When Al came to Isabelle's house at 6:30, she was not quite ready. She appeared at 6:40, looking radiant, but her good mood was quickly dashed when Al said angrily, "You're very late. My family will be waiting for us on the subway platform of 125 Street at 7:00 o'clock. We'll never make it on time!" Isabelle picked up her purse and said nothing. She wondered how being ten minutes late could make Al so angry and unhappy. The train ride to 125 Street was made almost entirely in silence. Any conversation was initiated by Isabelle and answered in monosyllables by Al. He was clearly deeply agitated because they were late.

They arrived at 125 Street five minutes late. When they alighted from the train, they immediately saw the six members of Al's family, unhappily huddled together. When Isabelle said "Hello," Eva said, "We've been waiting here for twenty-five minutes. Where have you been?"

"Twenty-five minutes?" queried Isabelle. "Weren't we supposed to meet you only five minutes ago?"

"Yes," said Al's brother, Harold, "but we all met here twenty-five minutes ago."

"Then you were too early," said Isabelle. "We're only five minutes late. We didn't make you wait a long time. Your coming too early made you wait for such a long time."

Just as Isabelle was making her angry retort, the train to Brooklyn roared into the station. All of them got seats scattered all over the subway car. Because they weren't sitting together, the conversation about lateness was terminated.

Al had regained his pleasant disposition, and he and Isabelle chatted amicably all the way to Brooklyn. The train ride took fifty minutes. They left the train at 7:55 P.M. It took them fifteen minutes to find the wedding hall that was their destination, so they entered the chapel at 8:10.

To their immense surprise and great discomfort, they were the only guests there! The bridal party hadn't arrived yet, either. But, there were other people in the chapel…. the cleaning crew was finishing their work and a florist was setting up floral baskets along the aisle.

Isabelle couldn't believe her eyes. She asked Eva what the time for the guests' arrival was on the wedding invitation. An embarrassed Eva answered "8:45."

"We arrived here at 8:10," thought Isabelle, angrily. "We were thirty-five minutes too early! Yet, when I was five minutes late, the entire family made a big 'to-do' over it."

The other guests began to arrive at 8:45. At 9:00, the ceremony began. It was completed by 9:35, when all of the guests repaired to the wedding hall to eat a lavish, late dinner and dance to popular music and to Jewish Klezmer-type music. Many of Al's relatives complimented or teased him about his choice of a girlfriend. For everyone, the entire mood of the wedding was festive, except for Isabelle, who felt gloomy. She tried to hide her feelings behind a big, false smile, but periodically her feelings came to the surface, causing her to feel scared and unhappy. She didn't understand Al's family's behavior concerning time. Al, too, seemed to share the same problem. She hoped that if she had to see this behavior again, it would be very infrequently.

It was not. In Isabelle and Al's long relationship, one of the sorest of sore spots was the issue of time. Isabelle, who believed she ran her life fairly efficiently, hated Al's time anxiety and his erroneous belief that without his prodding, she would be late to everything.

———————

Isabelle entered Hunter College in the winter semester of 1949 along with four other girls with whom she had graduated from Theodore Roosevelt High School. They had become Hunter College freshman in September, and in early November they were surprised to find themselves waiting outside the office of one of the Hunter College deans. They were in few classes together, so they could not figure out why all five of them had been summoned to see the dean at the same time. They surmised that the summons had something to do with Theodore Roosevelt, the high school from which they had all graduated.

The dean asked them to be seated, and then spoke gravely. She asked if they were getting along well at Hunter College. Did they feel that they could keep up with the workload? Were their grades good?

The girls all assured her that everything was going well.

"Good," said the Dean. "Then you will be the best batch of Theodore Roosevelt graduates that we've had. The history of the students at Hunter College, from your high school, is not good. Like you, previous students were bright and eager girls, who somehow came to a point where they couldn't or wouldn't apply themselves to the demands of our college. Our experience has been that generally half of Theodore Roosevelt's graduates, who attend Hunter, either drop out or fail. The other half goes on to graduation."

"The five of you were able to meet the qualifications for admission to Hunter, and I congratulate you for that. Yet, if you are like previous Roosevelt High School graduates, only two or perhaps three of you will graduate. Therefore, if any of you feel that the workload at Hunter is getting too difficult for you, please make an appointment with me. Perhaps I'll be able to help you cope with Hunter's demands and improve Roosevelt's graduates' performances."

When the girls left the dean's office, they were scared and insulted. They had the same credentials for acceptance to Hunter as students who had come from other high schools, and they believed that the dean was "out of line."

She wasn't! Of the five girls who entered Hunter from Theodore Roosevelt High School, only Isabelle and Rosemary Cadoro graduated. Marie Calgore, Marilyn White, and Claire Blatt dropped out of college, without graduating

———————

From 1949 to 1950 Isabelle enjoyed being a student at Hunter College. She felt as though a whole new world of learning had opened up for her. Her grades were good and dating Al was good too. Then Isabelle came down with the flu. The flu caused Isabelle to be absent from school for two weeks, and she had to work very hard to catch up in all of her subjects. One subject, however, eluded her. While she was absent, her College Algebra class was learning about permutations, combinations, and probabilities. No matter how hard Isabelle tried, she was unable to teach herself the algebraic material she had missed. In desperation, Isabelle finally turned to Al for help. Mid-term exams were in the offing, and she needed to know the math material she had missed, in order to pass her math mid-term.

Al came over to Isabelle's house with the best intentions in the world. Because he had taken business math in the City College School of Business, he had never taken College Algebra. But Al had a strong bent for mathematics, so he felt sure that by following the instructions in Isabelle's mathematics textbook, he could teach himself, and then teach her. He hoped to succeed where Isabelle had tried to teach herself by using her textbook, but had failed.

After Al had mastered the math that he needed in order to teach Isabelle, he began to show her what he had learned. Either he was a poor teacher or Isabelle was a poor student, because Isabelle simply didn't understand what Al wanted her to know. Very quickly, Al became irritated with her and began to yell at her and roll his eyes in disdain when she made her frequent errors, causing a devastated Isabelle to be very insulted. Al's loud voice, insulting remarks about her inability to learn the material, and his disdainful facial expressions were more than she could bear. Isabelle began to cry and tearfully ordered him to go home.

Al was horrified at what his well-intentioned efforts had brought about, and quickly changed his tone. "I'm so sorry Isabelle," he said, "I lost my patience. I shouldn't have yelled or said most of the things I said. Let's try again. You've got to learn this stuff in order to get a decent grade on your exam."

Isabelle calmed herself, and once more, gave Al her attention. He taught her gently and corrected her mistakes without insulting her. In a very short time, it seemed to Al that Isabelle understood and had mastered permutations, combinations, and probabilities.

When Al went home, things looked as if all was well between the two of them. As they parted, Isabelle thanked Al for his help and gave him a warm kiss.

———

Isabelle received an A on her math exam. She was very grateful to Al for having helped her to achieve this fete, but she was resentful about the fact that it had been such an emotionally trying experience. Try as she might,

Isabelle had some serious doubts about Al. She knew that he was well intentioned and that he cared for her deeply, but she frequently suffered his anger or disdain. She planned to confront him with her worries, so at the very next time that Al rolled his eyes and spoke with annoyance at something Isabelle had said, Isabelle told him about her concern and unhappiness over his frequent criticism. She said that she believed that it would be better for both of them to stop "going steady," date other people, and see how everything turned out. She gave the very reluctant Al, no recourse. Both of them were now free to date others.

———————

Shortly after Isabelle and Al stopped seeing each other exclusively, Isabelle's Uncle Irving came to the Bronx for a visit. He asked his niece about how school was going, and Isabelle told him it was going quite well. He asked Isabelle about how her "love life" was going, and Isabelle told him about her new freedom to date lots of boys.

"How do girls in your all-girls school meet boys?" Uncle Irving asked.

"Through introduction, or going to dances, or joining sororities," answered Isabelle.

"What do sororities do to help their members meet boys?" Uncle Irving inquired.

"They pair up with fraternities from other colleges for parties and dances," Isabelle said, "but there are dances at the 92 Street Y every weekend, and you don't have to be in a sorority to meet boys there," said Isabelle.

"Have you any intention of joining a sorority?" asked Uncle Irving.

"Oh no," laughed Isabelle. "Sororities are very expensive to join. I can meet boys in other ways, and I have plenty of girl friends at school, without having to join a sorority to make friends."

"I know you're hardly going to believe me," said Uncle Irving, "but last night I played pinochle, and all I could do was win! I couldn't understand how I could be so lucky. It seemed that I could do no wrong, and when I walked away from that pinochle table, I was quite a few hundred dollars richer."

"When I got into my car, crazy thoughts kept whirling about in my head. I somehow knew that I needed to come to the Bronx today. Now I know why. I came to the Bronx to find out why I was so damned lucky at pinochle last night. I came to suggest that you join a sorority, because my pinochle buddies have paid for your sorority entrance fees." With that Uncle Irving produced a huge roll of one, five, and ten-dollar bills. There certainly had to be enough in that roll for Isabelle to join a sorority. In fact, there should have been money left over.

Isabelle immediately protested. She refused to take the money saying, "Uncle Irving, I'm sure that you and your family can find fifty different ways to spend the money you've won. And while you're finding ways to spend the money, I'll find boys without joining a sorority."

"I have no doubt that we both can manage, and I wasn't thinking of a sorority as merely a dating bureau. I thought that belonging to a sorority helped a girl make new friendships and made a student's college experience complete. In any case, I honestly believe that last night's winnings were meant for you, so I'm going to leave the money here. Now, if you want to join a sorority, you can. Remember, my pinochle buddies have made it possible."

With that, Uncle Irving laid the roll of bills on the coffee table and prepared to take his leave of Bella and the rest of Bella's family.

———

Isabelle did join a sorority. She rushed and was accepted into the most coveted Jewish sorority at Hunter College. She dated fraternity boys from most of the finest colleges in New York City. Along with them, she also dated Al, and Al always seemed to be the one she liked best. In a very short time, she was once more dating Al exclusively, and sorority was just a place where she had female friends.

Isabelle would have remained in sorority until she graduated from Hunter, if she had not been made aware of the sorority's value system, concerning the acceptance of girls for membership, during *Rush*. Isabelle's sorority was greatly desired, and many girls tried to become members. Each sorority had its criteria for blackballing the girls that they did not care to have joined their group, but Isabelle was flabbergasted when she learned her sorority sisters' reasons for blackballing prospective members.

The leading criteria for acceptance to Isabelle's sorority seemed to be attractiveness. Most very pretty girls were accepted. Being a member of an influential or wealthy family generally gained a girl entrance to the sorority, too. And occasionally, an extremely high grade point average served to gain a girl's acceptance to the group. Isabelle disliked her sorority sisters' criteria for the acceptance of applicants to the sorority, and she really detested their behavior, when a very close friend of hers rushed and was blackballed.

Isabelle's friend Anne lived in the West Bronx. She and Isabelle had met at the beginning of their freshman year, and almost immediately, a close friendship had developed between the two girls. Anne was short and wiry and was an excellent athlete. She planned to major in physical education. While Anne was not attractive, she was not homely either. She was also not highly intellectual, but was greatly interested in people, and valued kindness in others. Above all she was a true and loyal friend. Isabelle thoroughly enjoyed Anne's company, so when Anne informed her that she was planning to rush Isabelle's sorority, Isabelle was delighted. The prospect of Anne being her sorority sister pleased Isabelle completely.

To Isabelle's horror, Anne was blackballed for reasons that Isabelle considered to be superficial and unkind. The general consensus was that Anne was not pretty enough for membership. Isabelle's descriptions of Anne's kindness and loyal friendship fell on the deaf ears of her sorority sisters. They did not believe that Anne possessed the criteria they sought in a sorority sister. After Isabelle protested and touted Anne's good qualities, one of her sorority sisters said, "Isabelle, I know you think we are wrong in blackballing a nice girl like Anne, but Anne is being blackballed for the good of all of us. If we allowed every kindly friend of a sorority sister to become a member, we would soon be known as a sorority that was made up of ordinary looking girls. The *best* fraternities would boycott us. We'd have to go to the parties of average frats."

The approving nods of a large number of Isabelle's sorority sisters clinched it! Isabelle was a sophomore when Anne rushed for sorority. She dropped out of the sorority at the end of her sophomore year. She used her relationship with Al and her impending engagement as her excuse for leaving.

——————

Now that Isabelle was, once more, exclusively dating Al, they began to be somewhat bolder in their sexual behavior. Their kissing became more frequent, more passionate, and more demanding. They were finally driven to satisfy their craving young bodies by fondling each other with heated urgency. They knew they were on dangerous ground as they headed into the summer of 1950. Both of them ascribed to the sexual mores of that time, and wanted desperately to abstain from sexual intercourse until marriage. Because Al respected Isabelle and viewed her as his probable bride, he truly believed that he should abstain from having sexual intercourse with her. (The mores of 1950 permitted boys to discreetly have consensual sex with girls they were not considering for marriage, but strongly urged against intercourse with the girl they might marry. All girls, however, were supposed to remain virgins until they married.) Isabelle, who fully intended to follow the rules for women, did not ascribe to the laxity permitted for males. She fervently hoped that she would be able to save her virginity for her marriage bed and expected abstinence from Al until that time.

Practicalities helped Isabelle and Al to follow 1950's rigid sexual rules. The absence of places where they could comfortably consummate their passion was a great contributor to their mutual chastity. It was very rare for either of their homes to be empty of family and available to them for making love. Heavy "necking" was something they abstained from in such public places as the beach or the park. Only places where they could maintain their privacy and where they would be unlikely to be discovered, served as sites for their sexual trysts.

Consequently, the summer of 1950 saw Isabelle emerge with her virginity intact. Both she and Al went to school every morning that summer; and every night the young couple went to bed frustrated and physically unfulfilled. Isabelle spent her afternoons that were free of schoolwork, on the beach. Al was employed by Moore's once again, but this was his last year there. Al was slated to graduate from City College in September of 1950, and planned to immediately look for a well-paying, full time job.

From the time Al's father died, when Al was only nine years old, Al had earned money. As a small boy, he had delivered groceries. As he grew older, he had taken many different part-time jobs to keep him solvent in his day-to-day travels to and from school. He also provided for most of his own clothing. Al liked to pride himself with the fact that from the time he had been nine years old, his earnings had bought every pair of shoes he had ever worn.

Isabelle, unlike Al, did not earn money when she was a small child. Isabelle took her first job when she was fourteen years old. Her work history included such jobs as being a sales girl in a bathing suit shop, working as a sales girl in a blouse shop on Fourteenth Street in Manhattan, and working as a packer for Klein's Department Store.

Isabelle had hated the bathing suit store job; because she was required to help her customers try on the suits. Some of the customers were sweaty or smelled bad, and Isabelle was disgusted by them. Isabelle stayed in that job for only a month. Bella's pampered daughter quit.

Isabelle's next job, in a blouse store, lasted six months. The manager of that store was often verbally abusive to the employees and frequently yelled at them. Isabelle thoroughly disliked him, even though he had never turned his venom on her. One day, however, he did. He angrily berated her about a blouse that had been left on the counter after it had been rejected by a prospective customer. Isabelle had not left the blouse there, but it didn't matter. She told the manager that he was a tyrant who didn't know how to speak politely. Then Bella's pampered daughter quit her job again.

Ordinarily, Isabelle would not have taken a job at Klein's, because their only part time jobs for girls were working as cashiers or packers. Klein's was a noisy, crowded, low-priced department store, and not at all an environment that appealed to Isabelle. She took the job there, because Al worked there, and on Saturday nights they could leave work together and go on their dates.

During her freshman year at Hunter College, Isabelle worked at Klein's as a packer. She was not allowed to be a cashier until she was eighteen years old and could be bonded. Because she was only seventeen years old, Klein's required a signed work permit, which she had to get from the high school that she had attended. This permit was required of all Klein's employees who were under the age of eighteen, whether they had dropped out of high school or had graduated. This requirement forced Isabelle to make her last trip to Theodore Roosevelt High School, where she had her last encounter with Mrs. Casey, the school's hated dean.

Isabelle stopped at Roosevelt High School at 8:00A.M. on a Tuesday morning. Her first class at Hunter College on Tuesday was at 9:30, so Isabelle believed that she could attend to her business at the high school and get to her class on time. When she entered the high school, she walked briskly to the office and asked the secretary to sign her form. As Isabelle stood waiting for the secretary to finish with the form, Mrs. Casey emerged from her office. In the school surroundings, Mrs. Casey immediately recognized Isabelle.

"What are *you* doing here?" the dean demanded.

"I've come to get a signed work permit," said Isabelle.

"Oh," said Mrs. Casey, venomously. "What happened? I thought you were going to be a college girl!"

"Nothing happened," replied Isabelle. "I'm a student at Hunter College, but I want to work too. I work part-time at Klein's, so I can earn pocket money and clothing money," replied Isabelle.

The dean's nasty face changed. Showing most of her large yellow teeth as she smiled benignly at Isabelle, she said, "I always knew that you would succeed, and now you're doing it. I'm proud of you."

Isabelle took her signed paper and giving the false Mrs. Casey a very dirty look, turned on her heel and left Theodore Roosevelt High School, never to return again.

———

Full-time and part-time packers at Klein's were required to attend a weekly meeting every Saturday morning. Their manager, an angry unpleasant, red headed, middle aged woman they called "Miss Cathy," would harangue them about how they should look and how they should behave when dealing with customers. After the harangue, she would assign them to cash registers, where they would remain for the day, bagging or wrapping the merchandise that had been purchased. Miss Cathy would roam the many floors of the large store, checking each packer's performance as the packer worked at her post.

Most of Miss. Cathy's full-time packers were high school drop-outs. Many of them dressed poorly and many of them wore bizarre fashions. Miss Cathy's Saturday morning speech often addressed the issue of proper working attire.

On Isabelle's second Saturday on the job, Miss Cathy caused her great embarrassment, because after she had harangued the packers about their terrible appearance, she pointed out that Isabelle was dressed appropriately. She made Isabelle stand up and praised her skirt, blouse, hair-do, and make-up. Even though Miss Cathy had been flattering her, Isabelle was seriously discomfited. Her discomfort increased when, very quickly, she became Miss Cathy's pet. Miss Cathy continued to embarrass her during Saturday morning meetings, but she also rewarded her. When registers were assigned, Isabelle was always assigned to either an easy register that just bagged small items, or she was assigned to gift-wrapping. In fact, the abrasive redheaded manager of the packers even spoke to Isabelle gently and politely. Therefore, what could have been a physically and emotionally exhausting job had been made quite easy, because of Miss Cathy's favoritism.

Al was a ticket collector at Klein's Department Store. He periodically collected the tickets that had been removed from purchased merchandise, by going from register to register. The tickets were then brought to the keypunch operators. In this era before computers, keypunch was the state-of-the-art tabulating method for a store, and Klein's had a very large keypunch department that was fed by collectors like Al.

When Al was on his rounds, he never failed to stop at Isabelle's register to chat with her. One afternoon, Miss Cathy saw them chatting. That evening, when Isabelle went to her locker, Miss Cathy, who had been waiting there, accosted her. "I saw you talking to that awful boy from keypunch," said Miss Cathy. "A lovely girl like you should be more discriminating."

"I like him," answered Isabelle. "What do you think is wrong with him?"

"He's got a nasty mouth and he's a Jew!" Miss Cathy exclaimed venomously.

"I know he's a Jew," retorted Isabelle. "And so am I!"

Miss Cathy's face turned as red as her hair. She didn't even make an attempt at an apology. She just turned and stalked off.

When Isabelle met Al that night, they both laughed at Isabelle's exchange with Miss Cathy. Al told Isabelle that Miss Cathy had tried to boss him around, so he informed her that she had no authority over him. "From that time on," he said, "Miss Cathy has been gruff and unpleasant with me. When she speaks to me unpleasantly, I answer her in kind."

When Isabelle came to work on the following Tuesday afternoon, she found that she had been assigned to work at the coat department. After a day at school, plus several hours of boxing heavy coats, Isabelle was exhausted when she came home.

For the next several weeks, Isabelle was always given the most difficult assignments. Bella saw her daughter's exhaustion and questioned her about it. Isabelle said it was nothing, because she didn't want Bella to know what was going on.

On the following Saturday, Bella decided to go shopping at Klein's. When she found her daughter, Isabelle was boxing heavy winter coats, without a moment's respite. She caught Isabelle's eye and asked her what time she was going to eat lunch. When Isabelle told her, Bella said, "I'll meet you in the restaurant across the street and I'll order for you, so that you can get back to work on time."

When Isabelle arrived at the restaurant, Bella spoke to her firmly. "I did not raise you to be enslaved for a couple of pennies per week that you throw away on clothes you don't even need. You are working much harder than a student should. If it doesn't destroy your health, it will affect your work at school. School is your first priority and I want you to quit this job!"

Isabelle liked her earnings. She spent them on clothes and other things that she could not expect her parents to provide. Even more, she liked meeting Al after work on Saturdays, but observing that Bella was adamant, Isabelle said in a conciliatory tone, "Mama, I promise you that if I feel too tired, or my work interferes with my school work, I'll quit."

Her mother, not wanting to be overbearing said, "We'll see; but we may have to talk about this again."

———

Miss Cathy continued to harass Isabelle, and during the first week in October, she called her aside and said that it was necessary for Isabelle to work from Monday through Saturday during the store's big Columbus Day coat sale. Miss Cathy had assigned Isabelle to one of the registers in the coat department and she expected her to pack coats every day of the sale.

Isabelle told Miss Cathy that she had been hired to work Tuesday evenings, Thursday evenings, and all day on Saturdays. She said that not only could she not work every day that week, she had been planning to ask for Tuesday and Thursday off, because she needed to prepare for mid-term exams.

Miss Cathy exploded! "This is a place of business! You had better set your priorities straight!"

"Done!" exclaimed Isabelle. "School is my priority. I quit!"

Isabelle did not even finish work that day. She walked away from Miss Cathy, and said angrily, "I quit! Be sure you have my check mailed to me!"

———

Isabelle's idol and mentor was her cousin Millie, who had recently been married. Millie had dropped out of college, when she married, and because she was extremely beautiful, was modeling high priced ladies' suits in the garment district. Now unemployed, Isabelle decided to follow Millie's suggestion, and try her hand at modeling again. Isabelle had had an unpleasant experience on her first and only part-time modeling job, when the firm's male showroom manager barged into the models' dressing room in order to issue some orders. At the time, the firm's three models, Isabelle among them, were in their undergarments. Isabelle was the only one who protested the manager's intrusion. Everyone else laughed at her reaction and good naturedly assured her that it was "standard operating procedures" for the manager to walk into the models' dressing room, unannounced. "We are always covered by our underwear," said one of the models. "No one can see anything important."

Isabelle quit that job that day and now that she wanted to return to modeling, she wanted to work somewhere other than in the garment district. She believed that modeling for a department store, part-time, would enable her to work in a place where her privacy would be respected. Getting a job as a model in a department store, however, was a difficult matter, because there were few such jobs available.

As if it were fated, on the weekend after she had spoken to Millie and had determined to try modeling again, Isabelle saw an ad in the *Help Wanted Female* section of the *New York Times,* saying that Macy's was looking for models to work part-time. She applied for the job, was hired, but was disappointed to learn that the job would last for only six weeks.

———

Macy's fabric department was holding a six-week fabric fair. They needed several full-time models and two part-time models who would model clothing made from the fabrics Macy's Fabric Department created. When there were no fashion shows being presented, the models would distribute little, brightly wrapped gifts of thread, buttons, trimmings, tape measures, and other sundries, while wearing extremely lovely suits made from the department's fabrics, and supplied to them by the store.

Macy's salary for the two part-time models was much higher than the salaries paid to Macy's part-time sales clerks, but was lower than the salaries paid to the full-time models. Isabelle however, could only work part-time, because, as she had informed the heinous Miss. Cathy, school was her first priority. Besides, Macy's promised the two part-time models sales clerk jobs, unfortunately with a decrease in salary, after the fabric fair ended. Hopefully, this would keep Isabelle employed for a long while. This job portended to be more permanent and better than previous jobs had been. In addition, Macy's was a finer store than Klein's. Isabelle accepted the job, feeling very positive about it.

Macy's fabric fair drew crowds of women. In 1949, many women still sewed clothing for themselves and for members of their families. They loved seeing the new styles and fabrics being displayed. They particularly liked the small gifts being distributed by the models they had recently seen modeling lovely clothes for them.

Lola was the other part-time model who had been hired to work with Isabelle. Lola and Isabelle were the only two college students modeling in the fabric fair, and the two girls quickly became friends.

Lola's auburn hair and pretty, freckled face contributed to her being presented as the perky model, modeling mostly sporty or casual clothes. Business suits, formal gowns, and dressy cocktail outfits showed off Isabelle's sultry good looks, as she walked across the stage that had been constructed for the fashion shows.

Lola was a student at Brooklyn College. She was engaged to be married to a boy whom she had dated since her high school days. She was a year older than Isabelle, and she and her fiancé, Sanford, were to be married in June of 1950.

After the fabric fair came to an end, Isabelle was offered a position in the lamp department, selling trimmings for lampshades. While most people in 1949 bought completely finished lampshades, there was a sizable market consisting of those who bought unadorned lampshades, which they trimmed themselves. Others bought the trimmings to repair or refresh lampshades that had become old and shabby.

Isabelle thoroughly disliked selling the boring lampshade trimmings, but Macy's considered it to be a job that demanded greater skill than ordinary sales. Consequently, while Isabelle's salary was smaller than the salary she had received when she was modeling her newly diminished salary was not quite as diminished as it might have been.

Lola was not as lucky as Isabelle. She was only offered an ordinary job, selling women's sweaters, for which she received a much lower salary than she had received as a model. Lola remained with Macy's until the end of the semester, when she dropped out of Brooklyn College and took a well-paying, full-time job. Her new employer was the telephone company, which had a history of never knowingly hiring Jews. Recently, they had changed their discriminatory policies, and Lola took a job with them that was considered quite a coup for a Jewish girl. Isabelle considered Lola's new job to be sabotaging her future. In 1950, many girls dropped out of college when they were contemplating marriage or had actually gotten married, but many other married female students stayed in school until they graduated. Unlike her cousin Millie and Lola, Isabelle planned to be in the latter group. If she married while she was still going to school, Isabelle did not plan to drop out. She knew that this was what Bella wanted, and she wanted it too.

Isabelle's friendship with Lola ended fairly soon after Lola left Macy's. They went to different schools, lived far away from each other, and would soon live very different lives.

Isabelle was, thankfully, transferred from lamp trimmings to Macy's Little Shop. In the Little Shop she sold extremely expensive designer clothing. Some of her customers were difficult, haughty, or spoiled women, but most of them were quite pleasant. Isabelle would have thoroughly enjoyed staying at her part-time job at Macy's, until she graduated from Hunter College, if one day her supervisor had not asked her to temporarily help out in the Bridal shop. An elderly couple had come in to buy a bridal gown for a girl who had not accompanied them. The supervisor thought that perhaps the wedding gown was for a girl who had passed away. (A wedding gown was sometimes purchased as the burial dress for a deceased single woman.) The couple had pointed out Isabelle as a girl who resembled their granddaughter, and they asked if she would consent to try on some wedding gowns, so that they could select one that would be becoming to her. Isabelle was spooked, but she tried on as many wedding gowns and veils as the elderly couple requested. They were very grateful and heaped great praise on Isabelle's manner and cooperation.

Before Isabelle knew it, she had been permanently transferred to the Bridal Shop. While this too was considered a prestigious selling position,

Isabelle found it to be an extremely difficult place to work. The gowns were kept in a loft, located up a narrow, winding flight of stairs. The sales staff were required to climb these stairs in order to return and fetch the heavy wedding gowns. They descended the terrible staircase while carrying the heavy wedding gowns that were to be tried on. Isabelle had quite a few near- accidents on the dangerous stairs; and finally when a full-time sales person fell down the stairs and broke her leg, Isabelle knew that she needed another job.

———

Isabelle's next job was truly the job that she intended to keep until she graduated from college. On Monday and Wednesday afternoons, Isabelle taught tap dancing for two Arthur Murray Children's tap dancing classes. She also taught three children's tap dancing classes on Saturday. She loved working with the children and choreographing dance routines that were on the children's levels. She surprised herself with how much she remembered from her dancing school days, but having danced seriously from ages 4-14, she reckoned some of it would never be lost. She was completely delighted to discover that the longer she taught the children at Arthur Murray, the better dancers they became and the better she became too.

The salary at Arthur Murray depended upon how many children were enrolled in each of Isabelle's classes. Isabelle made more money there than at any of her previous part-time jobs.

———

It was 2:00 P.M. on Tuesday, Isabelle's earliest day of the week for leaving school. Her Political Science Class had just ended and as she gathered her belongings to leave, she glanced at the side chalkboard. As usual, it was covered with announcements pertaining to club meetings and lectures. One announcement, however, was different from the rest. It stated that at 4PM, that very day, a member of Alcoholics Anonymous would be speaking to interested students. The talk would be given in the vicinity of Isabelle's Political Science classroom.

Isabelle decided to kill some time in the library and then come back to attend the Alcoholics Anonymous talk. As she left the library and walked down the hall, Isabelle thought about her ambivalent feelings toward her step-father. On the one hand, she loved him deeply for the love and total acceptance he had always shown her. On the other hand, she hated his repulsive, drunken behavior, as he snored in an easy chair with mucus running out of his nose into his open mouth. She detested constantly stumbling upon the empty wine bottles he had already drained, or on his partially drained bottles of *Sneaky Pete* (very cheap wine), which he thought he had carefully hidden in the family's tiny apartment. When Isabelle found one of his "hidden treasures," she poured the contents of the bottle down the sink or down the toilet. If Hymie was conscious when Isabelle made her find, Isabelle nastily informed him of her intentions. She said such things as:

"I'm pouring this garbage down the toilet. It may clean the pipes, but the toilet won't get drunk and cause everyone in the house to want to vomit in disgust!" or, "Watch this crap go down the drain Daddy. At least the drain doesn't have a wife or children who pine for its company and attention. The drain has no obligations to a family."

Hymie would become enraged when Isabelle disposed of his wine. He allowed himself very little money for his personal needs or his heinous habit. So that Bella could run the household, he gave her most of his small earnings. Consequently, it was difficult for him to replace the wine Isabelle had poured out. But, even more vexing, were Isabelle's hateful, sarcastic, disrespectful remarks. Their truth stung him terribly, and he feared he was losing the love of the step-daughter he adored and her mother, who was truly "the love of his life."

Isabelle knew that Hymie was a good man. She often wished she could find a way to help him. She had heard of Alcoholics Anonymous and the good work it did, but in the immigrant Jewish community in which she lived, there was very little problem drinking, and even less discussion about it. Isabelle fervently hoped that A.A. would show her a way to help Hymie, because while his drinking infuriated her, she deeply loved and valued the sober Hymie.

———

The room was practically empty, "Could it be," thought Isabelle, "that so few people at the college have no curiosity or need for this organization?

Could it be that such a small number of her fellow students were affected by problem drinking?"

The four students in the room listened intently to the speaker from A.A. She told them about the organization's beginnings, and how A.A. had turned her life completely around. She described how A.A. worked, and invited the four young women who had come to the meeting, to speak to her personally.

Two of the four students left the room without speaking to the speaker. Isabelle and one other girl approached her. The other student discussed her concerns about her fiancé. She thought he drank too much and she was worried about his prospective stability as a husband.

The speaker told the worried student that alcoholics were among the most difficult people to have as husbands or wives. She suggested that the young woman confront her fiancé on the issue of his drinking and observe him to see if he was capable of abstaining or drastically reducing his alcohol consumption. "If he cannot cut down sufficiently," the A.A. speaker said, "you should follow one of two courses.... either break off your relationship or get him to A.A."

The young woman left the room looking very worried and very frightened.

Isabelle told the woman from A.A. that there was no doubt in her mind that her step-father was an alcoholic. The A.A. program seemed to have strong possibilities for helping him. Isabelle asked the woman for the address of an Alcoholics Anonymous meeting place to which she could bring Hymie.

The speaker from A.A. consulted a list she carried with her, and suggested an A.A. meeting place that met on Wednesday nights at a Catholic Church in the lower East Bronx. This church was an easy bus ride from Minford Place, where the family lived.

Isabelle sincerely thanked the woman from A.A and they both expressed their hopes for Hymie's success with A.A.'s program.

––––––––––

When Isabelle came home, she immediately discussed A.A. with Bella. Bella was more than enthusiastic. She had had no idea that help existed.

286

She had believed that if a person with an alcohol problem wanted to be free from it, he had to do it by himself. Isabelle's description of the work of A.A. seemed practical to Bella, who became impatient for Hymie to come home from work, so that she could discuss it with him.

Hymie came home, already slightly tipsy. Bella angrily told him that she needed to discuss a very important matter with him, but would say nothing about it until he was totally sober. A contrite Hymie ate some supper and dozed off in his favorite chair. At 9:15 Hymie awoke, and was cold sober when he found Bella and Isabelle sitting at the kitchen table and chatting.

"What was it that you wanted to discuss with me?" he asked.

Isabelle then proceeded to tell him what she had learned from the speaker from Alcoholics Anonymous.

Hymie's eyes watered a little as he answered, "I've heard about them. They're a bunch of religious fanatics, claiming miracles where doctors have failed. If there was anyone in the world who wanted to stop drinking more than I do," he continued, "I'd like to meet him. But when the alcohol owns you, you can't stop!"

Bella interrupted, "I've heard enough of that." she exploded. "The A.A. meeting is on Wednesday. Isabelle and I will go with you; and it's totally non-negotiable! If you are not home on time to wash up, shave, and put on clean clothes, I'll never forgive you. I want you totally sober and thinking positively. I have a good feeling about all of this."

––––––––––

Hymie brooded over A.A. for an entire week. Then it was Wednesday of the following week- the day of the A.A. meeting.

Hymie did clean up and shave. He had donned his clean clothes and seemed ready to go, when he suddenly plunked himself down on the sofa and said, "the two of you- women that I love more than life- railroading me to a place where they'll probably lock me up and torture me!"

"Enough nonsense," scolded Bella. "Get yourself up. We're going to the bus stop. Even Phyllis is coming." A frightened Hymie slowly arose from the sofa.

As they walked to the bus stop, Bella took Hymie's left arm and

Isabelle took his right arm. He muttered and mumbled protests all the way, continued his protests on the bus, and protested loudest during the short walk to the church in which A.A. was having its meeting in the church's basement.

The large basement meeting room was packed with people. A table occupied by a man and a woman was placed at the back of the hall, right near the door. When Bella, Isabelle, Phyllis, and Hymie entered, the man at the table arose and introduced himself as George. He explained the A.A. program to the four of them. He said that he would probably be Hymie's sponsor, the A.A. member who would always be available if Hymie felt a need for companionship or for help in avoiding his first drink. Taking the first drink caused an alcoholic to resume his drinking, George explained. He also told them that A.A. liked new members to enter the hospital for a week, in order to be assisted in "drying out." After the hospital purged Hymie's body of alcohol, he would be ready to undertake the full program, and learn the ways of A.A. in assisting alcoholics to remain sober.

A skeptical Hymie asked, "Is it really a hospital that you're taking me to, or am I being put away?"

George laughed, "It's really a hospital. When you're truly sober, you'll laugh at your drunken fears. But now, the meeting is starting," he continued, "let's sit down and listen."

Three speakers spoke that night. Each told about his or her journey into alcoholism, the agonies of being addicted, and most of all the agony of not being in control of one's own life. They spoke of the joys of the sobriety A.A. had helped them to attain. None of their stories were the same, indeed, their stations in life were quite different; yet, each suffered anguish when under the control of alcohol, and each was jubilant at being freed from his alcohol addiction.

Hymie was deeply pensive on his way home from the meeting. After much thought, he told Bella that he would give A.A. a try.

True to his word, Hymie's sponsor, George, took Hymie through all of the hospital's red tape. The family was not permitted to visit Hymie while he was "drying out," but George was allowed to do so. After the week was over, George brought Hymie home. He looked happy and fit and he had not had a drink for a week. Best of all, Hymie announced that he didn't miss his drinks at all.

George informed him that he *would* miss them. He urged him to telephone when he felt the need for a drink. He said that he could help him avoid the drink at those times. If Hymie didn't call, George warned, he would have a *slip*. Slips were commonplace in A.A., and always loom as a threat to the recovering alcoholic. Some slips were terminal, leading to more and more drinking, and precluding a cure. "Alcoholism is a disease," George said. "Many of us beat it, but some fall by the wayside. Follow the rules you learned, Hymie, and we will be *sober* buddies forever."

George's words were prophetic. Hymie did have slips. But when Hymie finally got the "program" he was alcohol-free for ten years. During his ten years of sobriety, until his death at sixty-seven years of age, Hymie became the sponsor of many recovering alcoholics. Hymie even helped others during his early years of sobriety, when he, himself, was plagued by occasional slips.

———

People think they know the alcoholic in their family but they usually are mistaken. The person they think they know has masked many of his character traits and many of his abilities while in his alcoholic haze. When he becomes sober, these hidden traits and abilities often come to the surface. In Hymie's case, when he drank, he said very little and slept a lot. When he became sober, however, Isabelle learned that he was a wonderful and funny storyteller. He regaled her with stories of his childhood in Lithuania, his early youth in the Catskill Mountains of New York, and his experiences as a soldier in France during and following World War I.

Hymie's storytelling skills shone even more, when he took to the podium, during AA meetings. He spoke with pathos of his despair, when alcohol ruled his life; and he described the damage that drinking had done to his first wife, his children, and his present family. He usually managed to find a humorous note to interject to lighten up his somber story, and whenever he referred to Isabelle's role in bringing him to sobriety, he called his beloved step-daughter his *Civilian Sponsor.* He always spoke tenderly about his beloved Bella, whom he referred to as *his bride.*

———

Bella and Hymie's last years were marred only by the vicious pancreatic cancer that killed him. They loved and cherished each other and felt blessed in their family and in Hymie's hard-won sobriety.

———

One of Isabelle's sorority sisters, who lived on Staten Island, threw a big bash on New Year's Eve, 1951. Isabelle and Al were among her many guests welcoming in the New Year. The party was festive and gay, even though the United States was at war in Korea and many of the young men at the party would soon be drafted into the armed services.

Al and Isabelle sat at the table wondering aloud about what 1951 would bring. Al had been working at a small sheet metal company, where he was the office manager and Federal Contracting Officer. As the Federal Contracting Officer he did research to inform his company's owner of any bids he considered to be appropriate for the firm. Al, who had received his Bachelors Degree in September of 1950, would probably have been drafted into the military, if his employment as Federal Contracting Officer had not been classified as essential to the war effort. Because of this, he was still a civilian on New Year's Eve.

Isabelle asked Al to dance with her. As usual, when confronted with dancing, Al refused. Isabelle told him angrily that *he* should have been asking *her* to dance. The music was lovely and almost everyone was on the dance floor, making Al's refusal to participate even more upsetting to Isabelle. Seeing her distress, Al reluctantly led her onto the dance floor. The romantic music caused most of the dancers to move a little closer, and made many of them feel romantically inclined. As they danced, holding each other close, Al regretted that he had made Isabelle angry, and he whispered into her ear, "I love you. Please forgive me."

"I love you, too," she answered, "and before you're drafted, I'd like to see us married."

Al was flabbergasted! He had "hit the jackpot" without even having to propose! Having to propose had seemed unbearably difficult for Al, even though he loved Isabelle with all of his heart. Al, who was able to be "the life of the party," telling jokes and funny stories, was incredibly shy when it came to expressing his emotions. Al answered Isabelle's proposal with a long and wonderful kiss. When they separated he said, "We're engaged! We'll have to discuss the particulars concerning our being engaged and getting married."

Just then the television announcer started the countdown for the New Year. When 1951 arrived, Al and Isabelle felt sure that it would be the best year of their lives.

In early January there was an in-depth discussion about the purchase of an engagement ring and the planning for an engagement party. Isabelle had a personal philosophy concerning engagement rings. She believed that the ring should be the very best ring that the groom could afford to buy, because later, when they were married, their money would probably be spent on necessities. "Only now," said Isabelle, "can we afford to act frivolously about the ring I will wear for the rest of my life."

When they had first discussed an engagement ring, to Isabelle's immense surprise, Al had informed her that he had a significant amount of money deposited in the bank. Having heard Isabelle's philosophy about engagement rings, he said that they could use that money for the purchase of her ring. Al told her how he had earned the money during a freak, very severe blizzard that had paralyzed New York City two years before. At that time, Al had been employed by a neighbor who owned a parking lot very near the New York Coliseum in Manhattan. Al's job consisted of parking cars, collecting fees, and helping returning drivers to locate their parked automobiles. He performed these duties every day, after school at City College. Al had to turn in any money he received from people who had parked prior to 5:00 p.m. His salary was made up from any tips or fees he received from people who parked after 5:00 p.m.

When the snows came, the parking lot was full, because the Coliseum was having a trade show. When people came for their cars, very few of them could get them out from under the deep blanket of snow that had all but buried them. Al charged the frustrated automobile owners a stiff fee for digging out their cars. Freeing the cars from under almost two feet of snow was grueling labor, and Al worked at this intense labor for almost a week. Providentially school was out for winter break, causing Al's days to be free for digging the cars out for their owners. At the end of all of his digging, Al had banked enough money to purchase a truly lovely diamond engagement ring for Isabelle.

Al and Isabelle decided to skip school and work, so that they could choose an engagement ring. They had planned to go to the Jewelry Exchange, in Manhattan, where they hoped to find a lovely ring at a good price.

It was a bright, sunny, crisp, and very cold day in late January. Isabelle and Al alighted from the subway station and enjoyed the cold, clear air as they walked to the large wholesale jewelry center. They entered and left several shops that claimed to sell to both jewelers and to the public at wholesale prices. By going from shop to shop they got an idea of how diamonds were priced, and believed that they now could make an intelligent decision about a diamond ring.

A little before noon, the young couple stopped at a luncheonette for a light bite and some deep discussion about diamonds. When they finished their lunch, they planned to resume their perusal of the Diamond Market, but as they emerged on Fifth Avenue, they passed a large corner store that looked like a typical jewelry store, but proclaimed itself to be a jewelry pawnshop. The window of the store arrested Isabelle's eye. She stopped her rapid walk back to the wholesale diamond market to examine the merchandise in the pawnshop's crowded window. The window was filled with diamond jewelry of all kinds. One section of the huge window displayed diamond engagement rings, ranging from miniscule stones to solitaires that were vulgar because of their very large size. Isabelle's eyes stopped at a lovely round solitaire, flanked by smaller diamonds on each side. It was set in what appeared to be either white gold or platinum. Excitedly she pointed the ring out to Al and said, "We have a fairly good idea of what these rings should cost. I'd like to inquire about the diamond solitaire displayed in this window. If we like what the pawnshop jeweler says, and the ring is within our price range, I'd like to have it professionally appraised. If the price is right, I'd like to purchase that ring for my engagement ring."

Al agreed and that the ring was lovely, and they went into the store. The carat count, platinum setting, and brilliance of the diamond showed that its price was commensurate with the prices of similar diamonds the young couple had seen at the Jewelry Exchange. They made the proper arrangements for taking the ring to an independent appraisal agency. Isabelle hoped that the ring would appraise properly, because she had fallen in love with it.

To Isabelle's delight, the ring was found to be priced fairly, and Isabelle and Al returned to the pawnshop to complete their purchase. A deliriously happy young woman left the pawnshop, wearing her sparkling diamond engagement ring.

On the following day, the newly engaged young woman returned to her classes at Hunter College. She sported her lovely engagement ring and showed it to everyone she knew. During the second period, Isabelle had a double period of Zoology. She hurried to the large laboratory, planning to show her newly acquired ring to those classmates who were her friends. Isabelle's intentions were waylaid, because when she entered the lab, she was assailed by the strong, pungent odor of formaldehyde and the sight of her classmates busily setting up lab stations and beginning to cut into fetal pigs. Isabelle immediately understood that she needed to go to her professor to find out what she had missed on the previous day, and how she could arrange to catch up.

Isabelle's professor informed her that he had distributed fetal pigs, a syllabus, and surgical instruments to each of the students. Each girl was to dissect her fetal pig according to the instructions in her syllabus. The competed project was due in mid-April, after Hunter's Spring Break. He directed Isabelle to two large wooden barrels filled with formaldehyde. They were located in the back of the room. He instructed Isabelle to select a pig from a barrel and then return to him for further instructions.

Much to Isabelle's horror, there was only one pig left. *It was hardly a fetal pig!* It was a dead piglet whose development showed that it had been ready to be born! Instead of pink, soft fetal skin, this pig had black and white stiff fur, wet from formaldehyde that had grown out of a fairly tough young pig's hide. This last remaining piglet was bigger and much tougher than any of the other fetal pigs being worked on by her classmates.

When Isabelle returned to her professor to complain about the piglet, he commiserated with her and agreed that the tough, well-developed, little piglet would be more difficult to dissect than a small, pink fetal pig. "But," he said, "You have four hours per week for two-and-a-half months to work on your project. I'm sure that everything will be all right. "Besides," he concluded, "you have taken the last of the fetal pigs, and I have no other pig to offer you". Her teacher handed his distressed student a set of surgical instruments and explained the use of each implement. He then wished Isabelle well on her project.

Isabelle returned to her lab space, read the directions in her syllabus, and splayed out her pig as directed. She then proceeded to make the first incision in the pig's chest, but her surgical knife didn't seem to work. It didn't incise the chest at all. Isabelle requested help from the student working near her. The neighboring girl tried to get the first incision started for Isabelle, but she too failed. She then tried to cut Isabelle's pig with her own surgical knife. In no time flat, the incision was made.

Isabelle promptly went back to her instructor and told him about what had occurred. The professor surmised that Isabelle's surgical tools were dull and he exchanged them for the last set of surgical tools in his possession. This set of surgical tools proved to be slightly sharper than Isabelle's previous set, but was still dull enough to cause Isabelle great difficulty and frustration in her work. Isabelle now understood that the day she stayed out of school to purchase her engagement ring, would make the cost of the ring far greater than she had imagined. She would now have to dissect a very tough piglet with tools that were insufficient for a soft little, pink fetal pig. A large portion of her zoology grade would come from the fetal pig project. Isabelle sadly knew that *she had her work cut out for her.*

———

Spring Break arrived and Isabelle found that she had made small headway on her project, using her maddeningly dull instruments on the stubborn, tough piglet. Consequently, Isabelle wrapped the piglet, whose innards were dripping out of the major incision, in copious numbers of paper towels, and stuffed the entire odiferous, disgusting bundle into a shopping bag. She planned to take the formaldehyde-soaked, dead creature to her home and continue to work on her zoology project there during her spring holiday.

When Isabelle arrived at home, no one was in. She cleared a space in the refrigerator and deposited the damp towel-wrapped bundle on the center shelf. She then sat down in an easy chair in the living room and began to read a book. As she was reading, Bella arrived from Jennings Street with a shopping cart loaded with newly purchased food. She opened her refrigerator, to begin stowing away her groceries, when she spied the towel wrapped bundle. Isabelle was startled from her reading by her mother's loud screams. She went flying into the kitchen where she saw her piglet splayed out on a bed of formaldehyde-soaked paper towels, guts spilling out onto the table.

"Where did this disgusting, stinking, dead pig come from?" screamed Bella.

Isabelle tried to explain, but the highly over-wrought Bella, didn't let her finish. "Get this damn pig out of here!" screamed Bella. "Put it on the fire escape….I don't ever want to see it again!" Bella, who very rarely used even the word "damn," continued her off-color tirade. "How the hell could you put that vile thing near our food? Have you lost your mind?" Then, to Isabelle's horror, her mother sat down at the kitchen table and sobbed.

Isabelle immediately rewrapped the pig and put it on the fire escape. She knew that it would quickly begin to decompose there, so she knew that she must complete her despised project in the lab at school. She hated to have to make a daily trip to Hunter College during her spring vacation, but she knew that she had no other alternative. Her mother, who usually supported every one of Isabelle's school endeavors, had clearly shown that she would not countenance the piglet in her home. "Perhaps Bella's kosher antecedents were haunting her," humorously thought Isabelle. But, Isabelle really knew that her piglet's disgusting aspect and odor, plus the need to store this obnoxious corpse in the refrigerator to avoid decomposition, had pushed the bar of Bella's support or tolerance. Isabelle would have to finish her hated project at the school lab after she had earnestly apologized to her mother.

———

Al's long-widowed mother surprised everyone by getting married in late February. Eva had married a man, who many years before, had been her neighbor. Their families had lost touch, and neither Eva nor Al's stepfather, Max, had heard of each other's widowhood. When they met again, many years later, they were instantly attracted to each other. Their marriage occurred very soon after this meeting and proved to be a long and very good one. Everyone in Al's family approved of their union and truly liked and respected Max.

———

Al's mother didn't have time to catch her breath after her own wedding, when the engagement party of her son took place. Eva liked Isabelle very much, but considered her to be over-indulged by Bella. Eva knew that Bella had no extra money to spare, so she couldn't understand Bella's allowing Isabelle to spend all the money she earned on herself. She believed that Isabelle, like Al, should pay something toward her room and board.

The engagement party was held in a synagogue basement party room, located close to where Al lived. Everyone had a good time at the party. They enjoyed the delicious catered lunch and the opportunity to visit with friends and family. By 5:00P.M. all of the guests had left, and Al and Isabelle repaired to his house to look at their gifts. Most of the gifts were cash, so the engaged couple planned to open their first joint bank account.

———

April flew by with Isabelle, her future-mother-in-law, and Bella spending much of the month searching for a suitable, affordable, catering hall in which to hold the wedding. The bridal pair wanted to be married as soon as possible, because Al's one-year deferment from the draft was coming to an end, and there was a good chance that it would not be renewed. They fortunately found a suitable hall that was available in mid-June. It was available because another couple had cancelled their wedding.

Bella didn't have the money to pay for the modest wedding they were planning. She borrowed some of the money she needed from the bank account Isabelle and Al had established with the cash engagement gifts they had received. Al's mother paid for the music and for the bar at the wedding. To save money, Isabelle's wedding gown was borrowed from a friend and her bridal veil borrowed from another friend. Isabelle and Al were having a very humble wedding, indeed, but nevertheless, it pleased them greatly.

———

There was only one great extravagance for the wedding that Isabelle insisted upon- the diamond wedding band she would not do without. Isabelle had seen a lovely and unusual diamond wedding band on one of her classmates at Hunter College. The platinum band consisted of a row of small diamonds that went all the way around the finger. Isabelle fell in love with the ring, and determined to have one like it.

When Al's mother heard about Isabelle's wishes, she told her that there were two jewelers living in her apartment house. She would talk to them about bringing wedding rings to her home that matched the description of Isabelle's wished-for ring. Isabelle could come over and decide upon the ring she wanted. Either jeweler would probably sell it at a very good price.

When Isabelle came to her future mother in-law's home, Eva had four flimsy rings on display on her kitchen table. All of them had tiny chips instead of full-cut diamonds. On none of them did the tiny chips go all the way around the finger. What they all had in common, however, was that all four of them were inexpensive and unattractive. Isabelle said, "Obviously you didn't understand what it was that I wanted. I'd rather wear an unadorned wedding band than one of these flimsy, ugly rings. I won't even consider them."

Her future mother in-law replied in a patronizing tone, "You are young and you don't understand your responsibilities. You and Al will need to furnish an apartment, and you're both poor kids. You shouldn't even consider an expensive wedding ring; especially after the expensive engagement ring my son bought you."

"It's not a matter of my age," replied Isabelle. It's just that you and I have different philosophies about wedding rings. I believe that I should get the best ring I can, before I'm married, because later on I really *will* have responsibilities and will not want to use our money to upgrade a ring."

"And where will the money for this ring come from? You and Al spent all the money he saved from his digging out cars after the blizzard, to buy your engagement ring."

"Oh, I was planning to use the money we got as gifts at our engagement party," said Isabelle.

"And what about furniture?" demanded Al's mother. "You won't have any money to buy furniture!"

"You and my parents managed to furnish your apartments even though you were very poor. Do you think Al and I, both of us people who have gone to college, will be as poor as you and my family were? If *you* managed to get furniture, we'll get furniture too."

"You're a spoiled brat!" Al's mother answered angrily. "I feel sorry for both of you."

Isabelle answered even more angrily. "Don't ever try to run my life. I make my own decisions!" With that, Isabelle left Eva's house, slamming the door behind her.

When Al came home from work and was told about the event that had transpired that afternoon, he was horrified. His mother was terribly upset, and it hurt him, but he believed that Isabelle was right. His mother had no right to impose her will or standards upon them.

———

Al went to Isabelle's house and cooled her down. They made plans to go to the watch factory owned by one of Al's neighbors. Mr. Pressor manufactured very dressy lady's watches in diamond- rimmed cases. Al felt sure that Mr. Pressor would be able to make a wedding ring to suit Isabelle, and would treat them fairly, because he always said he owed Al a debt of gratitude. He said that his daughter, Esther, would never have graduated from high school, if Al hadn't tutored her in math.

When the engaged pair went to Mr. Pressor's watch factory, everything happened as Al thought it would. Isabelle described the ring she wanted and Mr. Pressor then allowed her to select the diamonds she wanted. He agreed with her choice, saying that the selected diamonds in a platinum setting would look beautiful with her engagement ring.

When the wedding ring was finished, it was, indeed, beautiful. Isabelle believed her wedding set was perfect, and she felt sure that she would love her rings forever.

———

One couple planned for married life, while another couple's married life was ended by death. On the morning after Isabelle had selected the diamonds for her wedding band, Sarah awoke and was surprised to find that Appleman was still asleep. She got dressed, ate her breakfast, and then went back to the bedroom to see if Appleman had awakened. He had not stirred. It being 9:30A.M., Sarah thought she should rouse him, because Appleman often had early appointments that sent him on his way before 9:00A.M. It was unlike him to sleep so late.

Sarah gently tapped Appleman's shoulder. He didn't move. Becoming alarmed, Sarah shook him very vigorously. Receiving no response, she realized that he was either unconscious or dead. She put a flimsy piece of paper under Appleman's nose. It did not stir. He wasn't breathing. Appleman was dead. Sarah was a widow once again.

Isabelle and Al, 1951

Chapter 15: 87 Street

Though very modest, their wedding was lovely. The bride was beautiful, the groom was handsome, and except for the Korean War, which clouded their happy future, Isabelle and Al were very happy and unafraid. Al continued his work at the sheet metal firm and Isabelle continued as a full-time student at Hunter College and a part-time teacher of tap dancing at Arthur Murray's Dance Studio.

Al and Isabelle moved into a large one room furnished apartment in a converted brownstone. (Brownstones are old luxury homes on New York's east and west sides. Some of these were converted into apartment houses.) When they returned from their one-week honeymoon in the Berkshire Mountains, they found the evidence of Bella's presence in their home. Their miniature refrigerator was crammed full of food. Milk, butter, eggs, cheese, fruits, and salad vegetables filled every inch of refrigerator space. On the floor, alongside the refrigerator were several halved potatoes spread with J.O. Paste, a very strong domestic insecticide, particularly effective for killing cockroaches. More of these treated potatoes were scattered around their living quarters and placed in the bathroom they were to share with their next-door neighbor, whom they had not yet met. Obviously, when Bella had come into the bridal pair's prospective home she had met the unwelcome pests, and had begun immediately, what would be an ongoing campaign of cockroach extermination.

The newlyweds had a considerable amount of money in their bank account, because most of their wedding guests had given them gifts of cash. These gifts ranged from paltry $10 gifts to the most generous gift of all, $300 from Isabelle's "first boyfriend," her Uncle Irving. Uncle Irving was usually generous to his nieces and nephews, but his generosity went further to Bella and her children. He still remembered, with love, his very young surrogate mother, guiding him safely to school through the deep and menacing Russian forest. And he still remembered the pleasure he felt because of a little black-haired girl's antics and accomplishments, when he was a young man living in his sister's apartment.

The newlyweds attacked their sizable bank account to purchase the necessities they needed for their new apartment. Even though they had rented a furnished apartment, many necessary things were missing from it, so the newlyweds went on a shopping spree.

Their first purchase was an expensive bridge set which they planned to use as their temporary dining table. They expected to use the bridge set as a game table, in some future more commodious home, and being the only piece of furniture that truly belonged to them, they cherished it.

Needing a stove, the newly married couple purchased a two burner electric hot plate, which they placed on top of the very small refrigerator the landlord had provided. Pots, pans, and dishes scavenged from both of their parent's homes were kept on a small shelf above the stove. Although they had received a lovely set of dishes and a wonderful set of pots and pans as gifts, they never disturbed the boxes these gifts came in. Those lovely things were slated for their future home, along with the cherished bridge set.

The newlyweds' purchases also included such mundane necessities as a broom, a mop, and a bucket. A toaster, iron, and ironing board completed their shopping spree. They were reluctant to buy any more, because they realized that their home on 87 Street could be quite temporary. More than likely, Al would be drafted into the army, and Isabelle would have to move back with her family until she graduated from Hunter College. If, at the time of graduation, Al was stationed in the United States, Isabelle would join him. If, however, he was sent overseas, Isabelle would remain in her mother's home until her husband's return.

Isabelle deeply regretted the promise that Bella had extracted from her. Even though she had promised her mother that finishing college would be her first priority, she longed to follow Al before she graduated. At whatever time her young husband was stationed in the United States, Isabelle longed to join him, but she knew that she and Bella did not break promises made to each other. Therefore, because of her promise she could join Al only after she graduated from Hunter College. There was not a chance that her mother would release her from her promise.

A necessity absent from the little apartment on 87 Street was a telephone. Isabelle and Al had applied for a phone as soon as they had moved into their apartment, but they were informed by the telephone company that there was a three months' wait for residential telephones. Living without a telephone was difficult, and the newly married pair looked forward to the day when they would have one.

———

Their next-door neighbor *did* have a phone, and it rang incessantly, often awakening Isabelle and Al. She also had a boyfriend who frequently spent the night with her. The newlyweds were aware of his presence, because they could hear the very frequent arguments between their German neighbor and her paramour. They heard the boyfriend's loud voice and their neighbor's tearful replies through the bathroom that they shared and that separated their apartments from each other. They were made even more acutely aware of the boyfriend's visits, because he regularly trashed the bathroom. His disgusting behavior in their communal bathroom was ignored by his weeping lover.

A very squeamish Isabelle, remembering Bella's aversion to the dirt in their communal bathroom when she was a little girl, now felt just as her mother had on 30 Street in Coney Island. Isabelle emulated her mother's behavior, donning long, rubber gloves as she scrubbed the abominable bathroom with great disgust and plenty of Lysol. Although she had not yet met her elusive neighbor or her neighbor's paramour, Isabelle had already developed a healthy dislike for the sloppy pair who constantly left her a dirty bathroom to clean and whose persistently ringing telephone and frequent arguments disturbed her peace.

One evening there was an unexpected knock at the door. When Al opened the door, a tearful, disheveled woman, in her mid-forties, stood before him. Speaking with a thick German accent, the woman introduced herself.

"Gut evening," she said. "Mine name ist Inga Berger. I liff next door to you. I vanted to meet you und speak mit you."

"Good evening," answered Al. He invited Inga Berger in and introduced himself and Isabelle. He quickly poured himself and Inga some scotch whiskey. Isabelle didn't drink, but she sat listening with rapt attention as Inga told her story.

"Hermann und me haf parted. I tink he vas taking advantage uf me. I am zo alone! I need somevun! He knew dat."

"I vas born in Chermany. I vas married to a vunderful man. His name vas Fritz und he vasn't Jewish. I am Jewish. Are you?"

"Yes," they replied in unison.

"In Chermany," Inga continued, "vas hard to be Jewish, but Fritz stayed by me, und suffered mit me. I vas a dentist. Soon da Nazis not let me be a dentist. Den dey arrest Fritz und me. I never see mine Fritz again. They kilt him." She cried harder than ever.

Isabelle tried to comfort her, but Inga Berger shrugged her off. She continued her baleful tale, "I vas sent to three different concentration camps. I pull teeth from dead peoples. It vas terrible, but I liffed. Now I in Amerika – all alone. I try to get licenses to be a dentist, but the examination – too much Anglish for me. I vant instead to nurse sick people. I have papers mit government kind uff langvitch. It is too hard. I need help. Vill you help me?"

Isabelle immediately agreed to help. She told Inga that she would get together with her to help her on Sunday.

"Vye not now?" demanded Inga.

"I have homework. I am a college student, and on Saturday I have a job," an irritated Isabelle replied.

Al interjected, "Go to bed, Inga. Isabelle will help you, but now you've got to let her finish her homework."

Because Al had kept refilling her glass, a slightly drunken Inga bid them a Teutonic good night, and left.

"Well," said Isabelle, "we've met our neighbor."

———

On Sunday Isabelle helped Inga fill out her papers. From that time on, Inga was a frequent visitor. The newlyweds pitied her, so if she didn't prolong her visit too much, they suffered her. But, on those interminable evenings when Inga seemed to need to talk and talk, Al would curtail the visit by constantly filling Inga's glass. Being full of scotch made it easier to help her sway drunkenly to her door.

———

The long-awaited letter came. They were getting their telephone. The telephone company would install it in two days. Isabelle and Al had lived on 87 Street for three months without a telephone. The telephone would be greatly welcomed.

Two weeks after the telephone was installed, the feared letter came. Al was drafted. In a month he was to report to the induction center. Isabelle would have to return to her family. In a month 87 Street would just be a memory.

Al U.S. Army, 1951

Isabelle, 1951

Chapter 16: Weekends Only

They spent the night before Al was to report to the Army induction center at Eva's house. No one spoke of Al's impending recruitment. Instead, they watched silly television programs on the small black and white set in the living room. They spoke only in monosyllables, during commercials, but no one was able to speak of the terrible ache each one felt within.

In the morning, Al made trite conversation with Isabelle, assuring her that everything would be alright. At breakfast, conversation was even more banal. Finally, Al put on his overcoat, picked up his bag, and pecked his mother on her cheek. He shook hands with his step-father and then walked over to where a very forlorn Isabelle stood. They embraced and kissed, and Al turning rapidly, left the apartment. Isabelle and Eva wept as his footsteps could be heard echoing down the hallway.

Al and his fellow recruits were sent to Camp Kilmer for one week. At Camp Kilmer each man was issued some of his uniform. Military outdoors wear was in short supply and the recruits were given permission to wear their civilian coats or jackets in the bitter cold. Introduction to some rudimentary facts of military life and assignment to their camps for basic training were the main functions of Camp Kilmer.

Al had been assigned to Fort Dix, New Jersey for his twelve-week infantry basic training. After his first week there, he notified Isabelle that she and his parents could come to Ft. Dix on Sunday. The recruits were allowed to have visitors from 1:00 to 5:00 p.m.

On Sunday, Eva, Max, and Isabelle took the long bus ride to Ft. Dix. All of the passengers on the bus were going to Ft. Dix to visit recruits. Sharing the seat with Isabelle was a young woman who had been married for six months. Behind them, sat her in-laws, and in front of her in-laws, sat Eva and Max. Friendly, sporadic conversation passed between the six of them.

When the bus arrived at Ft. Dix, a crowd of recruits stood in the bitter cold, waiting to meet their visitors. Isabelle spotted Al immediately. He looked peculiar wearing his blue civilian overcoat over his khaki military garb. On closer examination they could see that he looked thinner and looked wan. He explained, saying that he had been working very hard and had not eaten much, because he thoroughly detested the army food.

In order to get relief from the biting cold, Al took his three visitors to the Day Room, where they could sit on comfortable sofas and easy chairs. Apparently all of the recruits had the same idea, because the large Day Room was crowded with visitors and the soldiers they were visiting.

Al and his guests were discussing possible future postings when they were startled by an awful tumult and the big bang of a heavy table being overturned and hitting the floor. The father-in-law of the girl with whom Isabelle had been sitting on the bus, had over-turned the table in a fit of rage. His voice and his wife's and son's voices were raised to so high a pitch of anger that everyone in the crowded Day Room could hear what they were arguing about. They were arguing about their recruit's designation of beneficiary for his army life insurance policy. As part of their induction into the army, the recruits had been asked to designate beneficiaries, and the angry father had learned that his son had designated his young daughter-in-law as his beneficiary. The soldier's father and the soldier's mother were greatly distressed by this choice, because they believed that having been married for only six months was not enough time for their daughter-in-law to qualify as their son's beneficiary. They demanded that he designate either his mother or both of his parents as beneficiaries. When their son refused, his parents argued loudly and long. All through their noisy altercation, Isabelle's former bus companion wept pitifully.

Most of the people in the Day Room were scandalized by the loud scene they were creating. When the noisy family left the Day Room to carry on their argument elsewhere, everyone else was greatly relieved.

Isabelle commented that she held out little hope for that marriage. Her reason was the soldier's helplessness in quieting his parents. Eva and Max agreed. They both believed that the young couples' marriage had little hope of succeeding.

———

For the first six weeks at Ft. Dix, the recruits were not issued passes. Each soldier was allowed to have a visitor stay at the camp's Guest House on one weekend out of four. This rule set basic trainees minds in motion to figure out ways of circumventing the once-in-four-week ruling. Wily Al and his friends did find a way.

On Al's fourth weekend at Ft. Dix, Isabelle used his visitor's pass at the Guest House, using her own name. She made three more visits to the Guest House, using the privileges of other soldiers who had nobody that was going to use their passes. Each time Isabelle came, she posed as the sister of one of Al's buddies.

———

There were always never-to-be forgotten adventures at the Guest House. For Isabelle and Al, the most memorable was when Isabelle was sharing a room with the wife of a soldier who was posing as another soldier's sister. Isabelle was also posing as one of Al's buddy's sister. Both young women were very compatible, as were their real soldier/husbands. Over dinner, the four made a plan for the "best utilization" of the girls' sleeping room. After making and discarding several plans, the two married couples decided that each couple would have the use of the room for two hours, beginning right after dinner. When the room was in use by the one couple, the second couple could either spend their time at the post's movie house or in the Day Room. The couples would reverse their venues at 9:00 p.m. At 11:00 p.m., both couples would meet clandestinely in the girls' room at the Guest House, and visit together for another hour. At midnight, the men would have to sneak out of the Guest House. Their presence in the girls' sleeping room was strictly prohibited, and if they were caught and questioned, in theory, *all hell would break loose.*

Al and his buddy did get caught. With a wink and a nod the Guest House desk clerk permitted both married men to have sex with two women registered as their buddies' sisters. No questions were asked about what the soldiers did and who the women really were. After a weak verbal reprimand for being in the Guest House, the two soldiers were told to quickly return to their barracks.

In the waning days of 1951, the United States was deeply gripped by a pervasive prudery concerning sex. The fact that Isabelle and her roommate were married to the soldiers they were visiting was immaterial. Sexual contact was strictly forbidden at Fort Dix. This prohibition was generally an exercise in futility, because most of the soldiers and their young female visitors were perfect examples of "raging hormones!" Couples therefore coupled all over the camp, ignoring the rules and trying to ignore the bitterly cold weather. The straight-laced attitudes of the 1950's were disregarded as was the couples' good sense regarding the frigid weather.

One weekend when Isabelle visited, Al had not been able to get her accommodations at the Guest House. Instead, she and another young woman visitor were staying together at the motel located an easy walk from the camp's entrance. The two couples were to meet at the gate at 11:45 p.m., after spending the evening at the army camp, following their own inclinations. The men would then have fifteen minutes to hurry back to their barracks and the girls would walk across the road to the motel. Their husbands couldn't escort them there, because basic trainees who had been at Fort Dix for fewer than ten weeks, were not permitted to leave the camp.

The temperature had fallen to single digits. Yet, couples walking arm-in-arm were strolling all over Fort Dix. Al and Isabelle were among them, and they were freezing! There were two easily accessible places to go to keep warm. They could go to the Day Room, which was very crowded; or they could go to the movies. In neither place could the deeply in love newlyweds find privacy. They foolishly decided to stay outdoors until they could no longer bear the cold.

Al took Isabelle to a large sports stadium. Even though it was very dark, they knew they were not alone in the stands, because they heard occasional grunts, moans, sighs, and indiscernible whispers. They found a place that seemed to be totally quiet and deserted, and they sat down. Al opened his jacket and Isabelle snuggled up to him. In just a few minutes they were passionately kissing, and fondling each other's bodies. Their lovemaking was as complete as lovemaking could be with the participants wearing heavy winter coats.

Because Isabelle's skirts were raised, she was the first to become aware of the brutality of the cold. She began to shiver uncontrollably, and their frigid lovemaking came to a halt. They rearranged their disheveled clothing and rushed off to the Day Room. In the Day Room, it took quite some time for Isabelle's body to feel even close to normal. Isabelle went from uncontrolled shivering, to very painful hands and feet, to numbness in all of her extremities. Never before, or any time thereafter, did Isabelle ever suffer so much pain from the cold.

When they emerged from the crowded Day Room, with the intention of meeting the other couple at the gate, they saw a bread truck that was apparently making a late night delivery for the soldiers' breakfast the next morning. It was a panel truck that they had noticed when they had arrived at the Day Room. At that time, the truck's rear doors had been ajar. When they left the building, the truck's rear doors were closed and the driver was starting up his engine. They could hear hammering at the closed doors and frantic calls shouting, "Help! Let us out of here! Help!" A male and a female voice were screaming with fright, but were obviously not heard by the driver over the truck's motor, as he caused the vehicle to gain speed and drive away.

Al, Isabelle, and the other couples milling around, immediately understood what had transpired. A hormonal couple, wanting to make love with some protection from the intense cold, crawled into the back of the truck, closing and latching its doors behind them. The driver, who had spent quite some time in the mess hall, returned to his seemingly "empty" truck, not knowing that he had passengers. It certainly would have been interesting to know what had happened when the hot-blooded pair were discovered, but none of the amused onlookers ever found out. Al and Isabelle found the whole situation very funny, and laughed all the way to the Fort Dix' gate.

When Al had been at Fort Dix for ten weeks, he received a weekend pass. On Saturday morning, carrying a duffel bag stuffed with dirty laundry, he boarded the bus to New York City. He brought himself and his laundry to Bella's door, where the whole family gave him a joyful and boisterous welcome. The young couple stayed at Bella's house for about an hour, leaving Al's dirty laundry behind. Bella had insisted that they do this, so that Isabelle, Al, and Al's family were free to visit each other without the annoyance of having to take care of the laundry. She promised that when Al brought Isabelle back, the laundry would be done.

Isabelle had made some changes in her life. She was no longer employed. Instead, she used the money she received from Al's allotment checks for her needs and any monetary needs Al might have. She also suspended all schoolwork on the weekends when Al had leave. All of her attention on those weekends was directed toward her husband. And very soon, as Al's weekend passes increased in number, her lack of attention to her schoolwork took its toll on her grades. Her grades plummeted! She had fallen behind on her assignments, was doing makeshift work to satisfy her courses' requirements, and was writing English papers based on reading library synopses of assigned books, rather than reading the actual books. In time her A's became B's and her B's became C's.

Most of Al's weekend passes were spent visiting with members of his family. Eva kept making dinner parties and inviting family members to see Al. These dinners were an annoyance to the young couple, because they interfered with their time together and the time they wished to spend with their own friends. They, therefore, eventually requested that Eva rein in on the dinner parties. Eva was deeply insulted, but complied with their request, feeling ill will toward the young couple.

Eva and Max lived in a one-bedroom apartment. They, very thoughtfully, gave up their bedroom and slept on the pull-out-sofa-bed in the living room, when Al and Isabelle spent the weekend with them. The young couple appreciated their thoughtfulness and understanding, because they ached for the privacy afforded by the bedroom Al's parents had relinquished when they had their cherished short reunions. And cherished, indeed, were these reunions! A sword hung over Al's head, as it did over the heads of all of the basic trainees at Fort Dix. They all knew that the majority of them would be sent to fight in Korea. In Al's group, those designated for the war in Korea would make an interim stop at a base in Arkansas. From there, they would be dispatched to the war grounds. The mentality of America in the early 1950's was forged by America's attitudes during World War II. To be sure, there was a new enemy, but the popular wisdom held that just as the Nazis wanted world dominion, the Communists wanted to spread their system throughout the world. Therefore, the North Koreans had to be stopped, and that part of Asia had to be saved from the *Red Menace*. The young men being sent to fight in Korea went there convinced of the correctness of their mission.

Nonetheless, many of the young fighting recruits hoped against hope that they would be posted somewhere other than Korea. Al was among them. He hoped that he would be accepted into a program in which servicemen worked in the fields for which they had been educated. Those selected for this program were called *Scientific and Professional Personnel or S.P.P.'s.* While they worked at jobs that the army generally designated for officers, S.P.P.s never were allowed to become officers. The highest rank an S.P.P. could achieve was the rank of corporal. If, however, on entering the program, a man expressed his desire to be an officer, he was immediately commissioned. Why then, didn't all of the S.P.P.'s accept commissions, instead of remaining lowly privates or corporals? It was because they had seen young men who had been commissioned officers during World War II being called back into the Army at the whim of the Army. On the other hand, those men who had been enlisted men during World War II, could not be called back again for the war in Korea, without an act of Congress.

Al's weekends at home became evermore precious, because of the fear of his being shipped to Korea. With a feeling of self-righteousness, Isabelle replaced her study and reading weekends with her cherished visits from her soldier-husband. Though there was not enough time to keep up with her studies during the week, she really did try to do so. Her family tiptoed through the living room in which she was working. Everything was done to facilitate her efforts for school.

————

Early one Wednesday evening, loud banging thundered through Bella's apartment. Isabelle knew that the banging was coming from the apartment above them that was occupied by a man named Phil, his wife Rose, and their severely mentally challenged teen-aged son, Herbie. Herbie was a nuisance to everyone! Just a few days before, he had been standing in the courtyard of their apartment building, seriously harassing young women and teen-aged girls who passed him as they entered or left the building. He would leer at them and try to grab either their breasts or their buttocks, and to Isabelle's dismay she was one of Herbie's favorite targets. Entering or leaving the building in which she lived felt like "running the gauntlet."

On the day in question, Isabelle rushed past the hormonal Herbie and into Bella's apartment. Breathlessly, she described her encounter with the mentally challenged boy and her frequent aggravation upon entering or leaving the building when Herbie posted himself in the courtyard. To add insult to injury, he was now causing a commotion by banging on the floor above them. Isabelle proclaimed loudly that she was going upstairs to tell Phil and Rose to reign in their obnoxious son.

Her mother said, "Isabelle, I forbid you to do any such thing! Herbie is enough of a trial for his parents. They don't need your anger, too. You have been blessed with a fine, healthy mind. Use it! Obviously you can devise ways of dodging Herbie's misplaced attempts at love. He is an unfortunate boy. Don't add to his misfortune by forcing his parents to keep him under lock and key."

Isabelle saw the wisdom in her mother's reaction to Herbie's "amorous" behavior, but today was different. She needed to study, and Herbie's banging on the floor was deafening to those below him. Herbie's loud noise totally

314

precluded Isabelle's ability to study, and after attempting to do so for about a half hour, Isabelle exclaimed, "I've had it! I can't study in my own house! I'm going upstairs to speak to Phil and Rose, right now."

"No you're not," retorted Bella. "I know it's too noisy to study here, but certain branches of the public library are open late at night. You can go to one of them to study. Instead of heaping more troubles on the shoulders of poor Phil and Rose, be thankful that you *are able* to study and that you *are able* to go to the public library. Those gifts were never given to poor Herbie."

Isabelle packed her books to go to the library, thinking about how wise and kind her mother was.

———

Al had been out on a three-day bivouac at Fort Dix. The weather had been lovely the week before, but during the bivouac week, winter had come back with a vengeance. It was so cold that the water in the recruits' canteens froze. On their very long march to their bivouac site, they not only were suffering from the cold, but those, who like Al, had tender feet, developed painful and gargantuan sores and blisters. Al had always believed that his worse military experience had to be when the recruits were sent across an obstacle course where they were told live ammunition was being fired over their heads. Even though Al froze, rigid with fear, he was wrong in this assessment. This freezing cold bivouac was worse. The biting cold and Al's extremely torn-up feet, caused him such great discomfort, that simple as well as difficult tasks were almost impossible to perform. At first, pitching their two-man tent, starting a fire, cooking their food, and melting the ice that was their only source of water seemed impossible to the two young recruits, yet they were tasks they eventually managed to accomplish. After the most physically difficult three days of basic training, the worn-out, exhausted recruits painfully limped the long distance back to the barracks.

At the barracks, the recruits found new energy when they were given passes allowing them to leave the base for the remainder of Friday, and for Saturday and Sunday. Al, like most of the married soldiers, hurriedly showered, dressed in a clean uniform, packed up his dirty laundry, and limped off the base.

When Al alighted from subway station at Freeman Street, he began his painful three-block walk to Isabelle's house. The sun shone brightly as the handsome young soldier with a duffel bag of dirty laundry slung over his shoulder, limped past two elderly Jewish women, sitting on a stoop, enjoying the chilly winter sunshine.

"See…. vat dey do!" exclaimed one of them. "Dey take our beautiful young boys and send dem home to us as cripples!"

When the "poor, blue-eyed, crippled soldier" arrived at his mother-in-law's house, he was convulsed with laughter. He told Isabelle about the two elderly women's reaction to his limping. He then showed her the gargantuan blister on his "destroyed" foot and told her about his travails during bivouac. But most important of all, he told her that the coming week was probably the week when he would find out about his next posting.

Al returned to Fort Dix on Sunday night. From Sunday until Thursday both Isabelle and he could think of little else than Al's potential posting. Isabelle prayed every night that he would be posted as an S.P.P. at a nearby army base.

*Al's grandparents (Bubbe and Zada) at their
golden wedding anniversary, 1951*

*Rear l.to r. Al's brother Harold, Bubbe and Zada,
Front Al, 1937*

Chapter 17: Bubbe and Zada

Isabelle was not the only one praying for a safe, nearby posting for Al. Prayers and supplications for Al's safety found their way to God from his grandparents and his mother, as well.

Al often felt as if he was blessed with two loving sets of parents. In order to reduce expenses during the Great Depression, Al's family, consisting of his mother, his father, and their two very young sons shared an apartment with Al's maternal grandparents. Al called them by their Yiddish titles, *Bubbe* (meaning Grandmother) and *Zada* (meaning Grandfather). Al's parents and their two little boys moved in with Al's grandparents, because Al's father was having extreme difficulty finding employment during the Depression. His father's unemployment was followed by an even greater calamity, when after he had become employed, he died in an industrial accident. Al's father died on the job, when he was working for the W.P.A. (a New Deal Program instituted by the federal government to create jobs. It was called *The Work Progress Administration*.) When he died, he left Eva and his two little boys with only the five dollars Eva had in her purse. Needless to say, it was a blessing for Eva to be living with her mother and father and to be a recipient of their help.

Eva and Bubbe were very good friends, as well as mother and daughter. They shared the household chores and heaped their love upon Eva's two boys. Feisty little Al was clearly Bubbe's favorite. His hardheadedness and outspokenness greatly appealed to her; perhaps because she shared these traits with her little grandson. Harold, the older boy was more like Eva, generally quiet and acquiescent.

Zada was a very hard-working tailor. When, because of the death of his son-in-law, his responsibilities increased, he managed to find and work two jobs. The tall, quiet man, who seemed to be so overshadowed by his loquacious, plump, vivacious wife, never failed to provide for her, and when necessary, for his children and grandchildren. When at home Zada could always be found in the living room reading his Yiddish newspaper and smoking many cigarettes. He said very little, but was aware of everything that went on within his beloved family.

———————

Bubbe's and Zada's relationship was deep and of long duration. They were married in Russia when they were both twenty-one years old. Although, by Russian standards, Bubbe's family was quite well-off, Zada distrusted everything Russian, in much the same way as Isabelle's grandmother, Sarah, had. He constantly insisted that his family immigrate to America during the great emigration of Russian Jews in the late nineteenth and early twentieth centuries, but Bubbe was reluctant to do so, because her parents did not wish to leave. They were familiar with Russia and by Russian standards, they enjoyed prosperity. They feared to leave their relatively comfortable lives for conditions that were unknown to them.

Determined that his family would leave Russia, Zada departed for America by himself, intending to establish a home in America and then send for his wife and children. Upon his arrival in America, he was met by all of the adversity usually faced by immigrants coming to the new land. Although he was a talented tailor, wages for new immigrants were low and the housing available to them was very poor. Being a man alone, and abysmally lonely for his wife and children, Zada kept his expenses at bare sustenance levels, in order to amass the large sums of money necessary to send for his family. Within less than two years, he had furnished a respectable lower east side apartment, procured four tickets, and sent them to his beloved family in Russia. Bubbe and their three children: Eva – five years old, David – four years old, and Mary – two and a half years old rejoined Zada in 1906, and began a new life in America.

Her children were doing well, but Bubbe was miserable. She sorely missed her parents and the siblings she had left behind in Russia, so she determined that the only plausible thing to do was to go back to Russia to convince them that they must emigrate. Seeing his wife's misery, quiet devoted Zada took an extra job to help Bubbe achieve her goal. In addition, they lived even more frugally, until Bubbe was able to do the unheard of, she and her three children returned to Russia to begin her campaign to convince her parents to immigrate to the United States.

Bubbe could not understand why on a calmer sea than she had experienced on her first voyage, she felt so much more seasick than she had before. She couldn't wait for the long trip to be over and for her children and herself to be in the comfort of her parent's home. It took her the long ocean voyage and being at her parents' home for a month and a half to figure out the cause of her persistent nausea. How could she have missed all the signs? Bubbe was pregnant with her fourth child!

It was decided that Bubbe and her children would remain with her parents until after the birth of the baby. She would be well looked after in her family's home, and her trip back to America would be easier if she were no longer pregnant.

Throughout her pregnancy, Bubbe regaled her parents with the wonders of America. With pogroms against the Jews proliferating in Russia, she urged them to seek safety in America for themselves and her siblings. Above all, she threatened them with the greatest threat of all....Bubbe stated that they were breaking up her marriage and depriving her children of their father, because, she adamantly declared, she would not leave Russia and return to America without them!

Bubbe's campaign succeeded. Her parents and her siblings joined her and her four small children on their journey back to America and her reunion with Zada. When they set out on their journey, Bubbe's baby son was five months old. Bubbe's hard work and persuasiveness had totally changed the lives of her entire family.

Isabelle met Al's family when she was casually dating Al. She met them because Al had developed a fungal infection on his hands, and was unable to type a paper that he needed to turn in for one of his college courses. He had called her and asked her if she would do him a favor and come to his house and type the paper for him. Isabelle was a very weak typist, but no one in Al's family was able to type at all. She, therefore, agreed to do Al the favor.

When Isabelle arrived, she was introduced to Al's family. Very unexpectedly, Al's grandfather spoke very sharply to her. He said, "We want Alvin to graduate from college. He will be the first member of our immediate family to do so. You look like just the girl who would make him want to quit college and get married."

"Don't worry," Isabelle retorted. "There is nothing serious going on with Al and me. If there were, I'd *really* expect him to graduate. I'd never get serious with a boy who didn't have a college education. In fact, when I graduate from high school, I'll go to college too, and I too, expect to graduate. You have nothing to fear from me!"

From that day on, Zada thoroughly approved of Isabelle and Al's relationship, and the quiet old man became Isabelle's friend. During the long summer days in Coney Island, they often played gin rummy together, and to Zada's delight, Isabelle usually won. Zada completely approved of the dark haired teenager his grandson had fallen in love with.

―――――――

In 1950, very few couples lived to celebrate fiftieth anniversaries. When Bubbe and Zada were approaching their fiftieth anniversary, it was indeed a wonderful milestone. Their four children decided to celebrate the great occasion with lots of fanfare. A wedding hall was rented where their children threw a party that exceeded many wedding celebrations. The catered meal was delicious and the band played beautiful music as the guests danced. A sparkling diamond wedding ring adorned Bubbe's finger. The thin, simple gold wedding band that she had worn for fifty years was relegated to a jewelry box. Zada had given her this diamond wedding band on their fiftieth anniversary. Her children had given her diamond stud earrings for the occasion, too. These were the first diamonds that Bubbe had worn in all of her seventy-one years.

Isabelle, who was one of the guests at this Golden Wedding celebration, wept during the ceremony in which the elderly couple renewed their vows. She was also deeply touched that Bubbe and Zada's attendants were three of their children and their children's spouses. Eva was the Matron of Honor and Harold, Eva's eldest son and Bubbe and Zayede's eldest grandchild, served as his grandparents' best man.

––––––––––

When Eva married Max, Bubbe and Zada moved out of the apartment they had shared for so long with Eva and her sons. Max moved into the larger apartment in the east Bronx, relinquishing his lovely smaller apartment in the West Bronx to Bubbe and Zada. Al's grandparent's apartment was a long, but doable walk from Hunter College's Bronx campus, where Isabelle was enrolled for her freshman year. Al's grandparents had moved near the college in February of 1951, just at the time that Isabelle and Al had become engaged.

One day, Isabelle decided to drop in and see Bubbe and Zada. In her last class that day, they had been discussing the growth of the fledgling labor movement in the garment industry, in New York, during the very early days of the twentieth century. Isabelle was thinking about the discussion when she rang Al's grandparents' bell.

Bubbe answered the door wiping her hands on her apron. She had been cooking in the kitchen while Zada sat in the living room, smoking cigarettes and reading his Yiddish newspaper. They both greeted Isabelle warmly and then went back to what they had been doing. Bubbe chatted with Isabelle as she worked, telling her they had run into some people from their town of Zlotopol, in Russia. She had not seen these people since they had emigrated from Russia. When these people had arrived in America, they had moved in with Bubbe and Zada and stayed with them until they could get themselves settled. Times were very hard then, and Bubbe and Zada's small apartment was often greatly over-crowded with recently arriving immigrants.

Her conversation with Bubbe caused Isabelle to, once again, recollect the highlights of the class she had just left. She mentioned that she was studying about the big strikes in the garment industry in the early 1900's, and to her great surprise and immense pleasure, Zada, who often kept to himself, entered the kitchen and immediately joined their conversation. With sterling clear recollection, Al's grandfather spoke of the dreadful working conditions, the impossibly low wages, the violent long and angry strikes, and the immense hardships he and all of the garment workers had endured. He was able to site dates and locations and tell about his own participation in the strikes. Isabelle was particularly moved by the verbal pictures he drew of gigantic lines of hungry women and children, patiently waiting for charitable organizations or the union to distribute milk. Bubbe said that she was one of these women waiting to get milk for her children. The birth of the labor movement was clearly witnessed and participated in by Al's grandparents. When Isabelle listened to her professor lecturing about these events, she never envisioned these two quiet people as militants in strikes that would contribute to major changes for the workers of their adopted and greatly beloved country.

————

Isabelle had great respect and felt a warm affection for Al's grandparents, so she often dropped in to see them and usually thoroughly enjoyed her visits. On one lovely spring day, Isabelle walked over to the elderly couple's house right after she had to perform in her speech class. In this class, they had learned the International Phonetic Alphabet, and ostensibly were now able to pronounce foreign words just as native speakers of the foreign language pronounced them. They had been given an assignment to write, in the phonetic alphabet, a song in a foreign language that they would be able to pronounce like the native from whom they had gathered the song. Each student was required to write the song on the chalkboard, using the phonetic alphabet. Then she was supposed to sing her song for her classmates, sounding like a native. Finally, she was required to translate the words she had sung.

Finding a foreign person was easy enough for Isabelle. She told Bella about what she needed, and Bella, who loved to sing, immediately sang a folk song to her about a young man named Greetzu who was a "ladies' man." Greetzu loved the ladies and then left them, often breaking their hearts. The song described Greetzu's shenanigans with two different unfortunate ladies. After breaking the heart of the first lady, the chorus warns Greetzu that women can be dangerous, and he must stop trifling with their emotions. Greetzu ignores this advice and proceeds to break the heart of the second woman. Once more, the chorus warns him to stop being cavalier with women's feelings. Once more Greetzu ignores all advice and begins his supercilious behavior with a third woman. This woman, when she discovers Greetzu's fecklessness, poisons him and he dies! The song ends with a third repetition of the chorus that had warned the murdered Greetzu not to trifle with the hearts of the ladies.

The melody of the folk song about Greetzu is lively, and Isabelle's class and the teacher loved her performance. Isabelle had such fun with the song that she decided to entertain Bubbe and Zada with it too, so when she went to their house, she told them about the song she had just sung in class.

They immediately pressed her to sing the song for them, and when Isabelle did so, she was aghast at Zada's reaction. "Where did you learn that dirty song?" he demanded. "I cannot believe that you sang such a song to your class!"

Isabelle couldn't believe her ears. She told Zada that someone was greatly in error, because her mother had sung the song to her, proclaiming it to be an innocent folk song.

"It certainly is not!" said Zada. "The only people I ever heard singing that song were drunken *goyim* (gentiles), singing it at the inn in Zlotopol, where they drank until they were out of their minds."

When Isabelle got home she immediately asked her mother to explain Zada's reaction to the song. Bella chuckling, when she heard about Isabelle's visit with Al's grandparents, replied, "You caught Al's grandpa in a little white lie. You know *Tochter* (Daughter), most of the Jews in Russia lived in *shtetelach* (small Jewish towns) where everyone was Jewish and everyone spoke Yiddish. From the description of the town from which Al's family came, it was a fairly large one for a *shtetl*. In such a place, Hebrew was used for prayer and Yiddish was used in day-to-day life. Jewish businessmen who had dealings with gentiles spoke a heavily accented Russian, causing Russian gentiles to be able to spot a Jew by the way he spoke their language.

Al's family, living in the large, totally Jewish, *shtetl,* probably never learned Russian at all."

"Unlike Al's family, our family lived in a hamlet along with very few other Jewish families. We did not live in a *shtetl,* so while we spoke Yiddish at home, if we did not learn to speak Russian, we could not get along. None of us had Yiddish accents, except my Zada, who grew up in Narovle, a larger town with a somewhat larger Jewish population, who still had to learn to speak a rudimentary Russian in order to get along. Our family in Vashisht spoke Russian like the gentiles amongst whom we lived."

"I think that once Al's Zada said the song was dirty, he felt stuck with what he said. He was embarrassed by his lack of knowledge of Russian, just as most *shtetl* Jews were, when they were forced to show their ignorance of the language of the land in which they lived."

"You can discuss what I am telling you with Al's *zada,* or leave it alone," concluded Bella.

Isabelle, who had such a deep respect for Zada's intelligence, decided to discuss it with him. She told him what the song really meant, and gently asked him if he spoke or understood Russian.

Zada, slightly embarrassed, admitted his almost total ignorance of Russian. He knew a few rudimentary words, but had had to rely on others for communication with Russian gentiles.

Isabelle explained to him what Bella had explained to her. She added that the Yiddish speaking people of Europe had created a fabulous literature that was studied in many universities around the world. Yiddish-speaking Jews had absolutely nothing to be ashamed of.

———

The unbelievable good news Isabelle and Al were hoping for came on the Thursday after his pleasant three-day weekend pass with Isabelle. Al had been assigned to be as an S.P.P. at the Army Chemical Center in Edgewood, Maryland, where he would be the S.P.P. Personnel Officer for the Chemical Corps Procurement Agency. He would be stationed only three and half driving hours away from New York, and it would be very unlikely that he would be sent to Korea. Isabelle and Al felt quite sure that he would be given frequent weekend passes which would allow them to see each other quite often while Isabelle was still in school. After graduation, Isabelle would be able to join her husband in Maryland.

———

At Army Chemical Center Al found his work and most of his colleagues to be to be very interesting. His fellow S.P.P.'s ranged from young scientists doing very secret experiments in the labs at Edgewood, to administrative types such as accountants, lawyers, and people like Al, himself. Most of the commissioned officers at the Army Chemical Center were educated people doing work that was similar to the work of the non-commissioned S.P.P.'s. The only exception was the contingent of career military men on the post, called Troop Command. The job of Troop Command was to to keep the young S.P.P. scientists and administrators constantly aware of the fact that they were soldiers. These people were in charge of the enlisted men's living conditions, parades, and brush-ups in weapons handling. They set up the rosters for KP and other unpleasant duties. Troop Command consisted mostly of career officers and career non-commissioned officers for whom the whole concept of the S.P.P program was anti-military. Most of them had never set foot in a college or university. Not only did they lack understanding of the work their more educated military underlings were doing, they resented the S.P.P.'s work schedules, which they believed interfered with the normal military routine of the base.

The S.P.P.'s and the career military men were mutually antagonistic. Each group constantly tried to spite the other. Al's weekends with Isabelle were filled with stories – some funny and some disturbing, about each group's spiteful treatment of the other.

———

Isabelle was finishing college. She had one regular semester, a summer school session, and her student teaching semester to go. She was not "covering herself in glory" with her college grades, because every Saturday and Sunday Al came home, causing her to shirk her reading and studying responsibilities. Being an English major, Isabelle was required to complete a term paper in each English class, in addition to taking exams, and reading many, many books. Her term papers were dashed off on weekdays, and were of a poor quality that did not represent what Isabelle was capable of doing. For Isabelle, her first priority was her husband's weekly visit, and her grades showed it.

In order to go home from Hunter College, which was located on 68 Street and Lexington Avenue in Manhattan, Isabelle took a local train to 86 Street and changed to an express train going to Freeman Street in the Bronx. Quite often, during rush hour, she was lucky enough to get a seat on the local train. If this happened, she did not change trains at 86 Street. Instead, she would go all the way to Eva's house on the local train. She could read for school on the train until she got off at Parkchester Circle; and when she did this, she felt none of the fatigue she would have felt as a cramped standing passenger on the express train. Besides, Isabelle liked Eva and Max, and enjoyed dropping in on them.

Eva was delighted on the occasions when Isabelle dropped in. She liked her son's lovely, spoiled young wife, and if her dinner was not already prepared, Eva cooked things that pleased her. She loved Isabelle's friendliness and openness, and never tired of her unexpected drop-in visits.

Summer school flew by, and Isabelle was a senior, slated to graduate in January of 1953. Hunter, unlike most colleges that prepared students for careers in the teaching profession, did not offer a major in Education. The many Hunter students planning to pursue such a career were required to take Education as their minor. Because of the requirements of the State of New York, these Education Minors consisted of as many credits in Education as the student was required to take in her major subject. In essence, these students were doing two majors, leaving very few credits for electives. (Electives are the courses college students chose themselves, either because of a great interest in the course or because the course doesn't demand too much work.) Isabelle was among the many people at Hunter preparing for a career in education, and she too was denied the pleasure and/ or the leisure of a large number of elective courses.

In her senior year, Isabelle was required to student teach. It was her good fortune to be appointed to her chosen school, P.S. 61, the school she had attended from 3B to 6B. Her student teaching semester was divided into thirds – a first grade and a third grade taught by teachers who were unknown to her, and a sixth grade with the teacher she had most admired when she was a student attending P.S. 61….the fabulous Mrs. Rebecca Simonson.

Isabelle's first grade student teaching experience was adequate. Her supervising teacher was of average ability, and mornings in her class didn't drag too much. Her third grade experience, however, was poor and boring. Isabelle saw so many flaws in her third grade cooperating teacher's work, that it was difficult to keep herself from saying something about them. During that third of her student teaching experience, Isabelle was relieved when she was finished with her morning at P.S.61, and had gone home to eat her lunch with her mother. After lunch, she took the subway to Hunter College for her college course work. During this time, Isabelle greatly looked forward to her impending sixth grade experience, but even though she had been a student teacher at P.S.61 for two-thirds of a semester, she had scrupulously avoided contact with the woman who would be her sixth grade cooperating teacher, Mrs. Rebecca Simonson. She wanted to surprise the woman who had been her own cherished sixth grade teacher. And surprise her, she did!

———

"Isabelle Brodsky!" exclaimed the small woman, whose raven black hair was severely combed back into a bun. "You've grown into a lovely young woman, yet I would have recognized you anywhere. I didn't know it was you who was assigned to be my student teacher. What a surprise!"

"You're obviously married," she said, glancing at Isabelle's rings. "How old are you anyway?" queried Mrs. Simonson.

"I'm twenty years old, and I'm married to a soldier stationed in Maryland. I hope to join him when I graduate," answered Isabelle.

The older woman walked over to Isabelle, and let down her reserve long enough to give her former student a big hug. Then she introduced Isabelle to her sixth grade class.

"Boys and girls," said Mrs. Simonson, "this pretty young lady sat where you are sitting less than ten years ago. She was a good student that I remember well. She is now completing her studies at Hunter College and in a few months she will graduate and have her own class to teach. She is here to practice some of her teaching skills on you, and perhaps learn a few more skills from me. I remember a lot about this young lady when she was my sixth grade student. She was a very good student, and I'm sure with your help, she will become a very good teacher."

Isabelle took a seat at the back of the room, and as she observed Mrs. Simonson, the years melted away.

As a sixth grader, Isabelle was enthralled with Mrs. Simonson. Almost everything they did in her class was interesting or fun. And, everyone knew that there was no shirking or high jinks allowed in the little black haired woman's class. She taught her students with an iron hand encased in a velvet glove. She expected lots of good work and lots of respect.... and Mrs. Simonson got it! Yet most of her pupils felt that she loved them. Isabelle wished that she too would possess a magic that would reach *her* future students, like Mrs. Simonson's magic had reached her.

―――――――

Rebecca Simonson was not merely a master teacher. She was an historical figure in America's labor movement. This dignified, passionate, and dedicated woman was one of the founder's and one of the very early members of the American Federation of Teachers. She was in the front lines of the fight for better wages, better benefits, and a voice for America's teachers. Her efforts were centered in New York City, but the work of people like her, spread throughout the United States. Rebecca Simonson was the very first president of the American Federation of Teachers.

―――――――

Isabelle was a student teacher in Mrs. Simonson's class when Mrs. Simonson was in full bloom, professionally. Isabelle loved the way her sixth grade teacher kept order in her class, while at the same time, strongly encouraging verbal participation during the many class discussions. Isabelle made a mental note of this master teacher's techniques, and took particular note of how Mrs. Simonson taught and conducted choral speaking. Isabelle, like Mrs. Simonson, was quite dramatic. She determined to use drama and choral speaking as a tool in her teaching.

―――――――

One day, Mrs. Simonson told Isabelle that she needed to leave the room. The children had written autobiographies and at that time were reading them to the class.

A boy had just completed the reading of his autobiography and was receiving the applause of his classmates, when Isabelle's eye lit upon a sweet little brown-haired girl named Naomi. She requested that Naomi read her story. Naomi timidly walked to the front of the room and began to read. She had not read two full sentences when she suddenly began to tremble and weep.

Isabelle was undone. She put her arm around the weeping child and said, "What's the matter Naomi? You don't have to read if you don't feel like it."

Sniffling and wiping her nose on her sleeve, Naomi returned to her seat.

Not knowing what to do, Isabelle started a game of *Simon Says*. Within minutes of the start of the game, Mrs. Simonson returned, and Isabelle immediately told her about Naomi's weeping. Isabelle's distress over the child's crying was very apparent to the seasoned teacher.

"Isabelle," she said, "in your teaching career you will see many children cry. Some will cry because they are ashamed of something, others because they've been bullied, and still others because you have made them cry. In addition, unfortunate children will cry because they are disturbed. Naomi's tears fall into the last category. You will have to determine what you will do in each different situation, but you must not show your own distress."

"Naomi comes from a family that suffered greatly during the Holocaust. She and her twin brother were hidden by a farmer in their native Holland. When anyone came to the farmer's house, the small children were put deep into a root cellar, where they learned to remain silent while in hiding."

"The twin's parents were hidden on other farms, but they were eventually found by the Nazis. They were sent to Auschwitz, where Naomi's father perished. But, Naomi's mother survived. When she was liberated from Auschwitz by the Russians, she rushed back to Holland as soon as she could, in order to retrieve her two very small children."

"Naomi's mother eventually remarried. She, her new husband, and her two children immigrated to America in 1949. The war is still very much with them, and in addition, they have all of the problems that people have when they must adjust to a new culture."

"Naomi is a nervous and high strung child," Mrs. Simonson continued. "She can burst into tears for what appears to be nothing. It's never nothing! The child has an unusually large burden of memory to carry."

"If she is willing to accept it, a child like Naomi needs a lot of loving attention. If she won't accept it, allow her to mentally sort things out when she's feeling unhappy. Eventually she may come around."

Once again Isabelle witnessed bigotry's long evil arm attack the innocent. It made her feel very sad.

Rebecca Simonson was truly a master teacher. She ran her class with an iron hand that was encased in a velvet glove. She expected lots of good work and lots of respect…. and she got it! Still, most of her pupils felt that she loved them. Isabelle wished that she too would possess a magic that would reach *her* future students, like Mrs. Simonson's magic had reached her and was now reaching the lucky children she taught in P.S. 61.

Chapter 18: Maryland

It was the first week in January, 1953, and Isabelle would graduate from Hunter College at the end of the month. She seriously doubted that she would attend graduation exercises, because she hoped she would get a teaching position somewhere in the vicinity in which she and Al would live in off-base housing at Army Chemical Center, in Maryland. She felt certain that if she were lucky enough to land a job, she would be required to start work very quickly.

An excited Isabelle boarded the train to Baltimore, where she planned to meet Al. The train was crowded – every seat occupied. Isabelle sat in the window seat and an African-American young man, a few years older than she, sat down beside her. Isabelle's eyes were clapped on the landscape speeding by, while the man with whom she was sharing her seat read a New York newspaper. The train stopped at Trenton, New Jersey, discharged some passengers and absorbed some new ones. It then sped on to Wilmington, Delaware. Before its doors opened, at Wilmington, the conductor came up to the young man sitting next to Isabelle and said, "At Wilmington, all Negroes must go to the Negro car located at the end of the train. Here is your new ticket. It will allow you to ride in the Negro car until you reach your destination."

The well-dressed African-American took the new ticket, and with an extremely pained expression, stood up and went to the door where passengers who were going to Wilmington would leave the train, along with all of the African-Americans in the car. All of the African- Americans were heading to the special car designated for Negroes only, because Delaware was a state in which the races were separated on public transportation.

Isabelle pondered the humiliating injustice she had just witnessed. In 1953, laws in southern and Border States still forced African-Americans to sit in train cars separated from white passengers. A terrible insult was implicit in this, and yet, in many states, in our supposedly free country, this was the law and it made Isabelle feel heavy hearted.

For the rest of the trip to Baltimore, Isabelle sadly watched the landscape flash by. Only seeing Al on the train platform, in Baltimore, improved her mood. She couldn't wait for the train doors to open, so that she could be in the arms of her husband.

After a loving greeting, Al told Isabelle that on Saturday night they would be attending a Detachment party. He informed her that he had learned a great deal about the public transportation in the areas in which she would be having interviews. He assured her that she would have no trouble getting to any place she wanted to go.

Isabelle had scheduled interviews in Towson, Baltimore, and Bel Air. In Baltimore, she would be given a written test along with a personal interview, and that interview was scheduled for Wednesday. Because Baltimore was farther from Army Chemical Center than any of the other school systems to which Isabelle was applying, Baltimore was the least desirable place for her to work. Isabelle's appointment for a teaching position in the city of Baltimore was early on Wednesday morning. A gruff man interviewed her and sent her to the area in which she took the required written exam. Isabelle found the exam to be easy. When she turned it in, she was told that she would be notified by mail as to whether she was hired by the city of Baltimore. While Isabelle felt sure that she would be offered a teaching position in this big city, she hoped that Towson or Bel Air would hire her instead.

Towson was a lovely college town located south of Edgewood. The interviewer liked Isabelle, but could only offer her a teaching position starting in September, because Towson had no mid-year vacancies.

On Friday, Isabelle went to her last interview. Bel Air, the county seat of Harford County, Maryland appeared to be a lovely town consisting of residences, churches, county buildings, and stores. On the day Isabelle interviewed for a teaching position there, Al came with her and waited for her in a small park where he enjoyed the rare sunshine of a balmy winter day. Bel Air, bathed in this winter sunshine, appealed to Isabelle and lifted her spirits. She suddenly felt confident that she would land just the job she wished for in this charming little town.

The person who interviewed Isabelle was a middle aged, austere, prematurely white-haired woman. Her thin lips were pinched closed in a straight line, relaxing only when she spoke. Her small eyes darted up and down, examining Isabelle's appearance very carefully. Her unpleasant, seemingly dissatisfied and unfriendly body language, more than the questions she asked, made it difficult for Isabelle to answer in a confident manner. Yet, when the unpleasant woman finished questioning Isabelle, to Isabelle's surprise, she informed her that there was a third grade opening, which would begin the last week in January. The present teacher of the class was pregnant and was leaving on maternity leave. The unpleasant interviewer then asked Isabelle if she had any questions.

"Yes," answered Isabelle. "How many students are there in the class?"

"Forty-five," answered the white haired woman. "The school in which you will teach is a consolidated school, serving all of the third grade students of Harford County. Yours is the only third grade class, and because we are experiencing a tremendous baby boom in Harford County, your class is inordinately large."

"There must be a wide range in family incomes and pupils' intelligence levels," remarked Isabelle.

"Yes," replied the woman. "I believe that you will be teaching a share cropper's child in the same class as the child whose father owns the share cropper's farm."

"I didn't know that share cropping had moved as far north as Maryland", Isabelle said.

"Oh yes," replied the woman. "You will find that share cropping and many other seemingly southern practices can be found around here."

334

"Really," said New York-bred Isabelle. "Can you tell me if there are children of different ethnicities here; and if so, what provisions are made to assimilate them?"

The white haired woman pursed her thin lips, straightened her back, and glared at Isabelle. "We have only *two* ethnicities in Harford County and they are *Nigra* and *White*! We have *two* school systems in Harford County – *Nigra* and *White*! *Nigra* teachers teach *Nigra* children in *Nigra* schools! *White* teachers teach *White* children in *White* schools! I assigned you to our *White school*," she said, glaring at the black-haired young woman being interviewed. "I assumed you were *White*. Was I mistaken?" she asked sarcastically.

To Isabelle's everlasting shame, she lowered her eyes and replied, "No, you are not mistaken."

"Then we'll see you in late January," said the interviewer. "Good day." She no longer looked at Isabelle and started to shuffle some papers on her desk. Totally cowered, Isabelle quietly left the nasty interviewer's office.

When Isabelle met Al in the park, she burst into tears as she lit a cigarette with trembling hands. She began to tell him about her interview, but was interrupted when he said, "Put out the cigarette, Isabelle. Women in Bel Air probably do not smoke in public."

Isabelle angrily squashed out the cigarette with her shoe and told Al the unpleasant story of her interview. "I hate myself," she said, "for knuckling under to that bigot! And I know I'll hate teaching in this place!"

"You had to knuckle under. There is nothing you can do about the awful laws here. If you had said your piece, you would not have gotten the job you and I badly need when you move down here," said Al.

"I guess you're right," said Isabelle. "Like the *Nigras*, we do what we have to do."

Isabelle did not brighten up until the Detachment party on Saturday night. She was surprised to see how many wives, fiancées, and girlfriends of the soldiers in Al's detachment of S.P.P.'s had come to the party. The hall was crowded. Isabelle estimated that there were more than two hundred people present.

Recorded music came through a loudspeaker system that was poor, making it difficult to hear. Consequently there was very little dancing, but lots of drinking. Beer flowed freely. Chips were plentiful, and hard liquor was plentiful too. The rule was "Bring Your Own Bottle" and bring them they did. Al brought a full bottle of scotch. Because Isabelle only drank Coca-Cola, which was also plentiful, the entire bottle of scotch was at Al's disposal. Al's access to hard liquor was also shared by the many S.P.P.'s who had come to the party without female companions. The bottles these men had brought were also for themselves alone.

About an hour into the party, a game called "Chug-a-lug" was instituted. In this game, two soldiers faced off and drank beer, for as long as they could, without coming up for air. The winner was the soldier who was able to drink for the longest time.

Chug-a-lug was soon replaced with a more lethal game. Isabelle and Al and the people sitting at their table were supposed to drink hard liquor followed by a beer chaser, without passing out. The last person, sitting upright in his chair, was the winner. All of the young men at their table participated in this dangerous game. All of the young women abstained.

As the amount of hard liquor they drank accelerated, soldiers at Al's and Isabelle's table began to pass out. Eventually, every drunken soldier, except Al, had passed out. The only soldier who had remained conscious, and was therefore the winner of the game, was Al. The huge amounts of liquor plus beer seemed to have little effect on him. The only visible effect it seemed to have, was that normally reserved Al was making outrageous amorous advances on Isabelle in public. Isabelle knew that she needed to get Al away from the party before he embarrassed them both, so she steered him in the direction of the door, and hailed a taxi to take them back to their hotel.

Al kept making sexual advances on his wife in the taxi. Isabelle had a difficult time restraining her drunken paramour, and only the promise of satisfying all of his demands when they got to the hotel room, kept him off her body.

In the hotel room, Isabelle expected some powerful lovemaking. She got herself into bed and awaited the arrival of her husband from the bathroom, located right across the room in which she lay. Suddenly, Isabelle heard terrible retching and moaning. Isabelle realized that Al was in the bathroom, throwing up everything that was inside of him. She went to the doorway of the bathroom to see if she was needed. She saw Al in a puddle of vomit, retching and violently throwing up. He was on his knees, hugging the toilet, which caused Isabelle to be bitterly amused. She thoroughly hated drunkenness, but there was something comical about Al – the great, demanding lover, hugging the toilet. Not having the ability to stop Al's drunken heaving, Isabelle once again, got into her bed.

Quite a while later, Isabelle heard the sound of running water. Al was cleaning the bathroom and himself. Had he recovered sufficiently to return to their bed and make love to her? When the water ceased running, Al appeared in the bathroom doorway, looking very pale. He staggered and weaved the few feet to where Isabelle was lying, promptly threw himself down on the bed, and passed out in a drunken stupor. "So much for the *Great Lover*," thought the amused Isabelle.

The next morning, a very contrite, greatly weakened Al apologized to Isabelle. Isabelle accepted his apology, believing that his escapade was a once-in-a-lifetime occurrence.

Al's older brother Harold was a quiet man, six years Al's senior. Since Harold's discharge from the army, after World War II, the two brothers had become very close. Harold's marriage had created greater distance between the brothers, but they still communicated frequently.

Harold's wife, Gert, and Isabelle got along quite well, in spite of the fact that Gert had a tendency to try to dominate most situations. Isabelle wasn't fazed by this. She simply ignored Gert's pushiness and did things her own way. Because of this, the two sisters-in-law remained on cordial terms.

As was the case with many New Yorkers, Gert and Isabelle were unable to drive. Harold drove, and he and Gert owned a car.

Isabelle planned to join Al in Edgewood, Maryland at the beginning of the third week in January. She would miss her graduation ceremonies from Hunter College to begin teaching in Bel Air Elementary School on the Monday of the fourth week in January. She planned to bring as many household items as she could cram into a car, for use in their new home in Maryland. Getting to Maryland with their belongings, and procuring a car to do so, however, was a daunting matter.

Isabelle and Al didn't own a car. Neither did Hymie nor Bella nor Max nor Eva. What is more, neither older couple had ever heard of renting a car, so while Hymie stood ready to drive his step-daughter to Maryland, Isabelle would have to procure the car that Hymie would drive, and neither Hymie nor Isabelle knew how to go about it.

During the second week in January, Harold and Gert had purchased a new car. They did not plan to trade in their old car, because they were dissatisfied with the price they had been offered for it by the car dealership. Instead, they planned to run an ad in the newspaper to try to sell the old car themselves.

Isabelle knew none of these things. She only knew that Harold and Gert now owned two cars, so when Al came home on the second weekend in January, Isabelle suggested that he call his brother and ask to borrow one of the cars for one day. He was to explain that Hymie would drive down to Edgewood, and after they unloaded their belongings, would immediately drive the car back to them.

Al thought nothing of asking this favor of his brother. Harold would certainly understand their need to borrow a car, and besides, Harold had always been warm and generous toward his younger brother. Therefore, Al called immediately after Isabelle had made the suggestion.

The phone was picked up by Harold. After a minimum of small talk, Al explained the importance of his request, and asked Harold to lend him a car. To Al's surprise, Harold asked Al to hold on. He then presented Al's request to Gert, explaining the importance of the loan, just as Al had explained it to him.

Gert flat-out refused! She said that the old car needed to remain in their parking lot, because it had to be looked at by prospective buyers. As for the new car, she said she wouldn't let anyone, except Harold, drive it.

Harold repeated Gert's remarks to Al, almost verbatim. In great distress, Al quickly terminated the conversation. It took Al a very long time to forgive his brother and sister-in-law for their selfishness, at such an important time.

———

Isabelle, seeing Al's acute distress, tried to sooth him by saying that she'd call her Uncle Irving for the favor. Al said that her Uncle Irving had only one car, but Isabelle assured him that if it were necessary, Uncle Irving himself would drive her to Maryland.

A very doubtful Al listened as Isabelle called her uncle. He heard Isabelle make her request, and then saw her nodding her head, as her uncle answered her. Finally, Isabelle said, "Thank you Uncle Irving. You always come to the rescue. I'll tell Al our plan. He'll be very relieved. I love you!" Then Isabelle hung up the telephone. "Uncle Irving says we'll need a car in Maryland," Isabelle said. "You've got your driver's license, so you'll be able to drive it when we bring it down there. Uncle Irving knows that we can't get the credit to buy a car, because I'm still a student and you're a low-ranking soldier. He said that when I select our car, he'll take me to his bank to see if he can get us a loan. I'm going to go car shopping on Staten Island, where he knows an honest used car dealer who will give us a fair price. He and I are going shopping this week."

"When I have to make my move to Edgewood, Uncle Irving says he'll drive me down in the car we buy. He says he'll take the train home."

Al was greatly relieved and immediately began to look forward to Isabelle's arrival.

———

Isabelle selected a bluish gray 1950 Ford. Uncle Irving and the owner of the used car lot negotiated a price that seemed fair, and a very excited Isabelle went to the bank with her uncle to get a loan to buy their first car.

At the bank, the manager was very cordial to Uncle Irving. It seemed that the two men had done business together and had great respect for each other. After the bank manager heard that Isabelle was just starting a teaching job and Al was a Private First Class, he said sadly, "Irving, I would be breaking every rule of the bank to give these kids a loan. You'll have to find another way to get the car financed."

"Okay," replied Uncle Irving. "I'll buy the car for them, and I'll expect you to give me my customary rate of credit."

"Certainly," said the bank manager, and he immediately proceeded to process the loan.

Uncle Irving gave Isabelle the loan booklet. The car was registered in her name. The loan was in Uncle Irving's name. He would expect Isabelle and Al to send the bank a payment on the loan every month.

Isabelle and Al paid off the car loan very diligently. Uncle Irving never again heard about the loan he had made for them, but Isabelle and Al never forgot Uncle Irving's great generosity and trust.

———

The 1950 Ford was filled to its roof. Isabelle and her Uncle Irving were ready to go. Bella, Hymie, and Phyllis stood forlornly on the sidewalk as the car pulled away. Laughing, Uncle Irving rolled down his window and said, "She's not going off to another country for fourteen years. She'll be home for a visit almost every weekend." He rolled up his window, and they were on their way.

The trip to Edgewood, Maryland took three and a half hours plus the half hour stop they made for lunch. Throughout the trip, Uncle Irving entertained Isabelle with stories from his past and stories about the antics of his two young sons. The trip flew by and then they saw the sign pointing to Army Chemical Center. Before Uncle Irving made the turn, he stopped at a gas station and filled up the car. He said, "I want to deliver a wife and a full tank."

When the car pulled into the cul-de-sac in which Isabelle and Al's apartment was located, they saw Al on the first floor, through an uncovered window. He saw them too, and came running out of the house to greet them.

As the three of them entered the apartment that Al had rented, Al hastily explained how he had procured it. "Apartments are very scarce here," said Al, "but I know a fellow who was being transferred, and I struck a deal with him. He said that I could pick up his apartment, if I bought the furniture in it for $150. Sight unseen, I agreed."

"The furniture is pretty awful," Al continued, "but we'll fix it up. The apartment is very nice, and besides, I'll be leaving here in August, so we won't be living here very long."

With that, the three of them began their tour of the apartment. In the living room there was an extremely shabby sofa and an even shabbier easy chair. The carpet was frayed and the windows were uncovered. The dining area was worse than the living room. A large wooden table surrounded by six chairs occupied this area. No one could figure out how it had occurred, but the table's top was not flat. In the center of the table, the wood had lifted and had formed a column of waves running the entire length of the table. Nothing could be placed on its wavy center, but its flat narrow sides could possibly be used by someone who didn't require much space. Isabelle planned to cover the ugly table with a tablecloth to obscure its hideous wavy center.

The three of them now entered the apartment's small kitchen. It contained a tiny Formica table of questionable age, and two ugly chairs with green plastic seats and rusting chrome legs.

The worst was yet to come....

When the three horrified people inspecting the apartment entered the bedroom, they truly could not believe their eyes! Wooden vegetable crates, covered with the same ugly pea green sheets of plastic that had been used in the kitchen, served as the drawer space in this rather commodious bedroom. The vegetable crates paled when compared to the bed; the bed that was the greatest disaster of all! It stood on four cinder blocks. The blocks supported an uncovered broken spring, with a filthy, lumpy, stained mattress perched upon it. It was the most disreputable mattress any of them had ever seen.

Uncle Irving wasted no time. He whisked out his address book and placed a telephone call to Baltimore. On the telephone, he explained the situation he had encountered, and arranged for a brand new mattress and spring-on-legs to be delivered to Isabelle's and Al's apartment that very day. When he hung up the telephone, he turned to the young couple and said, "I cannot allow you sleep on this awful mattress, even for one night. The man I just called was someone with whom I have business dealings. Because he owes me a favor, he will deliver a mattress and spring from his store in Baltimore today. I'm sure it will be a lovely set you will enjoy using. When you leave here, you will probably get a decent price for all this junk, because of the new mattress set."

"Enjoy kids!" laughed Uncle Irving.

When Uncle Irving boarded the New York bound train, he left two extremely grateful young people in an apartment that they knew they would have to fix up very quickly.

———

Al had a pass on the following weekend. He drove his new car to Sears Roebuck in Baltimore, where he and Isabelle planned to shop for some of the things they vitally needed to make their apartment fit to live in. They bought inexpensive draperies for all of the windows and inexpensive rugs for the living room, bedroom, and dining area. Slipcovers were purchased to hide the shabbiness of the living room furniture. They also bought a vacuum cleaner to clean the place up.

The young couple didn't have to buy a bedspread, because Bella had taken the spread off her own bed and given it to them. The very lovely tablecloth that they had been given as an engagement gift was already covering the hideous waves on the dining room table. Engagement gifts and wedding gifts had also supplied them with all of the sheets and pillowcases that they needed. They had received too few towels as gifts, but Eva had fleshed out their supply from her own linen closet. Al and Isabelle were ready to keep house again.

———

Isabelle's nasty and bigoted interviewer for her teaching job in Bel Air was true to her word. Isabelle was teaching every white third grader in Harford County. If, as the interviewer said, being Caucasian was an "ethnicity," the children Isabelle taught, did indeed share only *one* ethnicity. But, even though they were all white third graders who lived in the same county, Isabelle's forty-five pupils varied greatly. Their variance was most evident in family income. There were a few children whose families were well-to-do, while the vast majority of the children came from comfortable middle class families. The few children who were the children of poor independent farmers or sharecroppers could be easily distinguished from the others by the shabbiness of their clothing.

The intelligence of the children in Isabelle's class ranged from extremely bright down to borderline mentally challenged, (called "retarded" in 1953). Surprisingly, regardless of their intelligence, the children behaved the same in their excellent compliance to their teacher's rules and requests. In addition to their good behavior, they seemed quite eager to learn. And if they were eager to learn, Isabelle was eager to teach them. Almost immediately, an excellent rapport developed between Harford County's third graders and their new, very young teacher. The children were interested in what their teacher said and in the stories she read or told them. They knew if they read and wrote well, their teacher would be pleased; and all forty-five pupils strove to please her.

When Isabelle had arrived in her classroom, she was happy to find the *Dick and Jane* series she had used when she had been teaching reading as a student teacher in the third grade at P.S. 61. But, unlike the New York City public schools, Harford County did not supply individual workbooks for their children to use. Isabelle believed that the absence of these workbooks placed her pupils at a serious disadvantage. The exercises in the workbooks reinforced reading principles that were taught with the textbook, and also facilitated the pupil's grasp of written English. Isabelle had been supplied with single copies of the workbooks that accompanied each of her five reading groups. She, therefore, either arrived at school very early or stayed at school very late, because she filled her chalk boards with those workbook exercises she felt would best benefit her reading groups. It was very hard work to fill two long walls of chalkboard with exercises copied from the workbooks, but her pupils were progressing well in reading, so Isabelle didn't mind the work too much.

The last week of January and all of February of 1953 were a time of getting acquainted. The principal and most of the staff of the Harford County Elementary School were friendly, and Isabelle was happy professionally. However, Isabelle was deeply puzzled by her own reactions to certain aspects of life in the border state of Maryland.

Every day, Isabelle saw disturbing evidence of Jim Crow in action. What she saw was in response to the laws prevalent, at that time, in the border states and the southern states. She saw Harford County school buses carrying African-American children past her school to go to the Negro School. She passed a restaurant daily, which displayed a large sign reading *Negroes*. This was the only restaurant in the entire area in which African-Americans were allowed to eat. All other restaurants were for White people only. Even at Army Chemical Center, a United States Army post, all restrooms and water fountains were clearly marked *Negro* or *White*.

At first, all of this evidence of Jim Crow completely horrified Isabelle, but as she became accustomed to her environment, she became somewhat inured to the gross indications of prejudice all around her. They had caused her great anxiety and unhappiness when she first arrived in Maryland, but now they seemed to have become a part of the landscape. This was very upsetting to Isabelle. How had she become comfortable with the bigotry in her environment? How did she grow used to it? She was unable answer these disturbing questions.

Another thing that surprised Isabelle about Maryland was the fanfare with which they revered Abraham Lincoln. Prior to Lincoln's birthday, Isabelle learned that she was expected to teach a unit about Abraham Lincoln. When she expressed her surprise at this reverence for Lincoln, she was informed that Lincoln wanted to preserve the Union. Maryland, though a slave state, never seceded from the Union. Lincoln was presented in the Maryland schools as the president who fought a war to preserve the United States. Almost nothing was said about his anti-slavery position.

———

Harford County Elementary School was not Isabelle's only new interest. On Valentine's Day, Al took Isabelle to Harford County's Animal Shelter. He knew that Isabelle's family had owned dogs through many of Isabelle's growing up years, so he thought she might enjoy owning a dog once again.

There were seven or eight dogs in the cages of the small animal shelter.

Some of them barked, some of them yipped, and one little dog lay still, as if he were dead. Isabelle approached the cage of the silent, dormant animal and began to speak to it and to make affectionate sounds. The animal lifted its head and raised its dark, velvety eyes to her. Isabelle continued to cluck at him and then quietly said, "Here boy, come here, boy; what a pretty boy."

The little dog slowly got to his feet. Even more slowly, head hanging, he walked the few steps from the back of his cage to the front, where Isabelle cooed, "That's a good boy. That's the doggie I love." After he approached Isabelle, he never moved his eyes from her face. Then the little, black, shorthaired beagle began to slowly wag his tail.

Isabelle turned to Al and said, "Let's take this one. He seems so sad, yet he responded to my voice, almost immediately."

"Okay," said Al. "If that's the one you want, we'll take him."

On the ride home, the little dog lay in Isabelle's lap. Occasionally, his skinny tail flopped up and down.

They named their dog Val, because he became a member of their family on Valentine's Day. He adjusted to them almost immediately. He didn't even seem to need any housebreaking. (They conjectured that Val's previous owner had already housebroken him.) In the morning they either walked him on a leash or let him roam freely in the large grassy areas surrounding their apartment complex. When he roamed freely, he never failed to come home after a ten or fifteen minute romp.

———————

Every third weekend, Al, Isabelle, and as many as three paying passengers drove to New York. Each soldier who traveled with them paid Al $3.50 for a round trip ride. The money helped Isabelle and Al meet their car payments, because Al's Private 1st Class salary was miniscule and Isabelle's teacher's salary was only $2,700 per year.

When they visited New York, Al and Isabelle stayed at Eva's and Max's house. Eva was not fond of dogs, at best....and Val was far less than endearing when he came to her house. Val harbored quite a few canine grievances against the trip to New York, but his greatest two grievances were his being cooped up in the car for three-and-a-half hours, and then traversing the never-ending pavement in New York City that he hated with a passion. Val was a country dog, who could not get it through his canine head that the paved city road was his big-city bathroom; so being walked on a leash on the sidewalk and then being led to the paved road held no meaning for him at all. Val, therefore, abstained from doing his natural elimination outdoors, when he was visiting the city. Instead, he found his instant relief on Eva's green living room carpet. He had no idea about why everyone was getting so upset with him, and he developed an instant dislike for Al's mother and step-father. Being a good dog, he just remained aloof and unresponsive in their presence, and this disdainful behavior toward them, along with his destructive behavior on their carpet, made them equally unfriendly to Val.

Val had belonged to Isabelle and Al for approximately six weeks when they noticed that he was not eating well. The little dog had become quite thin and was becoming listless. Isabelle decided to take him to the post veterinarian.

The veterinarian looked grave when he examined Val, and when he was finished with the examination, he sadly told Isabelle that Val was suffering from distemper. Although Val had gotten his distemper shot at the post's veterinary clinic, he was probably already incubating the disease, and the vaccination was given to him in vain. The veterinarian said that there was a treatment that was usually successful in curing a dog with distemper, but it would cost over $100. The veterinarian realized that Isabelle and Al could not cover so steep a fee, so he suggested two other alternatives....

They could soak stale bread in milk and hand-feed the little dog, which rarely, though sometimes, worked. Or, they could put Val "to sleep."

Isabelle would not hear of euthanizing her dog. Tearfully, she decided to try the route of the stale bread and milk.

The weather was already warm and very humid, so getting bread to become stale was quite a feat, because the bread usually became moldy. But, they prevailed, for quite often, they could get a small quantity of stale bread, which they then fleshed out with soda crackers. Isabelle hand-fed the bread and soda crackers, soaked in milk, to their ailing dog; and miracle of miracles, Val began to rally. After almost two weeks of hand feeding and lots of love, their little dog was weak, but he was well once more.

———

Sol's son, Mel, was fighting in Korea. With every Yiddish newscast about the ferocious fighting on that little known Asian peninsula, Sarah sent supplications to God, begging him to spare Sol's only child. In the winter of 1953, when she learned that Mel was to be repatriated from Korea, her thankfulness knew no bounds. After making a handsome donation to her synagogue, she made arrangements with her rabbi for Mel to read from the *Torah* on his first Saturday back in New York.

This done, Sarah continued her supplications to God on Al's behalf. Although Al was safely stationed at Army Chemical Center in Maryland, until he had completed three-fourths of his two-year enlistment, he could still be sent to Korea. Sarah fervently hoped that her prayers would spare her grand-daughter Isabelle's husband from the horrific experience of a battlefield.

Isabelle and Al were living in Maryland on the April Saturday in 1953 when Al read from the Torah at Sarah's synagogue in Coney Island. He had just turned twenty-three years old, and his Torah reading commemorated two personal blessings, his birthday and his having reached the time in his army service where he would be exempt from being sent to Korea. His deep young baritone voice boomed the Hebrew words with confidence. Isabelle was greatly surprised to hear such excellent sounds coming from the *Bema* (area where the *Torah* is read and the Rabbi delivers his sermon.) After services, when she left the segregated women's section of Sarah's Orthodox synagogue and was reunited with her husband, Isabelle asked him how he had managed to sound so proficient when he was reading Hebrew.

"Oh," he replied, laughing heartily, "they had a gyp sheet. All of the Hebrew was transliterated for my reading."

Isabelle laughed heartily too. She now understood how both Al and Mel had managed to sound so accomplished when they read the *Torah*. They were reading transliterations.

———

When Isabelle had been teaching in Bel Air for about two months, she was told that the third grade was expected to make an exhibit for the Maryland State Fair. Every year, each grade made an exhibit, and that year, the principal requested that the third grade do something about the important buildings in their town of Bel Air. "Such buildings as the churches, the jail, the courthouse, and the schools should be emphasized," said the principal.

The exhibit was a big undertaking. Isabelle and her class decided to make a three dimensional map of Main Street. Most of the churches, the jail, and the courthouse were located on Main Street. On their map, the children would put models of the important buildings. The schools and the Catholic Church were the only buildings located off Main Street. They would extend their map to accommodate these buildings.

On the day that Isabelle presented the state fair project to her class, she suggested that the children might like to do models of the churches they themselves attended. The Episcopal, Presbyterian, Baptist, Church of God and Pentecostal churches were rapidly snapped up by the children who worshipped in them. Two or three children could work together on making models of each church. They would use corrugated or shoe boxes and paints to make their models. Several children expressed interest in the various schools in Bel Air, while others chose the courthouse and the jail. There was also a committee that was responsible for making the huge map on which the buildings would be displayed.

When everything was designated, to Isabelle's surprise, she found that one church had been left out. Right behind the school that the children were attending, was a small clapboard Catholic Church. Alongside it was a small building in which two nuns lived. These two nuns ran the only kindergarten in Bel Air. Many Protestant children as well as most of the Catholic children attended this kindergarten, because there were no kindergarten classes in the Bel Air Elementary School.

Isabelle asked if there were any children who attended the Catholic Church, and if so, would they like to make a model of their church. No one came forward. She then asked if there were any children who had gone to the kindergarten run by the Catholic Sisters. Approximately fifteen children raised their hands. She asked if any of them would like to make the model of the Catholic Church, and she got several volunteers.

That afternoon, when Isabelle was escorting the children to the various school buses that would take them home, an adorable little freckle-faced, redheaded girl tugged on her teacher's sleeve. She whispered, furtively, "You made a big mistake today."

"What did I do?" asked Isabelle.

"You said that the church where the Sisters teach kindergarten is the Catholic Church. I go there every Sunday, and I ain't one of them!"

"Oh, Sweetheart," responded Isabelle, "if you go there on Sunday, you are probably a Catholic. And, being a Catholic is a fine thing to be. Be proud of it!"

The child entered her bus, looking bewildered.

Isabelle now realized that in Bel Air racial bigotry and religious bigotry walked hand-in-hand.

———————

There were three Jewish children in the Bel Air School. Two were brothers, whose father liked small town living, and commuted to his job in Baltimore every day. The other was a little girl, in Isabelle's class, whose father owned a clothing store on Main Street. Janet was quite bright and very popular with the other children. When she learned that Isabelle came from New York City, she told her that she wished she lived in New York City or in Baltimore.

"Why?" asked Isabelle.

"Because there are lots of Jews in big cities. I don't like being the only one here. *Are you Jewish?*" she asked.

"Yes," answered Isabelle.

Janet's face lit up in a big smile.

On the next day, Janet's mother was waiting for Isabelle at the close of school. She introduced herself and asked Isabelle if there was anything she could do to help her get settled in the area.

"Yes," said Isabelle. "Would you happen to know of a good cleaning woman I could hire."

"Indeed I do. I have an excellent cleaning woman who lives just outside of Bel Air. I'll tell her that you're interested, and she'll call you. She doesn't have a telephone, so you can't call her," said Janet's mother.

Isabelle thanked her, and the two women parted.

Two days later, Yula called. Isabelle wrote down directions to Yula's house, and promised to come there the following afternoon, right after school.

———

Yula lived over a rickety bridge that spanned a rapidly running creek on the outskirts of Bel Air. The bridge rattled and shook as Isabelle drove over it, causing her to wonder whether it would support her car. When she got to the other side of the bridge, Isabelle immediately spotted Yula's house.

The house was a run-down, clapboard two-story affair, with a porch running around its front. Toys and a dog occupied the porch which was missing half of its railing. The house was located opposite a small factory whose huge chimney belched dark grey smoke. The factory was made of wood that once was painted tan, but most of the tan paint was gone, showing the grey worn wood underneath. To Isabelle, Yula's unpainted grey house, the factory's unpainted boards, and the dark gray smoke being emitted by the plant's chimney produced an aura of a dismal gray world. Worse still was the extremely disagreeable odor being emitted by the plant. It was so bad that Isabelle found it hard to breathe.

Yula, a heavy set, very dark-skinned woman in her sixtys came out of her house and quickly entered Isabelle's car. They exchanged introductions, and no more was said until Isabelle was driving on the highway.

"What was that odor coming out of the factory across from where you live?" asked Isabelle.

In a gentle voice, Yula replied, "They render dead animals to fat there. The fat is sold to the soap factory."

Silence once more descended upon the two women. They remained silent until they arrived at Isabelle's apartment in Edgewood. Once inside, Isabelle showed the older woman her apartment and then invited her to sit down and have a cup of tea with her at the small Formica table in the kitchen. Yula appeared nervous and flustered. She explained that she had never shared a table nor eaten with a white person, and she remained standing.

Isabelle said, "Please sit down. Any person in my house who is eating or drinking with me, shares my table. What is more, while I understand that you are behaving as *you* were taught to behave, *in my house*, I'd like us to behave as *I* was taught to behave."

"If you feel comfortable calling me *Miss Isabelle*, I'll let you do it, but I don't feel comfortable calling you *Yula*. Where I come from, we call women in our parents' or grandparents' generations, by their last names. What is yours?"

"Gregg," answered Yula.

"Then I will call you *Mrs. Gregg*. Do you feel comfortable with that?"

"No Ma'am," replied the older woman.

"Well please grow used to it. I was not raised to address people differently because of their race. Only their age causes me to show them respect or to be familiar," said Isabelle.

"It ain't the way we talk around here," said Yula, "but if y'all wants me to, we can talk that way to each other."

"I hope that in the not too distant future, my way will be everybody's way of talking," said Isabelle.

Mrs. Gregg and Isabelle arrived at how much Isabelle would pay her for housecleaning, laundry, and ironing every second Saturday. Isabelle said that she would pick Mrs. Gregg up in the morning and take her home when her work was done. And all of the arrangements were made as the two women sipped tea together, sitting at the tiny Formica table in the kitchen.

In the course of Mrs. Gregg's employment by Isabelle, Isabelle learned that Mrs. Gregg had been widowed when all ten of her children were still living at home. The youngest child was less than a year old and the eldest was sixteen years old. Yet, every one of Mrs. Gregg's children had graduated from high school. Two of her children had gone to college. All of them had worked and had helped out with expenses while they were in school. None of them, Mrs. Gregg included, had ever taken charity.

While Mrs. Gregg was working for Isabelle, she was raising two of her grandchildren, whose father was in the army. He was divorced from his wife, who Mrs. Gregg said had bad habits and was a poor mother. Isabelle deeply respected Mrs. Gregg, and she was outraged that this industrious and very decent woman was considered inferior to anyone. Once more bigotry had made Isabelle feel angry and sad.

————————

Teaching positions in the New York City public schools were procured through competitive exams. If a candidate scored well on the written exam he or she took an oral and a medical exam. Isabelle had passed the written exam, which she had taken while she was living in Maryland. Along with the letter announcing that she had passed the written exam, Isabelle received notification of the date, time, and place of her oral exam. Once again she had to come to New York from Maryland to take this oral exam.

The oral test was being given in the early spring, while Isabelle was still teaching in Bel Air. She came to Bella's house, bringing a lovely suit to wear for the exam which she would take on Monday. To Isabelle's distress, a terrible thunderstorm was inundating New York City on the day of the exam. She was forced to wear her thirteen-year-old sister's skimpy raincoat and carry her mother's umbrella, as she trudged through the storm from Bella's house to the subway. The raincoat was too small and could not be buttoned all the way. What is more, the skirt of Isabelle's lovely suit hung below her coat, and as she crossed the street, a car came by and splashed her shoes, coat, and skirt.

The subway ride from the Bronx to Manhattan's east side was very unpleasant, because many of Isabelle's fellow passengers were wearing woolen clothing which had become wet in the heavy downpour, causing the subway car to smell unpleasantly of wet wool. The musty smell of wet wool triggered Isabelle's allergies and she sneezed and blew her nose during most of the trip.

The school at which the orals would be given was a high school located four blocks from the subway station. Isabelle felt like she was swimming there through the driving rain.

At the high school, crowds of people who were to be examined were directed by signs on the wall to an immense gym. The hordes of examinees were herded to tables bearing the first letter of their last names. A manila envelope containing instructions was handed to each examinee. Inside Isabelle's envelope was information telling her where and when her oral exam was to be administered. There was also a packet with hypothetical school problems that would be discussed during her oral examination and a sheet of words, many of them either obscure or tongue twisters, that she would be expected to read to her examiners. Isabelle had about half an hour until she was to report to her examination site. She took this time to carefully read her packet, think of some solutions to the hypothetical school problems, and to go to the restroom to restore her "drowned" appearance, as best she could.

At the appointed time, Isabelle reported to a science lecture room that consisted of a podium with a desk and chair, and rows of student's desks placed on large stairs that climbed much higher than the desk on the podium. At the very back of the room sat three men. They greeted Isabelle and told her to take a seat at the desk. They knew her name, but they never gave her their names.

Isabelle put her wet coat and umbrella on the student desk closest to the door. Taking the manila envelope with her, she walked to the teacher's desk in front of the room and sat down. The three men questioned her about her solutions to the hypothetical teaching problems presented in the packet. Isabelle answered all of their questions in the best way she knew; and then, at their request, read the long list of difficult words from her packet. When she was finished, the three men cordially said goodbye. The grueling oral exam was over.

Several weeks later an article appeared in *The Journal American*, New York City's evening newspaper. In the article, listed in the order of their scores, were the names of the people being hired by the New York City Board of Education for the fall term of 1953. (It was Isabelle's first notification of her success.) The article stated that all applicants who had served in the armed forces had received an additional ten points added to their scores. It further stated that all applicants would be assigned to low-performing schools, but the applicants whose scores were in the top ten percent, would be assigned to low-performing schools in the borough in which they lived.

Isabelle, who had sent in her application when she was living in Maryland, had used Bella's address in the Bronx to facilitate matters. She had scored in the top ten percent of the applicants, so using Bella's address she was assigned to a Bronx school. Isabelle was not perturbed over this, because she knew that at the beginning of her first school year, she would be living in Eva's house in the Bronx, which was located just a short ride away from the school to which she had been assigned. The serious housing shortage in New York City in the early 1950's made living with Al's family the expedient thing for Al and Isabelle to do.

———————

Summer in Edgewood, Maryland came early and was very hot. Al worked in an air-conditioned office, but neither the Bel Air School nor Isabelle and Al's apartment were air-conditioned. The unrelenting heat oppressed Isabelle. It was, therefore, with great delight that Isabelle learned of plans being made to go swimming at a resort located south of the army base, on the Chesapeake Bay. Soldiers from Al's office and from his detachment planned to get together with their girlfriends, wives, and families to spend a late May Saturday picnicking and swimming at the resort. A caravan of a little more than a dozen cars would go on the outing.

It was a long, hot, and intensely sunny drive. A thick, torrid breeze, laden with humidity, blew into the open windows of the cars, making the occupants feel hotter and more uncomfortable than ever. Isabelle and Al's car was the second car in the line of cars full of young people driving toward relief from the oppressive heat. The drivers in the long line of cars behind them, tried very hard not to get lost on their way to the resort. Suddenly, the turning signal of the first car began to flash. After the turn, they could see signs directing them toward the resort. As they approached the resort's entrance, Isabelle and Al saw an arched sign brazenly stating, *Gentile Only! No Jews Allowed!*

Neither of them knew what to do. If they pulled out of the caravan and headed for home, they knew that some of their friends would follow them, and others would guiltily enter the resort. Their action would spoil the day's fun for everyone. But, if they entered the resort, their entrance fee would support bigots who hated their people; and they certainly couldn't enjoy themselves in a place like that!

Isabelle and Al made a quick decision to enter the resort. They discussed the decision with their innocent, but nevertheless embarrassed friends, telling them that they didn't want to spoil everyone else's good time. Most of their friends said that their good time was already spoiled by the hateful sign.

When Isabelle entered the water, she deliberately urinated. As she did so, she thought, "This is what I think of this place! I'll simply forget about it and not think of it again." She was wrong. Whenever she read about or saw signs excluding African-Americans, she likened their feelings to her own on that hellishly hot day at a Chesapeake Bay resort in the state of Maryland in 1953.

When the school year in Bel Air was coming to a close, Isabelle was filled with sadness because she would soon be saying goodbye to the forty-five third graders she had grown to love. On the other hand, she looked forward to the time she would be teaching in New York City and would be establishing a home there, so she began the tedious job of closing up her school room in preparation for the end of the school year.

A week and a half before school closed, Isabelle awakened with intermittent sharp pains in her side. When the pains failed to go away, she went to see the doctor at the army base in Edgewood. After a careful examination, the doctor suggested that she go to the clinic at the Aberdeen Proving Grounds, a much larger army base with much larger medical facilities, located just a few miles away from Army Chemical Center. "At the clinic there will be OBGyn physicians, whose specialty is women's health. I believe that you need to see an OBGyn doctor," he said.

Isabelle followed the doctor's advice and made an appointment at the Aberdeen medical clinic, where an OBGyn doctor, much to her embarrassment, gave her her first internal examination. After the OBGyn specialist looked and looked, he requested that one of his colleagues do the same. The second OBGyn examination caused Isabelle's discomfort to increase more than exponentially! To her horror, the second doctor consulted with a third doctor, causing Isabelle to angrily exclaim "Is this a peep show? Am I on display here?"

Isabelle's outburst caused the three young army physicians to apologize profusely. They then left the room to consult, leaving Isabelle on the examining table with her feet still in the stirrups. After their consultation, the original doctor returned to Isabelle and said, "We believe that you have salpingitis. Salpingitis is an inflammation of the fallopian tubes. It usually occurs as a result of sex with a man who carries the infection."

"That's impossible!" retorted Isabelle. "I have only had sex with my husband, and to my knowledge, he has only had sex with me. Neither of us could have picked up an infection!"

"It is the opinion of the three of us that salpingitis accounts for your pain. If neglected, you can become sterile," said the young doctor. "We'd like to admit you to our hospital here at Aberdeen. We'll treat you with penicillin and destroy the infection." A very conflicted Isabelle agreed to be admitted to the hospital. She went home to tell Al and the school that she was entering the hospital in two days.

The ward contained twenty beds – ten on each side. About fifteen of the twenty beds had occupants. Isabelle's was the second bed from the door on the left. A woman who constantly slept, was on Isabelle's right, and an empty bed was on her left. On the wall facing her, all of the beds but one, were filled with other patients, all of whom were the wives of army personnel. Isabelle appeared to be the youngest patient and was mothered by several of the others. Those patients well enough to walk comfortably, were expected to make their own beds and replenish their water pitchers.

The ward's source of water was located in a sink at the end of the hall that led to the ward. The bathrooms were close to the sink, and diagonally opposite them was the nurses' station. The hall connecting the nurses' station and the ward had two closed doors on each side, which were the doors to the private rooms, in which critically ill patients lay.

The doctor came to see Isabelle several times a day. Because she wore Chinese styled pajamas, with satin pants, they called her *Fancy Pants*. Every three hours, around the clock, Isabelle's doctor or another doctor injected Isabelle with penicillin. (In those early days in the use of the drug, doctors were not yet fully aware of the allergic damage penicillin could do.)

On the opposite wall from where Isabelle lay, in the middle of the long ward, lay a German war bride from Dresden. Her English was heavily accented and she said very little to anyone. She had had abdominal surgery, and she walked with considerable difficulty. Yet, on the day before she was to be discharged from the hospital, she hobbled down the long room and came over to Isabelle. She said that she had noticed the Star of David Isabelle wore. The necklace and Isabelle's black hair had told her that Isabelle was Jewish. She said that in the 1930's, there was a Jewish family that lived in their apartment house in Dresden. She maintained that she and the Jewish family's daughter were good friends. Then, one day, the police came for the Jewish family. "I swear to you," the woman said, "none of the people I knew, knew what the Nazis were doing to the Jews. We knew the Nazis didn't like the Jews and wanted them out of Germany, but most Germans had no idea of the atrocities being committed against them."

"You do believe me, don't you?" the woman pleaded.

"No I don't," Isabelle answered bitterly. "Do you expect me to believe that the Jews killed themselves? It took lots of people to kill six million of us! I know that the murderers wrote home or told about the atrocities when they came home. I don't believe that the German people didn't know. Besides, we knew a lot about it here! If news of the atrocities reached the ears of the Jewish community in America, I know that it was not much of a secret to Germans."

"Look you're too sick to be standing here," continued Isabelle bitterly. "Go back to your bed."

Giving the German woman a venomous look, Isabelle rudely turned on her side. The German woman hobbled away sadly. She was discharged the next day, but Isabelle remembered her and her denial all of her life.

———

A beautiful flower arrangement was delivered to Isabelle's bedside. It had come from her class. Many cards and letters came from the children too. They spoke of how they missed her and how much they wished she would teach them in the fourth grade. The flowers and the good wishes of her children caused Isabelle's spirits to rise, but at the same time, caused sadness, because she would not be seeing her precious Maryland pupils again.

———

On the day before Isabelle's discharge from the hospital, the bed next to hers became occupied. Aides brought a sleeping woman down from the operating room to the ward. The woman was still sedated and sleeping soundly when she arrived.

A few hours later, while Isabelle was reading and relaxing in her bed, she heard the woman in the next bed calling out in pain. She was calling "Swester" and saying "Wasser." Isabelle, who had studied German for two years at Hunter College, and spoke Yiddish fluently, immediately understood that *"Swester"* meant either "sister" or "nurse" in German, *"Wasser"* meant "water." The woman was calling for a nurse, because she was in discomfort and was feeling thirsty.

For a swift moment Isabelle contemplated ignoring the suffering German woman. "Why should she help a member of the people who had slaughtered so many of her people?" Isabelle mused. But very quickly, the answer became apparent. This woman may have been innocent. As much as Isabelle hated the Germans for their deeds, she could not indict every German. As a moral Jew and a moral American, Isabelle knew that she needed proof of the woman's guilt before she could punish her by remaining silent and indifferent to her pain.

Isabelle rang for a nurse. When the desk answered, Isabelle explained that the woman next to her needed a nurse, because she was calling out for one in German. She further explained that the woman was in great discomfort and was thirsty.

On the morning of the day Isabelle was to go home, the German woman had become alert. *"Sprechen Sie Deutch?"* ("Do you speak German?") she asked Isabelle.

"Nein," replied Isabelle. Then she said in English, "I just know a few words."

The German woman, who had been more conscious the day before than Isabelle had realized, knew that Isabelle was avoiding conversation with her. She, therefore, said, in German, "You are angry with Germans. I am sorry about that; but thank-you for your help yesterday. You were a friend."

Isabelle understood most of what the German woman had said to her. She didn't know whether she should feel that she had behaved stupidly when she helped a German, or whether she had behaved morally as her religion and her upbringing had taught her. It was a question she couldn't answer. Isabelle remained conflicted.

———

Because New York City was still suffering from a serious housing shortage when Isabelle and Al came home in August of 1953, the city was in the midst of a gigantic building boom which started at the end of World War II and continued well past the couple's return. Most of the apartments being built were far too expensive for couples who were just starting out and didn't come from families able to give them financial assistance. Housing for the poor was being built by the city, in the form of housing projects, but the newly built projects accommodated only a miniscule percentage of New York City's poor people, leaving the remainder to live in their slums. Lower middle class neighborhoods in the Bronx were rapidly being turned into slums by the large influx of people from Puerto Rico and the large immigration of African-Americans coming north from the south. These new arrivals had a tendency of crowding two or three families into small apartments meant for one family, in order to be able to pay the exorbitant rents being charged for apartments in the city. Even though

New York City had placed a freeze on the rent of all pre-World War II apartments, the new arrivals had difficulty in procuring apartments that they could afford.

This dismal housing situation was particularly difficult for returning servicemen, just starting out in civilian life, but Isabelle and Al were among the lucky ones for whom there was a good housing solution. Al's cousin was on the board of Deepdale, a housing development in Little Neck on Long Island. This development was a sprawling apartment complex, consisting of two family, two story garden apartments surrounded by greenery and playgrounds, with a high quality public school to accommodate Deepdale's children. Al's cousin was able to assign an apartment that had not yet been spoken for to Isabelle and Al. It was located in a building on the edge of the Deepdale development, which was classified as a co-op, meaning that important housing decisions were made by an elected board of residents. All residents were expected to "buy" their apartment for a very modest sum. The erection of the Deepdale development was made possible by subsidies voted for by Congress, in order to help alleviate some of America's pervasive housing shortage.

The construction of Isabelle and Al's apartment would be completed in January or February of 1954. While they were awaiting its completion, the young couple would move in with Eva and Max. Of course, they would no longer use the only bedroom in Eva and Max's apartment, because they would no longer be weekend guests. They would be living with Eva and Max from August until either January or February, so they would be sleeping in the living room on a bed that folded out of a convertible sofa.

In August, just two weeks before Isabelle and Al were to move back to New York City, Isabelle developed small bumps on her scalp, a scabby sore on her face, and an oozing rash on her ear. She went to the doctor at Army Chemical Center and he said that he believed that she was suffering from a bad allergic reaction to the large amounts of penicillin she had received at the hospital in Aberdeen. He suggested that she go to the clinic at Aberdeen to have a specialist look at her.

When Isabelle went to Aberdeen, the specialist concurred with the diagnosis made at Army Chemical Center. He said that he'd like her to soak all of her affected areas in a solution she would make with warm water and a new and very potent drug called *cortisone*. The cortisone came in large white, hard cubes that Isabelle would have to break into tiny pieces with a hammer and then dissolve in water to make her soaking solution. Isabelle scrupulously followed the doctor's orders, though making the cortisone solution was tedious and messy. She found that the medicine was even messier to apply, and although she followed the instructions faithfully, she followed them in vain. Her nasty skin condition continued and even worsened. After using the cortisone solution in vain for two weeks, the doctor in Aberdeen said, "You're going home to New York soon. There are excellent doctors in New York. Ask around and find a good dermatologist. He'll get rid of your nasty condition."

The largest emotional jolt caused by Isabelle's leaving Maryland was not leaving segregation behind her, or her inability to move into an apartment that was hers and Al's alone. It was her inability to turn her deeply beloved dog into a New York City dog.

This great problem, concerning Val, worried both Isabelle and Al. While Al was to be officially discharged from the Army in October, he had accumulated so much leave time that he and Isabelle were able to sell their furniture and pack up and leave Edgewood in late August.

Isabelle and Al sadly knew that Val would not be a welcome guest in Eva's Bronx apartment, while the young couple waited for their Little Neck apartment to be ready for their occupancy. Fortunately, however, Al was acquainted with a career-army sergeant whose apartment was only a block away from Isabelle and Al's apartment in Edgewood. This soldier and his wife and children were looking for a dog to love. They took Val, when Isabelle and Al moved back to New York and became the non-paying residents sharing Eva and Max's very small space.

A year after they had returned to New York, Isabelle and Al were driving to Washington D.C. to attend a wedding in Al's family. When they approached the Edgewood cut-off, they decided to visit Val and his present family. They rang the doorbell of the sergeant's house and his wife opened the door. They apologized for barging in and explained their desire to see Val. A very flustered woman told them that after they had moved, Val had discovered his "manhood." When we let him out to do his stuff," the woman said, "more than likely he wouldn't come home for an hour or so. We expected that the little devil was carousing, and pretty soon our suspicions were verified." All over Edgewood and on the neighboring farms, litters of little black puppies, resembling Val, were being born. It seems that no bitch in heat, for miles around, was safe from Val's *amorous attentions.*"

———

"We had received several complaints about our roving canine Lothario, and we finally decided to put an end to it, by having Val neutered. The veterinarian told us that it would take Val several weeks before he realized that he was no longer able to perform. Other than that, he said that Val would be as he always had been."

"Val recovered from his operation very quickly, so we let him out to run and play. To our amazement, he behaved in a most unexpected way. Every day he went to visit a bitch and her new black litter at a nearby farm. He would stay with them for a few hours, before returning home."

"One morning," the woman continued sadly, "shortly after I had let Val out, he was run over and killed by a school bus. He was heading in the direction of the farm on which the bitch and litter he seemed to favor so much lived."

"My husband said that Val's death wasn't really an accident. He said that Val knew that he was no longer a *man*, and he committed suicide!"

All three people laughed at the woman's story; but then Isabelle suddenly realized that the little dog she had loved was dead, and she was filled with sadness. They said a sad goodbye to the woman, and resumed their trip to Washington D.C.

Max and Eva

Chapter 19: Eva's House

I sabelle followed the Army doctor's suggestion. Upon returning to New York and making several inquiries, Isabelle was told about a dermatologist in Brooklyn who was considered to be "state of the art," but by the time she could get an appointment to see him, large boils had also appeared on her buttocks. The trip from Eva's house, where Isabelle was living, to the dermatologist's office in Brooklyn, took more than an hour. Isabelle made the trip every Saturday from mid-September to December. The Brooklyn dermatologist treated Isabelle by shooting x-rays into her head, left ear, face, and buttocks. Yet the rashes, oozing ear, and boils persisted in these areas. Isabelle was becoming desperate for a cure, but even though she was unsightly, she continued to work and participate in life. While her condition did not cause her great physical discomfort, looking in the mirror and seeing the ugly sores on her face, or having to respond to the occasional inquiries made by curious, insensitive strangers were painful to her ego.

One of the most insensitive inquiries was made by an elderly woman in a crowded restroom of a Howard Johnson's restaurant on the New Jersey Turnpike. Al was driving Isabelle, Eva, Max, Bubbe, and Zada to Washington D.C. to attend his cousin's wedding. The crowded car had already made two stops to allow Bubbe and Eva to use the restroom. (Al's mother and grandmother suffered from the need to urinate very frequently.) At this, their third stop, Isabelle joined them. As she was

364

washing her hands, the elderly stranger, who had been staring at her face, said to her, "Oh Sweetie, have you been in an automobile accident that did that to your pretty face?"

"No," answered Isabelle. "It's an allergic reaction to something."

"To what?" asked the prying woman.

"I don't know," said Isabelle, "and if I did, I wouldn't want to discuss it with you."

The woman mumbled ashamedly, "Sorry," and walked away.

When Isabelle began her teaching assignment in the Bronx, one of the kindest recognitions of her skin condition came from a very timid little Puerto Rican child in her class. One Monday, little Maria Cuaderado whispered shyly to Isabelle, "Your sores will go away soon, because yesterday in the church, I lit a candle and told God about my pretty teacher who has sores on her face and an ear that leaks and makes her hair wet. I asked Him to make you better, and I know that He will."

Isabelle hugged little Maria and thanked her. She was deeply touched and never forgot the loving act of this little, exceedingly shy, Puerto Rican girl.

One night in early December, well after midnight, Isabelle began to shiver with the chills. She felt so sick that Al panicked and awakened his mother. Because of Isabelle's violently chattering teeth, Eva took her daughter-in-law's temperature, albeit with great difficulty. When the thermometer was finally read, they found that Isabelle was burning with fever.

Through her job as a teacher, Isabelle belonged to an insurance plan that provided for twenty-four hour doctors' visits to her home. Al put in a call to the doctor, explaining his wife's condition. Even though it was after 2:00 a.m., a young doctor arrived to look in on the sick young woman. Isabelle was examined carefully and told, "Ordinarily I would give you a shot of penicillin, but because the doctors in Maryland suspected an allergy to penicillin, I am going to give you this new antibiotic called aureomycin. I believe that your flu-like symptoms will be helped with it."

Isabelle's flu-like symptoms persisted for a full week. The new antibiotic didn't seem to help the flu at all. But while Isabelle's body had to heal itself of the flu, the medicine that had failed to cure the flu, greatly helped to get rid of Isabelle's rashes, boils, and the oozing lymph glands. Within one day, Isabelle saw great improvement. After three days, all of the rashes and boils had disappeared, the oozing had stopped, and what remained were red, irritated patches of skin that didn't return to their normal color for two more days. Aureomycin had done what cortisone soaks and x-ray treatments had failed to do. It had made Isabelle's skin normal once again.

In late 1953, the medical profession was not yet fully aware of antibiotics' abilities and inabilities to heal. They did not yet know that antibiotics could not heal viral infections, but that they could heal many types of bacterial infections. Isabelle's flu was a viral infection. Her body, therefore, had to heal itself. But, her persistent, nagging skin problems were caused by a bacterial infection. Her skin, therefore, quickly responded in a positive manner to the administration of the antibiotic.

———————

In the fall of 1953, Isabelle became a teacher at P.S. 124. It was located in an East Bronx neighborhood that had recently changed from a Jewish neighborhood to a Puerto Rican and African-American neighborhood. It was an easy bus or car ride from Eva's house, but a terribly long and expensive ride from Little Neck. When Isabelle would move into her own apartment, she would have to pay a 50 cent toll each way on the Whitestone Bridge. This extra $5.00 per week would be difficult to sustain on her very small $3,000 annual salary.

On Isabelle's first day at P.S. 124, she drove her car from Eva's house. Finding a parking spot on the congested streets that totally restricted parking on one side was a major feat. The street's restricted side alternated daily on weekdays to facilitate street cleaning. After searching the neighborhood, Isabelle finally found a parking space. She walked the several blocks from where she had parked her car to the large school building. The office was located on the second floor, and as Isabelle approached it another young woman who was just entering the office held the door for her. They smiled at each other, and there seemed to be an instant affinity between them.

The secretary directed the two young women to a bench outside the office. She said that there would be one more new teacher coming, and then Mr. Gallo would see them all.

No sooner had the secretary seated Isabelle and the other young woman, when a beautiful, statuesque blond rushed by and entered the office. Within minutes, she was escorted back out to join the two young women on the bench.

"My name is Carla," she said. "I've been assigned here as a new teacher."

"We've all been assigned here as new teachers," said Isabelle. "My name is Isabelle."

"Mine is Annabelle," said the other young woman.

"Where did you go to school?" asked Carla, turning to Isabelle.

"Hunter," replied Isabelle.

"I went to City College," said Annabelle.

"I went to City, too. Funny that we never met, "mused Carla.

Just at that time, a very short, trim, middle-aged man came out of the office. He approached the three young women and said, "I'm Mr. Gallo, the principal." Laughing, he continued, "I feel as though I should be the master of ceremonies at the Miss America pageant in Atlantic City. You three girls are certainly beautiful! But," Mr. Gallo continued, "you are not here because you're beautiful. You're here to do a very difficult job in a very difficult school. Mrs. Bronstein, our Assistant Principal, will get you started. She will be here any minute, but in the meantime, let me tell you your grade assignments. Mrs. Stern and Mrs. Tangini will be teaching second grade classes." He handed each of them a packet and then turned to Isabelle. "You will be teaching third grade," he said, as he handed Isabelle her packet.

Mr. Gallo was telling the three new teachers their room numbers when a brown haired, plump, middle-aged woman approached. She was introduced as Mrs. Bronstein, the Assistant Principal. Mrs. Bronstein continued the orientation, while Mr. Gallo disappeared into his office. She explained that because of the baby boom following the return of the service men after World War II, the New York City Board of Education had been unable to build enough new schools to keep pace with demand. Consequently, many New York schools had been placed on split session programs, P.S. 124 among them. If a school was on a split session program, the children in the first session came to school early in the morning and remained in their classrooms for four hours of instruction. The second session children came to school three hours after the first session had started. The second session spent their first hour in an assembly or having a gym class. When the first session, after their four hours of schoolwork, left their rooms, the second session children began their academic work in the classrooms that had just been vacated. They would remain in these classrooms for four hours. During the first hour of academics, for the second session children, the first session children would attend an assembly or have a gym class

It immediately became clear to the three new teachers that the children of P.S. 124's split session program received one hour less instruction than children in the schools that had retained the traditional six-hour school day. This was obviously one the many stumbling blocks facing the pupils they would teach. They would soon learn that many stumbling blocks stood in the way of their underprivileged pupils' ability to achieve parity with pupils in more affluent neighborhoods.

The school population of P.S 124 was 60% Hispanic. 99% of the Hispanic children were either born in Puerto Rico or had parents that had been born in Puerto Rico. The other 1% of Hispanic children were children whose families came from other Hispanic countries. 40% of the children attending P.S. 124 were African-American. Most of these were children born to parents who had recently immigrated to New York from southern states or children who had been born in the south and had immigrated to the north with either one or two of their parents. Both the African American and the Puerto Rican children were citizens of the United States by birth.

Most of the Puerto Rican children's parents had been rural people in Puerto Rico. The children's mothers and their children had immigrated to New York, where the mothers either worked in the garment industry or were employed at making artificial flowers. Earning their own money in New York, and not being ordered about by domineering husbands, frequently changed the timid Puerto Rican women from being meek and docile wives into wives who refused to obey their husbands' orders. While most of the women sent for their husbands to join them in New York, after they and their children were established, few of the couples remained together. This often happened because after their husbands' arrivals, the men tended to assert the same authority that they had asserted in Puerto Rico. In New York, however, they were confronted by wives who had lost their meekness. This, and the husbands' inability to find work were the two most prevalent reasons for the breakdown of the Puerto Rican family in New York in the early 1950's.

Puerto Rican women had been able to transfer their domestic skills to paying skills in New York City's factories. The men were unable to do so. Their agricultural skills were useless in New York City and didn't easily translate into job skills that were useful in gaining employment in the big city. Consequently, many Puerto Rican men were unemployed.

A similar situation existed in the African-American community. African-American women could find employment in small industry, the restaurant business, and when all else failed, in cleaning houses and office buildings. The men tended to limit themselves to unskilled work, usually requiring physical strength. Not much of this kind of employment was available in New York City in the 1950's, causing many African-American men to be unemployed.

Both the Puerto Rican and African American communities were characterized by female-headed, single parent households, or households in which the children's mother was cohabitating with a man who was not the children's father. In Puerto Rican homes, these men were called the children's *uncles*. Children of both of these ethnic groups, who attended P.S. 124, often lacked proper male parenting. Where the mother was very strong and deeply interested in her children's education, the lack of male parenting could be mitigated, but, more than likely, children had overworked mothers who were too tired and too preoccupied by other matters to be helpful guides in their children's education. Consequently, most of the pupils of P.S. 124 lacked parental guidance in their educational pursuits.

It took the new young teachers a while to understand the weak family structure from which most of their pupils came, but by the time they had been teaching at P.S. 124 for a month or two, they grew to understand it quite well.

A greater surprise for Isabelle and the other new teachers was the attitudes of many of the seasoned teachers in the school. These teachers were largely without hope for their pupils, and often without any patience at all. In addition, empathy for the children seemed to be a scarce commodity. Unfortunately the pupils of P.S. 124 often left dysfunctional homes to be educated by dysfunctional teachers, among whom compassion was an unknown emotion. Although New York City law forbade corporal punishment in the schools, many of the teachers at P.S. 124 slapped and shook their pupils. To be sure, most classes were unruly, filled with noisy, shoving children, but the teachers' yelling and the corporal punishment being meted out were not solving their pupils' problem. Other methods were badly needed.

––––––––

Isabelle decided that she would, indeed, use different methods! On the first day of school, she greeted her class with a big smile and told them how good looking they were. She assured them that if they did the things she asked, everyone would have lots of fun in third grade, but then, with a very grave and somewhat scary face, she threatened, "If you do not do as I say, I can promise you a very unpleasant third grade!"

Isabelle believed that if a teacher did interesting things with her children, they would reward her with good behavior and good learning. An example of how she did this was when she was teaching a science unit about the five senses. First, she discussed the human senses in a traditional classroom manner. When she felt satisfied that her pupils understood what their senses were and what their senses did, in a subsequent lesson she said, "Even though the senses tell our brains what is happening around us, sometimes our senses can mislead us."

"How many of you believe that your eyes, ears, and taste buds always tell you the truth?" she asked.

Most of the children raised their hands.

Isabelle then held up two lumps of white chocolate, each about the size of a small grapefruit.

"Does anyone know what these are?" she asked.

Not a hand went up. (White chocolate had just begun to be sold to the public in the early 1950's. It was sold at stores that sold expensive or unusual confections.) Isabelle knew that it would be highly unlikely that any of her students had seen white chocolate or heard of it yet.

She asked a child to come up to the front of the room and heft one of the chocolate lumps. "Tell the class how it feels, Juan," she said.

"It's pretty heavy," Juan answered. "It's sort of soft, but mostly hard."

"How many of you know the word *surface*?" Isabelle asked, writing the word *surface* on the board. There was no show of hands.

After Isabelle explained the word, she asked Juan to try again.

"The *surface* is sort of soft, but the whole big lump is hard. It doesn't feel like a white rock, because the *surface* isn't hard enough," said Juan.

"Well done," said Isabelle. "Marie, tell me what this lump smells like."

Little Marie Cuadarato, who had been so shy that she cried the first time Isabelle spoke to her, walked up to the front of the room. Her smiling teacher handed her the chocolate.

Marie smelled it.

"Do you recognize the smell, Marie?" asked Isabelle.

Marie whispered, "I've smelled this before, but I don't know what it is."

"Marie," said Isabelle. "That's a wonderful answer. Please say it louder so that Jose, in the back of the room, can hear it."

Marie repeated her answer in a louder voice.

"Well," Isabelle said, "we have used three of our senses and we still don't know what this big lump is. Can someone tell me which senses we have used?"

Hands shot up in the air. Bobby Caruthers, an African-American boy who had been labeled a "slow learner" said, "Sight, 'cause we can see it.

Touch, 'cause Juan touched it and so did Marie. And smell, 'cause Marie smelled it."

"Excellent, Bobby," said Isabelle. "How many senses have we left out?"

"Two," said Bobby.

Isabelle looked delighted with Bobby's answer. "Good work!" she said.

She listed the three senses that had been used, on the chalkboard. She asked Jenny, who labored very hard in reading, to read the three senses that they had used.

Jenny read, "Sight....Touch....and Smell."

"Good work, Jenny," Isabelle said. Then turning to the class she asked, "Can anyone tell me the senses we have not used?"

John Palmer, one of her best students, raised his hand. "Taste and hearing," he said.

"Do you think our sense of hearing will help us to discover what this white lump is?" asked Isabelle.

The children all called out "No."

"Well, we have one sense left. Does anyone want to taste this white lump?"

Not one child volunteered. After a slight pause, Miguel, the class dare devil, apprehensively raised his hand. Isabelle asked Miguel if he could break off a piece of the white lump. When he couldn't, she produced a knife and cut off a piece of the chocolate.

The previously very quiet class, laughed uproariously as brave Miguel, very tentatively raised the piece of chocolate to his mouth. As he ate it, he rolled his eyes and said, "It not only smells like chocolate, it tastes like chocolate. But it can't be chocolate, because chocolate is brown. Everybody knows that!"

Isabelle chuckled. "I don't, because now they are making white chocolate....and that is what you ate!"

The class laughed at Miguel's look of complete surprise. When they had quieted down, Isabelle said, "Our sense of sight fooled us. But, our senses of taste and smell finally helped bring us to the truth."

"Now that we know that the white lump is chocolate, let's all have some. But before you eat yours, be sure to feel it and smell it. It will help you understand how your senses work."

———————

Isabelle's methods of teaching the children seemed to work. Very little disciplining was necessary, because the children were usually interested in what was going on. High interest caused high jinx to be cut to a minimum. While discipline was a small problem, Isabelle realized that in her class of thirty-two underprivileged children, reading was the biggest problem. At best, every one of her pupils was a poor reader. Even the brightest of the children was not reading on grade level.

Isabelle, therefore, "declared war" on her pupils lack of literacy. Everything done at school required reading and usually writing. Isabelle started by labeling everything in the classroom. The labeling not only helped all of the children to read, it taught English vocabulary to her Hispanic pupils.

Even *Show and Tell* became a reading experience. Every afternoon, about half an hour before dismissal, at least three children presented either a story about something important, or presented an important object. When the presentations were finished, at least one of the presentations, and sometimes all of them, received write-ups in the classroom newspaper. The newspaper consisted of large sheets of newsprint, displayed on an easel. Isabelle wrote the class news on the newsprint, using markers.

A typical page could read, "Carlos has a new sister. Her name is Juanita. She cries a lot." Or it might read, "Marcy showed us a red sweater she made. Her grandmother taught her how to knit. The sweater is very pretty."

Isabelle supplemented the regular reading program, using such devices. Indeed, the printed word proliferated in her classroom and reading books became a fact of life for her pupils.

Isabelle's efforts paid off. At the end of the school year, twenty-eight of her students tested at reading levels on or above grade level. The remaining four pupils were reading almost at grade level.

Chapter 20: Little Neck

In February of 1954, Isabelle and Al joyously moved to Little Neck, a community located at the very edge of the borough of Queens and across the street from Lake Success. Almost as happy as the young couple, was the older couple, Eva and Max. The older couple had generously shared their small apartment with Isabelle and Al and had endured the overcrowding, but worst of all, what they considered to be rude obstinancy and disobedience on the part of their "guests." Eva often made suggestions about the furniture the young people were purchasing or negative comments about the late hours they were keeping. She hated their habit of sleeping, on the weekend, until almost lunchtime. Isabelle and Al almost never considered the inconvenience they were causing by sleeping late and keeping Eva and Max out of their living room. They ignored Eva's negative comments, as well as her suggestions about furniture, and were determined to live by their own lights. Like most young people, from time immemorial, they were blind to the generosity and love with which they were being treated. They considered Eva and Max's kindness their due. It took many years for them to understand the largess and love that Al's mother and stepfather had bestowed upon them.

———

Once settled in Little Neck, Isabelle found two male school teachers who taught in a Junior High School near P.S. 124, and with whom she formed a car pool, saving gasoline money and part of the heinous

374

Whitestone Bridge toll. When it was Isabelle's turn to drive the two men, she often found it quite unpleasant, because they criticized her driving unmercifully. While her driving was still a somewhat new experience for her, Isabelle really was quite proficient. Their negative remarks only served to erode her confidence and set her driving skills back. In later years, Isabelle would understand that her carpool mates were acting out the prevalent male chauvinism of the 1950's by pointing out the inferior skills of a female driver.

Although Isabelle loved her pupils and had become a close friend to Annabelle and Carla, she realized that the commute from her apartment in Little Neck to P.S. 124 in the Bronx was both expensive and tiring. She, therefore, asked Mrs. Bronstein about the procedures she must follow to transfer to a school closer to where she lived. The assistant principal informed her that she would have to teach at P.S. 124 for three years. After three years, she would either receive or be refused tenure. If refused, she would be fired. Mrs. Bronstein chuckled, "I know you won't be fired, because we are very aware of how well you teach. In fact, I suggest that after you have taught for the required four years, you should take the test for an assistant principal's position. By then, you will have finished your Master's Degree, which is a requirement; and then I'm sure you will have no problem getting an assistant principal's position."

Mrs. Bronstein's praise fell on deaf ears. To Isabelle, the prospect of two and a half more years of teaching in the Bronx, with the long and expensive commute from Little Neck, was awful. But Isabelle was helpless. She could not change the unfair rules.

Isabelle began to mentally enumerate the many unfair practices with which the New York City Board of Education burdened its teachers. It caused her to admire Mrs. Simonson even more than she had admired her when she was her student teacher. Perhaps a teacher's union could eradicate some of the injustices that irked Isabelle so much, and would bring relief from some of the injustices that existed and negatively impinged on the children.

It was common knowledge that brand new teachers lacked the expertise that they could possibly gain with additional teaching experience. Yet in

1953, all new teachers were assigned to schools in which teacher expertise was terribly needed to mitigate the children's heavy burdens from home. These burdens diminished their performances at school and required great expertise from their teachers. This expertise would probably be absent in brand new teachers. In fact, as Isabelle was to learn, a beginning teacher who showed a true talent for the profession improved her performance with each year of acquired experience. The best new teacher was better in her second year of teaching than in her first and still better in her third year of teaching, etc. A good, seasoned teacher usually has learned and developed the techniques that would facilitate learning for her pupils. Untried new teachers had, as yet, developed nothing.

In schools like P.S. 124, the hour of school that the children lost each day was a dreadful loss of instruction. This loss, due to split sessions, proliferated in schools located in underprivileged neighborhoods. More affluent neighborhoods seldom had their pupils' school hours reduced. Along with the flagrant subtractions of teaching time for children in impoverished neighborhoods, the Board of Education rarely considered the needs and comfort of the teachers in these areas. Isabelle, who had to drive from Little Neck to P.S. 124, was unable to avail herself of the New York City bus or subway systems, because they did not serve her part of the city. She, therefore, drove her car to school and needed a place to park in the very congested area in which she taught. Because alternate street parking existed for many blocks around P.S. 124, finding a parking place on the street on which the school was located was a virtual impossibility. Once again, Isabelle's miniscule annual salary of $3,000 was gouged for the cost of parking in an expensive neighborhood garage. New York City failed to see its obligation to supply parking for its teachers.

All of the aforementioned grievances were small compared to what Isabelle considered to be the lack of empathetic communication between many administrators and their teachers. Two glaring examples in Isabelle's experience typified the experiences many teachers faced.

Isabelle had been made aware of a peculiar attitude on the part of some administrators, on her second day at P.S. 124. Following the introductions of the new teachers to the rest of the staff, Mr. Gallo and Mrs. Bronstein held a meeting that explained schedules, rules, and recent occurrences in the neighborhood. After the meeting, as the members of the faculty either headed to their rooms or stopped to converse with colleagues, a small middle-aged woman rushed up to Isabelle. She introduced herself as Anita Brand. She said that she taught sixth grade and had been at P.S. 124 for fifteen years. She had witnessed the changes in the neighborhood and the changes in the school. Anita Brand explained that she was looking for Isabelle, because her brother, a principal in a Manhattan school that was to get eight new teachers, had been one of Isabelle's oral examiners. He had planned to request Isabelle for his school, because he was impressed with the way she had presented herself. But, when Isabelle's exam score placed her in the top 10% of the candidates, she had earned the right to be placed in her own borough. She was listed as coming from the Bronx, so if Anita Brand's brother wanted Isabelle to teach at his school, he'd have to get in touch with her and ask for her permission to take her out of the Bronx and into Manhattan.

"My brother thought that if he let you know about his admiration for the way you presented yourself, it would 'swell' your head," said Mrs. Brand. "He thought it might make you difficult to work with."

"I'm very flattered," said Isabelle. "Thank you for telling me, but why is it all right for you to tell me, but not all right for your brother to do so?"

Mrs. Brand answered, "Oh my brother doesn't know I'm telling you. He just brought the whole thing up when he learned that you had been assigned to my school. He asked me to look you up, and I decided to tell you. I think it's nice to hear good things, but many administrators are fearful of praising their teachers."

The second misuse of communication between supervisors and the professional staff was what Isabelle considered to be an act of intimidation. It happened when Isabelle's days at P.S. 124 were drawing to a close.

During the last quarter of Isabelle's third year at P.S. 124, Mr. Gallo came into her classroom and smilingly told her to stop in at his office before she went home. Isabelle didn't worry about it, because the principal had been smiling so happily.

She was correct not to be worried. Mr. Gallo had called Isabelle into his office to present her with her certificate of tenure. Having tenure gave her many job protections. Isabelle was quite pleased, but when Mr. Gallo expressed his admiration for her work and said that he hoped she planned a long career at P. S. 124, Isabelle was forced to tell him that her trip to school was exhausting and expensive, and though she loved the children, her colleagues, and the administrators at P.S. 124, she would have to seek a transfer to a school located closer to her home.

Mr. Gallo expressed his regret, but told Isabelle that he understood. He then told her that she would have to apply for jobs at the schools she was interested in, and when she landed a job, she had to make an appointment with her current District Superintendent and present her application to him. The District Superintendent was the person with the authority to release her from her present assignment.

After investigating several schools in Queens, Isabelle found placement, teaching fifth grade in Bayside. She would no longer need to pay a toll, and the trip from home would take less than twenty minutes. What is more, parking spaces were plentiful on the suburban streets surrounding the school. Consequently, a delighted Isabelle, immediately called for an appointment with Dr. Sullivan, the district superintendent for the district in which P.S. 124 was located. She needed Dr. Sullivan to sign her transfer papers, so that they could be sent to the elementary school in Bayside.

At her appointment time, Isabelle was kept waiting in Dr. Sullivan's outer office for almost thirty minutes. To her knowledge, no one was with the district superintendent, so another appointment was not the cause of the delay. When she was finally invited to go in, she entered a very long, somewhat narrow room. The blinds on the long wall of windows were tightly shut. The room was dimly lit by a lamp on Dr. Sullivan's huge, immaculately clean, and empty desk. The desk was located at the furthest point from the door to the narrow room, and the chair that was placed in the front of the desk clearly beckoned to Isabelle as the only chair she could sit upon. She would have to walk across the long room that seemed to be designed to intimidate. As Isabelle walked the long distance across the highly polished wooden floor, her heels clicked with each step she took.

By the time she reached the beckoning chair, she was greatly intimidated, indeed.

Dr. Sullivan's voice was loud and booming. "Why are you leaving our district? Has anyone been unkind to you?" he boomed.

"No," answered Isabelle. "The district is too far from where I live. What is more, the toll on the Whitestone Bridge is too expensive for me to pay. I love the children at P.S. 124, but practicalities force me to leave."

"If you must, you must, but don't fill me with the palaver that it hurts you to leave the children. You're looking for an easier job, that's all!" the superintendent boomed. Dr. Sullivan then tossed Isabelle her signed transfer. The paper sailed across the large, empty desk. Isabelle intercepted it rapidly and made her exit from the inhospitable, long, narrow room.

———————

Isabelle had spent three fulfilling years teaching needy children at P.S. 124. When they were promoted out of her class, she and they were greatly saddened. But, every child who left her class was less needy than when he had first entered it. Every one of Isabelle's pupils was no longer confounded by the written word.

To Isabelle the lack of empathy and the paucity of praise at P.S. 124 were of small importance. The achievement of her pupils and the love she felt for them and from them were the highlights of her three years of teaching in the inner city. She would never forget those years and the wonderful children who so completely filled her life.

———————

February was not a good month for moving. New Yorkers could handle the bitter cold, but a winter storm could often negate a move. Isabelle and Sarah were both lucky, for although both of them had moved in the month of February, neither of them had scheduled her move on a stormy, blustery day. Isabelle had moved to Little Neck in the early part of the month, and Sarah had moved from her tiny apartment on 29 Street in Coney Island to a larger apartment in a newly erected middle-income housing project on Surf Avenue, at the end of the month. Sarah's new apartment was located just one block from the beach and the boardwalk that she loved so much. Sarah's move, on the last day of February, was without incident from the weather. Both grandmother and granddaughter were spared winter storms, but neither of them spared themselves from the storms of domesticity they had created as they arranged and then rearranged the furniture in their new apartments.

On the first day of March, as Isabelle prepared to leave her home to go to work at P.S. 124, the telephone rang. To her surprise, it was her grandmother, calling her so very early on a workday morning. Sarah's voice was greatly agitated. "This new apartment is on the ground floor," she said. "The windows are completely uncovered and everyone who passes by can look in. I am forced to dress in the bathroom, because every other room of this apartment is on display....just like a store window! I want you to come over to my house today, or no later than tomorrow. I have purchased drapes to hang on the windows, but I have become too old to climb up to do it myself. Please come over and hang my drapes," Sarah said.

Sarah rarely made demands on Isabelle, and by the tone of her voice, Isabelle knew that her grandmother was in great distress. She would have liked to go to Coney Island immediately, but she was expected at P.S. 124 and she had classes for her Master's degree at Hunter College in the evening. An important paper was due that evening, and Isabelle was unable to miss her graduate class. She told Sarah that on the following day, she could go to work, and after work, travel to Coney Island to hang the drapes. She asked her grandmother if late, Friday afternoon was a satisfactory time.

"Not at all," said Sarah. "I don't want you hanging drapes here on the Sabbath. You'll have to be finished before it becomes dark." (The Jewish Sabbath begins on Friday, at sundown, and ends on Saturday, at sundown.) I don't understand the fuss about a paper. Why can't you turn it in on the next evening that you go to your school?" Sarah asked.

Isabelle realized that Sarah had no understanding of matters pertaining to school. She carefully explaining why she would have to go to her class and turn in her paper. She made it clear that she was very sorry about it, but it was non-negotiable.

"Bubbe," she said, "tomorrow I will rush to your house right after work and I won't leave until your drapes are hung. It doesn't matter that I'm hanging drapes on Shabbat. I'll be driving home on the Sabbath too, and you know that's not permitted either. You've always known that I'm not observant, yet you are always glad to see me when I travel to your house to visit you on a Saturday."

"You and all of my children and grandchildren have given up Jewish ways. I have forgiven all of you, because I love you so much, and I pray to God that He will forgive all of you too. My father, of blessed memory, said that in America Jews become *Goyim* (Gentiles). In a sense he was right. They don't become Goyim, but they behave like Goyim!"

"If Friday afternoon is the soonest you can come, come Friday afternoon. I shall be anxiously awaiting you," said the pragmatic Sarah.

———

Both Isabelle's and Al's grandmothers believed that imposing on a grandchild or ignoring a grandchild's privacy to satisfy a pressing need was completely acceptable behavior, because in their lives, as grandmothers, they were now entitled to certain prerogatives not available to others. Because Al's grandmother's ordinary audacity surpassed Sarah's, Al's grandmother's infractions of the rules of common courtesy, surpassed Sarah's too.

Al's Bubbe didn't display her audacity to Isabelle until the end of March. At that time, Isabelle was having a dinner party to which Eva, Max, Bubbe, Zada, Al's brother Harold, his wife Gert, and their little boy, Max were invited. The dinner party was not Isabelle's idea. Isabelle was so inundated at her job as a teacher, her graduate school work, and her domestic chores for the week, that she never would have initiated a dinner party at her home that weekend. But, Eva had asked for it. Eva said that none of the family had seen Isabelle's and Al's apartment, and Bubbe was clamoring for an invitation. Eva said that if the work was too much for Isabelle, she'd bring food and help with the clean-up.

Isabelle didn't tell Eva that Al's brother Harold and his wife Gert had already made several visits to the apartment. The dinner party, which Isabelle considered a terrible imposition, should have, in her opinion, been only for Al's parents and grandparents. Indeed, she did not believe it should have been held at all. But, like most of the young women of her generation, she acquiesced to her mother-in-law's proposal. She did, however, accept some of Eva's help. Eva brought deviled eggs, a huge salad, and a cake. Isabelle prepared the meat and vegetables.

When Al's family arrived, they all showed admiration for the lovely furnishings and the beautifully set table. Suddenly, Isabelle realized that Bubbe was not with them. Isabelle went to her bedroom doorway and stopped dead in her tracks! There was Al's grandmother methodically looking through the drawers of Isabelle's dresser.

"Bubbe," Isabelle demanded. "What are you doing?"

"Oh," answered Bubbe nonchalantly, "I was checking to see how neatly you keep your drawers. The true sign of a good "*balabuste*" (good housekeeper) is how she keeps her drawers." Bubbe smiled an innocent smile. She had no idea of how seriously she had infringed upon the rules of privacy in Isabelle's American culture. "You are a very good "balabuste," she continued, "and I might have predicted that. Any young woman who can earn as much money as you earn, would surely be able to be a good balabuste too. I was telling Zada that Alvin was as lucky as any young man who married a wealthy woman. The money that you're bringing into this house is as much or more than a rich girl would bring to her marriage," said Bubbe innocently.

To Isabelle's credit, even though she was both flabbergasted and angered by Bubbe's actions and words, she put them in perspective. She realized that Bubbe was behaving and stating what she had always seen and heard in her culture. In her sights, Bubbe was exercising her prerogative as a grandparent, in her grandson's home, toward her grandson's wife. Isabelle said none of the angry remarks of which she was thinking. Instead she turned and rejoined her other guests. Everyone enjoyed the dinner party that remained in Isabelle's memory for the rest of her life.

Fanny's two children were almost like siblings to Isabelle. When they all were little and lived in the house on Richmond Terrace, Millie, Fanny's eldest child, ruled. The other three children in the Richmond Terrace house; Marty, Fanny's youngest child, Isabelle, and Mel, Sol's only child, did Millie's bidding. Although she sometimes delivered a punch or a slap to her younger cousin, Millie's prevailing behavior toward Isabelle had usually been kind, gentle and tutorial. She introduced Isabelle to much of the good English and American literature that she herself constantly read. She also discussed political and historical events with her younger cousin and opened Isabelle's eyes to issues that would remain important to Isabelle for the rest of her life. Because both Isabelle and Millie loved to dance, they often performed interpretive dances, delighting Fanny and Bella. The two girls also played games together, discussed boys, and sometimes even shared clothes.

When Millie's first son was born, Isabelle was chosen to be the baby's godmother. Both Isabelle and Millie mourned the fact that they lived so far from each other and could only see each other sporadically. It was, therefore, a great joy for both of them when Isabelle moved to Little Neck. Once more, Isabelle would be living nearby her beloved Millie. Once more the young cousins could and did see each other frequently.

Isabelle's relationship with Millie was different from her relationship with Millie's younger brother, Marty. In Isabelle's relationship with Marty, Isabelle ruled. Because Fanny and Bella usually lived near one another, Marty, Millie, and Isabelle had great exposure to each other. When Isabelle played with Marty, she played ball, card games, and board game. She also insisted upon their doing imaginative plays that Marty hated. Isabelle would invent imaginary stories, forcing Marty to act out the prince's role, while she played the role of princess. Marty much preferred their bicycle outings, on the rare occasion that they were given money to rent bicycles. Isabelle's imaginative plays would then cast them as athletes or explorers. Marty, however, liked it best of all when they traveled great distances on their rented bikes and didn't pretend anything at all.

Isabelle's close relationship with both of Fanny's children, always remained deep in her heart. Even, when in later years, their communication was sparse, Fanny's children remained very important people in Isabelle's life.

———————

When Isabelle moved to Little Neck, Marty was serving in the Navy.

383

After going to college for one year, he had dropped out and enlisted in the Navy for four years. When Isabelle had seen him on one of his shore leaves, he regaled her with stories of the distant parts of the world he had visited. He particularly loved the Far East. Hong Kong and Japan especially appealed to him.

Marty was serving on a huge aircraft carrier called *The Bennington*. He was very proud of his ship, and he spoke fondly of his shipmates and the ship's officers who made the colossal ship operate. His four-year stint in the U.S. Navy appeared to be exactly the right thing for Marty to be doing at that period of his life.

One day, late in the afternoon, as Isabelle was driving home from P.S. 124 to Little Neck, the radio program to which she was listening was interrupted by a report of a U.S. aircraft carrier, located just outside American territorial waters near Boston had suffered a large explosion and was now on fire. A horrified Isabelle recognized the name *Bennington*. Marty's ship was burning!

Isabelle sped home and put on the television set. Several New York City channels were carrying the story, citing the numbers of dead, missing, and injured sailors aboard the great ship. Isabelle called her Aunt Fanny, who was already glued to her television set. Aunt Fanny was crying as she spoke optimistically to her niece, saying, "I know you will think I'm crazy, but I have an optimistic feeling about this. I had a peculiar dream last week, and it gives me hope."

"I don't want to keep talking on the telephone. The TV set keeps giving information. If I learn anything important, I'll call you."

Aunt Fanny asked Isabelle to tune into a different channel than the one she was watching. "Perhaps one station will give information that the other station isn't giving," said Aunt Fanny.

Isabelle and Al ate their dinner in front of the television set. The same news repeated itself over and over again, but at 10 P.M., the news changed. A rolling list showing the many names of the sailors killed in the accident, scrolled slowly before their eyes. Thankfully, Marty's name did not appear among them. After the listing of the dead, the scroll reported the names of the missing. Providentially, Marty's name was not among them, either.

The television commentator then promised the viewing audience that if they had loved ones aboard the *Bennington*, their men would be released to call them when the fire was extinguished. While the fire burned, the sailors would remain on board to fight it.

Isabelle and Al went to bed at midnight, worried, but mostly reassured that Marty was alright. In the morning, Isabelle called her aunt. The line was busy. After many futile attempts, Isabelle's own telephone rang. A jubilant Aunt Fanny said that Marty had called and he was completely unscathed.

———————

Two weekends after the fire, Marty came home on leave. His parents, his sister and her family, Bella and her family, and Isabelle and Al came to see him. As they all sipped coffee and tea and ate confections, Marty told his whole story.

"A week before the fire, I was supposed to have a weekend shore leave," Marty said. "A buddy of mine had a girlfriend in the Boston area. He asked me if I would cover for him by taking his watch and staying on board the ship for the weekend. Having nothing to do on shore anyway, I agreed to let him go. If I wanted to, I could take his shore leave on the following weekend and he would pay me back by taking the watch I had been scheduled for. By doing this, my buddy could see his girlfriend a week earlier. We swapped, exactly as planned. I took his uneventful watch, while he caroused around Boston," continued Marty.

"On the following weekend, I decided not to go ashore. When I went to sleep, a huge blast knocked me out of my bed. The explosion occurred exactly where my buddy was doing the watch for which I had been scheduled. He was paying me back, and sadly, he was blown to smithereens!"

"I feel terrible about his fate and the fate of all of the sailors who perished during the explosion and the fire. It makes me wonder if our fates are truly written in a *Book of Life* as they say in the synagogue on Yom Kippur."

"There is some sort of a Divine plan," said Aunt Fanny. "What about my dream the week before?" She then proceeded to recount her dream.

"A week before the fire, I had another dream about Husmann." Fanny then told them the awful story about Husmann following her to the train to Riga and about his dreadful threat. She said that he had come to her in a dream, and threatened her, right around. the time of Bella's terrible bus accident. His threats always seemed to have substance.

"In my dream a few weeks ago, Husmann laughed eerily and told me he was bringing me very bad luck, just as he had promised at the train. I was unable to speak or call out and I was paralyzed with fear. Husmann was laughing at my petrified state, when suddenly Papa and Zada appeared. They, just like Husmann, looked exactly as they had looked when they were alive," Fanny said.

Zada angrily took Husmann's arm. Our gentle Zada said forcefully, "Get away from her, Husmann. You're not welcome here! When it is her time for sorrow, she will have sorrow. This is not the time!"

"Both Zada and Papa embraced me and I awakened in a cold sweat," Fanny said. "I believe that Papa and Zada interceded for Marty," Fanny said, as she smiled lovingly at her handsome, sailor-son.

"I believe it too," said Bella.

The younger adults laughed, but as Isabelle thought about it, on their way home, she wondered if Fanny's dream had some efficacy.

———

The subway ended several miles away from Little Neck, necessitating the formation of a car pool that transported Al and several of his neighbors to the subway every weekday morning. In this time of one car families, and because all of the men came home at different times, the men were picked up in the evening, by their wives.

On one such day, when Isabelle was to pick Al up, she decided to get an early start on cooking their dinner. One of the things they were going to eat was French fried potatoes, so along with other early food preparation Isabelle decided to warm the oil for the French fries. It was her belief that the oil would hold most of its warmth long after she shut off the stove and went for Al. She thought that when she returned home, she would need less time to bring the already warmed oil to a boil.

Isabelle lit a flame under the pot of oil and repaired to the bathroom with a book. She became totally involved with her bodily functions and the interesting book she was reading, completely putting the heating cooking oil out of her mind. Suddenly, loud calls of, *Fire! Fire!* tore her away from her book. As she ran to the upper hallway landing, she thought, "Little Chuckie, the three year old boy who lives downstairs, must have started a fire."

At the bottom of the stairs, stood the man who had shouted, *Fire.* He yelled up to Isabelle, "I was driving by when I saw a fire in your kitchen, Lady!" Isabelle then remembered the oil, and ran into her kitchen. A column of fire reached from the pot on the stove to the ceiling. Isabelle's racing mind told her that one threw sand on an oil fire, but she had no sand! All she could see was an oatmeal pot filled with water. It had been soaking in the sink since breakfast. She grabbed the pot and threw the lumpy water onto the oily fire.

Fireballs of various sizes flew across the kitchen, through the kitchen doorway, and into the dining room. Along with the fireballs, big and small splashes of hot cooking oil whizzed by Isabelle, some of them burning her and her clothing. The fire on the stove had been instantaneously extinguished, but had converted into a mini firestorm by the contact of the hot oil with the water. Tiny fireballs dotted the dining room carpet and most flat surfaces in the kitchen. A decorative plastic, electric clock that hung on the wall over the stove melted and dripped down the wall like Dali's famous melting clock. When Isabelle saw the clock through the smoke that permeated the entire apartment, she burst out laughing, thinking of the Dali clock. Nonetheless, she continued to swat the small fireballs that were burning, with a dishtowel. Her fire fighting activities, the thick smoke, and then the firestorm had put Isabelle into a mild state of shock, but when four or five men burst into the apartment to see if they could help, Isabelle was finally able to put everything into perspective.

Isabelle's uncovered lower arms and her hands had sustained some minor burns from the flying oil. Her lovely sweater and her skirt had small burn holes in them, and her shoes were covered with oil. Not visible to Isabelle was her hairline, which had turned from black to red, because her black hair had been singed so badly that it had lost its color. She had also lost most of one eyebrow. Along with her eyebrow, there were small blisters on her face, where flying hot oil had burnt her. She did not yet feel the pain of these small burns, but they would cause her some considerable discomfort in the near future.

Isabelle's downstairs neighbor offered to go to the subway station to get Al. Isabelle gladly accepted his offer.

The walls, carpets, and draperies of the living room, dining room, and kitchen would have to be professionally cleaned. Painters would have to be hired, too.. Fortunately Isabelle and Al were insured against fire, and the repairs would be paid for by the insurance company. In the meantime, they would have to return to Eva's house until their apartment was made habitable once again.

Isabelle was worried about Al's reaction to the destruction her carelessness had wrought. She was sure he'd deliver an angry lecture, but she was wrong....When Al walked into the still smoky apartment, he rushed over to Isabelle and said, "Are you all right? Were you burned?"

Isabelle tearfully recounted the whole affair and her culpability in it.

"None of it matters," said Al. "All *things* are replaceable. You aren't! Thank God you're all right!"

*Sarah's Torah is being escorted to her synagogue. It is carried under
a Chupa (Bridal Canopy) by Sarah's grandson, Mel. He is flanked
by Sarah on his right and members of her synagogue on his left.
He is turning to converse with Isabelle, in the rear to his right.*

Chapter 21: Torah

Isabelle and Al returned to their apartment in a week's time. They resumed their busy schedules of working and going to graduate school. Isabelle would have her Master's degree in June. Al's degree would come later, because he had started work on his Master's degree later than she.

One Sunday afternoon, as Isabelle was doing schoolwork at her kitchen table and Al was doing schoolwork at the dining room table, the telephone rang. It was Isabelle's grandmother. She said that she was calling because she expected to see both of them at her house in Coney Island on the following Sunday. She wanted all of her children, grandchildren, and great grandchildren to be there, because she had fulfilled a lifelong wish to present a Torah to her synagogue, and she wanted her progeny, her *Ten Fingers,* to celebrate the great event with her.

After Sarah came to America, had paid off her debt to Anna, and had married, she began to save money once again. She no longer buried her savings under the chickens. She now put her savings in an American bank account. Sarah always lived extremely frugally, and now that she was a widow once more, and forced to accept the support of her more affluent four children, she lived even more frugally. She wished to be as light a financial burden on her children as possible. She longed to be independent, but since the death of Appleman, she had been forced to accept her children's help. Sarah stretched the dollars she received from them and still had money left for her small charities, the gifts she gave to her *Ten Fingers*, and to her growing bank account.

Sarah had an important goal. Just as she had obsessively saved money for her family's trip to America, she now obsessively saved money to purchase a *Torah*. (The *Torah* is a large parchment scroll containing the first five books of the *Bible*. It is believed that Moses had received the *Torah* directly from God. The *Torah*, containing the words of God, is the holiest and most revered symbol in Judaism.) It was Sarah's fondest wish to personally present a *Torah* to her synagogue.

Each *Torah* is copied by hand by a specially educated and trained, very religious man called a "scribe." No mistakes are permitted in the copying of the *Torah*. The *Torah's* parchment papers are wrapped around wooden staves which extend beyond the parchment. These extensions are used as handles, and when the *Torah* is "dressed" the extensions usually wear silver crowns. The *Torah* is always dressed lavishly, but it is dressed differently by Jews from different parts of the world. Sarah's *Torah* would be dressed in a beautifully gold-embroidered blue velvet mantel, characteristic of *Torah* mantels from central and Eastern Europe. It would also wear a silver breastplate attached by a silver chain.

Needless to say, the price of a new *Torah* is immense. Sarah had been saving nickels, dimes, quarters, and dollars for many, many years. She had denied herself most pleasures and many adornments for her home. And finally, the auspicious day had arrived! The *Torah* she had commissioned with the money saved by personal deprivation and with tremendous love was ready to be dedicated and placed in her *shul* (synagogue). This illiterate widow, from a tiny poverty stricken hamlet in White Russia, had achieved her own miracle. She now desired that all of her progeny share in her blessing and join in the holiness and joy of the occasion.

On the designated Sunday, all of Sarah's children, in-laws, grandchildren and grandchildren's spouses, and her great grandchildren had been summoned to her small apartment in the housing project near the sea. They found the apartment decked out as if a wedding was to be performed there. A blue velvet *chupa* (wedding canopy), supported by four wooden poles was standing in a corner of the living room. A long table, lavishly loaded with wonderful food, stood in the middle of the room. Members of Sarah's shul were already partaking of the delicious fare. As they arrived, Sarah's family joined in the eating.

Sarah explained what she had done to her wide-eyed family. She told them that *The Torah* was to be escorted, under the wedding canopy, to every *shul* on Coney Island. All of the grown male members of her family would take turns carrying the blessed *Torah* to its new home in the *Ark* of Sarah's *shul*. (The *Ark* is the special place in a synagogue in which the synagogue's *Torahs* are kept).

It happened just as Sarah had planned. All of the people who had been in her apartment, assembled on the roadway outside of the house. Sarah's eldest son, Harry, was the first man to carry the *Torah*. Four elders of her synagogue each held a pole supporting the wedding canopy which formed a home for the new *Torah*. Three musicians joined them, coming as if from out of nowhere, and began to play joyous Klezmer music. Everyone formed a parade behind the musicians, and some of the marchers even danced to the happy melodies. Bystanders joined the constantly growing parade. Walking alongside the canopy and her *Torah*, a proud Sarah smiled so broadly it looked as if her face would split. A designated synagogue member periodically told her when to change the male relative who was being honored by carrying the *Torah*. She did so, at his bidding, choosing her sons in age order, then her grandsons, then her sons-in-law, and finally her grandsons-in-law.

The procession stopped at each *shul* on Coney Island. Members of the *shul* being visited, came outside carrying every *Torah* from the *Ark* of their *shul*. Prayers of welcome for the new *Torah* were recited by those being visited, followed by prayers recited by the members of Sarah's *shul*. After each of the *Torahs* in each *shul* they visited, acknowledged and welcomed Sarah's new *Torah*, the procession continued on to another synagogue, where the same welcoming ritual was followed. The *Torah's* final destination was Sarah's *shul*, where after appropriate prayers were recited, the new *Torah* joined the other *Torahs* in Sarah's synagogue's Holy Ark.

A party in Sarah's apartment followed the dedication of her *Torah*.

During the festivities, a bemused Isabelle, standing against a far wall, sorted out the events of the day. She knew that she had participated in a rare and disappearing Eastern European ritual of welcoming and honoring the *Torah*. It was awe-inspiring. But even more awe-inspiring was its initiator, Sarah, who had brought her family out of the horrors of Russia and had just expressed her devotion and deep connection to Judaism in the most significant way. She had bought a holy *Torah* for her *shul* and she had brought her *Ten Fingers*, her deeply beloved family, to the *Torah*. Isabelle, who had often heard the story of Sarah's father's refusal to come to America, could only think, "No Zada, you were not correct. In America, Jews remain Jews!"

Chapter 22: A Marriage and a Widower

For the past two summers, when Sarah's family came to the beach, she would point out a handsome elderly man who sat surrounded by many elderly women. She would scoff at the man and at his besotted followers. "Hmpf!" she'd say. "An old gigolo, getting what he can from silly old women."

Having heard her ridicule of the old man for two years, Bella was astonished by her mother's telephone call. "You remember Friedlander, don't you?" queried Sarah...."the handsome man that all of the old women fawned over?"

"The one you called a gigolo?" asked Bella.

"Yes," said Sarah. "Well, he's been courting me in a very proper way, and yesterday we were married in my shul."

"Mama, I thought you despised him!" exclaimed Bella.

"I despised the way he sopped up attention from those silly old women. When he's serious, he's quite interesting, although we disagree on many subjects," said Sarah.

"Well, good luck to the two of you," said Bella, as she terminated the conversation.

Laughing, almost hysterically, Bella called Isabelle, "Doesn't this make Bubbie's fifth husband?" Isabelle asked.

"Yes," the still laughing Bella said, "I think from what your grandmother told me about this man, Friedlander, they are both in for a rough ride. Falling in love does not go smoothly for my mother!"

And a rough ride it was. From the very beginning, Sarah had financial dominance. Friedlander's children hardly bothered with him, while Sarah's children not only supported her financially, they doted upon her.

Friedlander was jealous, and Sarah rubbed it in. And that wasn't their only difference....

When Sarah felt cold, Friedlander felt hot. They constantly argued about the position of the windows and the thermostat....

They rarely listened to the same programs on the radio. Friedlander liked political commentators and Sarah liked music and religious programs....

But the biggest difference of all was their views on the practice of religion! Friedlander was an atheist. He also clung to the anarchist ideals that had propelled him as a young man, at the turn of the twentieth century. Sarah believed anarchy was worse than monarchy; and as for atheism- it was pure anathema to the deeply pious Jewish woman.

When Sarah's children and grandchildren visited, she complained about Friedlander long and bitterly. At these times, the beleaguered old man would retreat to another room.

Sarah and Friedlander remained together until Sarah died, quite a few years after their tempestuous marriage. Isabelle always believed that her grandmother truly loved the handsome old man and found his quirky beliefs to be interesting, as well as very irritating. Of her four previous husbands, Sarah had loved only Avroham, Irving's father. Michal, her first husband, and the father of all her other children, was a good man, but their marriage was practically arranged by their families. There was no great love from Sarah there. Nor was there great love for Eva's father, her third husband. While they deeply respected each other, theirs was a marriage of convenience, which gave comfort to both of them. Sarah's marriage to her fourth husband, Appleman started and ended as a business arrangement. In his own way, Friedlander, Sarah's fifth husband, brought fire into her life. Sarah liked the fire very much, and although she argued with Friedlander quite often, she never gave him up.

Al's mother was very happy with Max. He was a good provider and a quiet, loving man. Eva's happiness would have been complete if it had not been for Bubbe's illness. Bubbe and Zada had not lived in Max's old apartment in the west Bronx for more than a year, when Bubbe began to complain of unpleasant and strange digestive symptoms. After extensive medical tests, it was determined that Bubbe was afflicted with stomach cancer. Many different doctors and even some quack cures were tried in order to rid her of the advancing disease, but to no avail. Bubbe failed rapidly. The garrulous, outspoken, funny, and audacious woman now said very little. She could no longer maintain her high standard of housekeeping and had become very sad.

Eva was, once more, her mother's most frequent companion. Every day, Eva boarded the bus in the east Bronx and traveled to the west Bronx to care for her ailing mother, cook her parents' meals, and clean their apartment so that the deteriorating Bubbe would not be distressed by a deterioration in the cleanliness and neatness of her home. On rare occasions, when the pain of her cancer abated for a while, Bubbe was her old self again. She made clever and often funny statements about her disease and the professionals who were helping her to fight it. Bubbe fully understood that the fight was in vain, and a great sadness descended upon her family.

When summer came, Eva resumed the family's old practice of going to Coney Island. In order to save herself two grueling bus trips per day, and to enjoy an occasional sea breeze, Eva rented their old summer place for Bubbe, Zada, Max, and herself. Because the place shared only two distant toilets, between all of its tenants, and because Bubbe spent so much of her time in bed, Eva brought in a portable commode for Bubbe's use.

When Isabelle and Al made their last visit to Bubbe, her first comment was, "They've turned my bedroom into a toilet." She then began to regale them with her demeaning description of the unfortunate *Vatch Froi* (caretaker) Eva had hired to help with her toileting, bathing, and other ablutions. "She is no more than an insect with eyes," said the venomous invalid. "I may be dying, but if I wish to die in peace, I don't need to be surrounded by the likes of her!"

The visiting young couple could see that all of Bubbe's worst characteristics had taken control of her. They felt sorry for Eva and Zada, for having to be exposed to such venom, and were relieved when Bubbe had exhausted herself and seemed to be taking a nap. But just as they were saying goodbye to everyone, Bubbe opened her eyes. She beckoned to Isabelle, who came up close to her. "Diene lebben zul zein azoi shane vi du bist," (May your life be as beautiful as you are) whispered Bubbe. A tearful Isabelle bid Al's fabulous grandmother goodbye.

A great sadness descended on the family. They were losing their leader, a woman whose sharp tongue sometimes hurt, but whose courageous, generous deeds and loving kindness would be missed by all who had been lucky enough to be loved by her.

———————

After Bubbe's death, Zada moved back to the apartment in the East Bronx, to live with Eva and Max. On the one hand, Eva was delighted to have her father with her, but on the other hand, his old man's idiosyncrasies and his seeming helplessness drove Eva mad. He had also become the *Thrift Captain* of the apartment. Anything Eva wanted to throw away had to be disposed of out of Zada's line of vision. If he caught her disposing of food that had been in the refrigerator for days, he delivered a long sermon on thrift and wastefulness. But even worse was his helplessness. Everything Zada ate had to be served to him. Under Bubbe's aegis, he had never even brewed himself a cup of tea. Eva hated to leave him, because she knew that while she was away, the old man just sat reading his newspaper and being hungry. She knew that Bubbe's long years of serving him, had rendered Zada helpless to serve himself.

After much discussion, it was decided that Zada would fly to Florida for a two week vacation. He would stay and take his meals at a vacation hotel. If he fared well, a two-week vacation would be tried again, and this time Eva and Max would go off together for a two week vacation of their own, at the same time that Zada was gone.

Zada, who was gone on his first solo vacation, must have had many stories to share, but frugal Zada would not make an expensive long distance telephone call, even to tell his family about his first airplane flight and his first stay at a hotel all by himself. They knew that they would have to learn all about his Florida adventure after he came home.

Two days before Zada's return, Eva called Isabelle to ask if she or Al could pick Zada up at LaGuardia Airport on Saturday afternoon. Isabelle agreed to do so, because Al worked on Saturday.

On the day of Zada's arrival, Isabelle drove from Little Neck to the Bronx to pick Eva up. They would go to LaGuardia Airport together to meet Zada. It was a lovely day, but Eva was very jumpy. She was afraid she had enjoyed Zada's two-week absence too much. When Isabelle picked her up, Eva confessed her guilty thoughts, saying that life had improved immensely without having to put up with Zada's idiosyncrasies.

At LaGuardia Airport in 1955, passengers could be picked up on the tarmac. As Isabelle and Eva waited for Zada on the tarmac, they watched his fellow passengers alighting from the Florida flight. Passenger after passenger came through the open door and down the steep stairs that had been rolled up against the aircraft. There was no sign of Zada, so Isabelle and Eva continued to wait anxiously. Finally Zada, who was the second-to-last passenger to leave the airplane, carefully descended the stairs. When he reached the tarmac, his eyes fell upon Isabelle and Eva, and to their great distress, both women became instantly aware of copious tears coursing down Zada's wrinkled cheeks.

Isabelle ran to him, and as she hugged him asked, "Why are you crying, Zada?"

"Florida was beautiful," he said, "but I saw it alone. Bubbe always wanted to go to Florida, but I said we should wait until we saved more money. Now, I have seen Florida....alone."

"I want you and Alvin to remember this," Zada continued. "Go and do things together. Don't wait until you are completely sure that you can afford it, or you too may do it alone."

"I will remember, Zada," replied Isabelle. And she did.

Chapter 23: Jobs

When Al was discharged from the army, he believed that having graduated Cum Laude from City College, with his military obligations behind him, would cause employment opportunities to jump out at him. He was wrong.

Al's modus operandi was to study the "Help Wanted" ads in the *New York Times* and follow up on those that seemed to be appropriate to his abilities. For three or four weeks, he followed this procedure, with no luck. Large, well-known firms were often downright unfriendly, treating Al as if he were totally unqualified. Al often felt that he was coming face-to-face with anti-Semitism again. City College graduated mostly Jews, and Al's dark handsomeness, was definitely Semitic. In 1953, being Jewish was still a stumbling block to employment in many, many firms.

Al was determined to work in the private sector, so he didn't consider taking any of the civil service exams offered by either New York City, New York State, or the Federal Government. His search in the private sector, however, was quickly becoming very depressing.

Finally one interview worked. It was with a firm that neither Al, nor any of his family had heard of. The firm's name was "Bronx Box Lunch." The man who interviewed Al, made Al extravagant promises of a golden future. He was told that he was being hired to be groomed for a high executive position in the firm. As he advanced, he was promised that his salary and his responsibilities would increase. In the meantime, however, he needed to know the workings of the business from the ground up, so Al began his work at Bronx Box Lunch as a truck driver who delivered and sold box lunches to workers at industrial sites all over the New York City area. While it was certainly not the kind of work a college graduate, in the mid 1950's, would be expected to do, Al was patient. He took his employers at their word and performed the menial tasks as a beginning exercise in learning the workings of the business. After several weeks of delivering lunches however, Al began to suspect that he was being exploited. When Al discussed moving out of the truck to a more visceral type of work, he was refused. His suspicions of being exploited were confirmed, and he quit working for Box Bronx Lunch.

Al came home to Eva's house in a very dejected state. Eva, Max, Isabelle, and Al discussed Al's difficulty with anti-Semitism and discussed strategies for getting around it. Eva, who had worked as a sales clerk in Hearn's Department Store, casually commented on the fact that most of the managers at Hearn's were Jewish. After a lively discussion about Jews in retailing, Al decided to seek employment in that field.

———————

A beginning class of executive trainees was being formed at Orbach's, the store that was the grandfather of the modern, low-priced department store. Orbach's made its huge profits by buying quality merchandise at a low price. Huge volume and crowds of customers was Orbach's secret to success. Al loved his job at Orbach's and did very well. In a short time, he was promoted, becoming an assistant buyer, and then once again to an associate buyer's position With each promotion, there was an increase in salary, but not nearly enough to satisfy Isabelle and Al's needs. In their view, the money that Al earned was far from commensurate with his skills or with the innovative ideas he had brought to Orbach's.

Al believed that he would have to leave Orbach's in order to get the salary and recognition he deserved. He was brooding over these thoughts, when Orbach's promoted him to a higher position in their Newark, New Jersey store. Now, in addition to being underpaid, and in Al's opinion, under appreciated, Al had an unbelievably difficult commute to work.

Even though Isabelle was very happily employed, teaching in Bayside, they both knew that according to the mores of the mid 1950's, Al's was the primary job in the family. Consequently, they began to hunt for an apartment in New Jersey. If they moved there, Isabelle would have to find a new teaching job.

One Sunday, shortly after Al had started working in Newark, Isabelle and Al decided to spend the day apartment hunting. They went to New Brunswick, where lovely new apartments were being built. Isabelle and Al drove around these newly developed areas and seriously considered going back to New Brunswick on the following weekend to have a look at some of the apartments and perhaps sign a lease on one of them.

It had been a brutally hot Monday. As the torrid breeze whipped into the open windows of Isabelle's car, she thought of Al's hellish trip on two non-air conditioned trains, from Newark, New Jersey to the last stop on the subway line in Queens. She expected to be picking up a totally exhausted young husband, who would have little to say, and would be pining for a cold shower. Instead, when Al emerged from the rush hour crowds, he seemed to be very chipper and very excited, when he entered Isabelle's car.

"I had lunch with a fellow from one of the "head hunting" agencies with which I'm registered. He described a job that he thought might be right up my alley. It's in Cincinnati, Ohio, and it's for a job as buyer of five departments in a department store there. He wants us to fly to Cincinnati on Wednesday of this week to see the city and meet the merchandise manager I may be working for. We can take Wednesday, Thursday, and Friday and return to New York on Friday night. I'll call in sick at Orbach's for three days. It will be the first sick days I have ever taken," Al chuckled.

Isabelle called Bella to tell her about their impending trip to Cincinnati. A very unhappy Bella wished them well and told them that she would be anxiously awaiting their opinions on Cincinnati and on the job awaiting Al there.

The whirlwind trip to Cincinnati left many unanswered questions and many problems for the young couple to face. Al thought he'd like the Cincinnati job, so Isabelle realized that she would not be returning to her teaching job in Bayside, Queens. Labor Day was on the following Monday, and school started in New York on the Monday after Labor Day. Isabelle realized that she was giving the New York City Board of Education very little notice of her intention to leave. She believed that they deserved better, but she was unable to do better. (In 1957, a woman was expected to do what was best for her husband's career. If she had a career too, it was secondary to her husband's.)

Al and Isabelle had many practical matters to discuss. Because Al had to report to work in Cincinnati on the Monday after Labor Day, they knew that they should move to Ohio during the following week. The company Al was going to work for would pay for their move and for the storage of their furniture and belongings, until they found an appropriate place to live. In the meantime, they would live in the lovely Terrace Hilton Hotel, located in downtown Cincinnati. They had stayed at this hotel during their whirlwind trip to Cincinnati when Al was hired for his job at Rollman's Department Store. They knew it would be a comfortable place to stay until they found an apartment that suited them.

Isabelle fretted over giving notice to her principal in Bayside, but managed to get the unpleasant task done with grace. She hoped that telling her mother and the rest of her family about their move to Cincinnati would be as easy.

Rollman's had provided Al with the name and telephone number of the movers they would use. A moving date was set for the Thursday before Labor Day. Now their greatest remaining hurdle was telling their families about their plans. They planned to go to Coney Island on Sunday, to tell both of their families that they couldn't keep from moving, because Al had been promised a handsome salary that was almost twice the salary he received at Orbach's. What is more, Cincinnati had a lower cost of living than New York. Al believed that Rollman's was an offer he could not refuse, and Isabelle felt compelled to do what was best for her husband.

On the Sunday after their return from Cincinnati, Al and Isabelle went to Coney Island. Their first stop was the bungalow that Eva had rented for the summer. Zada was still morosely quiet, having never completely recovered from Bubbe's death. He, Eva, and Max were stunned by Al's news. Putting on brave faces, they congratulated Al and wished the young couple well in Cincinnati. Eva's lovely blue eyes, however, darkened a shade. She had never recovered from the loss of her mother, and now her youngest son was moving far away. Eva was deeply saddened by their news.

Heedless of the sadness they had left in the bungalow, the young couple headed for the beach and all of Isabelle's family that might be assembled around the blue umbrella with the white stripe. This particular Sunday saw a crowd of Sarah's progeny. Sarah's three daughters, their spouses, and their offspring were on the beach when Isabelle and Al arrived at Sarah's enclave. Just as they arrived, Uncle Irving, Uncle Sol, and their families arrived too. Sarah was lying down on an army cot, under her blue umbrella with the white stripe. Her family was parked around her on blankets that formed concentric circles. They had all conglomerated to spend a hot day at the beach together.

After greeting Sarah with a kiss, Isabelle and Al spread their blanket near a blanket upon which Bella and Fanny were chatting. Isabelle kissed her mother and her aunt and said, "I have some news to share with you.… Al has accepted a very good job in Cincinnati, Ohio. We will be moving there in less than a week."

Fanny and Bella gasped and then burst into tears. They tearfully requested particulars concerning the location of Cincinnati, the type of job Al was taking, how long a car trip took to Cincinnati, and what Isabelle was planning to do about her job. Bella looked bereft, and Isabelle cried with her. While Al was making the rounds telling people about their plans, Fanny exclaimed loudly, "And Husmann didn't even come to me! How can such an awful thing happen without Husmann coming to torment me?"

*Caption – Isabelle and her 8ᵗʰ grade class, 1957 at
Saylor Park School in Cincinnati, Ohio.*

Chapter 24: Cincinnati

It took Al and Isabelle two days to drive from New York to Cincinnati. Super highways took them through New Jersey and most of Pennsylvania, but through the remaining portion of Pennsylvania, and a small, very hot portion of West Virginia and through central Ohio into south-western Ohio, the young couple was forced to travel on state highways that often were no better than country roads. The tedious trip and the hot, sticky wind blowing into the car's open windows made them yearn to be at their destination, when suddenly the rural landscape became suburban, and eventually turned into the city streets through which they had been directed by their AAA Triptik. These streets took them to the downtown area of Cincinnati. As they drove though Cincinnati's downtown, they were shocked to see several large city buses carrying huge signs across their rear sections reading *Husmann*. Upon closer examination, they saw, in very much smaller print, *The World's Best Potato Chips*. Both Al and Isabelle laughed at the advertisement, but Isabelle felt a little uneasy. Her Aunt Fanny's tales of Husmann had left their mark, and inwardly, Isabelle wished that *The World's Greatest Potato Chips* had a name other than *Husmann*.

After they had checked into their hotel, Isabelle studied the Cincinnati telephone book for the names of school districts to which she could apply for a teaching position. She realized that she was at a terrible disadvantage, because the school year had already begun in Cincinnati, and there would be few, if any, teaching positions available. Her plan was to call school districts on the telephone and apply in person only where she was told that positions were still available. Only two school districts of the many she called, still had openings for the school year. One was Mt. Healthy, a suburban district in the north central part of the Cincinnati metropolitan area and the other was the huge City of Cincinnati School District.

––––––––––

Knowing how New York City filled its excellent schools with teachers very quickly, leaving troubled schools with vacancies that had to be filled at the last minute, Isabelle assumed that she was more likely to get a good position in a suburban district than in a big city school district. Consequently she scheduled her first interview with Mt. Healthy. It was her hope that after she interviewed with Mt. Healthy, she would not need to go to the interview she had scheduled with the Cincinnati School District.

––––––––––

It was a long drive to Mt. Healthy from her hotel in downtown Cincinnati. Cincinnati had not yet built its network of expressways and Isabelle had to drive through the busy city streets to reach suburbia. She found the site of her interview almost an hour after she left her hotel, but she had allowed for mistakes and getting lost, so she arrived on time at the brand new school building in which the Mt. Healthy Superintendent of Schools was to interview her.

When Isabelle entered the school on Compton Road, she was surprised to see workmen all over the place. She asked one of the workmen if he could direct her to the Superintendent's office, and he obliged her by putting down his paintbrush and escorting her to her destination. They had to pick their way over building debris and around workmen who were putting finishing touches on the floors and walls of the debris-strewn hallways, until they came to a large gym that seemed to be totally completed. On the shiny wooden floor of the gym were three tables laden with papers. One person, busily working, sat at each of the three tables. Two of the tables were occupied by women who were rapidly typing and the third table was occupied by a nice looking, middle aged man, whose steel gray hair was cut close to his scalp in a style popular with young men in the military. This very short haircut was called a crew cut and it made the attractive, middle- aged man look very severe.

Isabelle's high heels sounded loud as she walked across the gymnasium's newly lacquered floor. As she approached the man at the table, he rose politely and introduced himself. He said that he had been expecting her and asked her to be seated. The man with the steel gray crew cut had steely gray eyes, which appraised Isabelle slowly and thoroughly. He said, with a strong mid western country twang, "I could have picked you out anywhere. You look like you come from New York. Now tell me about your experience, teaching in New York.....but first let me remember my manners."

"I'm Rex Walker, Superintendent of the Mt. Healthy School District. We have a good suburban school district here, but we suffer from overcrowding. This school was supposed to be opened when the school year started, but it didn't make it on time. Believe it or not, I have been told that all of this building chaos will be cleared away in two weeks, and on the third week of school we will finally have pupils coming into this new building. At the present time, pupils are going to school in churches, meeting halls, and empty stores. To complicate matters further, one third grade class is being taught by a substitute teacher. When everyone moves into this new building, I'd like to have already hired a full-time teacher to take the substitute's place. You are one of the people I am interviewing for that third grade position."

Isabelle told Mr. Walker about her Maryland, East Bronx, and Bayside teaching experiences. He was impressed with her credentials – her four and a half years of teaching experience, her appearance, her manner of speaking, and her recently acquired Master's Degree. He said that she would be hired for the job, contingent upon his telephone call to the New York City Superintendent of Schools. He wanted the New York City's Superintendent to give him an assessment of Isabelle's work.

Isabelle stifled a laugh at Mr. Walker's naivety. She said as kindly as she could, "Mr. Walker, the Superintendent of New York City's Public Schools is in charge of a vast number of schools, teaching thousands upon thousands of students. He has observed very few of the thousands of teachers he is in charge of, and probably knows none of them by name. Not only is he ill equipped to assess me, he has never laid his eyes upon me. What is more, getting an appointment with him or a telephone call through to him is a virtual impossibility."

"Well then," twanged the annoyed Mr. Walker, "I can call your principal. He surely can assess your work."

"Yes," said Isabelle. "On this coming Monday, Mr. Goldsmith will be at the Bayside school getting the staff readied for the first day of school."

"School starts mighty late in New York," commented Mr. Walker. "I'll call Mr. Goldsmith today and then get in touch with you."

"What if Mr. Goldsmith is unavailable?" asked Isabelle. "He may still be away on vacation or away on a trip. He and his wife travel a lot."

"If Mr. Goldsmith is unavailable, I'll hire the woman I interviewed before you. Her credentials are not as impressive as yours, but I can reach her superintendent by merely dialing my telephone. In fact, her less impressive credentials are more believable than yours. I probably have no need to reach her superintendent at all."

"Do you think my credentials, as stated by me, are false?" asked Isabelle angrily, feeling very insulted.

"Listen here," sneered Mr. Walker, "I've had several nasty experiences with Easterners who interviewed for jobs and then turned out to be frauds. Why, last year a woman from Boston came here touting credentials as impressive as yours. She, too, told me how difficult it was to speak to highly placed people in Boston's huge public school system, so I started her here, foregoing the telephone interview with Boston."

"When she had been teaching here for four months, our schools' district's controller, for the second time, requested her Ohio certification. When she failed to produce it, he called Columbus to see if, indeed, she had been certified. She had not! For four months, a fraud was teaching in our school district – an uncertified fraud! I had allowed this to happen, because I was gullible, but I no longer am! Everyone from out-of-state that I interview for a teaching position at Mt. Healthy....especially if they come from the East....must be certified by their previous employer. We country boys are fooled by big city slickers only once. After that we are more careful," he said with sarcasm and lots of ill will.

Isabelle was appalled by his attitude and was insulted by his distrust and obvious dislike of people like herself. She bid him a cold goodbye, and left, determined to refuse his job offer, if he made any job offer at all.

Isabelle had an appointment for an interview with the Cincinnati Public Schools scheduled for later that afternoon. She, therefore, stopped at a luncheonette on her way to the Cincinnati Board of Education offices, ate a leisurely lunch, and continued on to McMillan Street, where her interview was to take place. When she arrived at the Cincinnati Board of Education building, she was directed to a waiting room on the second floor. The room was crowded with men and women applying for the teaching positions that Cincinnati might still have available, in spite of the fact that the school year was already underway. In Isabelle's view, the available jobs would probably be so awful, that she might be forced to accept work in the school system of the detestable Mr. Walker.

As Isabelle was thinking these depressing thoughts, a door to an inner office opened and a man entered the filled waiting room. "How many of you applicants have Master's degrees?" he asked.

Only Isabelle and a young man sitting at the other end of the room raised their hands.

"Those with Master's degrees, please remain. All of the rest of you may go. Cincinnati's teaching positions are now filled for this school year," he said.

The room emptied quickly, leaving only Isabelle, the young man with a Master's degree, and the man from the inner office. The latter said, "I'm glad that there were only two of you with Master's degrees. You've made it easier for me. I'll start with the young lady....you know *Ladies First.*" He beckoned to Isabelle to follow him into his office. When Isabelle was seated, the man, who was the personnel officer for the Cincinnati Public Schools, quizzed her about her experience and her educational philosophy. He then told her that Cincinnati had two openings left. One was for a math teacher of seventh and eighth graders in a downtown school, in a rough, high crime rate neighborhood. The other teaching position was in

Saylor Park, a sleepy small river town, located closer to Indiana than to downtown Cincinnati. No one understood how Saylor Park ever became a part of the city while other river towns had not, but understand it or not, Saylor Park was a part of the City of Cincinnati, and it had a teaching position that was still available. The personnel officer urged Isabelle to take the Saylor Park position, even though it was not a conventional teaching job. Saylor Park was one of the few remaining schools in the Cincinnati system in 1957, that was a kindergarten through eighth grade school, and the position offered to Isabelle was to teach seventh and eighth grade English and Social Studies, and to teach seventh and eighth grade Home Economics to the girls. It would be a full and interesting schedule, in a very pleasant little Ohio River town that was surprisingly a part of the City of Cincinnati.

Isabelle asked the interviewer about what Home Economics entailed. He said that he wasn't sure, but he thought it entailed teaching cooking and teaching sewing on a sewing machine.

Isabelle laughed out loud. "I don't know how to sew on a sewing machine, myself!" she said.

"The Home Economics supervisor will visit you right away. She'll get you started and tell you what to do, "explained the man.

"Where exactly is Saylor Park?" asked Isabelle.

"Just about as far west as Cincinnati goes. I assume that you have found a place to live?" the personnel officer inquired.

"No, not yet. My husband and I are living in the Terrace Hilton Hotel. We were waiting to find out where I will be working before we rent an apartment."

"I am guessing that you would be happiest living in Roselawn, but it's very far from Saylor Park. I think you'll have to rent your apartment, keeping in mind the distance it is from where you will work," he said.

"Thank you," said Isabelle. "I look forward to beginning at Saylor Park on the day after Labor Day. At what time should I report to work?"

"At Saylor Park, school begins at 8:30. It ends at 3:00 P.M. I shall call Mr. Johnson, the principal of the school and tell him about your arrival. I'd get there at 7:45."

When she left the interviewer's office, Isabelle called Al at Rollman's and told him the good news about her job. He said that they should begin their apartment hunting as quickly as possible.

The only people Al and Isabelle knew in Cincinnati were Harold and Anita. Their connection to Harold and Anita was less than ideal, because Harold was Gert's brother, and Harold and Gert had a very painful relationship. Al's sister-in-law, Gert, did not even speak to her brother, who was a highly respected surgeon in Cincinnati. Harold and Anita could have been a great contact for the new arrivals, but because of Gert's angry boycott of her brother and his family, the newly arrived couple felt awkward about getting in touch with them them.

When Al finished his day's work and came back to the hotel, he said that they'd have to "take the bull by the horns" and call Harold and Anita. He then asked Isabelle to do the job. Isabelle was reluctant to do so, because Gert was not even on speaking terms with her brother, and their rift was so severe that Gert had even boycotted Harold and Anita's wedding. She had also forbidden the timid Eva to attend the wedding, and Eva had fearfully complied with her daughter-in-law's wishes. While it would have greatly facilitated their move to Cincinnati to have someone they knew from New York to advise them about Cincinnati's neighborhoods, shopping, synagogues, etc. Isabelle did not want to get in the middle of Gert and her brother's feud. She, therefore, refused Al's request to call Harold and Anita. She said, "If in spite of the bad blood between them, you want to contact Gert's brother, you call them yourself."

Al said, "They will probably respond to a call from you in a more kindly way than to a call from me. I really don't want to call. Please do me a favor and call them."

Isabelle, reluctantly, gave in. She dialed the number and after three rings, the phone was picked up. When Anita answered, Isabelle said to her, "I'll bet you'll never guess who this is."

"Of course I know who it is," answered Anita. "It's Beverly. How are you?"

Laughing, Isabelle said, "I'm fine, but I'm not Beverly. Anita this is

Gert's sister-in-law, Isabelle. We met in New York, on a few occasions. We even went to see a play together. I remember you well. Do you remember me?"

"Of course I do! From where are you calling?" asked Anita.

"Al and I recently arrived in Cincinnati. Al has begun work at Rollman's. I have spent today interviewing for teaching jobs, and we'd really love to get together with you and Harold to catch up on what's going on in your lives and to tell you about what's going on in ours. We'd also like you to answer our questions about Cincinnati."

"Harold and I would love to see you tomorrow evening. Grab a pencil and paper and I'll give you directions to our house, but first tell me where you are staying"....

"Do you have a car?"....

"Of course you'll have dinner with us," Anita said excitedly.

Isabelle happily accepted Anita's gracious invitation and wrote down the directions to the house.

On the following day, Isabelle purchased a lovely hostess gift for Anita. After work, Al drove them to the rambling, very large Victorian house located in a neighborhood of beautiful mansions and old Victorian houses. The neighborhood was called the Rosehill Section of North Avondale.

Harold and Anita welcomed them as if they were beloved, close relatives. They showed off their three fetching young children, and never once referred to the great insult they had suffered from Gert. Indeed, they did not refer to their estranged relative at all. They kept their conversation focused on Isabelle and Al's adjustment to Cincinnati.

After a sumptuous meal prepared by Anita, Harold proposed that the children remain at home with the maid, while he and Anita showed Isabelle and Al around some of Cincinnati's neighborhoods. They drove up Reading Road through Bond Hill, which was a long established Jewish neighborhood. Just north of Bond Hill were Golf Manor, Roselawn, and Amberely Village. Harold explained that these were newer Jewish neighborhoods, Roselawn being the one that would have the most apartments for rent. Suddenly, Isabelle knew what her interviewer for her teaching position in the Cincinnati Public Schools meant when he said that he thought that she would prefer to live in Roselawn, but that Roselawn was too far away from Saylor Park. He had recognized that she was Jewish, and was trying to tell her where a Jewish neighborhood was located.

Isabelle told Harold and Anita that they would have to live on the western side of Cincinnati, because she would be teaching in Saylor Park. Harold laughingly said, "You'll be teaching in Indiana! Saylor Park is as far west as you can get, and still be in Ohio. And wait until you meet the Cincinnatians from the West Side! They're truly a breed unto themselves, and most of them have never known a Jew. You're in for quite an adventure!"

When they parted from Harold and Anita, Isabelle and Al knew that they would become close friends with these generous and friendly people. They could not know that their slim family connection would grow into a family bond respected by both of their families for a generation to come.

Getting an apartment on the west side was not difficult. Many lovely apartments were available in their price range, but none possessed all of the criteria the young couple required. They wanted the apartment to be spacious, to be air-conditioned, to provide parking, to be near shopping, and above all to be near a bus stop where Al could catch the bus that would take him to his job in downtown Cincinnati.

After a long search, they found an apartment that met all of their criteria. It was located on Foley Road, near Pedretti. The neighborhood was a cross between being rural and suburban. A large cemetery, located across the street from the apartment house they were contemplating, stretched from Pedretti almost to the corner of Anderson Ferry Road. The cemetery abutted a large public school with a building annex that housed a public library. The school was located at Anderson Ferry and Foley Roads. On the corner of Foley and Pedretti Roads, across the street from the cemetery and next door to where Isabelle and Al lived, sat an old ramshackled house, surrounded by lots of grass. One of the out-buildings of this house housed two goats who grazed on the grass, thereby making it unnecessary to mow the property. Alongside this house stood the newly built five family apartment house in which Al and Isabelle would live. For a fairly long stretch after their apartment house, there were no other structures at all. In the center of Foley Road, facing the cemetery, houses appeared once again. They were stretched in a continuous line towards Anderson Ferry Road. They ended at a recently built Methodist church, which stood on the corner of Anderson Ferry and Foley Roads, across the street from the school.

When Isabelle and Al moved into the left, upstairs apartment of the newly built apartment house, the building debris had not yet been cleared. Their landlord gave them a reprieve from their first month's rent in exchange for cleaning away the debris in their own apartment. They gladly accepted his offer.

During the first month of their tenancy, Isabelle and Al were the only people living in their apartment house. Construction crews were busy building three more four family apartment houses behind the building on Foley Road in which the young couple lived. The residents of all three of the apartment houses would share the large parking lot behind the building in which Isabelle and Al lived.

At the end of September, a young couple moved into the basement apartment of the house facing Foley Road. They were to be the caretakers of all three buildings. Doc was a busy medical student at the University of Cincinnati Medical School, so his young wife did most of the care taking. The young caretakers had come to Cincinnati from Iowa.

By October, the Foley Road apartment house was totally rented. A quiet, unfriendly, reclusive couple had moved next door to Isabelle and Al, and a very friendly, gregarious young couple had moved into the apartment beneath the quiet couple. Three people made up the family that had moved into the apartment beneath Isabelle and Al's apartment. They were a husband, a wife, and a child about six years of age. The man and his wife were very homely people, who never looked neat. To top off their unattractiveness, they were both very stout. Yet, unattractive as they were, these two homely people had parented an absolutely beautiful daughter, who had not inherited their stringy, dishwater brown hair, nor their coarse features Instead, their daughter had jet-black wavy hair framing an alabaster white complexion, whose pallor was relieved by dimpled pink cheeks. The child's huge grey eyes were fringed with long, thick, curly, black lashes. Her nose was small and straight, and when her lovely lips parted in a smile, they revealed small, straight, pearly, white teeth. Isabelle's downstairs neighbors' daughter was one of the most beautiful children Isabelle had ever encountered, and she marveled at such beauty coming from such homely parents.

Al and Isabelle soon became friends of the gregarious couple. This couple explained, to the recent New Yorkers, the demographics of Cincinnati, giving particular emphasis to the demographics of the West Side. People who had an interest in people with backgrounds different from their own, almost never lived on the West Side. Most of the people living on the West Side could trace their ancestry back to the thousands of German settlers who had come to Cincinnati in the mid nineteenth century. In many cases, they could trace their family's church membership to a particular Catholic church in a particular town or city in Germany. In these cases, they and their descendants built churches to be places of worship for people who traced their ancestry back to the same Catholic parish in the Old Country. Outsiders, even though they too were Catholics, never seemed to be fully accepted, and usually left to go to other churches where they could receive a warmer welcome.

True strangers like Isabelle and Al or the Iowans Doc and his wife, were suffered politely, but were never fully accepted. Yet, good manners and a patina of friendliness did exist.

When tenants of their apartment house parked their cars behind the Foley Road house, they usually entered in the basement and walked through the basement laundry room. Groceries or newly washed laundry had to be lugged up the stairs from the basement to their respective apartments. Isabelle never carried her groceries or laundry up to her apartment if one of her male neighbors was in the vicinity. Any one of the males living in the Foley Road house would insist that she immediately turn over her bags or laundry basket and allow him to carry them to her door. Isabelle had never witnessed chivalrous behavior like this in New York. Consequently, even though people from the West Side of town were insular, she still believed that they were accepting of outsiders.

Having basked in the warmth of Harold and Anita's attentions, and having succeeded in renting a truly lovely apartment close to the bus line and only a fifteen minute drive from Isabelle's school in Saylor Park, the young displaced New Yorkers felt very secure in what they thought was their successful move to Cincinnati. And then, their sense of security was destroyed by an accident.

During the second week in September, their belongings had been taken out of storage by the moving company and delivered to the house on Foley Road. Al and Isabelle had unpacked all of the corrugated cartons and Al had broken them down to be burned in a fire he had built in the far corner of the large parking lot. He kept taking the broken down boxes and flinging them into the blazing fire, when suddenly, as he twisted his body to fling a large box into the blaze, he heard a click in his neck. He then felt a tremendously sharp pain, and couldn't turn his neck to face forward again. Frightened, and in great pain, he went upstairs to tell Isabelle.

Isabelle's head was buried deep in a clothing closet, when Al arrived and told her his tale of woe. Greatly concerned, she suggested that he take a very hot shower. She hoped that the water's heat would loosen up his locked up neck.

The shower was worthless. Al hurt more than ever. Worse of all, they didn't know where to go or whom to call. Harold and Anita were in New York, because. Harold's youngest sister had just given birth to a baby boy. Harold and Anita and their three children had gone to New York to be present at the baby's *brith* (a *brith* is a circumcision ceremony in which a male infant is circumcised, named, and becomes an official member of the Jewish people.) While in New York, Harold and Anita also planned to visit their parents and other family members. Little did they know that their absence from Cincinnati would present a great problem for Isabelle and Al.

Having no one else they knew to call, Isabelle called the Cincinnati Academy of Medicine to ask for advice. When she asked them for a name of a local doctor, the Academy of Medicine suggested that Al be seen at a nearby hospital. They told Isabelle that the nearest hospital to them was Saint Francis.

Isabelle drove to St. Francis Hospital, following the directions given to her by a nurse in the hospital's Emergency Ward. She found the hospital with a minimum of difficulty, and Al was rapidly whisked into a small room in the emergency ward, while Isabelle sat in the waiting room. In the small room, a dark complected, black haired resident asked Al many personal questions. When he asked Al what his religion was, Al replied, "Jewish." The resident's head jerked up. He stared straight into Al's eyes and said, "Did you say Jewish?"

"Yes," replied Al.

"Well I'll be damned!" said the resident. "You're the first Jew I've seen in this hospital, and I'm almost finished with my residency." Laughing he added, "I thought my wife, my two kids, and I were the only live Jews on this side of town. There are plenty of dead Jews in the large Jewish cemeteries located on this side, but all of the live Jews live east of here."

Al explained that they had just recently come to Cincinnati and were living on the West Side because of its proximity to the school in which his wife was teaching.

The doctor, whose name was Walter, treated Al with muscle relaxants, and assured him that his neck would soon be better. He also said that his wife Nellie would call them. He was sure that she would be thrilled to learn that another Jewish couple was living nearby. He said that he hoped that they would all get together soon.

Al's neck enjoyed a rapid recovery, and the visit to St. Francis Hospital marked the beginning of a close friendship between the two couples. Nellie, Walter's wife, was bright and well read. She had been the only child of a teacher who had published several books in her native Romania. Even though they were Jews, Nellie's family seemed to be respected by their non-Jewish neighbors in the small city from which they came. Because Romania was ruled by a government allied with Nazi Germany, several annoying anti-Semitic laws were thrust upon Romania's Jewish population, but by-and-large, the Jews of Romania remained unmolested.

All of this changed when the German government began to exert pressure on the Romanian government to become more decisive in their dealings with their Jews. The result of the Nazi demands was that the Jews of eastern Romania were rounded up and deported to Romanian occupied areas of the U.S.S.R. Nellie and her parents were interned in a concentration camp established in the Ukraine. The camp was located in the midst of the flourishing farms of the Soviet Union's "bread basket," but the deported, starving Romanian Jews could only gaze longingly at the fields and gardens rich with food. While their Romanian guards did not kill them, they were rough and brutal about any transgression.

The prisoners were given very little food and were forced to live in overcrowded, unsanitary, unventilated, barn-like structures that were worse than the barns that housed most farm animals. When the brutal winter came, death also came to many of the camp's inhabitants. Many froze to death, while others starved to death. But, the majority of deaths, in this horrible camp were the result of disease that spread rapidly among the starving overcrowded prisoners. Nellie's father was among the first of the winter's dead.

When the prisoners thought that the conditions of the camp could not be worse, the Romanian guards were replaced by German guards who shot prisoners without even a pretext. They also reduced food rations and increased the prisoners' workloads, causing the rate of death among the prisoners to accelerate precipitously. Only a small remnant of the Romanian Jews in the camp survived to be liberated during the Soviet's counterattack which routed their Nazi guards.

After the war ended, Nellie and her mother were returned to Romania. With great courage and stealth, they made their way to a displaced person's camp in Germany. The Australian government accepted them as immigrants, and Nellie and her mother resided in Australia in peace. Young Nellie even resumed her education there.

Walter had been a pre-med student in college. To his acute dismay, he was unable to gain admittance to a medical school in the United States. He was able, however, to gain admittance to an Australian medical school, and while he was there, he met Nellie. They fell in love, and because Walter was an American citizen, Nellie was able to enter the United States as his wife. But because of the heinous quotas on Romanians, Nellie's mother would be forced to wait to enter the United States until Nellie became an American citizen. As a mother of an American citizen, she would be able to circumvent the tiny Romanian quota, and finally come to the United States. In the meantime, she would have to remain in Australia, without any family.

After Walter graduated from medical school in Australia, he was required to complete several years of residency at two American hospitals. It was when Walter was in his last year of residency at St. Francis Hospital, that Isabelle and Al met him.

When Isabelle met Nellie, she liked her immediately. She was bright, well read, and interesting. She felt sorry for Nellie, however, because Nellie harbored some bad feeling toward her mother and seemed to be down on herself concerning her appearance. To be sure, Nellie had a matronly figure, because she had done nothing to help herself regain and maintain a lovely girlish figure after the births of her babies. What is more, Nellie was a fabulous cook, who thoroughly enjoyed eating the delicious foods she constantly prepared. Her figure not withstanding, Nellie had a pleasing face and a wonderful mind. Isabelle secretly believed that if Nellie emphasized her good traits and stopped brooding about her deficits, she would be much happier. Isabelle also believed that when Nellie became an American citizen and brought her mother to America, she would be much happier. Because Isabelle keenly missed Bella, she was sure that beneath all of Nellie's criticism of her mother, lay a strong love. She was sure that Nellie really missed her mother as much as she missed Bella.

Isabelle was young and innocent. In later years she would have a better understanding of the differences between people and their different outlooks on life. Isabelle was rarely jealous of anyone, consequently, it was difficult for her to discern the envy that might be eating away at someone else. She was totally unconscious of the fact that Nellie envied her bigotry-free upbringing in the United States. Nellie also envied Isabelle's relationship with Bella, and she envied the education Isabelle had received, that deportation to Russia had robbed from her. Isabelle even had a graduate degree, and this rankled Nellie, too. This envy should have been enough to poison Nellie against Isabelle, but there was more. Nellie envied Isabelle's slim young figure and the lovely business clothes Isabelle wore when she went to work.... It was absurd that Isabelle, who wasn't usually stupid, had remained totally innocent in her understanding of Nellie's feelings. For Isabelle, her frequent visits and interesting conversations with Nellie completely masked the envy and hatred eating away at the older woman whom Isabelle believed was her friend.

Chapter 25: The West Side

Isabelle started to teach at Saylor Park School in early September, and quickly began to understand the lay-of-the-land. The charming, sleepy river town had several layers of housing. Most of the town was made up of modest, small brick and clapboard one-family homes, which housed mainly blue-collar workers who were employed in the many factories that peppered western Cincinnati. Closer to the river stood the lovely, stately Victorian houses in which the families of professionals and successful businessmen lived. These executive types usually commuted to downtown Cincinnati from their large Victorian homes in Saylor Park There was a drug store, a grocery store, and a meat market in the village. Several churches were peppered throughout the town. The post office, a small Catholic school, and the much larger public school, in which Isabelle was to teach, completed the town's public buildings.

The ramshackled houses of Saylor Park's African Americans were located on Hillside Avenue, a road that ran on the northern periphery of the town. Like many of the white inhabitants of Saylor Park, many of the African American families' ancestors had settled in Saylor Park in the nineteenth century. Some few of them, could trace their roots to escaped slaves who crossed the Ohio River and settled in the town. In modern Saylor Park, most of the African Americans were employed in the factories located on the West Side.

Further east on Hillside Avenue was a trailer colony. It housed people from the Kentucky, West Virginia, and the Tennessee hills. Most of these people had left the coal mines and had come to Cincinnati seeking jobs during World War II.

Children from all of the aforementioned communities were pupils in the Saylor Park School. Isabelle was to teach seventh and eighth grade English and Social Studies and also teach Home Economics to the girls of the seventh and eighth grades. It was a daunting assignment, but twenty-five year old Isabelle was ready to take it on.

On Isabelle's first day at the Saylor Park School, Mr. Johnson, the school principal, walked her around the school building, explaining the school's demographics. He stopped outside of the room in which she would teach and said, "I'm an old *Hoosier*, and I like to tell things straight."

"What is a *Hoosier*?" asked Isabelle.

Mr. Johnson laughed. "A *Hoosier* is a person from Indiana. We pride ourselves with telling it the way it is."

"New Yorkers like to think that *they* tell it the way it is, too," countered Isabelle.

"Good," said Mr. Johnson. "Then you and I will get along quite well."

He then turned and pointed to a bank of lockers strung out against the wall of the hallway in which they were standing. "We do not have enough lockers to provide each student with his own locker. You will have to assign each locker to two children. Be sure that you do not assign a locker for both a white and a Negro child to share. And of course, you will be sure to assign all lockers to partners of the same sex."

Isabelle was astounded …. segregated lockers! Did Mr. Johnson think that the children's coats would damage one another? But Isabelle did not tell it the way it was. Isabelle said nothing.

Mr. Johnson then showed Isabelle her home economics room, the auditorium, the gym, and through a window, the swimming pool. He explained how the pool was used.

The swimming pool was an outdoor rectangular pool to be used only by the children of Saylor Park. It was put into use on Memorial Day weekend and remained open seven days a week until the Tuesday after

Labor Day. Mr. Johnson explained, "From Wednesday through Monday the white children of Saylor Park swim in our municipal pool. On Tuesday, the Negro children may swim. The pool closes at 5:00 P.M., on Tuesday, and on Tuesday evening it is drained, cleaned, and refilled with clean water. On Wednesday, the white children resume their occupancy of the pool, turning it over to the Negro children once again on the following Tuesday."

Isabelle grimaced as she listened to Mr. Johnson's bigoted explanation. The principal noticed her disapproval and came to the defense of Saylor Park's pool practices by saying, "I see that how we run our children's pool offends your New York sensibilities. I'm sorry about that, but I must inform you that your pity is misplaced. All swimming pools in Cincinnati are segregated, entirely eliminating their use to Negroes. Ours in Saylor Park is the only one I know of that makes some provision for Negro children. The Negro children in Saylor Park are better off than all of the other Negro children in southwest Ohio."

Isabelle did not answer him. She knew that any of her arguments about fair treatment would fall on deaf ears and would turn Mr. Johnson against her.

———

Mr. Johnson escorted Isabelle into her room. He introduced her to her eighth grade homeroom and then exhorted the students to be helpful and obedient to their teacher. When he left the room, Isabelle asked a boy who was sitting near the window to open all of the windows as wide as they would go. The closed up room must have been 85 to 90 degrees.

After assigning lockers to the children, Isabelle began to distribute textbooks. She asked four students to help her in this endeavor, and instructed all of the students to write their names on the inside covers of their books.

A very handsome, tall African American boy caught Isabelle's attention, because he mostly kept his head on his desk, and when he deigned to look up, his handsome face wore a very sullen expression. Because the boy was wearing a heavy woolen jacket in the extremely warm classroom, it distressed Isabelle, so turning her full attention to him she said, "It's very hot in here. Why don't you take off your jacket and hang it in your locker?"

The boy turned his unpleasant gaze on his new teacher and said in a soft, but very unfriendly tone, "I like wearing my jacket. I guess my jacket is really my business."

"Do as you like," said Isabelle, in an even tone. She then turned to the class at large, and began to teach a lesson appearing in their English literature textbooks.

————

Isabelle was not the only one trying to professionally "get her house in order." While she struggled to adjust herself to Jr. High School children who lived in a little river town in southwest Ohio, Al was trying to acclimate himself to the difficult job of being a buyer of five different departments in a department store located in a city in which he was a stranger.

Seeking to achieve success, Al made a buying trip to New York very early in his employment at Rollmans. He concentrated his efforts on the departments from which he expected his best returns; spending his time buying hosiery, sox, and cosmetics, and giving only a cursory glance at cameras. His camera department consisted of one counter and a showcase located beneath an escalator. Clearly, cameras and photographic paraphernalia were not important items at Rollmans.

While Al was perusing the photographic equipment market, he sometimes came in contact with people selling telescopes and binoculars, as well as cameras. One such merchant presented the young buyer with an offer Al found difficult to refuse. The merchant said that he would sell Rollmans his telescopes and binoculars on a "guaranteed sale basis." This meant that after one month, Rollmans would only have to pay him for the units that were sold. All unsold units could be returned to him. In addition to the very advantageous terms of sale, the salesman offered to pay for a full-page ad on the telescopes and binoculars. The ad would run on the Sunday after the goods were delivered.

————

Sometimes the Fates can be cruel and kind at the same time. The United States was horrified and embarrassed to learn that the Soviet Union had sent a satellite into space. This first satellite, put into space by humans was called, *Sputnik,* and caused great embarrassment to the American government and the American scientific complex. They immediately set forth on a huge space program that would eventually put other satellites into orbit, put a man on the moon, and establish radio contact with places far out in space.

But, it was little *Sputnik,* the Russian's great achievement in space in 1957, that grabbed the imaginations of people all around the world. Even in Cincinnati, hoards of ordinary people thronged to Rollmans to buy the telescopes and binoculars in Al's department They had seen the full-page ad for them in Sunday's *Cincinnati Enquirer,* and the stampede was on!. The man on the street in Cincinnati, bought the telescopes and binoculars in the hopes that he could visually track *Sputnik.* While the United States government and its scientific community deemed Sputnik to be their failure, the new buyer at Rollmans had become a hero because of the sale of telescopes and binoculars that would fail to show their viewers the Russian satellite.

———————

For Isabelle, teaching English and Social Studies to seventh and eighth grade classes was a "piece of cake." Teaching Home Economics to the girls of the seventh and eighth grades, however, was as daunting a task as Isabelle had ever attempted. She looked forward to a visit from the Home Economics supervisor for the Cincinnati Schools. Perhaps this expert could set her on a successful course, but in the meantime, Isabelle began both of her home economics classes with the Food Section of the curriculum. To this end, Isabelle brought home the Course of Study in Home Economics for both grades and studied their food sections late into the night. To her great disappointment, she found that she disliked most of their suggestions. She, therefore, decided to go her own way, unless the Home Economics Supervisor disapproved of her independence.

In each of her classes, Isabelle assigned the girls the task of creating menus for the three meals of the day. She checked each girl's work, and when she returned their menus, she instituted a discussion about breakfast. They talked about the nutritional value of the foods, the ease or difficulty in preparation, the time it took to prepare, and the costs of the various foods. The girls were then divided into family units of four. They planned a family menu that was voted upon by the members of their family. Then the class compared the family menus and selected the one that appealed to them the most.

The seventh grade class voted on a menu of orange juice, poached eggs, goetta, and hot cocoa. Isabelle knew that she would not partake in the poached eggs, because she found poached eggs to be detestable. She had not yet formed an opinion on goetta.

Although it was a local favorite, goetta was a food with which Isabelle was unfamiliar. When Isabelle first looked at the uncooked goetta, she immediately recoiled squeamishly. The goetta, which was made of cooked oatmeal, ground beef, and ground pork had an unappealing gray, sticky, lumpy aspect to the uninitiated. The German immigrants who had brought the goetta to Cincinnati, prepared it by slicing the unappealing mass and frying it until it gained a crispy, attractive exterior. It became a favorite breakfast food in western Cincinnati.

When the odor of the great quantities of fat that filled the pan in which the goetta was frying permeated the kitchen it caused strangers like Isabelle to dislike it even more than when the goetta was raw. Isabelle knew that it was unlikely that she would ever eat this popular food.

Things were better in the eighth grade. The older girls' menu consisted of fresh fruit salad, containing strawberries, blueberries, cantaloupe, bananas, and grapes. Their main course was pancakes with maple syrup. They too, selected cocoa as their breakfast beverage. Isabelle liked eating every item on the eighth grade's menu, and partook of their entire breakfast.

Dishwashing and cleaning-up were part of Isabelle's homemaking curriculum and there were discussions about the health hazards caused by slipshod cleaning. The girls also discussed and displayed their knowledge of table-setting aesthetics.

Preparing lunch was lots of fun in both classes. Isabelle did not interfere with the girls' planning, and each "family" produced a different lunch. Appetizers ranged from homemade and canned soup to elegant fruit salads. Some families ate sandwiches, while others ate salads. All of the food was appealing to the eye, and all of the "families" enjoyed preparing and eating what they had made.

Isabelle interfered with lunch preparation only when dessert was discussed. She imposed her will on her students by saying, "I would like every 'family' to bake a chocolate cake. You will draw lots as to which family uses a cake mix and which family bakes its cake from scratch. I want every girl to list the cost of ingredients used, the time spent in preparation, and the difficulty or ease with which the cake was produced. We will taste each other's cakes and compare them to one another. First we will decide which cake tastes best. Our final decision as to which cake *is* best will be made by considering the cost, the taste, and the recipe's difficulty.

The chocolate cake project grabbed every girl's interest. Everyone kept careful records, and after lots of tasting and comparisons of the cost and effort entailed in creating the cakes, the surprising results became known. Cake mixes, far and away, were chosen over cakes baked from scratch. The ease of their preparation, coupled with most of the mixes' excellent tastes, far out balanced the more difficult preparation and lower cost of from-scratch-cakes. If any difference was perceived in taste between cakes made from scratch and cakes made from mixes, it was miniscule.

Not so for the chocolate icing on the cakes. Isabelle's classes unanimously chose chocolate butter cream icing that was made from scratch, using a double boiler, and requiring a good deal of work. Its taste was so superior to the tastes of all of the icing mixes purchased in the grocery, that both the seventh and eighth grades enthusiastically endorsed the icing made from scratch.

Dinner was handled more by discussion than by the actual preparation of the meals. After all of the discussions, in November, it was decided that both the seventh and eighth grades would join together to create a mammoth Christmas buffet to which they would invite their parents. Several turkeys, stuffing, cranberry sauce, mashed potatoes, broccoli, carrots, jello molds, cakes, and pies were prepared by the seventh and eighth grade girls. On the Thursday night before their winter break, the students and their parents partook of the girls' Christmas feast. It was a wonderful and an unforgettable event for all.

Isabelle had encountered no difficulty in getting her students to supply either money or supplies toward their cooking projects. But, as with her difficult introduction to goetta, sometimes her background, which differed so much from that of the students, caused misunderstandings based on different uses of terminology. For example, great confusion occurred with the names of two commonly used vegetables. The girls spoke of using mangoes and green onions in their salads. Isabelle stated that mangoes were tropical fruits, sometimes difficult to obtain. She further stated that she had never heard of green onions. Her students laughed at her ignorance and refuted her definition of mango. One student said that her mother grew mangoes and green onions in her garden. She promised to bring some to school the next day. Isabelle thought, "This I've got to see!"

The student's mango turned out to be a green pepper. Green onions turned out to be the salad onions New Yorkers called *scallions*. Isabelle's usage had been correct about mangoes. The students' usage was correct about green onions. Teacher and students humbly looked up both of the names in the dictionary. They learned what a scallion really was and they learned to be leery of terms they had used all of their lives. From then on, Isabelle and the girls in her class were open to correction when a familiar term was challenged by someone coming from another part of the country or from a different culture.

After the Christmas buffet, the girls dismantled the tables and Christmas decorations, and mentally prepared themselves for their second course of study in their home economics class....sewing.

When the Home Economics Supervisor had visited Isabelle in October, she had explained budgets for home economics supplies and informed Isabelle that there was money in the budget for her to take a sewing course at the Singer Sewing Center. She also explained that if what Isabelle planned to do went over budget, she could ask the girls to contribute toward their own supplies. She further stated that students were expected to buy their own cloth for major sewing projects.

Isabelle's learning experience at the Singer Sewing Center was not a good one. When she completed the course, she did not feel sufficiently proficient to instruct a class in sewing. She, therefore, developed a plan to get around her deficient sewing skills. She asked the girls in the class to raise their hands if they had ever created a piece of clothing by using a pattern and sewing on a sewing machine. Several girls in each class answered in the affirmative. Isabelle selected five of these girls in each class. She dubbed them "*teachers*," and said that because her sewing skills were so poor, it would be their job to help her and their classmates in their sewing projects. Each seventh grade girl would sew a wrap around skirt using lightweight cotton, suitable for spring and summer wear. In the eighth grade, each girl would sew a wrap around skirt using heavier material, such as corduroy or wool, suitable for fall and winter wear. The "teachers" would help their classmates and help Isabelle, as well, because Isabelle planned to make a skirt for herself in each class.

The sewing project was a huge success. Much to Isabelle's delight and surprise, she was able to conduct two very successful Home Economics classes during each of her two years at the Saylor Park School.

The sullen African American boy, who had defied Isabelle when she had suggested that he take off his jacket, was named Bobby Greene. He turned in correct, but uninspired papers in both English and Social Studies classes. He never participated in class discussions, and his eyes never met Isabelle's eyes when he spoke to her. Bobby often got into trouble with his other teachers, but in Isabelle's classes he caused no disturbances.

Eighth grade achievement tests were given in October. Much to Isabelle's surprise, Bobby Greene's overall test was one of the highest in his class, and his reading achievement score was higher than any of the other student's. Isabelle knew that she needed to discuss his achievement scores with the angry boy, and deeply wished that she might gain his confidence. To this end, she summoned him from his gym class, because his gym class was during her free period. She wanted to talk to him when no other student was present.

Bobby came into Isabelle's classroom, his face covered with perspiration. He was wearing his gym shorts and his sweaty, handsome face was frowning with anger, and exhibited some perplexity. He walked over to Isabelle's desk and asked in a quiet voice, devoid of any emotion, "Why did you send for me?"

Isabelle smiled at the seemingly upset boy and said, "I sent for you because I needed to talk to you privately, and this is my free period, when I am alone in my room. I'm sorry that you're missing part of your gym period, because I know that your gym class is one of your favorite times at school."

"First I want to tell you that I've always wanted to be your friend," she said, "but unfortunately I know the feeling isn't mutual. You avoid conversation with me and even seem to have a difficult time looking straight into my face. I have always suspected that you are very, very bright. Your schoolwork is good, and sometimes what you say is so insightful, that it grabs my attention. Being insightful means that you have a deeper understanding of a subject than one would expect you to have."

"Bobby, your achievement tests were outstanding. Your scores are among the top scores in the eighth grade and your reading score was the highest reading score in the grade. You must enjoy reading. Do you read a lot at home?"

"Yes," answered Bobby. "I take books and magazines out of the library all the time. Thank you for telling me how high I scored….now may I go back to the gym?"

"No," you may not go back to the gym until I've finished talking to you," said Isabelle. "Bobby there is a spectacularly good school in Cincinnati called Walnut Hills. Students are accepted to Walnut Hills if they do well on the high school's competitive entrance examination. I know that you would do well, and if you go to high school at Walnut Hills, a boy like you would probably do well enough to get a scholarship to a good college. I know that Walnut Hills is far away from Saylor Park, but other students from here manage to get there, so I suspect that we could probably find you a ride."

Bobby interrupted, "I know that you mean well, but you are very impractical. Colored kids don't go to college very often, and when they do they have plenty of backing. I have mapped out a more practical plan. I'll go to an ordinary high school and I'll graduate. That will make me the first member of my family to graduate from high school! After I've graduated, I'll apply for a job with a big overland trucking firm. Some of them have started to hire colored men. They pay very well, and my family and I could certainly use the big bucks."

"You're naïve if you believe that in Cincinnati, there are great opportunities for colored kids. They are very few and far between. There may be more opportunities in the future, but I mean to stick to my guns and make it as an overland truck driver, way before that time comes."

Isabelle realized that she would be unable to penetrate Bobby's stubborn resolve. Although she was very disappointed, she sent him back to his gym class.

But, from that day on, a far more animated Bobby willingly participated in class discussions and always had a shy smile for his teacher whenever their eyes met.

In May, Bobby announced that his family was moving to the nearby river town of Addyston. Addyston was a small town located quite close to Saylor Park, but Addyston was not part of the City of Cincinnati. Bobby would be going to a consolidated high school called Taylor High School that served several of the small, sleepy towns that stretched along the Ohio River as it meandered toward the neighboring states of Kentucky and Indiana.

———————

One day, during Isabelle's second year at Saylor Park, an agitated message came into her room over the intercom. One of the school's secretaries said that Bobby Greene was intercepted by a teacher on the stairs leading to Isabelle's room. The teacher, and indeed the school secretary, knew that Bobby no longer attended the Saylor Park School, so they believed that the "troublesome" ex-student had no business in the school building. The secretary said that Bobby insisted that he was in the school because he wanted to visit Isabelle, and the secretary said that she was just checking his *unlikely* story.

Isabelle immediately left her class and ran down to the office where an angry Bobby Greene stood, looking more handsome than ever. Isabelle gave the secretary a dirty look, took Bobby's hand, and joyfully escorted him to her room. She introduced him to her class and then asked him why he wasn't in school.

Bobby said that Taylor High School was closed for a conference day. He said he took the opportunity of a day off to visit some people in Saylor Park.

Isabelle questioned him about his future plans. She was disappointed to learn that his plans had not changed.

After Isabelle hugged Bobby and thanked him for his visit, she never saw him again. She often wondered what had become of the handsome, gifted African American boy, smoldering with anger and accepting mediocrity because of the racial climate in south western Ohio in the 1950's.

––––––––

At Christmas, during Isabelle's first year at Saylor Park, Isabelle's class performed a play written by their teacher. In those days, a very popular television program called *This Is Your Life* came into American living rooms on small black and white television sets, and enjoyed tremendous popularity. When Isabelle learned that her eighth grade class was expected to perform a Christmas play, she decided to write a play for them called *This Is Your Life, Santa Claus*. She followed the format of the popular TV program, by having Santa Claus be the surprised guest who is called up from the audience. Instead of relating stories from his childhood and youth, as the T.V. program usually did with their guests, the history and development of the myth of Santa Claus was presented by the eighth graders as they enacted and explained the places and the cultures that contributed to the Santa Claus story. The play was an overwhelming success. Parents, student spectators, eighth grade performers, and stage crewmembers thoroughly enjoyed the eighth grade rendition of *This Is Your Life, Santa Claus*.

Christmas may have been enjoyed by all, but Isabelle would have preferred less explicit presentations than the numerous nativity scenes that proliferated in the Saylor Park School. She also disapproved of reading from the *New Testament* at the beginning of the Christmas Assembly. However, because all of the students and all of the staff, with the only exception being herself, were Christians, the Christian atmosphere did not truly upset her. Although no one at Saylor Park cared that the Christmas assembly flew in the face of the United States' Constitution's assertion of the separation of church and state, nothing offensive had been said, and Christmas passed as a happy holiday for all.

Not so with Easter. No Easter programs were required in the grades that Isabelle taught. A story about the Easter Bunny was dramatized by the third grade during the Easter Assembly. Everyone was required to attend this assembly which began with Mr. Johnson reading a passage from the gospels in which it was written that the chief priests and scribes of the Jews "vehemently accused" Jesus. The principal of the Saylor Park School went on to read another passage showing that Pilate, the Roman leader, and Herod, the Jewish king, found no fault with Jesus; but that the Jewish mob yelled, "Crucify him, crucify him!"

As Isabelle heard these blatant anti-Jewish remarks, she squirmed in her seat. The *New Testament*, the Christian *Bible*, was casting blame for Jesus' death upon the Jews. Because of this blame, on Good Friday, for hundreds of years, Christian mobs had attacked and killed innocent Jews, calling them *Christ Killers*.

As they all sat in the Easter Assembly in Saylor Park, work was underway in the Vatican toward the negation of the aforementioned murderous allegations against the Jews. The Catholic Church, grieved by the recent blood bath of the Holocaust, was hard at work examining the facts that would lead to its official exoneration of the Jewish people of any guilt for the crucifixion of their fellow Jew, Jesus of Nazareth. The Church's official statement clearing the Jews was not issued until *Vatican II* in 1979, but in its statement, *Vatican II* not only exonerated the Jewish people of any complicity in the death of Jesus, but officially apologized for the past outrages perpetrated against Jews because of these allegations.

Yet in 1958, in the quiet Ohio River town of Saylor Park, children in a public school were still being taught that the Jews were responsible for the death of Jesus. This blatant anti-Semitism sickened Isabelle. She wished that she were miles away, but she remained seated, and she deeply mourned the Saylor Park School's "fall from grace."

Another "fall from grace" occurred in the apartment house on Foley Road, in which Isabelle lived. She had become friendly with her neighbors and loved the helpfulness of her male neighbors when they came to her aid at the times they saw her maneuvering bulky laundry or heavy grocery bags up the two flights of stairs to her apartment. She believed that her wonderfully friendly and helpful neighbors behaved as amicably as they did, because they liked and accepted the New York Jewish couple who had moved in among them.

One warm spring afternoon, Isabelle returned home from school feeling very tired. Al was working late that night, so Isabelle decided to open her window, let the fresh air in, and take a nap. She planned to nap on the sofa in the den. The den's window opened out onto the building's back parking lot, and when Isabelle opened the window, she heard the voices of her homely downstairs neighbor and Doc's wife. The two women were discussing the impending birth of Doc's baby. Doc's wife was in her last month of pregnancy and was looking forward to shedding the huge burden of weight she was carrying. She said, "I can't wait until the baby is born. I'm so curious about its sex and its appearance. It's kind of scary, thinking about what the baby will look like. I sure hope it's beautiful and healthy."

Isabelle's downstairs neighbor answered, "You've had a healthy pregnancy, so I'm sure you have nothing to worry about concerning the baby's health. As for its appearance, let me warn you that most newborn babies are very ugly. You know how beautiful my daughter is....well, she was born so ugly she looked just like a Jew!"

"Shhh," said Doc's wife. "Her window is open. She'll hear you. Besides," she continued, "all of them aren't ugly. She's pretty good looking."

"Yeah," said Isabelle's truly homely neighbor. "She's the exception that proves the rule."

After that overheard conversation, Isabelle no longer accepted assistance from her neighbors and greeted them coolly with curt hellos and curt goodbyes.

Walter and Nellie no longer lived on the West Side. Walter had taken

434

over a practice in a suburb that was due north of Cincinnati. He had learned of the practice's availability from Harold, when Isabelle and Al had introduced the two couples. At that time, Walter was completing his residency at St. Francis and was glad to be able to take over the practice of the retiring doctor to whom he had been led by Harold. Walter and Nellie had purchased a home in Finneytown, a lovely, booming suburban community of one family houses and excellent public schools. A small, active young Jewish community lived in Finneytown, and the area had a large Women's B'nai B'rith chapter to which most of the young Jewish women belonged. When Nellie told Isabelle that she had joined the Jewish organization, with a great sense of forlornness, Isabelle said, "Al and I are probably the last living Jews on the western side of Cincinnati." She wistfully said that as soon as a baby was in sight, they would leave the west side to the dead Jews who were buried there, and move to an area where she and Al were not the only live Jews.

They may have been the last two living Jews on the West Side, but that summer on Foley Road turned out to be a wonderful summer for Isabelle. After making a two-week trip home to New York, she returned to Cincinnati, sweltering in an extreme summer heat wave. She went swimming with Anita and her children at their swim club, visited with Nellie and her babies, but most of all, she spent her days lounging in the sun on her uncovered porch – listening to classical music and reading.... reading....reading. The lazy, satisfying days passed uneventfully, and if Al had been happy at his job at Rollman's, or if she had become pregnant with the baby for whom she fervently yearned, that summer of 1958 would have been the best summer of her life.

Al, however, was deeply dissatisfied with his job. He was working much too hard and his boss was a tyrant. Al was seriously looking into changing his place of employment.

To complicate the young couple's lives further, although they deeply desired to become parents, Isabelle had not gotten pregnant. After extensive fertility testing in Cincinnati and in New York, it was determined that while conception was possible, it was unlikely and that they would probably be best served by looking into adoption.

One hot summer day, as Isabelle was eating her breakfast, the telephone rang. It was Walter, who told her that he had just delivered a baby girl to a Jewish woman who lived in the town in which he practiced. He said that the woman looked enough like Isabelle to be her sister. His patient had tearfully told Walter that the baby was not her husband's, and to save her marriage, she was placing the baby for adoption with Jewish Family Service of Cincinnati. Walter strongly urged Isabelle to call Jewish Family Service to see if she and Al could adopt the baby.

Isabelle called Jewish Family Service immediately. An appointment was made, which began the grueling investigation that would determine their eligibility for becoming adoptive parents. Isabelle believed that Walter's telephone call was a good omen….and perhaps it was. In 1958, when Isabelle and Al began their journey into adoption, there were several ways to achieve their goal. Some couples adopted babies privately, through doctors or lawyers who had learned of a baby's availability and worked with the biological parents and with the adoptive parents. There were sometimes difficulties with this method, and periodically one read in the newspaper of a child being returned to its biological parent quite some time after its adoption. This wrenching pain for both the adoptive parents and the child was too difficult for Isabelle and Al to even contemplate. Therefore, they earnestly pursued the agency route of adoption. In 1958, in most states, agency adoption carefully followed religious lines. Therefore, in Cincinnati, there was a *Jewish Family Service*, a *Catholic Family Service*, and a *Family Service*. The latter handled Protestant adoption, although, supposedly, it was open to all because it was a government supported agency.

Isabelle and Al, like many prospective adoptive parents, cared nothing about the baby's religious background. But they were strongly cognizant of the frequent newspaper articles relaying the horrific experiences of adoptive parents whose children were yanked away by biological parents of differing religious persuasions. The courts generally supported biological mothers who, because of religious differences, were unhappy with their babies' adoptive placements. In some cases, these extremely painful disruptions occurred years after a child was adopted.

In order to avoid such a heartbreaking event, Isabelle and Al's adoption efforts were concentrated with only Jewish Family Service. They were assigned a caseworker at the agency, with whom they worked for many months. The entire process lasted from early November, 1958, when Jewish Family Service began their interviews in earnest, to late September, 1959, when their interviews were completed.

In Isabelle's second year at the Saylor Park School, a foul smelling, often disheveled, very disagreeable man in his mid thirties was hired to teach seventh and eighth grade mathematics and science. Isabelle and Mr. Whitman developed an instant dislike for each other and gave each other plenty of space. Nonetheless, Isabelle was still made quite aware of him because in the home economics classes she heard the students' less than complimentary anecdotes concerning his unacceptable remarks and poor teaching techniques. Then, one day, a truly frightening story was told to Isabelle by some of her students. Because Barbara, a girl who was, far and away, the prettiest eighth grade student in the school was absent from home economics class, Isabelle asked if she was ill. "No," replied one of her students. "Barbara is being kept at home until the problem with Mr. Whitman is resolved. Mr. Whitman has been stalking Barbara and constantly telling her how much he loves her. Yesterday, Mr. Whitman parked his car on the street on which Barbara lives. He stayed there for two hours. Barbara didn't leave her house, and when her father came home from work, she told him about what had been going on. Barbara's dad bolted out of the house, carrying a shotgun. He went right to Mr. Whitman's car and threatened that he would kill Mr. Whitman if he went anywhere near his daughter. Mr. Whitman was scared and immediately drove away."

"Barbara called me," said the student who was narrating the story, "and told me the whole thing. She said that she and her father were coming to school today to talk to Mr. Johnson."

Mr. Johnson upon hearing about Mr. Whitman's behavior toward Barbara immediately suspended him. The Board of Education then fired him. The people at the Saylor Park School never saw him again, but they did hear about him. Several months after Mr. Whitman's suspension and subsequent firing, Isabelle was smoking with some of her colleagues in the small basement room located next to the boiler. (It was the only designated smoking area in the school.) It was there that another teacher finished Whitman's tale. She said, "My husband works at the Courthouse in downtown Cincinnati. I had told him the story about that Whitman creep stalking Barbara. In complete shock, he told me that Whitman was now working at the Courthouse as a juvenile counselor for the city. That bastard probably knows someone powerful. I certainly hope that he doesn't harm some other kid down there!"

To Isabelle's shame, neither she, nor any of the staff at Saylor Park School, nor the teacher's husband who worked at the Courthouse, did anything about Whitman. Everyone feared for his or her own position and waited until a distraught parent would "blow the whistle" on the obnoxious juvenile counselor. No one wanted to get embroiled in a dirty case that Whitman, with whomever his connections were, could very likely win.

If Barbara was the prettiest girl in the eighth grade, Alvin Compton was certainly the most handsome boy. Barbara, who came from a quiet family that had recently moved to Saylor Park from the hills of Kentucky, epitomized the well-behaved, gentle country girl. Alvin, whose family originally came from the hills of West Virginia, came to the Saylor Park School from a rough, under-privileged neighborhood along the Ohio River, called Anderson Ferry. Alvin epitomized all of the baser elements found in the transplanted mountain people, and he possessed none of their many virtues. He easily resorted to violence to get what he wanted, and if angered, foul language usually accompanied the violence. While he was far from stupid, his negative attitude toward schoolwork had caused him to fail two grades.

When Isabelle taught him, Alvin was almost sixteen years old. He was over six feet tall, slim, muscular, and extremely handsome. He had not remained in her class for more than three months, when he was suspended from school for an offense committed in another teacher's classroom. His suspension would last until the Christmas break, during which time, Alvin would turn sixteen. It was Mr. Johnson's prediction and fervent hope that Alvin would drop out of school when the Christmas break was over.

One day, Isabelle was walking into town with some of her students, with the express purpose of purchasing a tree that the class would decorate for Christmas. Every classroom in the Saylor Park School was required to either put up a Christmas tree or create and display a creche. (The Christmas season of 1958 occurred before the United States Supreme Court prohibited prayer and religious displays in public buildings. This prohibition was enacted by the Court, because religious displays in public buildings were deemed to be in violation of the constitutional clause calling for separation of church and state.)

As Isabelle approached the lot upon which the trees were being sold, Alvin Compton sauntered over and made some lewd remarks, rife with sexual innuendo. The five students accompanying Isabelle were shocked, but they giggled with amusement at their teacher's discomfort. Alvin continued to follow the group, dropping explicit and highly inappropriate remarks. He laughed as he followed them.

Isabelle angrily ordered him away. She threatened to call the police if he persisted.

Finally, still laughing, the handsome, almost sixteen-year old, sauntered away.

When Isabelle returned to school on the following day, she told Mr. Johnson about her encounter with Alvin. He told her that he was unable to deal with Alvin off the school grounds. The school grounds, however, were in his jurisdiction, and if Alvin transgressed there, Mr. Johnson assured Isabelle that he would take care of him.

On the following Sunday, Alvin made several suggestive telephone calls to Isabelle's house. Isabelle had been the one to answer the calls, and when she heard Alvin's voice, she hung up. The last call of the series, however, was picked up by her husband Al. Alvin Compton said, upon hearing Al's voice, "So this is the other Alvin! You've got a good-looking wife. What do you look like?"

Al replied, "Listen you little pervert, you leave my wife alone, and stop calling here or I'll call the police!"

"Pay attention, *other Alvin*," answered the nasty teenager, "I'm not afraid of you or your snooty wife. If you're not careful, I'll come over there and beat the shit out of you!" Alvin Compton then hung up.

Al was furious. When he threatened that he'd get physical with the nasty teenager, Isabelle said, "Don't be a fool. That kid is bigger than you are and meaner than you'd ever plan to be. What is more, he's the third brother in his dreadful family. His two older brothers are in jail! All of the people he bothers with are probably criminal types."

On Monday afternoon, when Isabelle went to the school parking lot to get into her car in order to go home, Alvin Compton was sitting on the car's hood. Isabelle saw him there, as she stood in the doorway of the school building. She quickly turned around and went to Mr. Johnson's office. She told Mr. Johnson about Alvin's harassment on the telephone during the past weekend, and said that as they spoke, Alvin was sitting on the hood of her car in the school's parking lot.

"Great," said Mr. Johnson. "Today is the day we will cure Alvin of his lecherous thoughts about his teacher."

Mr. Johnson and Isabelle went to the parking lot. Alvin quickly jumped off her car when he saw them coming.

Mr. Johnson said, "Alvin, you're still a student in this school, even though you're suspended. You will remain a student in this school until you are legally released when you quit school or are promoted. I believe you've expressed your wish to quit school when you've completed your suspension. We have every intention of allowing you to do so, if we have not placed any charges against you that can send you into a reformatory or put you in jail. Right now, I want you to come up to my office. You, your teacher, and I have some business to attend to."

Alvin reluctantly followed, and when the three entered Mr. Johnson's office, the principal closed the door. He asked Isabelle to take a seat and turned his attention to the sneering boy. "I hear that you were making phone calls yesterday," said Mr. Johnson. "I guess the other kids your age were in church on Sunday, or doing something with their families, because I heard that you alone were making telephone calls to your teacher's home. You weren't calling your teacher for help on some school problem, you were calling her to harass her sexually! Alvin….Alvin….I could get you sent away for that!"

"Until I sign your papers permitting you to drop out of school, you are still a student in the Saylor Park School, and I have jurisdiction over you. When I came out to the parking lot with your teacher, your body was sprawled all over the front of her car. You have no right to do that, and you certainly have no right, as a suspended student, to be on school grounds preparing to do some ugly mischief."

Mr. Johnson asked ominously, "Were you laying in wait for your teacher, so that you could continue your harassment? Answer me truthfully….your whole future may depend on it."

Alvin, no longer sneering, but looking very frightened, answered quietly, "Yes I was," he spoke in barely more than a whisper.

"When a student is disrespectful to a teacher, the smallest punishment I give is a swatting. You have not only been disrespectful, you have exhibited criminal behavior toward your teacher and her husband. You're lucky, Alvin. Because you will soon be leaving school, I will not send your case to Juvenile Court, where they would probably send you to a reformatory. Instead, I will only give you a good swatting. We will keep your unlawful behavior on record if the police ever have to refer to it, but I believe that being in the outside world and going to work will cause you to grow up enough to know that there are consequences in harassing and threatening people. I believe that you'll probably always remember what I'm telling you. You can go to jail for the kind of behavior you have been displaying!"

"I have asked your teacher to be present, because Ohio law requires that another school professional must be present to witness a swatting. You see, Alvin," said Mr. Johnson, "she's the teacher – she's the professional! You, Alvin, are the student!"

"Now empty your pockets," said the principal.

Alvin did so.

Mr. Johnson went to a closet and took a large wooden paddle from a shelf. "Bend over," Mr. Johnson commanded.

The sneer returned to Alvin's face, as he bent over. Mr. Johnson delivered a hard swat to Alvin's backside. The boy's knees buckled slightly as the paddle struck. Four more sturdy swats were delivered to Alvin's buttocks and by the third swat, tears spurted from the arrogant teenager's eyes. After the fifth and final swat, Alvin was truly crying.

"Now," said Mr. Johnson, "apologize to your teacher and leave us. Remember – a school swatting is much easier than even a week in jail. Behave yourself and see that you stay out of jail!"

"Sorry," said Alvin, not even looking at Isabelle. Then, head bent and totally humiliated, he left the room.

Isabelle had never before seen anyone swatted. Corporal punishment was against the law in New York, and although Isabelle had witnessed occasional shakings, grabbing of clothing, and even two or three slaps, the swatting stunned her. She hoped that the chastised Alvin would mend his ways, but she doubted that the swatting would accomplish this end. The swatting did, however, end Alvin's harassment. She never saw nor heard from the obnoxious teenager again.

The last account that Isabelle had of Alvin was that when his suspension was over, he did, indeed, drop out of school. For a few months he had a job working at a gas station on River Road near Anderson Ferry. During that time, he was dating lovely Barbara.

What finally became of handsome, ill-mannered Alvin, Isabelle never heard. She hoped that his fate was better than the fates of his two jailbird brothers.

———————

The Easter break was only three teaching days away. Isabelle had spent most of Saturday shopping. She had purchased a large fashionable hat to wear with her beautiful new gray flannel suit. Al had presented her with a gift of exquisite stone marten skins to wear draped over her shoulders. She couldn't wait until she arrived in New York wearing all of her finery. She wanted to preen, but even more, she wanted to have wonderful long talks with Bella. She missed her mother dreadfully. This was a greatly anticipated trip for Isabelle.

After Isabelle's busy shopping day, she was to pick Al up. She, therefore, parked their green Plymouth at a meter located in an alley alongside Rollmans. Al had already given Rollmans his notice, and was to start working at Cincinnati's major department store, Shillitos, in one week's time. His attaché case, crammed full of important papers needed for his new job, was on the back seat of the Plymouth, along with Isabelle's purchases on this very fruitful day of shopping.

When Isabelle and Al arrived at their car, they were horrified to see that the Plymouth had been broken into. The rear seat of the vandalized automobile was empty. All of Isabelle's purchases and Al's attaché case had been taken. Al immediately called the police.

A squad car with two Cincinnati policemen came very quickly. They took down the description of the missing contents of the Plymouth, and then put the young couple in their patrol car and rode into the West End, the downtown African-American section of the city. The police felt certain that they would find most of Al's papers scattered in certain sections of the neighborhood. As for Isabelle's purchases, one of the policemen said, "Forget about them. They have been distributed to the thieves' women. On Sunday, he said, "you'll see a fat nigger woman swaying her ass proudly as she leaves the church wearing the hat her boyfriend stole for her!" The policemen laughed as he painted his distasteful and very prejudiced verbal picture.

Isabelle, even though she had been robbed, was offended by the policeman's words, and never forgot them. Because some thieves, probably African-American, had robbed her, the policeman seemed to be damning the whole African-American community.

Al's papers were scattered all over an empty lot, just as the policeman had predicted. Al, Isabelle, and the policeman gathered what papers they could, and then the patrol car returned the couple to their damaged car.

"We will write up a report on your robbery," said one of the policemen. "Don't ever park in an alley again. The niggers are afraid to rob cars parked out on the crowded street. Park there, or in a parking lot or garage. The alley invites the crooks to rob you."

When Isabelle returned to school on Monday, one of the school's secretaries said, "My husband told me that your car was broken into. He's a policeman, and he saw your police report. He saw that you worked at Saylor Park School, and he told me about your robbery. I'm sorry about it, but my husband says you'll never get your stuff back."

"I know," said Isabelle. Most of the stuff was clothes that I planned to wear on my trip home. I'll live. I've got other clothes."

With that, Isabelle went to her classroom and taught her classes. At the end of the day, she went to the office, where she encountered Connie, the first grade teacher, who was laughing with two other teachers, who quickly shared their hilarity with Isabelle. Upon hearing their story, Isabelle doubled over with laughter.

Elizabeth, the school secretary whose husband was a policeman, was the mother of two beautiful little girls who were pupils at the Saylor Park School. Elizabeth was often judgmental and prejudiced and she was also extremely straight laced.

The laughter that Isabelle had encountered was in response to what Carlie, the secretary's smallest daughter, had shared with her first grade classmates during *Show and Tell,* which occurred in first grade at the end of each school day. During *Show and Tell,* children either showed their classmates things that they thought would be of interest or told stories that they thought would interest them. Carlie had begun her tale by saying, "My sister broke her tooth on Saturday night. It happened 'cause I woke up in the middle of the night 'cause I was thirsty. I wanted a glass of water, but I was ascared to get it 'cause my house is so big and dark, and sometimes makes scary, creepy noises at night." (Carlie and her family lived in one of Saylor Park's lovely, large old Victorian houses.)

"I tiptoed over to my sister's bed and woke her up to go with me when I went to get a drink," continued Carlie. "We were going to go downstairs to get the water, when we saw a light coming out from under the door of the room where my mom and dad sleep. We didn't want them to know that we were out of our beds, and we wanted to know what they were doing in their room with the light on so late at night. Patty said that she'd look through the big key hole to see."

"Patty said they were doing something very strange. She said my daddy was on top of my mommy and both of them were naked! She said that Mommy was hugging Daddy with her legs. But it was when Daddy started to jump up and down on Mommy that Patty moved her head down too hard 'cause she was so scared and surprised; so she hit her tooth on the door knob, and broke it!"

Connie could not contain herself. She left her first grade class and ran out into the hall to laugh. After she composed herself, she went back and dismissed her class. She then went down to the office and told Carlie's tale to every adult she encountered. Straight laced Elizabeth, blushing profusely, immediately left the office. It took her a long time to live down the popular story of her daughter's broken tooth.

————————

The last two Jews, on the western side of Cincinnati, were planning to move. They were in the process of being interviewed by a lovely social worker named Mrs. Wolfenstein, who had been assigned their case at Jewish Family Service. They had come to the conclusion that they would improve their chances for adoption if they lived in a neighborhood in which there were other Jewish families. They also believed that if they were homeowners they would have a better chance of adopting a child.

The likelihood of a successful adoption was slim. In 1959, at Jewish Family Service in Cincinnati, one in ten couples applying for adoption was found to be acceptable. The couple had to be less than thirty-five years old, in good health, have enough money to provide for a child, and pass the grueling interviewing process of the agency. If a couple was found to be acceptable, there had to be a baby that the social workers thought would match them. There were too few available babies to allow the social workers the luxury of matching physical resemblance. But, they worked diligently to match a baby's intellectual background to the couple who would be the baby's parents. There were lots of applicants deemed to be acceptable by

Jewish Family Service, but a pitiful few were given babies. The agency's supply of babies hinged on how many young Jewish women were placing their babies for adoption. These young women usually placed their babies, because they were unmarried, couldn't or wouldn't obtain an abortion, or were married and had aberrational problems within their marriages which necessitated placing their babies for adoption.

———————

Isabelle and Al could not afford even an average priced house. They usually looked at houses whose prices were below average, but none of these houses seemed to suit them, because they were either too small or in a terrible state of disrepair. Then, providentially, one of the realtors with whom they were working brought them to Glencoe. Glencoe was a fairly large, inexpensive, relatively new development of basementless ranch houses built on slabs. They consisted of three bedrooms, a bath and a half, and a large living room with a small dining area attached to it. The dining area sat beneath a pass through from the small kitchen. Glencoe was located in Springfield Township, and Glencoe children went to the Mt. Healthy Schools.

Compared to all of the other houses they had seen, a certain Glencoe house, which was located at the edge of the development, right across the street from houses that were in Finneytown, seemed more spacious and was finally found to be acceptable to the young couple. They had hoped to live in Finneytown, where Nellie and Walter lived, but the Finneytown houses were too expensive for them. This house in Glencoe was nearby, and they planned that when they accumulated more money, they would move to a better house in another community. Their Glencoe house was being purchased as a stepping-stone toward a better house in the future.

After much discussion, Isabelle and Al went to the lending institution recommended by their realtor, where they believed that they could procure a mortgage. When Isabelle checked their application, after the mortgage company had gone over it and made some changes, she found that her salary had been altered. The lending company had cut her salary in half. Isabelle asked why this had been done. She was told, "You will most likely become pregnant, and quit your job to stay at home with your children.

Because of this we can only credit married women's salaries at half of the amount of money that they earn. Isabelle felt cheated, but could do nothing about it. 1959 was not a good year for women's equality.

Isabelle spent her last three weeks at Saylor Park, having to make the horrendously long drive from her new home in Glencoe, on Daly Road, to the Saylor Park School. She looked forward to her summer vacation, during which she would have the house painted and would plant flowers in her own backyard.

One of the house painters kept making remarks and eyeing Isabelle in a lascivious way. He frightened her, so she called Fred, a friend who was divorced and lived alone. Fred, who was a manufacturer's rep, was often available, when he was not traveling. She explained her discomfort to Fred and he came over to stay with her. The errant painter no longer bothered her, and Fred and Isabelle enjoyed their day together.

The weather was beautiful and they decided to escape the paint fumes and sit in the yard. They discovered a strawberry patch planted by the previous owner and sat on the grass eating succulent strawberries, plucked from the stem. As they sat in the sunshine, Fred told Isabelle some of his story.

Fred was the only child of a Catholic mother and a Jewish father. He was born in Budapest, where his family was quite comfortable. Because Hungary was an ally of Nazi Germany and had its own fascist government, it had not yet imposed the terrible anti-Semitic laws of the Nazis on Hungarian Jews. Life was somewhat frightening for the Jews of Hungary, but throughout the 1930's they still felt reasonably secure. Fred's father had converted to Catholicism, making his family feel even more secure.

One day, a high ranking executive in Fred's father's company quietly warned Fred's father of the danger Hungary's Jews might face if the Germans put more pressure on the Hungarian government or if the Nazis decided to march into Hungary. This highly placed man said that if he were Jewish he and his family would immigrate to the United States. He urged Fred's father to do so, and if they chose to go, he promised that he would do what he could to facilitate the family's emigration.

The family was conflicted. They hated to leave beautiful Budapest, interrupt Fred's education, leave their loved ones behind, and begin a brand new life in a country whose language and customs they did not know. On the other hand, it had already become somewhat difficult to live peaceful lives, free of religious slurs and harassment. Furthermore, the advice they received came from a very highly connected man, who easily could be privy to secret information about plans that did not bode well for Hungary's Jews. His warnings needed to be heeded, because he could easily be correct.

After a great deal of soul searching, Fred's family made the decision to emigrate. They arrived in New York City in 1940, where Fred quickly mastered English and graduated from high school. In early 1942, the family moved to Cleveland, Ohio where Fred enrolled at Case Western Reserve. His college education was interrupted when he entered the United Stated Army in late 1942.

Fred's knowledge of German and Hungarian were invaluable to the army. Except for a brief stay in an army hospital to recover from minor wounds, he served in several unusual intelligence capacities, using his linguistic knowledge.

Ironically, in the case of Fred and his family, fascist bigotry hurt the fascists themselves. The work Fred did inflicted serious losses on America's enemy. And, when Fred returned to civilian life, he married, raised a lovely family, and was an upstanding citizen of his adopted country. Hungary's loss was America's gain.

Chapter 26: Stroke

The jangling telephone tore Al and Isabelle awake. It was 6:00 A.M. and Bella was on the phone. She said in a tremulous voice, "I'm sorry to be awakening you so early in the morning, but your grandmother has suffered a serious stroke and is presently in the hospital, unconscious. I'm calling this early, because if you plan to drive to New York, I want you to have enough time. Call me and let me know what you will do."

What Al and Isabelle did was begin to pack. By 8:00 A.M., when Al could reach the proper person at Shillito's, he notified him that he and his wife were heading to New York, because his wife's grandmother, to whom she was deeply attached, had suffered a severe stroke that could be fatal. He promised to call to apprise Shillito's of his plans and of the date on which he would come back to work.

Isabelle called Bella at 8:10 A.M. and told her that she and Al were on their way. They then began their twelve hour drive to Bella's house.

Because Isabelle was so worried about her grandmother's condition, at 7:00 P.M., when she and Al stopped at a roadside restaurant for dinner, Isabelle called her mother for a progress report. To her great relief, she learned that Sarah had regained consciousness, could speak, but was not in control of her extremities. She could not feed nor dress herself, nor could she stand or walk. The doctors at the hospital were planning to send her to a nursing home that served kosher food and provided physical and occupational therapy for their residents. "She might even be moved tomorrow," Bella told Isabelle.

Much relieved, Isabelle and Al continued their trip, but now they were heading to Eva's house. Once again, they chose to stay with Eva and Max, because they had more room there than at Bella and Hymie's apartment.

On the next day, after a hearty breakfast at Eva's house, Isabelle called Coney Island Hospital, where Sarah was a patient. Sarah was unable to take calls, and the nurse who was giving Isabelle information suggested that she call the medical resident in charge of Sarah's case. Isabelle was told that the resident would know more than the nurse knew about the hospital's plans for Sarah.

When Isabelle reached the resident, he told her that social services was making arrangements for Sarah's transfer to a facility in which she would be comfortable with the food and would be able to receive the post-stroke therapy she needed. He gave Isabelle the telephone number of social services.

When Isabelle called social services, she was informed that Sarah would be moved right after lunch to the Beth Israel Nursing Home, located on Ocean Parkway in Brooklyn. The social worker suggested that Isabelle wait until the early evening to see her grandmother, because the facility's intake procedures could possibly take hours and the social worker didn't know the exact time that Sarah was leaving the hospital.

Isabelle and Al decided to visit Sarah at 5:00 P.M. The weather was beautiful and they had left the Bronx early enough to miss the worst of rush hour traffic. Isabelle was so relieved that her beloved grandmother had survived the stroke, that she found the drive to the nursing home, even in New York City traffic, very pleasant. The bright sunshine matched Isabelle's mood as they drove down Ocean Parkway toward the nursing home and Sarah.

As they approached Beth Israel Nursing Home, they saw many patients on the lawn of the facility, some with visitors and others sitting alone. Suddenly, Isabelle spotted a patient who looked like her grandmother sitting slumped in a wheel chair under a large shade tree. She told Al to stop the car and let her out. She told him to park and to find her under the tree with Sarah. When Al stopped the car, Isabelle got out and ran to the woman slumped in her wheel chair. It was her grandmother! "Bubbie," shouted Isabelle. "It's me – Isabelle," she said in Yiddish.

Sarah looked up. A tear trickled down her face. "Isabelle," she said quietly, "I'm sick."

"I know," answered Isabelle, "but with therapy, you'll get well. You have had a stroke. We're all so lucky that you're alive and can think straight and can even talk."

"I can't walk or use my hands," said Sarah sadly.

"They will teach you how to use your hands and legs again, Bubbie."

"I'm so glad you are here, *Tochteril* (little daughter), you look well and beautiful."

"I am well, Bubbie. Oh, here comes Al. He was parking the car."

Al kissed Bubbie and told her how glad he was that she was coming along so well. His conversation was terminated by the arrival of an aide who had come for Sarah. She explained that it was dinnertime and she was taking Sarah to the dining room.

Isabelle told her grandmother that she and Al would go to a restaurant and have some dinner, and then would return to visit with her.

Sarah told her to buy a hairbrush for her. She said her hair was awful and she wanted Isabelle to brush it after dinner.

Laughing at Sarah's still healthy vanity, Isabelle and Al ate dinner nearby and purchased a hairbrush at a corner drugstore. They then returned to Beth Israel, where they learned that Sarah was still at dinner. They, therefore, walked over to the large dining hall, where seated at a long table from which her dishes had been cleared, Sarah was listening intently to an African-American aide who asked her in English, if she had moved her bowels that day.

Isabelle knew that Sarah understood English and that she understood the aide's question. "No," answered Sarah in English. Then in heavily accented English she said, "I am constoopate. I not can moof my bowvels."

Isabelle rushed over to Sarah. "Oh Bubbie," she said in English, "You can speak English!"

"Don't be a fool," snapped Sarah in Yiddish. "I understand English poorly and cannot speak it at all. Don't speak English to me, or I won't answer you," she threatened.

Isabelle laughed out loud. In Yiddish she said, "Oh Bubbie, I've caught you. You tried to force all of us to learn Yiddish, and you succeeded with some of us. With the others, they speak to you in English and you answer in Yiddish, if you know they understand it. The few who don't understand it get it interpreted for them, so that you can continue to force us to speak Yiddish."

"You're wrong!" said Sarah angrily. "I wish I was smart enough to get away with what you are saying. I'd do it, because I like to hear my grandchildren speaking a Jewish language. All too few of us are left that can speak Yiddish. But I don't force anyone! I just can't speak English."

"What language were you speaking to the aide?" asked Isabelle.

"You're dreaming," said Sarah, sticking to her deception.

Isabelle and Al decided not to discuss Sarah's ruse any further. The discussion was upsetting her. They stayed with Sarah a while longer, speaking Yiddish, and discussing many things. When they left Sarah, they promised that they would see her again, before they returned home to Ohio.

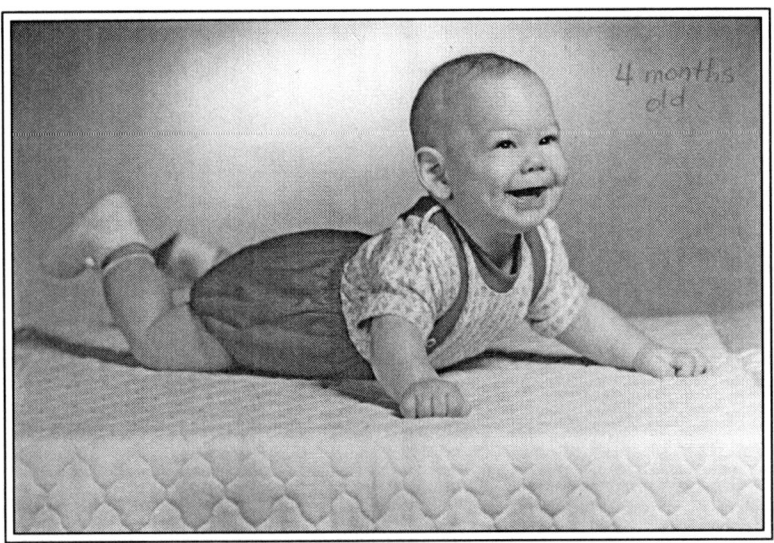

Ricky, 1960

*Ricky's membership in the Sky Cradle Club when
he flies to New York to meet his family*

Chapter 27: Ricky

Isabelle began the next school year teaching at Kirby Road School in Northside. In late November, 1959, her teaching career was interrupted by a telephone call from a Miss Greenstein, on a Friday, at 4:30 P.M. Miss Greenstein was calling from Jewish Family Service to tell Isabelle and Al that a baby boy had been born that Jewish Family Service believed should be their son. She told the trembling Isabelle that she and Al should come to her office at the agency on Monday morning to discuss the particulars.

It was the slowest moving weekend of both of their lives. If they weren't on the telephone with Bella or Eva, they talked to each other excitedly about the baby boy who would probably be theirs. Both of them could think of nothing else.

Finally Monday arrived. When they met Miss Greenstein, they learned that she would be their caseworker from then on. She told them about the health, weight, and biological background of the baby. She said that he was two months old and was presently living in the foster home he had been living in since his birth.

Miss Greenstein was a sober, tight-lipped type. She was in her fifties, and had been at this work a long time. When she concluded her description of the baby boy that would be theirs, she dropped her guard for a moment, smiled at the dazed young couple, and said, "I know you are getting a fine little boy, and he is getting wonderful parents. I have no doubt that all three of you will be very happy with each other."

454

"Have you chosen a name for your son?" she asked.

"Yes," replied Isabelle, "Eric Franklin in memory of Al's father."

"You may meet Eric on Wednesday. I will have him here at 11:00 A.M. Then, if everything is all right, I'll bring him to your house on Friday. I will ask you to have no one at your house for one week, except the person who will help you care for the baby. We frown on too much excitement during the first week."

Isabelle and Al went on a crash program of shopping and borrowing. Eric's crib was borrowed from a distant cousin of Al's, who lived in Cincinnati. His layette was purchased at Shillito's that very day. An ancient baby buggy was given to them by a friend and kept under the deep eaves that hung over the back patio. It would remain there to serve as the place Eric could nap if the weather was lovely. A chest of drawers and pretty baby decorations for Eric's bedroom were purchased to complete the nursery. Nothing was left but to await Wednesday, with anticipation greater than either of them had ever known.

On Wednesday morning, they ate a hasty breakfast, dressed quickly, and then realized that it was too early for them to go. They waited for the appropriate time to leave, and arrived at Jewish Family Service at 10:45 for an 11:00 A.M. appointment. When they took their seats in the empty waiting room, Al took Isabelle's hand and said, "Don't expect too much. All babies look like Winston Churchill when they're very new!"

Isabelle didn't answer. They remained in silence until Miss Greenstein appeared at exactly 11:00 A.M. "Isabelle," she said, "come with me. We'll bring Al in a little later."

Isabelle followed Miss Greenstein into an empty room. Miss Greenstein left Isabelle, walked through another door, and disappeared into another room. Isabelle tingled with excitement and anticipation when Miss Greenstein returned carrying a bundle wrapped in a blue blanket. She placed the baby on a bare table against the wall. Isabelle removed the blanket and the baby began to flail his little arms, kick his chubby little legs, and cry at the top of his lungs. She picked him up and cradled him in her arms, but he continued to cry, flail his arms, and kick his feet. She cooed at him and spoke to him, but to no avail. Her little son continued his distressed crying.

Then Isabelle had a plan. She put the crying infant back on the table and removed the gold charm bracelet she was wearing. She dangled the bracelet before the baby's eyes. He stared at it with rapt attention and then reached for it with his chubby fingers. Once again, still holding the bracelet above the baby's beautiful face, Isabelle picked him up. No Winston Churchill here! Little Eric, very soon to be called Ricky, was absolutely beautiful! A small amount of reddish, blond hair covered his perfectly shaped head. His nose was tiny and his round pink cheeks dimpled when he cried or made cooing noises to the bracelet. Suddenly, he turned his gaze on Isabelle. She whispered to him, "Hello, little son. You are the most beautiful human being I've ever seen! I already feel such love for you that my chest is bursting. I'll always love you better than life itself."

As if little Ricky understood, he looked straight at his mother and gave her a wonderful gummy and dimpled smile. At that very moment, Al was ushered into the room by Miss Greenstein. He looked at the beautiful smiling baby boy that was his son and said, "He's beautiful, Isabelle! What a beautiful kid!"

"Yes," said Isabelle. "We are the luckiest people in the world!"

Miss Greenstein took the baby after the couple had cooed at him for a few more minutes. She left the room with the baby, promising to return quickly. When she returned she said, "I guess I don't have to ask you how you feel. Use this day for last minute preparations. I will bring Eric home to you on Friday, at 10:00 A.M."

Isabelle and Al spent most of the rest of the day on the telephone. Arrangements were made for Bella to arrive in Cincinnati on the day after Eric's arrival at home. She would stay with Isabelle and Al for a little more than a week. Not only would she enjoy the baby, she would teach Isabelle some of the things Isabelle needed to know about infant care.

After Bella left, Isabelle and Al would be on their own for four days, and then Eva and Zada would arrive. They too would stay for a little more than a week. They would become acquainted with the new baby, and Eva would help Isabelle as she became more and more proficient in the care of her infant son.

―――――――

As expected, Bella was immediately enthralled with Ricky. She believed that he was the world's most beautiful baby and she never tired of feeding, dressing, bathing, and playing with him. She and her daughter were having a splendid visit, when one evening, Bella's face became quite grave and she said, "Isabelle, your grandmother is having a difficult time with this adoption. It is a concept that is brand new to her, and when she was trying to come to grips with it, one of her stupid cronies really messed things up. Bubbie's cronies often discussed the news with her and Bubbie also gets her news from the Yiddish station on the radio. Because she is unable to read the newspaper, a friend of hers, often tells Bubbie about the sensational news carried in the *Der Tag*, a Yiddish tabloid. This time the stupid woman *hit the jackpot*!

"Bubbie called me before I came here," said Bella. "She told me that the woman asked her if it was true that one of her grandchildren had just adopted a baby boy. When Bubbie answered in the affirmative, the woman said in a catty tone, "I don't think it is such a good idea." She then proceeded to tell your startled grandmother that in that day's newspaper, it was reported that the teenaged adopted son of a couple living in Brooklyn, had murdered his mother. She said to Bubbie, that in an adoption, you just don't know what kind of child you are getting."

"Bubbie called me," continued Bella, "to relate the story to me, and she said that she didn't feel good about your adopting a baby."

"I got very angry and told her she was a disappointment to me. I told her that she was acting ignorant and that no one knew what any baby would grow up to be, whether a baby was born to them or adopted by them. When I hung up, it was with a cool goodbye, and I haven't spoken to Bubbie since then."

"Mama," said Isabelle, "don't be mad at Bubbie. She just doesn't understand. She shot her babies out as if she were making popcorn. She doesn't understand my situation. I'll write her a letter explaining our physical limitations, how we came to get Ricky, and that he was born to a Jewish woman who was unable to keep him."

Isabelle wrote Sarah a letter in Yiddish and one of Sarah's literate friends read the letter to her. Isabelle said many things in the letter, but chief amongst them was their baby's ability to instantly cure the ache they felt about their infertility. She strongly stated that creating a baby did not make the child's creator a parent. If it did, there could be no adoption, for no one could part with a baby she had created. "Raising and loving a child makes a child yours," wrote Isabelle. "I feel nothing for George and everything for Hymie, because Hymie has been my loving father," she wrote. She further stated that Ricky and any other baby she might adopt would be hers as deeply and meaningfully as Bella and Sarah's children were theirs. She reminded her grandmother of how she always spoke of her children and their children as her *ten fingers*. Sarah often said that she had ten fingers that were very precious to her. She said that none of them could be spared, because each and every one of them was irreplaceable. Isabelle said, "Ricky is another one of your "ten fingers" and he is the beginning of my "ten fingers." How he came to be ours is irrelevant," she wrote. "My son is ours! He is a Vashishter!"

When the letter was read to Sarah, she did what was unheard of. Frugal Sarah had someone place a long distance telephone call to Isabelle. (In 1959 long distance calls were very expensive.) She and Isabelle and Bella laughed and cried over the wonderful addition to their family. She asked Isabelle when she could expect to meet the baby.

Isabelle replied that she and the baby would fly to New York in May, for Mother's Day. She would introduce the baby to the family at their large annual Mother's Day get-together.

———

Ricky's arrival caused the mailman and delivery men lots of additional work as they stopped very frequently at the little house on Daly Road. Every day packages arrived. Beautiful baby clothes, extravagant toys, and such infant apparatus as a high chair, an indoor swing, and a hobbyhorse were among the many baby gifts. The laughing mailman said he believed that a "crown prince" had arrived at the little house. Isabelle knew that it was a king that had arrived.

———

The second time Isabelle saw Zada cry was when he beheld his great grandson, Ricky. Tearfully he said, "He is a beautiful little boy. Bubbe would have been so happy to see Alvin's baby."

Zada and Eva enjoyed their visit. Eva bathed and fed the baby with such enjoyment, that Isabelle remarked, "I've never seen you smile so broadly as when you are taking care of the baby."

"That's because," said Eva, "I never bathed so young a baby before. Bubbe didn't let me bathe my boys until they were six months old."

Isabelle didn't continue that conversation. It opened up aspects about Al's mother and grandmother that Isabelle didn't want to touch.

When the time came for Eva and Zada to leave, Eva burst into tears. She said, "Gert never let me do things for her son when he was a baby, so I really have greatly enjoyed doing things for Baby Ricky. Thank you for sharing your baby with me. I shall miss this fun."

"Ricky is your baby, too" replied Isabelle. "Hurry back and see us."

———

During Ricky's first week in his new home, Isabelle spoke to her Cincinnati friends on the telephone, but did not invite them to see the baby, because Miss Greenstein had plainly said that, except for the care-giving relatives (i.e. Bella), there were to be no visitors at the house during the baby's first week there. Miss Greenstein stated that the baby needed to adjust to his new home quietly, with no excitement. "What is more," she warned, "an agency person will drop in, unannounced to see how everyone is getting along."

Isabelle adhered to Miss Greenstein's admonitions, but Nellie did not. On the second day that Ricky was with them, Nellie arrived at the little house on Daly Road. She angrily thrust a package into Isabelle's hand and stomped through the house to the baby's room. She stared at the sleeping baby for several minutes, turned and stalked out to the front door. Turning to Isabelle angrily, she said, "I know how to welcome a baby, even when I am not welcome!" She slammed the door behind her.

Isabelle was nonplussed. She and Al had liked Walter and Nellie very much. They had moved to the area in which they were living, because Nellie and Walter lived there. Al had just recently served as Nellie's witness for her naturalization as an American citizen. Isabelle and Nellie generally spoke on the telephone daily. Isabelle had even spoken to Nellie on the day that Ricky arrived. She had had absolutely no idea that Nellie was angry with her about anything.

Isabelle opened the package that Nellie had thrust into her hands. It contained a cute thermal bag for the baby's bottle. These bags were sold for a dollar in every drug store. A small, enclosed card said, "Congratulations!" It was signed Nellie and Walter.

The insulting gift card and the whirlwind, angry visit completely puzzled Isabelle, but she had no time to ponder them. Almost upon Nellie's footsteps, Miss Greenstein and Mrs. Wolfenstein arrived. Both social workers had come to see how well the new baby and his new parents were adjusting to each other. Isabelle invited them in and told them that Ricky was asleep. She served them cookies and tea and the three of them chatted about recent events.

"Have you had any visitors?" asked Miss Greenstein.

"No," answered Isabelle. "I adhered to your instructions and kept all of my friends away. Only one friend came by without an invitation.... Nellie....one of the people I had chosen to be a reference for our adoption, dropped in, against my wishes."

"I'll bet it was an unpleasant visit," commented Mrs. Wolfenstein. "Nellie was one of the most unusual references I'd ever interviewed. Your other references....let's see, you had your friend and almost relative Harold and his wife Anita....and Frank Lazarus, a friend of yours and a member of the family who are the principals of the Federated Department Stores. All of them behaved as expected. They glowed about both of you, and strongly recommended you as adoptive parents."

"Then there was Nellie....not only did not glow, she damned you as a prospective mother. She said that you, Isabelle, were shallow and only cared about your appearance. She said that she feared that you would care nothing for a child, because she believed that you do not care enough about

Al. She said that this is apparent because you don't cook enough, and seem to spend most of your time reading or fussing over your appearance."

"I considered Nellie's assessment of you to be the words of a woman consumed with jealousy. I had interviewed you, Isabelle, and I could see that you love Al and care deeply about household matters. Nellie's harping about your appearance was the utterings of an extremely jealous woman. I ignored them. But you must understand, Nellie is no friend of yours!"

"I learned that during her visit today," said Isabelle. "She must be a wonderful actress, because I was completely unaware of her negative attitude toward me. Thank you for overlooking them. I am certainly glad that I understand Nellie now."

Sarah always gave $100 in cash as a gift to a newborn great grandchild. (In 1959, $100 was a princely sum.) While talking to Isabelle on the telephone, Sarah said that Baby Eric's gift would be coming a little late. She said that she had paid a woman who was an excellent knitter to knit a sweater, booties, and a cap for the baby. They would be ready to be sent out at the beginning of the following week.

Isabelle believed that Sarah had commissioned the sweater, booties, and cap as Ricky's gift, because at that time she did not rank Baby Ricky as an equal great-grandchild to her others. Sarah's actual gift spoke legions of her altered opinion and complete understanding of Ricky's place in the family. Ricky was indeed one of Sarah's "Ten Fingers." The box that she sent contained a lovely, hand-knitted sweater, cap, and booties, the gift Sarah had originally commissioned. On the top of the knitwear was a money order for $100, the same princely sum she gave to each of her great-grandchildren at the time of his or her birth In a stranger's hand, Ricky's great-grandmother had written:

Welcome to our family, dear Great-Grandson. I look forward to meeting you.

With great love,
Your Great-Grandmother,
Sarah

In May, when Isabelle's beautiful baby boy was seven months old, Isabelle and Ricky flew to New York to properly introduce the baby to both of his parents' families. Eva prepared a buffet lunch and invited her brother, Abe, and his family, Max's daughter and her family, and Harold and Gert and their boy, Max. Everyone ate heartily and greatly admired the baby.

Out of nowhere, Zada suddenly said, "Isabelle, sing *Nechaditsy Gritzue.* Although she was embarrassed, Isabelle complied, singing the lively Russian folk song to her baby son. Suddenly Baby Ricky and Isabelle found themselves in the middle of a circle of clapping relatives, as Max's daughter and son-in-law, who were committed Zionists, sang a medley of Hebrew songs from the Zionist movement. Everyone was jolly as they welcomed little Ricky into his daddy's family.

Sunday was Mother's Day. It would be a different Mother's Day from the ones Sarah's family had celebrated at her home in the past. Because no one went to work on Christmas or Mother's Day, every year Sarah would cook a huge dinner on those holidays. Every one of her descendants and their spouses came to these dinners, and although Sarah was a terrible cook, there were a few dishes that she cooked to her family's delight. She knew how to roast turkeys, and she roasted two of them for the huge crowd that gathered in her small apartment. She also made gefilte fish that her children loved, but her grandchildren and in-laws detested. Isabelle and many of her descendants loved Sarah's *gedempte* (stewed), *potato latkes* (potato pancakes). Those who had married into the family often disliked their gray, slimy appearance so much, that they wouldn't even taste them. There were both fans and detractors of Sarah's *luckshun kugle* (noodle pudding), but best loved of all, according to Sarah's progeny, were her *kichalach* (small pastries) made with lots of cinnamon and sugar. Many of Sarah's in-laws disliked these too, but Sarah's descendants licked their chops as they devoured them.

In the past, Sarah had spent weeks preparing the food for the onslaught of her huge family. On the day of the dinner, each female head of a family served her immediate family. Cleanup was done by Bella and Fanny.

But this Mother's Day many things would be different. The *Vashishter*

Clan would once again gather at Sarah's small apartment, but they would not feast on Sarah's cooking. Instead, they would eat cold cuts and salads brought in by Irving and Sol from a local kosher delicatessen. The neighborhood Jewish bakery would supply the many desserts brought in by Anna, Fanny, and Bella. They would bring in bread for sandwiches from the bakery, too. Everything would be eaten on paper plates with plastic cutlery, and as usual, Fanny and Bella would clean up.

There was no table upon which to eat. Everybody ate in the chairs that ringed the room. Sarah sat in her wheelchair, which she announced she would be abandoning for a walker during the coming week. She told them how her visiting therapist was helping her to regain her prowess and once again be self-sufficient. She could already dress, feed, and wash herself without help. Soon she would be walking with a walker, and would be able to discard the hated wheelchair.

Sarah's wonderful progress would have been enough to make her family very happy, but the visit of Isabelle and her baby from Ohio, made this Mother's Day very special indeed. Everyone knew that Isabelle and Baby Ricky had flown into New York two days before, and everyone was eagerly awaiting Baby Ricky's arrival.

Isabelle and her baby arrived to hearty greetings. The baby was taken from her arms and began a trip around the room, being held, cooed to, and then passed to the next relative. One would think that the extremely beautiful seven-month-old baby would balk at being taken from his mother's arms and handled by so many strangers. Not so with Ricky! He either thoughtfully studied the person holding him, or he smiled. If someone jiggled or tickled him, he laughed out loud.

Half way around the room, he was placed in Sarah's arms. She laid the baby on her broad lap and slowly unbuttoned his sweater. Then she removed his matching cap, and lifted his shirt and undershirt, whereupon she gazed intently at the baby's bare chest. She stroked his reddish blond hair and his fat dimpled cheeks. She held his fat little hand in hers and then removed his shoes and gazed at his toes. Throughout her examination, Ricky stared up into his great-grandmother's face with great concentration. Everyone in the crowded room remained silent.

When Sarah had finished her examination of the baby, she kissed his forehead and in Yiddish announced to the whole room, *"Er ist a katsop!"* (He is a *katsop*!)

"What is *katsop*? asked Isabelle.

"A *katsop* is a sturdy Russian farmer," explained Bella. "Bubbie means that Ricky is strong and beautiful.

Hearing Bella's explanation, Sarah interjected, "Very beautiful! My great grandson is very beautiful, indeed!"

In July of 1960, Isabelle made another trip to New York. Ricky could crawl and stand and he could walk while holding on to furniture along his way. He understood everything said to him and called Isabelle "Ma Ma" and Al "Da Da." He was trying very hard to speak, and his understanding of what was being said to him indicated to everyone that he was clearly a very intelligent child.

On that summer visit, Isabelle decided to visit Sarah in Coney Island. Bella, Phyllis, Ricky and she drove to Coney Island in the car Isabelle had rented. To Sarah's complete delight, they got there in the late morning. Much to Isabelle's delight, her beloved grandmother was walking once again, albeit walking very slowly. Sarah directed them to carry her beach gear and set it up on the beach. Sarah walked to the beach very slowly, accompanying Isabelle who pushed Ricky's stroller.

At the beach, Phyllis and Isabelle set up the very faded, old blue umbrella with the white stripe. Like its owner, the umbrella had faded with age, but it still opened and closed and shielded them from the sun. Like Sarah, the umbrella was still viable. Isabelle set up an army cot under the umbrella for Sarah to lie upon. Ricky's stroller was set right beside the cot, but the baby was put on a nearby blanket to play with Bella and Phyllis.

After an early lunch and lots of supervised play in the sand, Isabelle took Ricky to the ocean. When he touched a wave that came up to the shore, Isabelle told him that the wave was water. She pointed to the whole broad expanse of very green ocean and told the baby that it was the ocean and that the ocean was made of water.

Isabelle then slowly walked into the calm ocean, carrying Ricky and gently splashing water on him as she walked. When she was in as deep as her abdomen, she began to bob up and down with the baby in her arms. Ricky was euphoric! He giggled, laughed, and shrieked with joy. Suddenly he became quiet, looked into his mother's eyes, and shouted "Wa wa, Ma Ma, wa wa." It was the first time Ricky had strung together words.

When Isabelle returned to the faded blue umbrella with the white stripe and began to dry her baby, Sarah pounced on her. "You're careless and foolhardy. God has given you an incredibly beautiful son, and you carelessly take him into the ocean. He's much too young for that. It will be a miracle if my great-grandson survives your light-headedness," she said angrily.

Isabelle didn't take Ricky into the water again that day. She didn't want to upset the still recovering Sarah. The tongue-lashing Sarah had delivered to her beloved granddaughter certainly showed everyone that Sarah had turned into a complete proponent of adoption.

Chapter 28: Stay-at-Home Mom

When Isabelle returned to her home in Cincinnati, she returned to her life as a stay-at-home mom. She loved being with Ricky and filling her life with volunteer work, her friends, and her totally absorbing, deeply loved, baby boy.

Isabelle had joined B'nai B'rith, a Jewish philanthropic organization to which many of the Jewish women living in her area of Cincinnati belonged. At B'nai B'rith she met many young women with whom she felt she could develop friendships. Chief among them were Joan and Rocky. Joan had a baby boy who was a few months older than Ricky. Isabelle and Joan's affinity was based mostly on their babies, but they did many things together and became good friends.

Rocky lived in Glencoe, just four blocks away from Isabelle. Her husband, Norm, worked at Shillito's, as did Al and an unmarried man named Jim. The three men formed a car pool, freeing their cars for their wives' use, or in Jim's case for his mother's use. Rocky and Isabelle liked each other very much and agreed, if possible, to be available for each other when either of their husbands drove the Shillito's carpool. This provided peace of mind for both of the young women. Each of them felt the security of having an automobile at their disposal at all times.

Even though Rocky, who grew up in Cincinnati, had many friends and relatives in the city, her proximity to Isabelle, their sharing of cars, the young women's fondness for each other, and Rocky's immense attachment to Isabelle's baby, all contributed to the building of a relationship between the two women that was blossoming into a very strong and enduring friendship.

One evening, at a B'nai B'rith meeting, a young woman approached Isabelle and said, "Isabelle, do you remember me? I'm Elaine Paulson. We were sorority sisters at Hunter College."

"Of course!" replied an astounded Isabelle. "Do you live around here? What a surprise!"

"I do," said Elaine. "My husband works for Federated Department Stores, and I have three little girls. I certainly never expected to meet you here….and let me tell you….you look great….just as you did in college. I had heard that you looked awful, and that you behaved badly too!" said Elaine.

"Oh my God!" exclaimed Isabelle. "I know just where you got that report. You lived in Brooklyn, didn't you?" queried Isabelle.

"Yes," said Elaine.

"Laura Kalin lived in Brooklyn too. You must have been in touch with her," stated Isabelle.

"Yes," said Elaine. "She's the one who told me the story of how awful you looked."

Isabelle laughingly told Elaine why Laura had told her that story. "My husband and I were with my friend Annabelle and her husband on a trip to French Canada. When we were in a small Canadian border town, I bought some cigarettes out of a vending machine that sold both Canadian and American brands. I, therefore, knew the Canadian vending machine's price for both American and Canadian cigarettes. Cigarettes are always more expensive when purchased from a vending machine than when purchased from a clerk in a store, so I was vaguely aware of what I'd have to pay for them in a store."

"On our first morning in Montreal, I went to breakfast with my husband, wearing clean, white pedal pushers and a clean red shirt, but my hair was unset and I wasn't wearing any makeup. Breakfast was very uninspiring, so I ate lightly and then left the restaurant to begin our exploration of Montreal. Almost immediately, we came upon a pushcart peddler selling the most beautiful fruit I have ever seen. My mouth watered for one of the peddler's gigantic peaches, so I bought one. I bit into the ripe and juicy piece of fruit and peach juice squirted all over the place, badly staining my peddler pushers and my shirt. In short, I really looked a mess!"

"We walked several more blocks, when the appearance of the city made a sudden change. We found ourselves in a busy, cosmopolitan, downtown area of Montreal. It was a commercial area with very tall buildings, into which poured crowds of well dressed, rushing people. It was 8:45 A.M. and the hurrying, well-dressed crowds were going to work. I felt ill at ease wearing my dirty, inappropriate pedal pushers, in the midst of these well dressed, sharp looking crowds, but I assuaged my feelings of discomfort by assuring myself that I couldn't possibly run into anyone I knew while my appearance was so disheveled."

"I went into a Rexall Drug Store that was teaming with people. I wanted to try a pack of Canadian cigarettes, so I waited my turn in the line at the counter and when I reached the clerk, I asked her to tell me the name of the most popular brand of Canadian cigarettes. She answered my question in heavily French accented English. I told her that I'd like to buy a pack, and she proceeded to ask me for an outrageous sum of money for the cigarettes. Remembering the prices I had seen in the vending machine the day before, I angrily demanded, "What would the price of the cigarettes be if I weren't an American?"

"The French-Canadian clerk began to scream at me in French. I left the cigarettes and turned to leave the store, when whom should I see observing the whole ugly commotion, but Laura Kalin! Laura looked beautiful. She was on her honeymoon and she introduced me to her new husband. I could see that she was embarrassed to do so."

"Annabelle, our husbands, and I laughed at my being caught in so embarrassing a situation. It never occurred to me that Laura would be telling the world that I had lost my mind," Isabelle chuckled. Elaine chuckled too.

Almost immediately, a close friendship grew between Isabelle and

Elaine. Both young women particularly relished the fact that they were linked to each other from college and home, but unfortunately, the connection to school and home was not enjoyed for very long, because tragedy hit Elaine's family and hit it very hard....

It all began when Elaine's husband Ira lost his job. He immediately began to search for work in the New York area. His job searches produced a number of appointments for interviews in places in or near where Elaine wanted to relocate; and Elaine really wanted to go home.

During one of Ira's trips, Isabelle was in her house. She was reading while her baby son was napping. The loud jangling of the phone startled her out of her book, and she was alarmed even more when she heard Elaine's frantic voice at the other end of the line saying, "I was just showering and I think I felt a lump in my breast. I'm not sure, so I need someone else to feel it to see if it is really a lump. Isabelle, can you come over right away? I'm petrified! I need someone else's opinion."

Isabelle answered, "Ricky is napping, but I'll wake him up and we'll be right over." She then woke the sleeping baby, who good-naturedly smiled at his mommy and played with her for a short time. Then he was whisked into the car, and mother and little son rode over to Elaine's house.

They found Elaine in a great state of anxiety. Isabelle was unable to allay her friend's fears, for when she felt Elaine's breast, she too, felt a lump there.

That was the beginning.... then followed the trip to several doctors.... and finally, Harold's performance of a mastectomy to remove Elaine's cancerous breast. Elaine and Ira were now faced with both his unemployment and her serious health problem.

After Elaine's operation, it was deemed necessary that she receive radiation treatments over an eight-week period. Isabelle offered her assistance during this period fraught with so much worry for her friend. She offered to be available to drive Elaine to and from her treatments when chauffeuring was needed. Because Ira was often out of town, on several such occasions, Isabelle found herself driving Elaine to and from her radiation treatments. During these times, Isabelle frequently had to refuse Joan's invitations for play dates or dates for the mommies to do things together. Much to Isabelle's surprise, Joan was petulant about Isabelle's inability to join her at the times when Isabelle was busy taking Elaine to the hospital for her treatments. Joan's selfishness and lack of understanding annoyed Isabelle, and their friendship cooled.

Ira eventually found employment in New York and Elaine and her family moved back home. Isabelle sorely missed Elaine, and even more, she missed having a friend who shared some of her life experiences in New York.

————

Al was in New York on one of his routine business trips. On the first morning that his daddy was gone, Ricky awakened, but he didn't call his mommy. When Isabelle checked Ricky's room, wondering why she had not heard the baby's call, she found that his face was very flushed and hot. But more worrisome than his fever, was Ricky's extremely labored breathing. Isabelle set up a vaporizer to help the baby's breathing, and then called his pediatrician.

The doctor told Isabelle to bring the baby right in. When he examined Ricky, the doctor told Isabelle that the baby had croup. He emphasized the gravity of the baby's illness, told Isabelle to watch him closely, and if she observed what seemed to be difficulty in the baby's breathing, to sit in a steamed-up bathroom. This was to be done by running the hot water in the bathtub and in the sink. Isabelle was to sit in the steaming bathroom with Ricky until he was breathing more easily.

Aside from the great amounts of time Isabelle spent in the steaming bathroom with her sick little boy, she spent the remainder of that day and that night in the rocker in Ricky's room. She never shut her eyes for fear that the baby would start choking once again.

In the morning, Rocky called. Isabelle told her about Ricky's croup, and within a few minutes Rocky was at her door. She offered to sit in the rocker watching Ricky, so that Isabelle could get some sleep. Isabelle gratefully declined her friend's offer, because she feared to leave her ailing baby with anyone. Isabelle preferred to keep a personal vigil.

When Al called from New York, Isabelle asked him to come home. He said that he would catch a plane that evening.

Al arrived at home at 11:00 P.M. Isabelle had maintained her vigil from 7:00 A.M. the previous day. She had stayed awake for forty hours.

When she saw Al, Isabelle quickly instructed him about what he must do, and told him to awaken her if he had the slightest doubt of his ability to carry out her instructions. She told him that Ricky seemed better, but she still wanted Al to give the sleeping baby his undivided attention. She then left Al sitting in the rocker she had vacated, and she tumbled into her bed.

When she awoke, Isabelle immediately went into Ricky's room. At 6:00 A.M. the baby was sleeping blissfully. His chubby cheeks were pink, no longer red. Best of all, he was breathing normally. Isabelle sent his tired father to bed, marveling at how she trusted Al so completely that she was able to go to sleep and leave him with her sick baby. Her mind told her that she could have trusted her dear friend Rocky in the same way, but her heart only allowed Ricky's parents to care for him, when his mortality was in question.

After Ricky's bout with croup, Rocky was almost a daily visitor at Isabelle's house. She would come in the door and immediately call out, "Where's my boy?" Ricky would run to her and jump into her arms shouting, "Here your boy!" After chatting and playing with Ricky, Isabelle, Rocky, and Ricky usually went to a restaurant for lunch. One of their favorite restaurants was Carters, where Ricky always shouted, "See, see the kitchen!" His mother and Aunt Rocky were bemused by the baby's excited shouts. The restaurant's kitchen was not visible to the baby, making his excited shouts a puzzle to the two women.

One day at Carters, Rocky told Isabelle about her infertility woes. Getting pregnant would be difficult, but not impossible for her. She had had an ectopic pregnancy, which almost cost her, her life, but she and Norm still hoped for another pregnancy....this time a healthy one.

Isabelle saw Rocky's poignant yearning for a baby every time her friend played with Ricky. One day she said, "Why don't you and Norm adopt a child? If you get pregnant, you'll have two children. I see how you love my little boy. You need a child of your own, and trust me, an adopted child is your own child."

As if on cue, twelve-month old Ricky put an end to their serious discussion. He interrupted the two women's conversation with his familiar cry of "Kitchen! Kitchen!" But this time the baby pointed and cried out, "Kitchen on wall!" Isabelle abruptly understood. Painted plastic plaques molded into the shapes of large roosters were mounted, as decoration, on one of the restaurant's walls. Because Ricky was unable to say *chicken*, he was calling a plastic, decorative rooster *a kitchen*.

"Yes, Ricky," said a smiling Isabelle. "On the wall there are chickens."

A few weeks later, Rocky told Isabelle that she had heeded her advice. She and Norm had discussed the advisability of their looking into adoption, and had decided to do so. They were in the process of being studied at Jewish Family Service, the beginning of their journey into adopting a child.

After Ricky's first birthday, he had begun to speak more and more fluently. By fourteen months, he not only strung words together, but he was having simple conversations with his mother, asking about and sharing his baby observations of many of the things in his environment. Around this time, it was Isabelle's practice to keep current magazines in a pile on a slat bench located under her bookshelves in the living-room. Ricky often was drawn to pictures on the magazines' covers, and when he was fourteen months old, he spied a *Life Magazine* at the top of the pile of magazines collecting on the bench. He brought the large magazine to his mother saying, "Mommy, see dutty man and funny hat." The "dutty man" Ricky referred to was a very dark-skinned African tribesman, dressed in full dancing regalia. The man wore an enormous headdress consisting of many brightly colored feathers.

Isabelle explained, "The man is not dirty, Ricky. His skin is very dark. That is the color of his skin." Then, pointing to the baby's arm, she said, "See, your skin is lighter. This is the color of your skin."

"Ricky clean! Man dutty!" said the baby dropping the magazine on the floor and walking away.

That Saturday, Isabelle, Al, and Ricky had their dinner in a neighborhood restaurant. The African American waitress who waited on their table, played with the baby each time she came by. As the waitress was pouring water, Ricky touched her very dark arm and said, "You dutty!" His parents gasped in horror, but the wonderfully understanding waitress said, "No Honey, I ain't dirty. I'm black. My skin is black." And pointing to the black table she said, "See, the table is black too."

Ricky grinned at her and said, "Black table, black mommy. Not dutty mommy." (At this time in Ricky's development, he referred to all women as *mommies*.)

Al and Isabelle marveled at the intelligence shown by the waitress in the manner in which she had instructed the baby. They also considered their son to be very intelligent in the way he learned and understood the color *black*.

————

Eva and Max were coming to Cincinnati for a visit. It was early December, 1960, and Ricky, who was just fourteen months old, was all excited about their visit. Isabelle put Ricky in the back seat of the car, where he played on the seat and on the floor with some small cars and trucks. Isabelle listened to the car radio and chatted with her baby as they traveled down Hamilton Avenue on their long trip to the airport. Suddenly, at a very busy corner, a car sped out of a side street, causing the car in front of Isabelle to come to a screeching, sudden halt. Isabelle slammed on her brakes, missing the car in front of her by a hair. Little Ricky came flying from the back seat, through the separation between the two front seats, and hit his right eye on the open ashtray jutting out of the car's dashboard. The baby hit the ashtray hard, and began to scream at the top of his lungs.

Isabelle abandoned her car in the middle of the heavily trafficked street, and with her screaming baby in her arms, ran into a drugstore that happened to be on that corner. She walked very rapidly to the pharmacy area in the back of the store, walked to the place on a back wall that housed a sink, dampened some paper towels sitting on a ledge, and gently wiped away the blood in the area of Ricky's eye. To her immense relief, she saw that the eye was intact. The blood was coming from a wound on the baby's eyelid.

Isabelle immediately came to the realization that the eyelid would require some stitches. She called her good friend Harold, and arranged to meet him at Jewish Hospital, where he could assess the seriousness of the wound, and treat it. She then called Al and told him to pick Eva and Max up at the airport. She explained the situation and told him she would see them all at home.

After thanking the pharmacist for the use of the pharmacy's facilities and telephone that she had used without thought or permission, Isabelle returned to her abandoned car and drove to Jewish Hospital, where she met Harold, as arranged. He looked at Ricky's eyelid and said that the baby was in need of several stitches.

Getting the eyelid stitched was a harrowing experience for both the baby and his mother. Harold had Ricky wrapped tightly in a blanket so that he would be unable to move during the stitching or anesthetizing of the eyelid. Becoming immobilized greatly frightened the child, and he screamed as loudly as his young vocal cords would allow him. Harold ordered Isabelle to the outside hallway saying, "It's best for mothers not to be present when their small children are being stitched. Mothers have been known to faint when they are in the immediate vicinity of their child's treatment."

Standing in the hall, hearing Ricky's screams, tormented Isabelle. When the stitching was finally completed, and her baby freed from the paralyzing blanket, Isabelle took him in her arms, kissed him and said, "Let's go eat our lunch where Santa Claus is." She thanked Harold, and she and the baby headed for the *Big Boy* restaurant in which Isabelle knew they had a Santa Claus roaming around for their small guests. Lunch was great fun. Santa Claus gave Ricky a small toy bus to add to his fleet of motor vehicles. He then stayed close to Isabelle and Ricky's table, talking to the delighted, recently injured baby throughout most of their lunch. Ricky was extremely happy, and in Isabelle's solicitude for her injured little boy, she totally forgot that Al and his parents were waiting for them at home, and probably worried out of their minds. When lunch was finished, the thoughtless Isabelle and her very happy baby headed for home. Upon their arrival, a tight-lipped Eva informed Isabelle that she had caused them great worry and needless concern. A very contrite Isabelle thought, "What a great way for a visit to begin!"

To compound the less than ideal atmosphere, on the second day of the visit, normally delightfully behaved Ricky was totally out of sorts. His favorite word was "No!" He refused to eat, put away his toys, or obey his mother or his grandparents. Exasperated, Eva threatened, "If you don't start listening and doing what you're told to do, I'll tell your daddy to come home with me. Your daddy is my little boy, and I can take him home with me."

Ricky glared at his grandmother and replied, "You not take my daddy home! You go home! You not stay here!" The angry little boy did not speak to his grandmother for the rest of the day.

While Ricky napped, a distraught Eva asked Isabelle how she could return to her grandson's good graces. Isabelle suggested that she take the little boy to a hardware store and buy him a new flashlight. "Ricky's favorite thing in the whole world is a flashlight," she said.

When Ricky awoke they drove to the nearest hardware store, where Eva bought the little boy a wonderful flashlight that could blink as well as give steady light. In addition, the marvelous flashlight shone in three separate colors…yellow, red, and green. Ricky was in paradise! He had never received a toy he liked better than his wondrous flashlight, and he played with it for the rest of the day. His flashlight lay beside his plate while he ate dinner, and followed him to the bathroom while his mother gave him his bath. As he was dressing in his pajamas, the marvelous flashlight blinked its green light at him. Then the wonderful flashlight was placed inside Ricky's crib when he went to sleep. No toy ever seemed to please the little boy as much as the flashlight his grandmother had given him.

Around midnight, while everyone in the house should have been asleep, Isabelle was wrenched out of her dream by the sound of a loud laugh. When she opened her bedroom door, a red beam of light flashed against the ceiling of the hallway outside her mother-in-law's room. Again, she heard the laughter, but this time, Ricky's laughter had joined the adult laughter. When Isabelle entered her in-law's room, she saw her mother-in-law sitting up in her bed. Ricky was sitting between her and a sleeping Max. The baby was shining light on his grandmother's ceiling, and it made them both laugh. Throughout all of this fun, Grandpa Max slept.

Eva explained, "Ricky climbed out of his crib and came looking for me. He wanted me to play with him and the flashlight. I guess he's no longer mad at me." She kissed the baby and handed him to his mother.

The rest of Al's family's visit was lovely. All of the adults and Baby Ricky enjoyed one another. When Eva and Max were taken to the airport, both of them seemed to be sad to be leaving their Cincinnati family.

_____

Isabelle, Al and Ricky did not leave the airport for two more hours. They ate their lunch at an airport restaurant and then spent time watching the airplanes taking off and landing. They were waiting for the arrival of the next plane arriving from New York, which would he bringing Ricky's other grandmother for a one-week visit.

Bella's plane arrived on time. She and Ricky seemed delighted to be in each other's company. Ricky promptly told her about his day. "Ga-Ma," he said, "we see yats of pwayns. Pwayns zoom up in the sky and pwayns bump down on the gwound." In the car, grandmother and grandson entertained each other until Ricky fell asleep.

_____

Whenever Bella visited Cincinnati, she was seen professionally by Harold. Since her first visit, when Harold had questioned her about her misshapen leg, he continued to examine the leg and checked the ulcer activity on it. On that very first visit, he had prescribed Neosporin, a new antibiotic ointment. In Bella's many visits to clinics in New York hospitals, she had always been told to apply Vaseline to her ulcers. Harold's prescription of Neosporin had produced wonders. While Neosporin didn't close all of her ulcers, it closed the two smaller ones and greatly reduced the size of the bigger one. Bella considered Harold to be a genius, and the new drug Neosporin to be a wonder drug. She planned to see Harold at his office to show him her excellent progress.

On the day after Bella's arrival, Ricky had an appointment at Harold's office to have the stitches on his eyelid removed. It was arranged that Harold would examine Bella's leg at that time too. As grandmother and grandson sat in Harold's outer office, little Ricky turned to his grandmother with big, round, frightened eyes, and said, "Ga-Ma, I faid! You faid?"

Ever-wise Bella understood that little Ricky knew that she too, was a patient waiting to see Harold. She marveled at the baby's perceptiveness and understanding and said, "Yes Ricky, I am afraid, but I really shouldn't be. Uncle Harold will make us both better. When he scared you, it was only to make your eye all better. He didn't want to scare you, but he couldn't help it."

Bella's wise words were turned over in the baby's head. "Uncca Harold scare Ricky. Now Ricky faid!"

At just that time, Ricky was called into the office. After a hug and a hearty welcome from Harold, Ricky was put up on the examining table. Harold came at the frightened baby with his medical instrument, and in the span of a blink of an eye, the job was done. "Well Ricky, the stitches are all out," said Harold. "Now I'll see your grandma."

Ricky ran to his grandma, where she still sat in the outer office. He excitedly said to her, "Ga-Ma, not be faid. Uncca Harold not hurt Ricky and he not hurt Ga-Ma too." Everyone laughed with pleasure, at the bright little fourteen-month old boy's fractured English.

———

When Ricky was eighteen months old, Isabelle needed to do some shopping at Shillito's, and she took the baby with her. They were in the store's book department, when Ricky saw two nuns. Ricky still referred to all adult women as mommies, but the nuns in their flowing black and white habits were a mystery to him. "Mommy," he said, pointing his pudgy little finger at the nuns, "What's that?"

"Those are ladies," Isabelle answered.

A month later, when Isabelle was in a supermarket with Ricky, they were discussing the cashier's role. Isabelle said, "The cashier is the lady to whom Mommy gives money to pay for the groceries she buys."

"She not yadey," said Ricky. "No Yadey in store."

Isabelle didn't know what her baby meant until the following week, when they were driving along the street on which two nuns were walking. Ricky, all excited, pointed at the nuns and shouted, "Yadies, Mommy…. Yadies….See Yadies!"

Laughing, Isabelle said, "Those ladies are *nuns*. We call them *nuns*."

––––––––––

One afternoon there was a knock on Isabelle's kitchen door. When Isabelle opened the door, Rocky besotted with acne, said, "I'm getting a baby boy! I'll see him on Monday. As she spoke, more pimples sprouted on her excited and happy face. To say that this was a happy and thrilling time for Isabelle's dear friend would be a gross understatement and Isabelle knew that her first priority was to properly prepare Ricky for his Aunt Rocky's big event. Ricky was very attached to his Aunt Rocky, who came into his house several times a week calling, "Where's my boy? Where's my boy?" How would Ricky respond to a new baby that his Aunt Rocky would refer to as *her boy.*

While Isabelle was bathing Ricky, on the day on which Rocky's baby was brought to live with Rocky and Norm, Isabelle said to her little son, "Sweetheart, something very wonderful happened today. Aunt Rocky has gotten a baby boy of her very own."

"She not need a boy," said the wet eighteen-month old baby. "I her boy!"

"No, Sweetheart," said Isabelle, "You are my boy, my very own boy that I love so much."

"No Mommy," said Ricky. "I your boy *and* I Aunt Rocky's boy, *too.* Aunt Rocky say that!"

"Oh Sweetheart, Aunt Rocky loves you, but she needs a little boy who is her very own boy, just like you are my very own boy."

Ricky began to whimper, "I her boy! I her boy!" Isabelle knew that they had a problem on their hands.

––––––––––

A week after Baby Jeff came to live in his new home, the big day came. Isabelle was going to Aunt Rocky's house with Ricky to introduce him to the new baby. For almost two weeks leading up to this event, Isabelle had been preparing Ricky. Now they would see his actual reaction to Rocky's baby son.

When they arrived at Rocky's house, she greeted Ricky warmly, and talked to him for a while. She told him that she had a baby boy named Jeff, and that when Jeff grew up to be a little bigger; he and Ricky would play together. She said that Baby Jeff had just gone to sleep, but when he awoke Ricky could see him.

Isabelle had brought some of Ricky's favorite toys. Therefore, while Isabelle and Rocky sat at the table drinking coffee and chatting, little Ricky sat on the floor playing with his toys.

Suddenly Isabelle turned around and worriedly said, "Where's Ricky? He was here just a minute ago!"

Both women rushed into the new baby's room. Standing at Baby Jeff's crib, with an angry look on his face, was nineteen-month old Ricky. "Him not a nice baby," said Ricky. "Aunt Rocky need a nice boy. Ricky a nice boy!"

Rocky picked Ricky up. She looked straight into his little face and said, "You are a nice boy! You are the nicest *big* boy in the whole world! Aunt Rocky loves you so much that she got herself a *little* boy who will grow up to be just as nice as you are."

"Your mommy is very lucky. You are her very own wonderful big boy. And now, I'm lucky too. Jeff is my very own little boy, who will grow up to be a wonderful big boy just like you!"

Isabelle said, "Aunt Rocky will always love you, Sweetheart. But you will always be my very own boy to love. I'll always love Baby Jeff, but he will always be Aunt Rocky's very own boy to love."

———————

Isabelle elected to do volunteer work at Rollman's Mental Hospital. B'nai B'rith made a monthly party for the teenaged patients at Rollman's. Three women from B'nai B'rith brought and laid out the refreshments for the teenagers and then circulated among them and chatted with them during their party. The teenaged partygoers were patients that the professional staff deemed healthy enough to participate in co-ed parties. Ordinarily, the boys and girls were kept separated. It was only at a few functions per month that the boys and girls fraternized, and this was one of them.

As Isabelle circulated amongst the youngsters in the mental hospital's canteen, she spied a very handsome boy, approximately fifteen years old, leaning against a wall in a booth. He was sitting all alone, and he seemed to be crying.

Isabelle slipped into his booth, and with the handsome teenager sitting opposite her, gently asked, "Can I help you?"

"No one can help me," whispered the handsome boy. "I've been destroyed by an operation those doctors gave me."

The boy in the booth, speaking with a very strong southern accent, was clearly in acute distress. Isabelle said, "Please tell me about the operation. Sometimes talking about things helps."

In a faltering voice, the boy said, "I can't remember the name of the operation. They did it two days ago. They cut my wiener and now I'll never be able to be a man!"

Do you mean you were circumcised?" asked Isabelle.

"Yes," replied the boy. "That's it!"

"Being circumcised does not take away your manhood," said Isabelle. "Many men and boys are circumcised. In my religion all males are circumcised when they are babies. My husband and son are circumcised. Because you are not a baby, your circumcision was probably done for reasons of health. In fact, today, most baby boys are circumcised for reasons of health. Circumcision never interferes with the workings of a male's penis."

A broad smile covered the handsome teenager's face. He was completely relieved. He thanked Isabelle profusely for telling him the good news. Isabelle suggested that he join some of the other boys and girls and have a good time. Once again, the boy thanked her, and then went over to a small group of teenagers standing around a juke box.

Isabelle wondered at the insensitivity of the doctors who had treated the boy. He obviously needed mental help if he was a patient at Rollman's, and keeping him ignorant of the results of an operation on his genitals, certainly couldn't help his mental or emotional state.

Chapter 29: On and On

A jangling telephone awakened Isabelle and Al at 4 A.M. Isabelle, in great fear of what the call was about, asked Al to answer the telephone. He did so, and Isabelle could tell by the expression on his face that he was not hearing good news. Sorrowfully, Al handed the telephone to his wife.

Bella was on the phone. When she heard her daughter's voice she said, "Bubbie died at 1 A.M. this morning. Don't make a sound until you hear what I have to say. Bubbie always talked about being eighty-four years old, and having lived a very long life. She did live a very long life and was strong for all of us. I know that you want to cry, but cry only a little. Bubbie would want all of us to be strong!"

Bella sobbed a little, and then continued. "Bubbie will probably be buried later today, because it's Friday, and there can be no funerals on Friday evening or on Saturday, because it is the Sabbath. I'll find out the exact time of the funeral and call you. In the meantime, call Eva when you know your flight time, and ask her to make arrangements for picking you up. Call me with your arrival time, and I'll call Eva with the time and place of the funeral."

"Goodbye *Tochter* (Daughter). Be strong."

"Bye Mama." Isabelle hung up the phone and wept for her terrible loss. While she was crying, Al was on the telephone making the earliest reservations he could get for her and Ricky.

481

Isabelle collected herself, and then called her mother-in-law. Eva took down the flight information and assured Isabelle that she would be at the airport to get her. She said that Isabelle would be driven to either the funeral parlor or the cemetery, depending upon the time of the events. Eva said that she would tend to little Ricky.

Isabelle packed and dressed quickly. She was unable to eat breakfast and was relieved when Ricky awoke a little past 6:00 A.M. She dressed him, fed him his breakfast, and told him that he was going to New York on a big airplane. She said that when he got there he would see his grandmas, grandpas, and aunts and uncles. She told him that he would have lots of fun in New York.

Their flight left Cincinnati on a beautiful, sunny day, just after 10:30 A.M. They were scheduled to land at LaGuardia Airport at about noon. Bella had told Isabelle and Eva that Sarah would be interred at a cemetery quite close to the airport at about 1:30 P.M., approximately twelve hours after her death had occured.

Sarah would have approved of the manner in which her burial was being carried out. Because *Shabbat* (the Sabbath) started that evening, her funeral occurred even more rapidly than the funerals of most observant Jews.

Sarah would also have approved of the manner in which she had died. Thursday night had been Selicot. Selicot occurred one week prior to Rosh Hashana, the Jewish New Year. Selicot marked the beginning of introspection and evaluation of one's deeds during the preceding year. Rosh Hashana and Yom Kippur, called the High Holy- days are spent in prayer, introspection, penance, and promises of rectifying sins committed against other people. Selicot turns the worshipper's attention to the themes of repentance, forgiveness, and spiritual renewal. Jews leave the Selicot service at around midnight, feeling, as they head to their beds, that they have taken the first steps toward bringing them closer to God.

On Sarah's last night on earth, she attended Selicot services at the synagogue in which the *Torah* she had commissioned resided. Having renounced her sins and having fervently prayed for forgiveness, she walked back to her home through Coney Island's dark streets, arriving at home after midnight. She immediately took a very hot bath, hoping that the heat would remove some of the ache of her rheumatism. She left the tub, dried herself, donned her nightgown, and headed for her bedroom; but she never made it through the bedroom door.

Sarah's non-observant husband was awakened by the thud of Sarah's body hitting the floor of the hallway. He hurried to where she lay crumpled in a heap, and tried to revive her. When he realized that his efforts were in vain, he called Anna, Sarah's eldest child, who was the child who lived nearest to Coney Island. Sorrowfully, he told her that Sarah had died.

———

Little Ricky was a very good boy on the flight to New York. He entertained his grieving young mother with constant chatter and questions. It was as if the almost two- year old little boy understood that his mother needed distraction.

After what seemed like a very quick, uneventful flight, the pilot's voice came over the intercom, saying "Ladies and Gentlemen, we are only fifteen minutes away from LaGuardia Airport, but it seems that most of the east coast is socked in by a soupy fog that has completely destroyed visibility. Don't be fooled by the beautiful blue skies you are seeing. We are flying above pea soup! There is no way that any aircraft can land in New York until the fog clears."

"Our plane has lots of fuel. We will circle around New York for what should be enough time for the fog to lift. If the fog doesn't clear in enough time for our fuel to keep us circling above it, I'll fly the aircraft to Philadelphia. Visibility is good there."

As the plane began a series of interminable circles around the New York area, Isabelle really began to believe that she would be forced to miss her grandmother's funeral. At 12:45 P.M. the pilot, once again, came over the intercom. This time, he didn't inform them that they were starting another circle around New York. This time, he happily told the stressed passengers that the control tower had cleared them for landing. Because of the large number of aircraft needing to land, their plane would be allowed to land at 1:00 P.M.

Isabelle was sure that she would be too late for Sarah's funeral. Eva, greatly relieved that they had landed safely, greeted her, and picked up little Ricky, to give him a kiss. Eva expressed her condolences, and told Isabelle how wild with worry she had been while the airplane was circling above the dense fog. All of this conversation occurred while Eva and Isabelle ran to the baggage claim area. Isabelle did not have her luggage, nor did she meet Al's brother Harold at the car until 1:45 P.M. They then rushed through the heavy New York traffic to get to the cemetery, hopefully on time for the burial. Isabelle thanked Eva and Harold for coming to get them at the airport, and expressed her wonder at Harold's being able to take time off from work. Harold assured her that his office was very family-friendly, and allowed him to go without any difficulty, whatsoever.

After getting lost in the huge cemetery, they finally came to Sarah's grave. As Isabelle had feared, the graveside service had already been conducted, and all of the mourners had left. Two gravediggers were shoveling dirt from a nearby mound of earth onto the fresh grave. They notified Isabelle that everyone from the funeral had left only a few minutes before.

As Isabelle stood on the grass alongside her beloved grandmother's grave, she thought, "There is a purpose in my missing Bubbie's funeral. I was not meant to see her dead. For me she will always be alive, and all my memories of her will be living memories. For me she will never really die. I shall think of her zest for life, her generosity, her piety, her strength, and her love as she enveloped all of her "*Ten Fingers*." I shall remember *her*, not remember her eulogy. I'll remember the vibrant life that touched me with an endless love."

After her musings at the graveside, Isabelle returned to the car. She kissed her baby and then began to chat with Eva and Harold. Her uplifting thoughts had brought her relief form heavy mourning. She would continue her life as Sarah would have wanted her to and would always think of her grandmother as a force that would continue to help her throughout her life.

When Isabelle returned to Cincinnati, after her four-week stay in New York, she called Rocky. After expressing her condolences, Rocky began to fill Isabelle in on events in B'nai B'rith and about the antics of her four-month old son, Jeff. Isabelle told Rocky about events in New York, and just as the two women were going to terminate their conversation, Rocky said, "By the way, one of my friends who happens to know Miss Greenstein, saw her when she and her little girl were at the pediatrician's office. Miss Greenstein was there with a fat, middle-aged woman who was holding a very new infant. She told my friend that the baby boy she was holding was born in early September. My friend said the baby was adorable. I'll bet that little boy is up for adoption," said Rocky.

"You're probably right," said Isabelle. "Let's get together soon. Call me."

"Bye," said Rocky. "I'll call you."

Isabelle digested Rocky's information for a few minutes then lost no time setting up a plan. She called Jewish Family Service, and asked to speak to Miss Greenstein. When Miss Greenstein got on the phone, Isabelle said, "I've just returned from a visit to New York. Ricky wowed all of his New York relatives, several of whom asked me when I planned to apply for a brother or sister for him. I thought this was a good time to do so, so I'm calling you to see if we can start setting things up for a second baby."

"I'm surprised that you called today," said Miss Greenstein. "You were not supposed to call until Ricky's adoption is finalized in December of this year. This is October, so you really are calling too early; but I find myself with some spare time, so we can actually begin now. Would you like to come in at the end of this week?"

"Yes," said Isabelle, and an appointment with Al and Isabelle was made for the following Friday.

———————

On Friday, armed with the knowledge that a baby boy was available, Isabelle and Al entered Miss Greenstein's office. She asked them about Ricky's progress, and after their glowing reports, notified them that she would like to make a home visit to see their son.

She then proceeded to tell them about the agency's new philosophy for placing babies. The agency's supply of new babies was so small, and the demand for babies was so great, that the agency used to do it's best to accommodate as many couples as they could. They were very frustrated to find that demand still so greatly out-weighted supply, that they ceased concentrating on trying to give babies to as many couples who qualified as possible; but instead placed their greatest emphasis on what was best for the babies. By doing so, some worthy couples were left childless, but the new change in philosophy benefitted the babies.

"We have always realized that our greatest obligation was to the babies we placed, so ours was never a first-come, first-served operation," said Miss Greenstein. "We tried to carefully match a baby's intellectual background to his adoptive parents' intellects. We placed babies where we believed they would flourish, but then we realized, that if a child were to be in an optimal environment, that environment would not only possess loving parents, it would possess a sibling for the child as well. Therefore, wherever possible, we are now giving second babies to adoptive families, because in doing so, we are providing both children with a sibling."

"You are here for a second child. So far only two couples before you have become the adoptive parents of a second baby, so you are here to participate in a new program for Cincinnati's Jewish Family Service."

"We're honored," said Isabelle.

"Yes," concurred Al.

"Well," said Miss Greenstein, "I need to know about some of your preferences. Isabelle, do you prefer a girl for your second baby?"

"Personally, I'd like a little girl," Isabelle replied, "but Ricky would do better with a little brother. Two boys would supply each other with greater companionship; and I guess, just as in a pregnancy, what one hopes for, doesn't matter. You have already blessed us with such a wonderful little boy, that I trust your judgment in blessing us with his sibling," Isabelle replied.

"What about you, Al?" asked Miss Greenstein. "Do you have a sexual preference?"

"No," said Al. "I, too, trust the agency's judgment in placing another wonderful child in our home."

Both Isabelle and Al knew that a little boy was available. In no way did they wish to jeopardize their consideration for this child, hence their very guarded responses as to sexual preference.

––––––––––

To Isabelle and Al's immense delight, Miss Greenstein processed them for a second child very rapidly. Within three weeks, they had received their approval, and now awaited the yearned-for telephone call, which came eight weeks after Sarah's death. When they met their adorable second son, and were asked the name they had chosen for him, they replied, "*Stephen Scott.*" Sarah now had a beautiful little boy whose first name, *Stephen*, was in honor of her first name; and whose middle name, *Scott*, was the English name derived from *Sroil* or *Isroel*, the people Sarah cherished above all others. Sarah's first great-grandchild to enter her family after her death was Isabelle and Al's second adopted son. Stephen Scott had become a member of Sarah's family only two months after she had died.

Isabelle knew why her second son became a member of her family as fast as he did. Stephen represented *life*. Sarah's descendants represented her immortality. She would live on through her "*Ten Fingers*" and the little "*fingers*" that would follow them. Isabelle's second son, carrying Sarah's name and the name of her people already testified to the fact that Sarah continues....

Epilogue

Vashisht is dead! If land and water can be killed, the horrible deed has been done. Vashisht is as dead as the bones in the pit's the Nazis forced the hapless Jews of Vashisht and neighboring towns to dig in the endless Russian forest surrounding their homes. There, during World War II, the Nazis shot their Jewish victims, leaving the hamlets and larger towns of the area *Juden Rein*, (German for "Clean of Jews" or "Without Jews). Now in the radiation poisoned forests, the only remnants of human life having ever been in the area, are the bones of the murdered Jews remaining in the pits they so piteously dug.

Vashisht is dead, but Sarah is not dead! Her descendents will soon number in the hundreds. They already include teachers, lawyers, doctors, accountants, people owning businesses, this writer, and many others.

Stephen is named for Sarah, as are others who followed him. Her *Ten Fingers* have spread over the land Sarah had yearned for, and eventually, providentially, attained for her fortunate family. None of Sarah's descendants are left in Russia. They are spread from New York City, north, south, and west over the United States.

While most of Sarah's progeny remained Jewish and even married Jewish spouses, some of her great grandchildren married non-Jews. Unlike Esther Sarah's descendants never needed to hide their non-Jewish spouses. These non-Jews became valued members of their Jewish spouses' family. Sarah even has great-grandchildren who have married Asians….a brilliant electrical engineer from Vietnam whose immigration to the Golden Land rivals Sarah's, and an attractive and intelligent young woman from Thailand. Sarah has an adopted Asian great, great-grandson and two beautiful Eurasian great, great-granddaughters. The girls live in Houston, Texas, and are Isabelle's great-nieces.

When Isabelle recently visited her niece and her family in Houston, an Asian store clerk admired the beautiful Eurasian little girls, whose lovely honey-blond mother was clearly not of Asian descent. Hoping to discover the origin of the girl's Asian features, the store clerk asked the eldest what her background was. The beautiful, six-year old Eurasian child answered proudly, "I'm Jewish."

Clearly, Sarah has not died. And clearly, Bella's pious Zada, in far away Vashisht, was wrong. Jews in America did not become *goyim* (non-Jews). They either remained very observant Jews, whose religious practices were like Zada's, or they entered Jewish denominations that had altered and modernized their practice of Judaism. But, his American descendents did not leave Zada's religion, as Zada had predicted they would. All denominations of Judaism respect and revere *Torah*, and Sarah's descendants always knowing who they are, respect and revere the *Torah*, as well. They know that they are Jews and the proud descendants of Sarah, a woman who loved *Torah*, even though she herself could not read. They are the proud descendants of a woman whose strength and wisdom conquered adversity and who succeeded in bringing her children and herself out of condemned Vashisht. Sarah's strength lives in her progeny, and her progeny, unlike tragic Vashisht....*lives!*

CPSIA information can be obtained at www.ICGtesting.com
Printed in the USA
LVOW081122290113

317698LV00002B/39/P